ECONOMIC ANALYSIS AND THE MULTINATIONAL ENTERPRISE

Other books by John H. Dunning

American Investment in British Manufacturing Industry
Allen & Unwin, 1958

with C. J. Thomas
British Industry
Hutchinson, 1961, 1963 and 1966

Economic Planning and Town Expansion
Workers' Educational Association, 1963

Studies in International Investment
Allen & Unwin, 1970

(Ed.)
The Multinational Enterprise
Allen & Unwin, 1971

with E. V. Morgan
An Economic Study of the City of London
Allen & Unwin, 1971

(Ed.)
International Investment
Penguin, 1972

United States Industry in Britain
Financial Times, 1973
with R. D. Pearce

The World's Largest Companies
Financial Times, 1974

ECONOMIC ANALYSIS AND THE MULTINATIONAL ENTERPRISE

edited by

John H. Dunning
Professor of Economics, University of Reading

London   George Allen & Unwin Ltd
Ruskin House   Museum Street

ISBN 0 04 330246 7

Printed in Great Britain
in 10 point Times Roman type
by Unwin Brothers Limited
The Gresham Press
Old Woking, Surrey

Acknowledgements

I wish to acknowledge the generous grant awarded by the Shell International Company which helped the writing of this book, and also the encouragement given by a number of the Shell executives throughout its preparation.

My gratitude is also due to the Rockefeller Foundation both for making the Villa Serbelloni in Bellagio available in September 1972 for authors of the book to exchange views on early drafts of their chapters, and for assisting in the travel costs of participants.

Among my academic colleagues, whose names do not appear above the chapters in this book, I would like to thank Professor E. Penrose, Professor Michael Beesley, Mr David Robertson, Mr Nils Lundgren and Mr George Yannopoulos who were among the discussants at the Bellagio Meeting.

Finally, my warmest thanks to Mrs Gillian Barron who has compiled the index of this book, to Mrs Mary Handslip who helped check the references to the text and to the secretarial staff of the University of Reading, and in particular to my past secretary, Mrs Pat Wylie, for their willing and efficient contribution.

References and notes appear at the ends of chapters, and a bibliography at the end of the book.

J. H. DUNNING
July 1973

Contents

Acknowledgements   *page* 7

1. The distinctive nature of the
   multinational enterprise   13
   JOHN H. DUNNING

2. The theory of the firm   31
   THOMAS O. HORST

3. The determinants of investment   47
   GUY V. G. STEVENS

4. The location of economic activity   89
   RAYMOND VERNON

5. Industrial organisation   115
   RICHARD E. CAVES

6. Technology and technological change   147
   EDWIN MANSFIELD

7. The theory of international trade   184
   W. M. CORDEN

8. Long-run capital movements   211
   GEORGE H. BORTS

9. Monetary policy   234
   GEOFFREY W. MAYNARD

10. The theory of development policy   252
    PAUL STREETEN

11. Wage determination and collective bargaining   280
    SUNE CARLSON

12. Income distribution and welfare considerations   300
    CONSTANTINE V. VAITSOS

13. Size of firm and size of nation   342
    CHARLES P. KINDLEBERGER

14. Conclusions   363
    JOHN H. DUNNING

Bibliography   375
Author Index   398
Subject Index   403

Contributors

GEORGE H. BORTS
Brown University

RICHARD E. CAVES
Harvard University

SUNE CARLSON
Uppsala University

W. M. CORDEN
Oxford University

JOHN H. DUNNING
Reading University

THOMAS O. HORST
Harvard University

CHARLES P. KINDLEBERGER
Massachusetts Institute of Technology

EDWIN MANSFIELD
University of Pennsylvania

GEOFFREY W. MAYNARD
Reading University

GUY V. G. STEVENS
Federal Reserve Bank,
Washington

PAUL STREETEN
Oxford University

CONSTANTINE V. VAITSOS
Lima

RAYMOND VERNON
Harvard University

Chapter 1

THE DISTINCTIVE NATURE OF THE MULTINATIONAL ENTERPRISE

John H. Dunning

Why is the multinational enterprise a subject worthy of study by economists? What new insights do its operations and effects offer on the workings of the international economy? What distinguishes this institution from other economic phenomena? Why, bearing in mind the already substantial body of literature on the subject, is another book needed? It is the purpose of this chapter, which serves as an introduction to those which follow, to try and answer these questions.

One simple answer to the first question is the importance, and increasing importance, of the multinational enterprise in the modern world economy. Firms which own and control income-generating assets in more than one country—the broad definition of the multinational enterprise adopted by this book[1]—now account for one-fifth of the world's output excluding the centrally planned economies (United Nations, 1973); their production, for some years now, has been growing at the rate of 10 per cent per annum, nearly twice the growth of world output, and half as much again as world trade; in 1971, of the 613 world's largest companies, 437, accounting for four-fifths of the total sales, operated three or more foreign producing affiliates[2]; in that same year, the liquid assets of all kinds of multinational institutions were put at twice the size of the world's gold and foreign exchange reserves (US Tariff Commission, 1973). Ranking nations, by gross national product, and multinational enterprises, by gross sales in 1971, we see that of the 99 largest nations or firms, there were 39 corporations and 60 nations (Brown, 1970).[3] In every respect, multinational enterprises are among the most powerful economic institutions yet produced by the private enterprise system.

To these data, can be added others which illustrate the role which multinational enterprises, or their affiliates, play in the particular economies in which they operate. Again the facts—such as they are—have been well documented.[4] To the home countries, their importance is usually expressed, at a macro level, as the share of the gross national product accounted for by the foreign activities of domestically owned multinational enterprises, to gross national product; and at a micro level, by the percentage of the sales, assets, profits or employment of a particular company or industry generated by foreign production. For example, more than 30 per cent of the profits of UK companies are currently derived from their overseas operations, while of the leading 342 United States firms, the sales of their foreign affiliates accounted for 25 per cent of their total sales (Dunning and Pearce, 1974). In 1970, the world-wide sales of foreign manufacturing affiliates of US firms were almost three times the value of exports of manufactured products (US Senate Committee on Finance, 1973). In the case of some of the smaller capital exporters, e.g. Switzerland, Holland and Sweden, the proportions are even higher. At a sectoral level, a substantial and increasing proportion of the world's output of several industries, e.g. motor vehicles, chemicals, pharmaceuticals, computers, processed foods, oil, etc., is produced by the foreign affiliates of multinational companies. At an individual firm level, some companies, e.g. Nestlé of Switzerland, Philips of Holland, produce only a small proportion of their total sales from domestic production units. Foreign affiliates also play a more traditional role of supplying investing countries with essential primary commodities.

To many recipient countries, the role of affiliates of foreign owned multinational firms is crucial. In several economies, both developed and less developed, such affiliates account for more than one-third of the output of the manufacturing sector and a major part of their resource industries. Examples include Australia, Belgium, Canada, Ireland, Norway and Sweden among the developed countries; and Brazil, Ethiopia, Fiji, Ghana, Malaysia, Mexico, the Philippines, Sierra Leone, Singapore and Taiwan among the less developed nations. The concentration of activity is most marked in import-substitution or export generating sectors supplying branded products, and in which competition is oligopolistic.

It is, however, less the distinctive features of multinational enterprises and more their distinctive behaviour, and the consequences of this behaviour for national and international resources allocation, which makes them of special interest to economists and policy makers. This distinctive behaviour stems from the fact that multinational enterprises directly control the deployment of resources in two or more countries and the distribution of the resulting output generated between these countries.

There are three near relations to the multinational enterprise. These are:

(i) The national enterprise which operates production units in different parts of the nation state in which it is incorporated, i.e. the multi-regional national enterprise. Like it, the multinational enterprise owns income-generating assets in more than one location and uses these, together with the locally owned resources to produce goods and services. As the affiliates of multi-regional national enterprises possess certain advantages over their local competitors, due *inter alia* to their being part of a larger economic unit, and the opportunities for specialisation this confers; so do multi-national companies enjoy similar benefits over national companies. But, unlike the multi-regional national enterprise, the multinational company owns and operates its assets and controls the use of its inputs in different national states, each of which, are sovereign political units.

(ii) The national firm which produces in the country in which it is incorporated but exports part of its output,[5] i.e. the international trading firm. Like it, the multinational enterprise sells its output across national boundaries, thereby introducing an element of openness and interdependence into both the exporting and importing economies. Unlike the international trading firm, however, its activities involve a transference of income-generating assets, and part of its trade is not between independent economic agents, at arm's-length prices, but within the same enterprise, at transfer prices, which, in so far as it is possible, will be fixed to serve the interests not of any particular affiliate but of the enterprise as a whole.

(iii) The national producing firm which exports part of its factor inputs, e.g. material or human capital. Like it, the multi-national enterprise exports income-generating assets; but, unlike it, supplies these as a package deal and maintains control over the use made of them.

Likewise, the foreign *affiliates* of multinational enterprises also may be distinguished from indigenous firms in the countries, in which they operate. They have two near relations. First firms which import factor inputs from foreign sources, and second branch plants of multi-regional national firms. In the first case, while both groups of firms are dependent on foreign sources for (some of) their resources, only the foreign affiliates are controlled from abroad in the use of these resources. In the second case, both firms are part of larger enterprises, and so their activities are likely to be truncated in some way or another (Gray, 1972); the difference here lies mainly in the extent to which division of labour is practicable and in the intercountry distribution of the proceeds of the output.

Although it may be argued that these differences are ones of degree rather than of kind, and arise largely because the world is divided into a number of sovereign states, they do confer a certain distinctiveness on multinational enterprises and their affiliates; the extent and character of which will vary according, *inter alia*, to the industries and countries in which they operate and their organisational strategy. However, wherever they occur, the response of multinational enterprises and their affiliates to the economic environment of which they are part, or changes in that environment, will, to some extent, be different from that of their near relations.

Partly because of this, and also because part of the output generated by the affiliates of multinational enterprises in one country will accrue to the owners of resources in other countries, both the international allocation of resources and the distribution of economic welfare will be affected. Since the operating objectives of affiliates will be geared to those of the enterprises of which they are part, rather than those of the countries in which they operate, clashes with host governments over some aspects of their behaviour are inescapable. These clashes are likely to be greater, *inter alia*, the more a country pursues a policy of economic isolationism, the more the activities of multinational enterprises are in response to market imperfections, e.g. barriers to trade in goods, inappropriate exchange rates, etc., and the greater the differences in incentives or/and penalties exerted by governments which cause multinational enterprises to shift resources, or claims to resources, across national boundaries.

The task of this book is to examine how far the distinctive characteristics of multinational enterprises necessitate modification to received economic analysis. Economic analysis is concerned with explaining the way in which resources possessed by economic agents are (or could be) used, and how the resulting output is (or could be) distributed. In so doing, it is interested both in the formulation of empirically testable hypotheses, and in advancing understanding about the relationship between economic phenomena. Economic policy deals with more normative matters. It is concerned with identifying and evaluating ways in which resources may be allocated to achieve certain goals, both economic and non-economic. The twin questions of how multinational enterprises affect our basic understanding of the relationship between economic phenomena and the way in which the policy objectives can best be achieved is the subject matter of these studies. Several authors also touch upon the broader issues of economic theory, and of evaluating the effects of the behaviour of multinationals. The book focuses attention on three of the main goals which guide most policy makers in their attitudes towards the allocation of resources for which they are responsible. These may be summarised under three heads: viz. efficiency, equity and sovereignty.

(1) *Efficiency* is concerned with the volume and composition of output produced by a community from the resources available to it, and its rate of growth over time. In the present context, it is the contribution of multinational enterprises (or their affiliates) to gross *national* output which is relevant; this is equal to gross *domestic* output, plus income earned on assets owned abroad minus income earned on foreign owned domestic assets.

(2) *Equity* (in this context) is a function of the way the proceeds from production or the rate of growth of production are distributed between the contributing factor inputs, customers and tax authorities, both within the country of production and between that country and others which provide part of the resources for the production.

(3) *Sovereignty* is a catch-all word which may be loosely defined as the ability of a country to run its own affairs and retain the maximum freedom of choice in the allocation of its resources. Within this heading one might include such sub-goals as economic nationalism, participation in decision taking, cultural identity and so on.

The extent to which these goals are realised will, of course, depend on the achivement of various sub-goals; for example, the need to cure a balance of payments deficit may act as a constraint (in the short run) on maximising efficiency; moreover, both goals and sub-goals may sometimes conflict with each other. The implicit assumption of our analysis is that the behaviour of multinational enterprises is different from that of other economic agents and that this will affect the success of countries in achieving their goals.

Clearly, it is of interest to the economist to study these differences, the reasons for them, and their effects on the realisation of both micro and macro economic objectives, but before looking into these more fully, a comment about the current state of economic analysis and the multinational enterprise may be in order. Until recently, the subject held little appeal to the academic economist. The main body of economic literature has remained substantially unaffected by it, and only in the last five or six years have articles on it begun to appear in the leading journals. This apparent lack of concern could be because economists believe that the subject matter is not sufficiently distinctive to warrant separate attention; or that the existing tools of analysis are adequate to deal with it; or even, that economic analysis has little to contribute to an understanding of it.

On the other hand, it may be that economists have insufficiently appreciated, either the extent of the multinational enterprise, or its implications for economic analysis. We are inclined to take this latter view, or, at least, suggest there is an *a priori* case for it. Certainly, even the most cursory look at the empirical work done on the subject makes one uneasy about its implications for received theory. Notwithstanding, that much of this work has been descriptive, and most of the discussion outside academic circles has been politically oriented, traditional economic doctrines have been frequently called to task. Is this because the theories are wrong, or because they inadequately take account of the distinctive characteristics of the multinational enterprise? Or, could it be that the critics do not properly understand the theories?

These are question worth answering and much of this book seeks to do just this. In the final chapter, we highlight some of the main conclusions. Here, all we seek to do is establish that there is an *a priori* case for investigation.

There are three ways in which a new institutional phenomena might affect existing explanations of the structure of resource utilisation. The first is that existing assumptions about the behaviour of institutions may no longer be appropriate. Take, for example, the goals of conduct. To what extent are multinational enterprises likely to be differently motivated than other enterprises? How far does their presence affect the goals of other economic agents including governments? For example, are consumer tastes likely to be more interdependent or cosmopolitan as a result of the closer links they make possible between people of different cultures. Will the community's welfare function be more geared towards economic nationalism? What too, of the assumptions about the value of exogenous variables, or those one usually chooses to hold constant? Foremost among these in microeconomics are that prices are determined by the actions of independent buyers and sellers. Where the exchange of goods is between different parts of the same economic agent this latter assumption may no longer hold good. New tools of analysis may be needed to explain these prices and, hence, behaviour dependent on them.

Second, new institutions may require economic analysis to be reconstructed or extended to take account of new independent variables which might influence their behaviour. In the present context, these arise partly because the multinational enterprise introduces a new dimension to both the theory of the firm and the theory of international relations, and partly because behavioural variables which may have been previously unimportant are now important (or *vice versa*).

Third, an explanation of the relationship between variables may be affected because the *value* of variables is no longer appropriate. This does not affect analysis itself but rather the conclusions to be drawn from the analysis.

Put in simpler terms, the multinational enterprise may influence resource allocation and economic policy through affecting: (i) the goals of economic agents; (ii) the means of achieving these goals, i.e. the availability and efficient use of resources; and (iii) the mechanism by which means are related to ends, e.g. the economic system. We shall now discuss each of these from the viewpoint of the three broad aims of governments set out earlier.

EFFICIENCY

Several of the chapters in the book analyse the ways in which multinational enterprises or their affiliates affect the level and composition of output in the countries in which they operate, and the distribution of the proceeds of that output between participating countries. Questions related to the efficiency of individual firms are analysed by Horst, Stevens, Vernon and Mansfield and touched upon by Carlson and Vaitsos; questions concerning the market mechanism in which firms operate are dealt with by Caves and Corden; questions about the role of government policy are discussed by Borts, Maynard and Streeten.

Given these assumptions, there seems no *a priori* reason to suppose that, at the firm level, the multinational enterprise should influence the *principles* of the efficiency of resource allocation, although it may well affect the level of efficiency actually achieved. Both Horst and Stevens, in fact, believe that the multinational enterprise is motivated basically like any other large enterprise and that there is no need for a separate theory of corporate behaviour on this count. Its operations across national boundaries introduce no new principles of resource allocation over and above those guiding the decision to spatially diversify production within a country. Vernon supports this conclusion but suggests that the impact of the multinational enterprise on the market structures in which it operates may cause it to behave differently than a group of independent firms, and that there are certain implications for the theory of oligopoly worthy of special attention. Institutional arrangements are taken up by Caves in his essay. He asserts that, for a variety of reasons to do with the possession of enterprise specific assets, the effect of the multinational enterprise on market structure is a distinctive one. Mansfield illustrates one area of this distinctiveness, viz. technology, but like Caves, believes that the existing tools of analysis, *if used properly*, can accommodate these differences.

What each of these writers is suggesting is that the fact that the world is organised into separate sovereign states, *by itself*, need make no difference to the way in which firms exploit markets. However, given the fact of multinational enterprises, and that individual governments *do* operate policies to advance the economic welfare of their own citizens, the allocation of resources may be different than would exist in the absence of separate governments. These actions might be independent of the operations of multinational enterprises, but may also be affected by them. Mention might be particularly made of their impact on monopoly policy, regional policy and demand management policies. None of these raise new conceptual issues; they arise equally at a regional level wherever affiliates of multi-regional national companies are operating. The question as to whether the advent of multinational enterprises makes for more or less economic power, thereby affecting the efficiency of resource allocation is a separate one, but this again, is touched on in Caves' and Vaitsos' essays.

The impact of multinational enterprises on world output arises partly from the extent to which the enterprises are themselves more efficient (relative to other enterprises), as a result of their multinationalism; and partly by the response of such companies to government policies designed to advance their own economic and social goals. These policies differ widely across national boundaries. Examples include different tax rates and fiscal provisions, exchange rate policies, differential monopoly and regional policies, import substitution and export promotion policies. Such policies, of course, affect all firms, but to the enterprise producing in more than one country they represent discriminatory treatment; and since their options—with respect to geographical resource allocation are wider—they are able to respond to differently than indigenous companies.

The analogy with a spatially diversified national firm is a particularly apposite one as, by it behaviour within the framework of both regional and national policies, it can affect the location of economic activity both between industries and between regions. It can influence the level and rate of growth of real income, and its distribution between regions. It can do this in a way which may increase the efficiency of resource usage in the region in which it operates yet lower its real income. It can create disturbance problems in the same way as can exogenous structural changes, and it is likely to do this more easily than a uni-regional firm partly, at least, because of its wider spatial choices. As far as the government of the nation state, of which the region is part, is concerned, this may be an acceptable price to pay where it advances national economic welfare, as it is able to alleviate, in part at least, undesirable distributional effects by appropriate compensatory policies. Moreover, in the last resort, it has power to directly influence the locational choice of the multi-regional firm.

At an international level, this is not the case. There is no *a priori* presumption that the presence of (say) US affiliates in Britain will make for a higher economic welfare of the UK, even if they are more efficient than indigenous firms. One can easily imagine takeovers of UK companies by US firms which may benefit both the investor and the US economy and, indeed, the combined welfare of the US and UK economies, yet may not be in the best interests of the UK economy. The reason for this lies partly in the greater immobility of resources, and in particular labour, across national boundaries than within national boundaries, and partly in the fact that there is no machinery by which the UK can share in the increased wealth accruing to the US economy, which directly arises from the employment of its own resources. In the case of a UK company taking over a firm in the North East of England, the same thing may happen, but at least devices are open to the national government to ensure that the North East can share in the prosperity of the country as a whole.

The identification and measurement of the international resource allocative effects of supplying markets from alternative production locations are questions which concern both location and trade economists. Is there any reason to suppose that a firm supplying the national market with only one production unit will behave very differently than one which is spatially diversified? On the other hand, there is a separate branch of economic analysis concerned with trade between nations rather than regions within a nation. As Corden emphasises in his essay, the analytical threshold which distinguishes the two sorts of trade is the immobility of factor inputs; while intra-country differences in the institutions and actions of governments also differentiate the determinants of external trade from those of internal trade. Presumably, the theory of capital movements, once national boundaries are crossed should also take on a new meaning, though Stevens, in his chapter, sees no reason, at a micro-level, to suppose that the determinants of international investment are significantly different from those of domestic investment.

Perhaps one important difference between multi-regional and international trading enterprises, on the one hand, and multi-national enterprises on the other revolves around the question of *ownership*. A market for a particular product may be serviced in three main ways: (i) by domestically owned firms producing within that market; (ii) by imports either from (*a*) foreign firms, or (*b*) the foreign affiliates of domestically owned firms; and (*iii*) by the affiliates of foreign firms producing in that market. Location theory is concerned with explaining the choice of firms between options (i) and (ii*b*) or (ii*a*) and (iii): trade theory is largely concerned with explaining the choice between options (i) and (ii*a*). It is only by using *both* approaches that one can appreciate why neither, by itself, is sufficient to explain the choices open to multinational enterprises. For example, how does one explain the share of a market serviced from a given location by indigenous firms and affiliates of foreign firms or importing goods from foreign firms or affiliates? Trade theory is deficient because its assumption about the immobility of factor inputs is inappropriate. Location theory is deficient because it cannot explain why firms of different ownership vary in efficiency. Both theories fail to appreciate that where there are barriers or imperfections in the transmission of knowledge between firms over space, this will tend to increase the concentration of ownership, but widen the options open to firms to service their markets. Such advantages may be *enterprise*, *industry* or even *country* specific. *Enterprise* specific advantages include access to particular markets or sources of inputs, the economies of integration and the possession of knowledge protected by patents. *Industry* specific advantages include those of a market structure and technological kind. *Country* specific advantages include the educational system and State policy towards research and development.

These specific advantages may be a function of many factors apart from the multinationalism of firms, and some e.g. economies of integration, apply to multi-regional as contrasted with uni-regional firms, or firms of one nationality rather than another. Again, however, there are some advantages which only arise if firms produce in more than one country. Sometimes these are matters of degree, e.g. the extent to which an American firm in America might possess a comparative advantage over a UK firm in the UK compared with a UK firm in Birmingham over a UK firm in Southampton. Since the difference between the two locations is more pronounced in the first case, so will be the comparative advantage of their firms. Perhaps more important is the case where firms trade with another at other than 'arm's-length' prices, i.e. the terms of trade that would operate in independent transactions. Although in a world context, this is primarily a distributional question; from that of a particular country, it will influence its efficiency of resource usage, and the gross national product.

Such intra-group trading, whether it be of goods, services, money or assets, at other than arm's-length prices, emphasises the distinction between the international trading and the international producing firm. There are other ways in which the latter type of enterprise may have more control over its market, than the former, but these are similar in kind to those available to the multi-regional firm. The extent to which a multinational enterprise will wish to earn income in one country than in another depends very much on conditions outside its control, in particular, the policies of individual governments and the international monetary system. In their essays, both Maynard and Vaitsos emphasise the way in which fixed exchange rates may affect the resource allocative policies of firms.

In his contribution, Corden looks at the impact of the multinational enterprise on the pure theory of international trade and concludes it can be easily incorporated into its framework. After all, *most* of the ingredients of received theory remain—notably, the immobility of certain productive factors, e.g. land and most kinds of labour. On the other hand, because of a common ownership of factor inputs, some features immobile between independent firms across national boundaries, e.g. knowledge, information and various kinds of services, become mobile in the case of the multinational company. Moreover, because of intra-group pricing, the *terms* of trade and hence the allocation of resources and composition of trade may be different. This point has also been recognised by Baldwin (1970) who pleas for a more systematic incorporation of the movement of inputs in trade theory. Several empirical studies have also shown that international investment and trade are closely linked (Robertson, 1971).

Several essays in this book touch upon factors external to the multinational enterprise, but influenced by it, which impinge upon economic efficiency. Foremost among these is Caves' examination of the impact of multinationals on market conduct and performance and Maynard's discussion of their effects on macro-economic demand management. Mansfield's essay on technology deals with some of the externalities of technological transmission, while Vaitsos examines the differences between private and social welfare which the operations of companies across national boundaries might generate.

Most authors in this volume are concerned with both the *positive* and *normative* implications of multinational enterprises. It is, for example, well recognised that their effect on economic welfare is strongly influenced by both Government policies and institutional mechanisms. Elsewhere, several writers have asserted that market imperfections favour multinational companies more than national companies (Lundgren, 1973). It is also clear that second best Government policies lead to lower efficiency; a protectionist import policy is one example. Like other institutions, multinational enterprises respond to economic signals; if these signals are inappropriate they could lower rather than raise welfare, and make it more, rather than less, difficult for governments to achieve their social goals. By their behaviour, for good or bad, multinationals may also force Governments or markets to modify established policies. An example of a beneficial impact (according to some economists at least) is the adoption of flexible exchange rates by countries following some of the financial activities of multinational enterprises: but such companies may cause Governments to take restrictionist meaures, with less welcome consequences and economic well being. However, in spite of recent research (US Tariff Commission, 1973), we are only at the beginning of our understanding of the interactions between the behaviour of multinational enterprises and Government policy.

EQUITY

We have suggested that the economic welfare of individual nation states is likely to be influenced by multinational enterprises and their affiliates by the effect they have on the distribution of income between investing and host countries. This has its parallel in international trading, where the terms of trade will determine the share of the gains from trading accruing to the participants. Given the output created by an affiliate of a multi-national enterprise, the question of its distribution between the citizens of the host nations in which the affiliate is located and those of other nations providing resources to that affiliate is of critical importance. It is, for example, possible that an affiliate may be more efficient than an indigenous firm, in the sense that its contribution to the gross *domestic* product is higher, but that all or more of this accrues to the investing country, so that gross *national* product is unchanged (or lowered). Higher efficiency of foreign affiliates does not guarantee an increase in gross national product, as it does when achieved by indigenous firms, where the issue is entirely one of distribution of the product between sectors within a nation state.[6]

This, indeed, is a noteworthy difference between the effects of multinational enterprises on the nation states in which they operate, and those of national enterprises in the regions in which they operate. Both affect the economies of the area of their adoption, but only in the latter case is wealth created and available for distribution in a way that *all* participants might gain. Again, it is worth emphasising that the effects differ primarily because the world happens to be organised into sovereign nation states, each with its own economic and social objectives, and its ways of achieving these, which may be very different from each other.

The determination of the benefit/cost ratio for companies and countries, and the extent to which it is as high as it might be, is central to any study of the economic consequences of multi-national enterprises. Rarely, of course, is the bargaining conducted in an easily identifiable way. The components of costs and benefits are many and varied, and some defy easy measurement. To the host country, they include all the externalities, or spill-over effects, both positive and negative, arising from presence of the affiliates of multinational enterprises. This is a subject on which there has been a great deal of research, at both a macro and micro level.[7] The share of the benefits directly created by the affiliates, which is then distributed to the investing company, (or other affiliates) includes not only profits, interest, royalties, technical fees and contributions to managerial and administrative overheads, but income resulting from the intra-group exchange of goods and services at above arm's-length prices charged to the affiliate.[8] In his paper, Vaitsos argues that the true income accruing to multinational enterprises is often well in excess of the profits recorded, and that some countries, particularly developing countries are paying well above their opportunity cost for the assets, goods and services provided.

All Governments are concerned with assessing the contribution of producing economic agents to their economic and social goals. For income generated by national enterprises, this reduces to a question of the distribution of the proceeds between factor inputs, notably between capital and labour within the country. The share does not directly affect the size of the national income except in so far as it affects incentives. With affiliates to multi-national enterprises, the situation is very different for reasons already given; this is why the bargaining process becomes all important. How far are existing models, e.g. that of bilateral monopoly, relevant? Both Streeten and Vaitsos in their essays take this as a central part of their themes although other con-tributions are also concerned with establishing the extent to which distribution of welfare is affected. It is here where economic analysis leaves much to be desired. Certainly there is no direct parallel in the case of the multi-regional company; nor with international trading company, where the question of terms of trade is the relevant one.

Perhaps, here, it is the national company which obtains its inputs separately from independent foreign sellers which offers the nearest parallel. In this case, the economist is interested in assessing the differential affects of control over the use of local resources and the decision of whether or not to supply the foreign resources which is implicit in international direct investment on the benefits and costs of this investment. What is the difference in economic terms? It is partly a question of price. In the case of licensing fees and interest on local capital negotiated by firms in the open market one knows the price in advance. Even in the case of equity capital one knows the range of benefits and costs and is prepared to make a choice on this basis. In the case of a company whose price can be affected in so many different ways and does not always wish to act in the way it would on an open market, there is a large difference. In addition, there is the question of concentration of economic power. Investment by the large multinationals is often indivisible. An investment by a dozen companies of £100 m is very different from the same investment by 1000 companies.

Because of the complexity and uncertainty surrounding the behaviour of multinational enterprises; because of their economic power; and because of ignorance surrounding their pricing strategy, they do seem to have established a new set of rules in the bargaining game. As Carlson points out, the bargaining options open to the multinationals do suggest a reconsideration of traditional theories of wage determination. Although one can site illustrations of bargaining strengths and weaknesses, we are still awaiting a satisfactory theory to explain the distribution of income generated by the multinationals.

A secondary question concerns the factors influencing the distribution of income *within* a country arising from multinational enterprises; Carlson also addresses himself to this question. Again, from the viewpoint of economic analysis, it is possible to examine these effects on the distribution of income as being caused by different goals of multinational enterprises, or of means to achieve these goals or of the system in which they operate. Does one need a new theory to explain the share of the benefits accruing from the operation of affiliates to the investing company, where that company is domiciled in a different country? Possibly, in so far as the multinationals have more opportunities to use the income they earn, modification is required. Stevens does suggest certain differences in distribution of profits policy. Far more important, however, is the bargaining position of the multinational company with domestic authorities. Here there is no comparable model economic analysts can call upon.

Summarising then, the multinational enterprise introduces a new institutional situation which may expose weaknesses in existing mechanisms of resource allocation, either at a national or international level. Where the effects of domestic economic policies of governments are confined to firms earning income only within their jurisdiction, the fact that these policies may be different across national boundaries may have no effect on the international distribution of income. For companies earning in different parts of the world, this becomes an imperfection in the market system, and affects behavioural patterns, which will not necessarily be in accord with policies of governments. A national firm which operates management policies to maximise its receipts is operating in the country's best interests: but, by becoming international and pursuing the same objectives, it finds itself in conflict with the governments of one or more of the countries in which it operates. The fact that it is the structure of the international economic system which causes this and not any change in behaviour of the companies (whose interests only coincide with nation states in so far as it pays them so to do) does nothing to endear them to governments.

Lastly, what of the means by which multinationals achieve their ends of the optimum distribution of income? The answer in the case of efficiency lay in technology and the economies of integration and size. The answer here, also, lies in some of those of these same variables and particularly those which affect bargaining and competitive strength. Of these size, flexibility in operation, access to information about international goods and factor markets and sheer professional skill and adroitness in international management, explain how distribution of income may be affected by additional means open to multinationals. However, as some observers have pointed out (Manser, 1973), sometimes the bargaining strength is on the side of nations, particularly where nations by grouping together (e.g. Organisation of Petroleum Exporting Countries, the Andean Pact countries) can evolve common strategies towards multinational enterprises.

This book is not about the practical ways in which nations can improve their own positions in dealing with multinationals, but, in their essays, Kindleberger and Maynard point out that the growth of these global organisations are having important implications on the optimum size of nation states. The reader is also referred to the substantial literature on the interactions between the two bodies. For further details, see a very interesting annotated bibliography by the Foreign Policy Research Institute (1971). Here suffice to mention that the economic analyst would do well to consider the strategy of international relations in the formulation of his theories relating to income distribution.

POLITICAL ASPIRATIONS AND ECONOMIC SOVEREIGNTY

We said that this volume is primarily about the ways in which the multinational enterprise may cause explanations of the relationship between economic phenomena or the techniques of economic analysis to be modified. Positive economics takes political ends as given, but the cost and benefits of attaining political ends have economic consequences. In the end, a country may wish to be as politically independent as it can. This is its right. Economic nationalism is a 'good' in itself, the opportunity cost of which, like that of any other good, may be evaluated in economic terms.

Here, we would just mention that the economist must be clear on what grounds he is making decisions which may affect the behaviour of multinational companies. When a country nationalises or expropriates the assets of a foreign affiliate in its midst; when it imposes a tariff or import controls to encourage inward direct investment; when it seeks to control the movement of funds from affiliates to parent company (or vice versa); when it insists on a certain proportion of the equity capital of the affiliate being locally owned or a minimum of local representation on the Board of Directors; when it requires the affiliate to purchase a certain quantity of its inputs from local firms and to recruit its management from indigenous sources; when it discriminates against local subsidiaries in its purchasing policies, or in their use of local capital markets; when it insists on research and development being undertaken locally; does it pursue these and similar policies to promote higher efficiency or to achieve a more acceptable distribution of income, or because, by so doing, it is better able to control the use of its resources or achieve non-economic goals? On the first issue the economist can make a direct assessment, though, in practice, this may be an extremely difficult thing to do. On the second, he can still estimate the economic trade off between alternative courses of action to the decision takers to make the final choice. In both cases, his role may be a valuable one that it enables more informed and rational decisions to be taken.

CONCLUSIONS

The growth of the multinational enterprise and the production of firms across national boundaries, adds a new dimension to various branches of economic thought, the theory of international trade, the theory of the firm and the theory of bargaining being perhaps the most affected. Factors which appear irrelevant or insignificant for analysing the behaviour consequences of the multi-regional or international trading firm take on a new meaning with the multinational firm. Foremost among these are the presence of intra-group pricing across national boundaries, the distribution of the final output of multinationals between the nation states in which they operate. We have also suggested that the interaction between multinationals and domestic economic policies and mechanisms gives rise to new tensions. These arise because the growth of multinationals has coincided with developments in technology, communications, patent systems and with the increasing intervention of governments in economic affairs. They are both the creatures of these circumstances and have helped fashion them. Policies or mechanisms appropriate in their absence may no longer work in their presence; they may also give rise to a completely new set of problems. The usual response of governments is to try and control the multinationals so that they behave in a way consistent with the policies and mechanisms. But sometimes a country's goals may be better served if the policies or mechanisms are themselves changed. On such normative issues the economist may be able to give important advice.

References

1 For a comprehensive analysis of the various definitions of the multinational (or international) enterprise, see Aharoni (1971) and United Nations (1973).

2 Parker (1973).

3 For a criticism of this approach see Kindleberger (1971).

4 In particular, mention might be made of the studies by Andrews (1972), Dunning (1958, 1971), Stonehill (1965), Johnstone (1965), Safarian (1966), Brash (1966), Kidron (1965), Deane (1961), Stubenisky (1970), Hughes & Seng (1969), Watkins (1970), Steuer (1973) and Van den Buldke (1973).

5 Elsewhere (Dunning, 1971) we have distinguished between the multinational trading firm and the multinational producing firm.

6 Although these effects may be important and influenced by multinational enterprises.

7 In addition to the reference cited in Footnote 4 see particularly Little & Mirless (1969).

8 In other cases affiliates may be charged below arm's-length prices, e.g. subsidised inputs, cheap loans, machinery at knock-down prices, etc.

Chapter 2

THE THEORY OF THE FIRM[1]

Thomas O. Horst

INTRODUCTION

The general subject of this paper, multinational enterprise and the theory of the firm, is a remarkably broad one. A multinational firm is a complex organism, and an analysis of its many activities calls for a theory of the firm with many facets. To complicate matters further, every one of these activities leads directly to another area of economic analysis—the location of economic activity, the determinants of investment, industrial organisation and market structure, and so forth. If one were to take the broadest view of this topic, virtually every contribution in this volume infringes upon this chapter; if one were to take the narrowest view, everything said here might be better said elsewhere.

Rather than divining a theoretically correct solution to this conflict, I have sought a pragmatic one. Although the theory of the firm may be applied in many contexts, 'the theory of the firm' also represents a separate and often abstract body of economic literature. This theory of the firm gives much attention to what motivates a firm's behaviour in general, and little to what constrains that behaviour in any particular instance. By way of contrast, the study of multinational enterprise has been a highly empirical topic. Although the general motivation of multinational firms has been questioned here and there, it has typically been in a rather and loose and casual way.

This paper explores the possibilities for, and the desirability of, bridging the gap between the theory of the firm and the study of multinational enterprise. The first section below accordingly reviews recent contributions to the theory of the firm with special reference to the question of firm motivation. Readers interested in more comprehensive surveys should find one of the recent offerings (Archibald, 1971; Machlup, 1967, Marris, 1971 and Simon, 1962) to their liking. The second section below explores the potential for applying the newer theories to the study of multinational enterprise. The potential would appear to be large: the behavioural assumptions of the newer theories appear well suited to the descriptions of the typical multinational enterprise, and the methodological barriers to generalising the theories to a multinational setting are small. But in practice, the benefits may be small because differences in motivation translate into essentially the same foreign investment behaviour. If so, the theory of the firm and the study of multinational enterprise will probably continue their separate existences.

SOME RECENT DEVELOPMENTS IN THE THEORY OF THE FIRM

Most of the recent work on the theory of the firm derives from a basic dissatisfaction with the classical assumption about the motivation of a firm, viz. profit maximisation. The classical assumption has been argued on two grounds, both of them subject to challenge. The first argument was that competition in product markets would force prices down to the level of long-run average costs, so that a firm would have to maximise its profits if it were to break even. If perfect competition ever was a good working assumption, industrial organisation studies suggest that various forms of imperfect competition are to be found in many important industries today.

Evidence of high concentration ratios and excessive rates of return, the hallmarks of imperfect competition, undermined only the first defense of profit maximisation. Although profits under imperfect competition may be excessive in a normative or hypothetical sense, they presumably are never excessive in the green eyes of a firm's owners. More is always better than less. But here, too, there is some damning evidence. The research of Berle and Means (1932) clearly established that shareholder ownership and managerial control were separate from one another in most large corporations. That management might have interests other than profit maximisation was convincingly shown by Gordon (1945). Gordon argued that managers' primary concern, once the survival of the firm was assured, was for growth. Although some discipline was imposed by 'the market for corporate control' (gross neglect of profits could lead to white-collar unemployment), management nonetheless would retain some leeway in pursuing their separate interests.

Most new contributions to the theory of the firm over the last 25 years have centred on corporations large enough to exercise some power in the markets to which they sell and independent enough of their shareholders to deviate from profit-maximising behaviour. Since large size and investing abroad go hand in hand, newer theories of the firm appear tailor-made for the analysis of multinational firm behaviour. It is appropriate, therefore, to begin this paper by recalling important contributions to the theory of the firm over the last 10 or 15 years. Rather than treating these contributions chronologically, I will organise them into three fairly distinct groups: the static optimizing theories, the dynamic optimising theories, and the behaviouralist-organisationalist approaches.

STATIC OPTIMISING THEORIES

William Baumol's 1959 study, *Business Behavior, Value and Growth*, was the first to incorporate into a formal model Gordon's earlier suggestion that managers would seek only some minimal level of profits and devote their further resources towards expanding the size of the firm. To many, the difference between maximising profits and maximising firm size (measured by sales or assets) was less than apparent. After all, advertising and other forms of sales promotion had obvious advantages in attracting new customers and investors impressed by apparent success, in maintaining a distribution network for the firm's product, in raising employee morale and in enhancing the firm's market power. Profit maximisation itself would dicate that the firm advertise its products and engage in other activities aimed at expanding the size of its markets.

But eventually diminishing returns to advertising and other marketing efforts set in, as the cost of expanding the programmes begins to exceed the additional revenues they generate. The essence of Baumol's argument is that a management-controlled firm will push the size of these efforts beyond the point where marginal benefits equal marginal costs, beyond the point their shareholders would have them stop. But since shareholders will stand for only so much before they revolt (the notion of shareholders revolting against managers indicating who normally is in control), management's concern for its own job security will prevent the complete dissipation of profits on size-expanding expenditures. Although Baumol's analysis has been refined and extended in many directions, his general formulation of firm behaviour (managers maximising with respect to their own goals subject to a shareholder-imposed constraint on minimal profits) has been widely accepted in subsequent writings.

B

Williamson (1964) argues that managers are even more hedonistic than Baumol suspects. Williamson cites no less an authority than Adam Smith, who claimed that the consequence of a grant of perpetual monopoly to any firm 'is merely to enable the company to support the negligence, profusion, and malversation of their servants, whose disorderly conduct seldom allows the company to exceed the ordinary rate of profits in trades which are altogether free" (Smith 1937, p. 712). In Williamson's model the 'negligence, profusion and malversation' of management may take many forms: higher salaries, fringe benefits, expense accounts, more expensive office furnishings, larger head-office staff or a higher level of retained earnings to invest at the management's discretion. Although Williamson's model presents an interesting contrast to Baumol's, it is easy to emphasise their differences, rather than their similarities. Baumol's managers, in expanding the size of the firm, are promoting indirectly the very same ends that Williamson's managers are seeking directly. The two models differ in detail, but not in spirit.

Baumol and Williamson both emphasised the consequences of managerial control of a firm for the *static* allocation of the firm's resources. In each case, shareholder profits are diverted to uses closer to managerial interests—size-expanding expenditures in Baumol's case, managerial emoluments in Williamson's. In focusing on a purely static misallocation of resources, both models leave aside the difficult question of how a firm's managers prepare for an even better tomorrow. To study the possible misallocation of resources over time, requires a theory of the growth of the firm, and to that topic we now turn.

DYNAMIC OPTIMISING THEORIES

The theory of the growth of the firm is both the subject and the title of Edith Penrose's treatise published in 1959, the same year as Baumol's study noted above. At first glance, the two books have much in common: both assume the separation of ownership from control and the preference of management for size rather than for profit. But while Baumol was focusing on the present size of the firm and ignoring the question of its growth over time, Mrs Penrose went to the opposite extreme of ignoring present size and concentrating on an optimal investment strategy for making the firm grow.[2] By focusing only on new investment, she came to an unorthodox rationale for profit-maximising behaviour. Since investments must be financed and current earnings offer the surest source of funding, the more profitable the investments selected this period, the more money available for investing next period. In the selection of an investment strategy, then, *growth maximisation was tantamount to profit maximisation*. The critical difference between having managers rather than shareholders at the controls comes with the decision of how much of the maximised profits to pay out as dividends: the powerless shareholders in a managerially controlled firm receive only some ill-defined minimum, while the lion's share is retained to finance the further expansion of the firm.

But more important than any financial constraint on the growth of a firm is the firm's limited endowment of managerial services. New expansion requires careful planning, and careful planning requires managerial time and effort. If managerial services could be hired from outside and easily integrated into the existing management cadre, then no worth while investment would ever be passed over for lack of managerial time. But new managers can be brought into the existing 'team' only at a limited rate, so that a firm's inherited managerial resources effectively restrain the firm's ability to grow. This emphasis on the integrity of the managerial 'team', and conception of a firm's management as an experienced administrative *unit*, is the keynote of Mrs Penrose's approach.

Because Mrs Penrose does not set down a formal model of a growing firm, the reader is left to determine for himself the exact roles played by the availability of funds, the endowment of managerial resources and the profitability of new investment opportunities in determining a firm's overall rate of growth. If my reading is correct, however, Mrs Penrose intends to put primary emphasis on the availability of managerial services and to presume that new investment opportunities and the requisite financing will typically be sufficient. If so, then this reliance on an internal limit on the firm's ability to grow, rather than on the availability of new investment opportunities, sets Mrs Penrose's theory off from both the neo-classical theory of the firm and the more recent, steady-state growth models described below.

This attention to a firm's internal resources and capabilities naturally lends itself to an analysis of the *direction* of a firm's expansion. What determines whether a firm will move horizontally into a new geographical market, integrate forward or backward, or even diversify into a new industry? In addition to the managerial resources available to plan all types of growth, any firm, according to Mrs Penrose, is bound to have a bundle of other unused or underutilised resources. Highly specialised labour and machinery, unused by-products of current production, as well as technological advantages in particular fields push the firm into complementary areas of specialisation. In moving into a new field, a firm develops new capabilities, finds another set of productive resources underutilised and thereby sets the stage for another round of expansion. In short, new investment opportunities come not so much from outside changes in the firm's economic environment, but from inside changes in the firm's ability to exploit existing market opportunities.

Over the last decade, the problem of determining a firm's rate of growth has received considerably more attention than that of specifying the direction of its investment. Robin Marris's *The Economic Theory of Managerial Capitalism* (1964) is the most ambitious and best known contribution in this field and well worth noting here. Marris begins with an elaborate, well constructed defense of why the primary goal of management would be to maximise the growth rate of the firm. In addition to the purely economic advantages conferred by size, sociological and psychological pressures push managers towards a primary concern for growth. Salary bonus schemes, often designed by the managers themselves, tend to reward success in growing and thereby reinforce management's preference for growth. But, Marris argues, even the most cynical and self-serving management cannot ignore shareholder interests. Why not? Managers themselves may hold stock in the firm and thereby have a direct economic interest in high stock market values. Robust prices also facilitate the issue of new capital in the stock and bond markets and, thus, indirectly contribute to the growth of the firm. But most importantly, depressed share prices invite takeovers by larger firms and thereby threaten the autonomy and even the job security of the existing management. The market for corporate control exerts some discipline through the threat of a takeover. Managers must accordingly temper their primary interest in growth (or high salaries, etc.) with a secondary concern for the stock market value of their firm's shares.

Unfortunately, the theory of stock market share values is in a crude and early state, and it is not obvious exactly what management can do to keep stock prices high. Marris turns more in desperation than by choice to long-run, steady-state analysis in which stock market prices equal the discounted value of a constant stream of future dividends. In such models, the firm's dividend policy takes on prime importance, since the dividend rate simultaneously determines the availability of retained earnings to finance new growth and the stock market value of the firm's shares. The implicit relationship between growth and share values can be represented in a simple diagram (see Fig. 1).

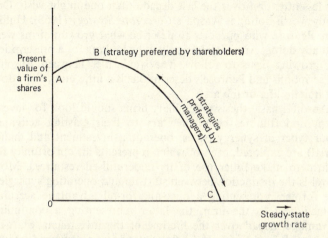

Figure 1.   Implicit trade-off between the present value of a firm's shares and its long-run rate of growth.

Between points *A* and *B* faster growth brings higher dividends and, consequently, higher stock prices. No conflict between manager and shareholder interests exists up until point *B* where the value of the firm's shares are maximised. But as we move from *B* to *C*, higher growth rates can be financed only by lowering dividend payments. The more willing management is to risk a takeover by sacrificing shareholder interests for higher growth, the further to the right of point *B* towards point *C* the management is willing to operate.

Steady-state analysis thus offers a rigorous answer to a difficult question: what determines a firm's rate of growth. In using this method, one must postulate a stable 'super-environment' of new investment opportunities as well as a constantly increasing capability of the firm to exploit these opportunities. By making the analysis homogeneous enough to yield a clearcut answer to how fast a firm will grow, one loses track of the heterogeneous capability of firms and, consequently, the changing directions of a firm's growth. Because foreign investment represents a particular direction for growth, steady-state analysis may have relatively little to contribute to the study of multinational enterprise.

Considerably less elegant, but potentially more useful in the analysis of foreign investment behaviour, are models explaining the *direction* of firm growth. Regrettably, this topic has received far less attention over the last decade than one might wish. One study worth noting is Ansoff's *Corporate Strategy* (1965). Unlike Mrs Penrose who purports to describe what growing firms were actually doing, Ansoff claims only to be looking for a prescription for growing firms to follow. The similarities between Ansoff's prescriptions and Penrose's descriptions is a little unsettling: does art imitate life, or life art?

Ansoff's basic thesis is familiar: firms should look for investment opportunities complementary to their existing activities. Four types of synergy (sales, operating, investment and managerial) are explored, each of which represents an opportunity for a firm to make fuller use of its underutilised resources. More novel is the distinction between start-up and operating synergies, the former representing a once-and-for-all advantage accruing immediately to the firm, the latter representing a continuing advantage spread over the lifetime of the investment. Start-up synergy often obtains when a firm introduces a new product into a market where it has some past experience, whereas operating synergy is often found where two or more activities can share common production or distributional facilities. Whether these notions could be fruitfully applied to the analysis of actual investment programmes remains to be seen, but they probably would provide as good a beginning as any.

BEHAVIOURAL AND ORGANISATIONAL APPROACHES

The behavioural-organisational approach to the behaviour of the firm has been developed by a number of economists and organisational theorists.[3] The approach differs fundamentally from the classical theory and the models of behaviour outlined above in its basic postulates about both individual and group behaviour. Unlike the classical assumption that an individual has a well-defined set of preferences and a willingness to choose the best alternative available, the behaviouralists assume only that an individual has expectations about what is satisfactory and accepts the first alternative he finds which satisfies his expectations. Individuals are not optimisers, but 'satisficers'—to use the simple phrase that Simon coined. Because an individual's notion of how much is enough, together with his process of looking for satisfactory alternatives, are largely determined by his past experience with similar decisions, only by studying an actual decision-making process over a period of time can one understand and predict individual behaviour.

In addition to these different postulates about individual behaviour, Simon *et al.* take a different approach in their analysis of group behaviour within a firm. In traditional theories of the firm, the behaviour of the firm is determined by the preferences of a single individual or group—formerly the owners, lately the managers. In the behavioural-organisational model, the firm is less a monolith and more a mosaic of several groups: share-holders, directors, managers, secretaries, clerks, salesman, fore-men, workers, etc. While all groups have a common interest in the survival of the firm and a consequent willingness to co-operate, each has separate interests to be pursued once survival is assured. The behaviour of the firm is the product of the interaction of the several groups, so rather than being predictable from profit or growth considerations alone, the behaviour is an uncertain and shifting compromise among the several interest groups.

The essence of the behaviouralist-organisationalist approach is clearly revealed in actual practice. To take a particularly apt example, consider Aharoni's 1966 study, *The Foreign Investment Decision Process*. The very idea of a decision process spread over a period of time and a sequence of decision makers, rather than a once-and-for-all choice by a single decision-maker, is characteristic of this general approach. Aharoni breaks this decision process down into sequential steps: the decision to look abroad, the investigation process, the commitment to invest, and follow-up reviews and refinements. The most significant distinc-tion, according to Aharoni, is between the initial decision to look abroad and the following steps, since the first step appears to be the most critical. Whether or not the firm pursues the initial idea of investing abroad depends not on hard information about profit and growth prospects, but on the strength of the initiating force (an outside proposal from a credible source, the threat of losing an export market, the drive of a top executive, etc.). If and when a decision is made to investigate the foreign investment opportunity more fully, then more reliable information is gathered and the project picks up further momentum. Aharoni traces the decision process through to completion, noting how information passed within the firm is often distorted to serve the goals of the sender, and how perceptions of the project change over time and at different levels of the managerial hierarchy. The foreign investment decision, if repeated, is often institutionalised in an international division within the corporation, a significant development in creating both expertise and a vested interest in further foreign investments.

A most interesting topic in the theory of the firm today is the synthesis of the behavioural-organisational approach with optimising theories of the firm. Economists of each persuasion believe that a reconciliation is both feasible and worth while, but so far success in joining the two has been limited. Leibenstein's work (unpublished) on individual preferences and behaviour, although very classical in its basic postulates, gives a theoretical foundation to satisficing behaviour. Chandler's study (1962) of the relationship between a firm's strategy for growth and its administrative structure offers considerable insight into the linkages between a firm's objectives and its observed behaviour. Although Chandler's thesis is that administrative structure is ultimately determined by strategic objectives, his case studies convincingly demonstrate that, in the short run at least, structural relationships impinge upon a firm's behaviour. This, of course, is the essence of the organisationalist hypothesis. In recent publications Williamson (1971) has explored the information and control content of different administrative structures and concluded that the modern administrative structures are more conducive to optimising behaviour than the older administrative structures were. If firms continue to adopt new administrative structures, the orthodox economist may shed the image of a reactionary for that of a visionary!

These then are some of the recent developments in the theory of the firm. A common practice in all the writings is to reject the notion of a firm as an agent of its shareholders and to replace it with that of an organisation with both a will and a personality all its own. Although important issues concerning the motivation of firms remain unresolved, most writers would agree that as long as the survival of the firm is not in jeopardy, the primary objective of the firm is to grow. Firms are also increasingly credited with having distinctive personalities. Although these personalities are difficult to characterise for analytical purposes, most profiles would include the distinctive resources and capabilities of the firm, the apparent preferences and inhibitions of its top management and perhaps the administrative structure through which these preferences are (or are not) implemented.

THE STUDY OF MULTINATIONAL ENTERPRISE

The preceding section sought to recall the more salient developments in the theory of the firm over the past 15 years. Much of the newer theories is geared to the behaviour of a corporation large enough to earn some excess profits and, thus, large enough to give its managers some discretionary influence over its activities. Accordingly, the newer theories would appear to be well suited to the study of multinational enterprise. By almost every account, the typical multinational firm is an oligopolist in its own domestic product markets. But this accordance between the new theories of the firm (excepting the behavioural theories) and the new reality of multinational enterprise is largely an illusion. As Guy Stevens shows in Chapter 3, the familiar profit-maximising models of the firm have worked as well in empirical studies as the newer size-maximising models. The purpose of this section of my paper is to show how this could be so, and why differences in firm motivation are fine distinctions in most empirical analyses of foreign investment behaviour. I intend to show that, even at the level of pure theory, differences in objectives may not lead to differences in behaviour, or if they do, the differences in behaviour are far too subtle to be detected with existing data. For the empirical analysis of foreign investment behaviour, the newer theories of the firm may represent much ado about nothing.

To demonstrate this proposition, I need to develop a simple, theoretical model of multinational firm behaviour which will allow me to contrast profit-maximising with size-maximising behaviour. Virtually any aspect of foreign investment behaviour could serve as the basis for this demonstration; let me focus on the familiar problem of choosing between exporting and foreign subsidiary production.

Since I wish to make only a few, simple points, the analysis below can be kept at an elementary level. Suppose that the marginal cost to a firm of serving a foreign market with exports (including all tariff and transport costs) is the same for all levels of supply. Suppose further that production within the foreign country entails some fixed, overhead costs as well as constant marginal costs. Assuming the firm has some monopoly power in the foreign market, the various supply and demand curves might be as shown in Fig. 2.

The optimal strategy for the firm depends, of course, on what is being optimised. Let us begin with the most familiar assumption —that the firm is trying to maximise profits. We can limit our attention to two points: (1) the profit-maximising export strategy (point B in Fig. 2) where the marginal revenue from foreign sales equals the marginal cost of exporting: and (2) the profit-maximising foreign-production strategy (point C in Fig. 2) where the marginal revenue from foreign sales equals the marginal cost of foreign production. The choice between exporting and foreign production depends on whether the savings in variable supply costs (represented by the trapezoid *ABCD*) is greater or less than the fixed costs of foreign production.

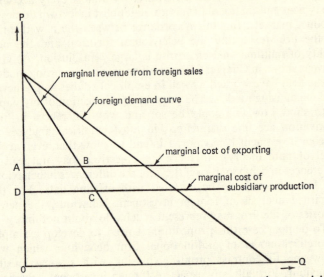

Figure 2. Maximising foreign sales subject to a constraint on minimal profits.

This simple, static analysis can be used for simple, dynamic analysis by imagining, for instance, that the foreign market is growing and the foreign demand curve is shifting out over time. Even if the firm initially finds exporting to be more profitable than producing abroad, the time may come when the balance between the fixed-cost savings of exporting and the variable-cost saving of foreign production is reversed. Figure 3 shows a 'product cycle' type of response—exports are replaced by foreign production as the preferred source of supply. Notice the quantum jump in the volume of foreign sales when the changeover occurs.

The behaviour described above is the optimal strategy for a profit-maximising firm. If the firm's primary concern is for something other than its profits, its response to its foreign market opportunities will be different. Suppose, for purposes of comparison, that the firm wished to maximise its sales in the foreign market subject, of course, to a constraint on minimal profits. In operational terms, it may be willing to lower its price and sacrifice profits in order to expand its foreign market. The nature of this optimal strategy is shown in Fig. 4. If exports are the source of supply, sales can be expanded until the diminished profit rectangle, *ABCD*, just equals the minimally acceptable level. If subsidiary production is the source, sales will be expanded until the profit

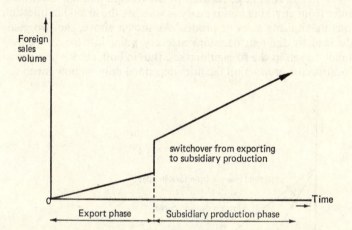

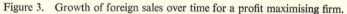

Figure 3.   Growth of foreign sales over time for a profit maximising firm.

rectangle, *ABEF*, less the fixed costs of production (not shown) just equals the minimum. The choice *between* exporting and subsidiary production in this instance is based on which source permits a larger sales volume in the foreign market. Notice that as long as the profit constraint does not force the firm to maximise profits, the sales-maximising firm would always be selling more and earning less than the profit-maximising firm.

This simple, static analysis can also be translated into simple, dynamic analysis by assuming (see Fig. 5) that the foreign demand curve is shifting out over time. Here, too, exports may be preferred initially, but as time passes and the foreign market expands, the firm will establish a producing subsidiary in the foreign country. Figure 5 depicts the growth of foreign sales over a period of time. The principal differences between the response of the sales-maximising firm here and the profit-maximising firm above are (1) the sales-maximising firm is always larger: (2) the switchover to subsidiary production comes sooner (but at the same critical volume of sales); and (3) the switchover is not punctuated by a quantum jump in the level of sales. The optimal strategy of the firm does indeed depend on what the firm is optimising.

With this analysis in mind, we are in a good position to assess some of the difficulties of inferring a firm's motivation from its foreign investment behaviour. Let us begin with a completely hopeless case. Suppose one were trying to estimate an investment function relating changes in the size and location of a capital stock to the volume of its sales to the foreign market. Could one infer from anything in this analysis whether the firm(s) in question was maximising sales or profits? As shown above, the two goals do lead to different decisions at every point in time about how much to sell in the foreign market. But, in both cases, the optimal location for production facilities depended only on how much the

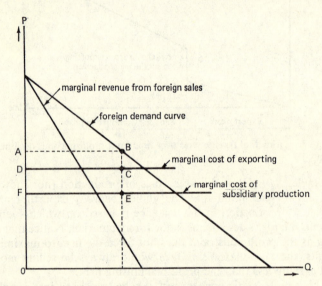

Figure 4.   Maximising profits from selling abroad.

firm wanted to sell abroad, and this relationship was the same in the two instances. Furthermore, the optimal capital-output ratio is strictly a cost-minimisation problem, and both types of firms, profit maximisers and sales maximisers, are cost minimisers, In short, the investment function does not depend on whether the firm is maximising sales or profits, so an analysis of investment behaviour reveals nothing of the ultimate goals of the firm.

An analysis of how much a firm sells abroad is only slightly more revealing. As noted above, given the same demand and cost conditions, a sales-maximising firm sells more and earns less than a profit maximising firm. In theory, differences in the objectives of firms should reveal themselves in differences in foreign market size. But in practice, one rarely has reliable data on the demand and cost conditions in any two instances. At most, one has some information on the levels of exports and subsidiary production over time or across firms, and this data may shed little light on

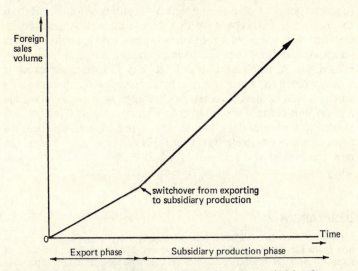

Figure 5.   Growth of foreign sales over time for sales-maximising firm.

the underlying motivation. In both the profit- and sales-maximising cases, one observes a transition from exporting to foreign subsidiary production. The histograms in Figs 3 and 5 look much the same, and it would be difficult to distinguish between differences in motivation from differences in demand and cost conditions. The only qualitative difference in the two histograms was the quantum jump in sales accompanying a profit-maximising shift from exports to subsidiary sales, and such a jump may be too small to observe in practice.

One encounters similar problems in studying the way firms respond to changes in their economic environment. Tariff changes, an acceleration in the growth of the foreign market, increases in factor costs, technological breakthroughs at home and abroad all produce qualitatively similar responses by firms with different goals. Without the appropriate information on the firm's cost and demand conditions, the behaviour of a firm may reveal little about its ultimate objective.

CONCLUSIONS

In the end, one must come to rather negative conclusions. The newer theories of the firm are very plausible in arguing that a large corporation today probably doesn't have to maximise profits constantly if it is to survive, nor if it is to forestall a shareholder revolt. They are also plausible in claiming that the 'market for corporate control' is too imperfect to force profit-maximisation to discourage a takeover by outsiders. But what appear to be clearcut differences in motivation—profit maximisation versus size maximisation—turn out to imply rather subtle differences in behaviour. A firm maximising size has a foreign investment strategy much the same as a firm maximising profits. Old theories work as well as new theories, not because they are as plausible *a priori*, but because they predict as well *a posteriori*. Until we are treated to far better data than those at hand, or until we focus on areas of activity where motivation makes more of a difference, the new theories of the firm will shed little light on the empirical study of multinational enterprise, and vice versa.

References

1 Research on this project was supported by a National Science Foundation grant for the study of foreign investment behaviour. I am indebted to several people for helpful comments on a preliminary draft of the paper— George Borts, Richard Caves, Edith Penrose and Guy Stevens among others.

2 The difference between size and growth maximisation was confusing, and it was only with the publication of Williamson's article seven years later (1966) that the confusion was resolved. By expanding an advertising programme or lowering prices, a firm can sacrifice current profits for current size—Baumol's proposition. Current profits are needed to finance new investments, so growth maximisation requires profit maximisation—Penrose's proposition. Putting the two together, we have the ineluctable trade-off between present size and further growth—Williamson's proposition. The presumed preference of managers for 'size' turns out to be far more complicated than it first appeared.

3 Notably Simon (1957a, 1957b, 1962), Cyert and March (1963) and Cohen and Cyert (1965).

Chapter 3

THE DETERMINANTS OF INVESTMENT

Guy V. G. Stevens[1]

INTRODUCTION

In 1970, fixed investment spending of US foreign affiliates reached 20 per cent of the domestic total for manufacturing and 16 per cent for all industry. For specific industries the 1970 figures are even more dramatic: chemicals, 38 per cent; transportation equipment, 45 per cent.[2]

Moreover, the faster growth of foreign operations of US firms implies higher percentages in the future. Since 1957, when the figures were first collected, foreign plant and equipment expenditures in manufacturing have increased from $1 \cdot 3$ billion dollars and an 8 per cent share to its 1970 level of $6 \cdot 5$ billion and 20 per cent; for all industry the figures are $4 \cdot 9$ billion and 12 per cent in 1957, to $13 \cdot 1$ billion and 16 per cent in 1970.

In view of the rapid growth and present importance of the foreign component of US fixed-investment spending, it is fitting to ask what, if anything, this implies for the determinants of corporate investment. Do studies of the multinational enterprise provide new evidence on the theoretical or empirical determinants of investment?[3] Might such findings affect studies of domestic investment, as well as foreign? As it turns out, these are not idle questions; as we will see below, many unusual hypotheses have been offered to explain the investment spending of multinational enterprises.

Closely related to the answer of the primary question is an evaluation of the state of theoretical and empirical research into the determinants of multinational investment. Where do we stand? Are researchers at the frontiers of investment theory? Are they making adequate use of the available empirical data? Do we have moderately bright chances to solve the important questions before us—such as the reasonably accurate explanation and forecasting of foreign investment, both real investment and the financial flows that are so important to the balance of payments; such as the estimation of the effects of past and, especially, proposed policies to influence the flow of foreign investment for the purposes of balance-of-payments equilibrium or economic development?

In this chapter, 'the determinants of investment' will be interpreted broadly, to include both investment in real assets and the concomitant financial investment. Real investment and its financing are related in any case, but, in the study of the multinational firm, financial investment has an extraordinary importance. Most of the worries about the effect of the multinational firm on the balance of payments are worries about *financial* investment. Talk about the 'flow of direct investment', or 'the net capital outflow', is talk about financial flows—in the first case, the change in a country's net worth or ownership position in foreign-based business firms; in the second, the major financial flow (along with repatriated dividends) that enters the balance of payments.[4] These important questions cannot be answered by studying real investment alone.

This chapter is divided into five parts. Following the introduction, the next section briefly surveys the present state of the theoretical and empirical analysis of investment; both real and financial investment are covered, but research into the determinants of plant and equipment is emphasised—mainly because most of the progress has been in that field. The third section attempts to assess the implications of research on the multinational firm for the determinants of real investment. In much less comprehensive fashion, in the fourth section, the same is attempted for financial investment. The final section is concerned with the suggestions for future research which come out of this analysis: research to test more adequately some of the hypotheses discussed in the previous two sections and research which, in the author's estimation, is necessary in order to achieve the most important goals in the study of the investment of the multinational firm.

FIRM INVESTMENT: A VIEW OF THE STATE OF THE SCIENCE

Looking at the current state of theoretical and empirical knowledge of corporate investment, one is presented with a paradoxical picture. In some respects, it is a picture of vigorous, steady progress; in others, one of controversy reaching to the very foundations of the science. The theory of real or fixed investment and the theory of corporate finance are deductions from an underlying theory of the firm. There is considerable dispute today over what this underlying theory should be. At the same time, however, there has been dramatic progress both in refining the traditional theory—based on the neo-classical model of profit maximisation —and in empirically estimating investment functions.

CONTROVERSIES OVER THE FIRM'S OBJECTIVE FUNCTION[5]

For 40 years—at least since Berle and Means (1932) argued that the firm's owners do not control its managers—there has been a more-or-less continuous debate over the model that best describes business behaviour. Do managers really attempt to maximise the market value of the firm—or its equivalent under certainty, profits—as the traditional owner-oriented theory says? Or does the separation of ownership and control allow managers to do something else? Or, as hypothesised more recently, does operation in an uncertain environment *force* them to do something else? Clearly the answers imply much for the theory of capital and investment.

As far as its application to the empirical analysis of investment is concerned, the traditional theory has had its fullest development in the work of Jorgenson and his associates, and Bischoff.[6] So far the theory has been fully developed only under conditions of certainty or certainty-equivalence; under these conditions, the objective of the managers of the firm is to maximise the discounted sum of present and future net cash flows.[7] Out of this maximisation comes, among other things, the firm's optimal plan for capital and investment. As molded by Jorgenson, the theory is neo-classical—in the sense that the firm's investment policy is assumed to respond to all the product prices, factor prices, interest rates, and tax rates that affect profits. As will be discussed in more detail below, much empirical work has been devoted to confirming and measuring the impact of these variables on domestic plant and equipment expenditure.

Competing, non-profit-maximisation theories, have arisen for a number of different reasons. The assumption that managers are at least partially independent of stockholder control is the groundwork of a class of theories that state that what is maximised is the utility functions of the managers. Specifically, much has been made of the possible fact that managers' remuneration is more closely correlated with the size of the firm than with firm profits.[8] This suggests that it is rational for managers to sacrifice profits to achieve greater firm size and growth. For this reason, a major challenger to the traditional theory is some form of *growth* maximisation, a theory associated with the names of Marris (1964), Baumol (1962) and Galbraith (1967). The managers choose to maximise the corporate growth rate, subject to some constraint on profits or dividend payments—this latter to placate the stockholders and avoid takeovers. What does this theory say about the firm's capital and investment? First, with respect to the choice of factors to produce any given level of output, Williamson (1966) has shown that the solution under growth maximisation and profit maximisation will be the same: because of the profit or dividend constraint, profits will not be sacrificed unless they contribute to growth. However, it is easily shown that, under growth maximisation, the firm's optimal capital stock is larger at any point in time than that under profit maximisation. At the margin, investment and related variables such as R & D and advertising are pushed beyond the point where net returns are equal to the market-determined cost of capital.

Although sometimes linked with the foregoing, there are separate causes for the espousal of non-profit-maximisation theories of the firm. The difficulties connected with working in an uncertain environment have been emphasised by the 'behavioural school' as causes of firm behaviour that is inconsistent with profit maximisation.[9] Cyert and March (1963) set up a model which consists of: (1) the existence of established firm goals or rules of thumb in every relevant area of firm decision; (2) a rule of choice among alternative actions which calls for the selection of the first solution perceived that satisfies the goal; (3) a search procedure for discovering alternative solutions to be activated only if no 'satisficing' solution can be found. It is an open question whether this system is always inconsistent with profit maximisation under uncertainty, especially if firm goals are adjusted over time.[10]

With respect to their implications for investment functions, behavioural theories seem to make investment choices the vehicle for satisfying simple firm goals such as a constant or growing market share.[11]

THE STATE OF EMPIRICAL RESEARCH ON THE DETERMINANTS OF INVESTMENT

If we were to limit our attention to the existing state of empirical research on corporate investment, we would hardly be aware of the controversy raging around its theoretical foundations. For example, in a recent compendium containing papers by most of the major contributors to empirical investment analysis, there is not a mention of growth maximisation or behavioural theories.[12] All investment equations were based directly or indirectly on the foundation of profit maximisation. This is not meant as an indictment—although it is intellectually unsettling to be in a situation where the foundations of a discipline are seriously questioned. Rather, the continued ascendency of the neo-classical model can be defended by noting that: (1) by using it, significant progress has been made in the last ten years in explaining and predicting investment; (2) alternative theories have been very slow in throwing up testable hypotheses that could be substituted for the neo-classical investment functions. And when, in the very recent past, alternatives have been suggested, they have proved to be empirically indistinguishable from the neo-classical functions.

Concerning the second point, to the author's knowledge, the first attempt to derive and test an investment function from a non-traditional set of postulates—in this case growth maximisation—is a very recent one, published in 1972, by Grabowski and Mueller (1972). Moreover, the empirical results obtained by Grabowski and Mueller made it impossible for them to accept the growth maximisation investment function and reject the neo-classical. In particular, in their tests of a 'managerial variant' of the investment function, the significant variables explaining investment were a series of sales change and cash flow terms; both of these variables are frequently part of neo-classical investment functions. Although Grabowski and Mueller did not successfully supplant neo-classical investment functions, their results cannot be interpreted as a blow for the traditional theory of the firm: in testing equations for the other decision variables in their model—dividends and research and development—they found considerably more evidence for the managerial model.

On the other hand, there has been the appearance and, probably, the reality of steady progress in estimating investment functions based on the neo-classical model. In the first place, resulting mainly from the pioneering work of Jorgenson, there has been a link forged between the theory of profit maximisation and empirically estimated investment functions. In Jorgenson's theory, as in some of its predecessors, investment occurs as the firm attempts to adjust its actual capital stock to its desired level. Jorgenson's major theoretical contribution was to deduce from the profit-maximising conditions a precise functional form for the desired stock of capital and its precise dependence on factor prices, the rate of depreciation and tax rates. In most of Jorgenson's articles desired capital, K^*, is equal to:

$$K_t^* = \frac{a p_t Q_t}{c_t},$$

where p_t is the product price (at time t), Q_t is expected output, c_t is the rental price of capital and a is a constant derived from the assumed Cobb–Douglas production function, the elasticity of output with respect to capital. The rental price of capital, c_t, is in turn a function of the price of capital goods and its rate of change, the cost of capital or the rate of interest, the depreciation rate and various tax rates.

Given the desired stock of capital, investment is viewed as a gradual adjustment of actual capital to that desired level— a modified version of the flexible accelerator introduced by Chenery (1952).[13] A second source of progress has been the development of more sophisticated procedures for estimating the above adjustment process—the polynomial and rational distributed lag estimation procedures of Almon (1965) and Jorgenson (1966).

These developments have improved the explanatory and forecasting ability of investment functions. Bischoff (1971a), Jorgenson and Siebert (1968) and Jorgenson et al. (1970a, b) have compared the neo-classical investment functions in various ways with the existing alternatives and have concluded that the neo-classical function out-performs its competitors. In particular, the neo-classical model has been tested against the simple accelerator model (where desired capital is assumed to be a constant times expected output), liquidity and cash flow models first suggested by Meyer and Kuh (1957), securities valuation models, where desired capital is assumed to be proportional to the market value of the firm, and combinations of the three. Many types of tests have been performed: comparison of standard errors of the residuals and multiple correlation coefficients within the sample period; comparison of the sign and significance of estimated coefficients with those predicted; the relative ability to predict turning points; and the relative forecasting ability outside the sample period. In virtually every case some form of the neo-classical model out-performed the alternatives.

CONTROVERSIES AND UNSETTLED QUESTIONS' CONCERNING THE
NEO-CLASSICAL INVESTMENT FUNCTION

Despite the empirical successes of investment functions derived
from the neo-classical model, much controversy and many
unsettled questions remain.

Most of the advocates of growth maximisation, behavioural
theories, and other non-traditional approaches are still uncon-
vinced by the evidence supporting the neo-classical investment
function. For one thing, none of the empirical results specifically
reject the alternative of growth maximisation; as we discussed
above, the article of Williamson (1966) implies that it will be
difficult to distinguish between these two alternatives on the basis
of tests of investment behaviour alone.[14] Moreover, there are
enough arbitrary elements in the present formulation of the neo-
classical investment model that it is easily argued that the supporting empirical evidence is slight confirmation of profit maximisation. The use of output or sales as an independent variable in
most neo-classical investment functions is hard to justify, and
raises the complaint that the new functions are really little
different from the old flexible accelerator. The failure to relate
the distributed lag structure of the model to profit maximisation
is a second fundamental objection. Finally, the obvious unreality
of the assumptions of perfect competition and perfect certainty
provide an easy mark for critics maintaining that the neo-classical
model says little about firm behaviour in the real world.

The validity of these objections is acknowledged by many of
the supporters of the neo-classical model. Undoubtedly they
hope—not without evidentiary support—that the relaxation of
the arbitrary assumptions will be possible without the jettisoning
of the underlying theory of profit maximisation.[15] In any case,
these and other questions are as much the subject of debate and
research within the neo-classical school as without.

One of the most important unsettled questions, and an area
where future research on the multinational firm is most likely to
make a contribution, is the place of liquidity or cash flow variables
in the investment function—in addition to the other neo-classical
variables. This is intimately related to the basic question of
whether there is any simultaneity in the determination of real
investment, the cost of capital and the financial plan of the firm.[16]
In a recent survey, Jorgenson (1971) concludes that there is no
evidence that supply-of-funds variables have any marginal
impact on investment. The evidence he cites suggests at best a
small impact of such factors relative to sales and price variables,

but it is probably claiming too much to say no impact.[17] In any case, Jorgenson concludes that all the evidence supports the proposition first stated by Modigliani and Miller (1958) that the firm's cost of capital and investment are independent of sources of finance. However, two types of evidence call this conclusion into question. First, a number of other, recent, studies by Coen (1971) and Klein and Taubman (1971) support both empirically and, to some extent, theoretically the dependence of investment on the supply of internally-generated funds. Second, it seems to be the general opinion in the financial field that the real world is not a Modigliani–Miller world. All agree—including Modigliani and Miller (1966)—that the deductability of interest for tax purposes should imply a preference for debt over equity or retained earnings. On othe other hand, other costs, such as those that may be associated with bankruptcy or the flotation of external sources of finance may push the corporation away from debt finance. These considerations imply that the value of the firm is not independent of the sources of finance.

Although few seem to accept the original Modigliani–Miller propositions, entirely open questions are the precise determinants of the firm's optimal financial plan, its relation to the cost of capital, and the interdependence between the optimal financial plan, the cost of capital, and investment in fixed and other assets.

All of this, of course, affects the choice of investment function for plant and equipment. It also affects the explanation and prediction of the firm's sources of finance. This latter is a relatively neglected area of the theory of the firm, but one, which we will see below, is extremely important for studies of the multinational corporation.

In summary, the present state of investment theory seems to be one where considerable progress has been made in the past decade on linking empirical work to theory and improving the explanatory and forecasting ability of empirical investment functions. However, the reigning champion, the neo-classical theory, is under attack from all directions, both from without and within, from those who feel the whole idea of value or profit maximisation is wrong and from those who object to particular parts of any given neo-classical model. This is not just an academic debate, devoid of practical consequences. Although it might be argued that we are getting fairly adequate short-run forecasts of investment,[18] empirical investment functions are not developed to a level where we can adequately predict the impact of new or proposed policies.[19]

IMPLICATIONS OF THE GROWTH OF THE MULTINATIONAL FIRM FOR THE DETERMINANTS OF FIXED INVESTMENT

The purpose of this section is to determine what the growing importance the multinational firm implies, if anything, for the theory or empirical analysis of investment.

Until now, the analysis of domestic investment has progressed in isolation from considerations of the internationalisation of production. What inter-action there has been, has, in fact, been one way: international researchers borrowing from the domestic. However, there has been much done on the multinational firm which is quite independent of any domestic influence.

Do any of our results concerned with the international operations of the firm *compel* changes in investment theory or its applications? The conclusion from what follows below is: no, not yet. The reason is the same as that used to defend, in the preceding section, the continued reliance on the neo-classical investment model: in order to replace a theory you have to demonstrate that you can do its job better with something else. If the goal is explaining past data or forecasting, no alternatives or additions to the neo-classical model suggested by studying the multinational enterprise have been proved superior to what we already have. This assertion holds for data at all levels of aggregation. Further, it should be argued that no other goals have been seriously defended.

However, the author also feels that there are some findings based on the study of foreign investment that may, with further verification, prove important. Some of these findings suggest new factors to be taken into account, generally, in investment functions; other support one side or the other in important debates discussed in the previous section.

In this section, the discussion will be organised around the following questions:

(1) The implications of research on the real and financial investment of the multinational firm for the firm's objective function.
(2) The application of standard neo-classical models to the multinational firm.
(3) The incorporation of variables specific to international activities into the neo-classical model.
(4) The possibility of interactions between domestic and foreign real investment expenditures.
(5) The explanation of investment in new subsidiaries, in

addition to the explanation of the expansion of existing subsidiaries.

(6) The possibility of oligopolistic interdependencies.

The succeeding section will cover, in less detail, the implications of multinational operations for the theory of corporate finance.

THE OBJECTIVE FUNCTION OF THE MULTINATIONAL FIRM

The argument of the previous section was that, despite considerable controversy over the basic objectives of the firm, virtually all empirically verified investment functions (that have been deduced from any theory of the firm) have, in fact, come from the neo-classical theory. Many, many researchers on the international operations of the firm have had something to say on the firm's objective function and, therefore, directly or by implication on the theory of investment. Some of these findings give quite unusual pictures of how multinational firms behave—differing, not only from the neo-classical profit-maximisation theory, but also from all the other theories discussed above. It is time to attempt to catalogue these disparate theories, to try to assess their significance and their implications for the theory of investment.

Table 3.1 is an attempt to categorise the most important studies that the author has read that say something about the multi-national firm's objective function or investment policies. The general interpretation is that both the majority of researchers and the weight of the evidence support the maintenance of the profit-maximisation theory. But that is the conclusion to a long story. In what follows the focus will be on the dissenters from profit maximisation. These are the ones to concentrate on if we are to determine whether research on the multinational firm tells us anything *new*.

Table 3.1. Studies on the Investment and Financing Decisions of the Multinational Firm

Name	Theories Supported*	Decisions Studied	Type of Evidence
Aharoni (1966)	Behavioural	Location	Interviews
Aliber (1970)	Profit maximisation	Location	Relies on other studies and general knowledge (O.S. + G.K.)
Balassa (1966)	Profit maximisation	Location	O.S. and G.K.†
Bandera & White (1968)	Profit maximisation	Flow of direct investment (financial)	Regression: macro data

Name	Theories Supported*	Decisions Studied	Type of Evidence
Barlow & Wender (1955)	Behavioural and 'gambler's' earnings	Location; finance	Interviews
Behrman (1962)	Profit maximisation; growth	Finance	Interviews
Behrman (1969)	Growth; profit maximisation	Real investment, finance; location	Interviews; macro and micro data
Berlin (1971)	Profit maximisation	Finance; real investment	Regression: micro (Office of Foreign direct Investments)
Billsborrow (1968)	Profit maximisation	Plant and equipment	Regression: micro (Colombian Subsidiaries)
Brash (1966)	Profit maximisation	Location; finance	Interviews and micro data (Australia)
Carlson (1969)	Profit maximisation —subject to risk	Finance	O.S. and G.K.†
Caves (1971)	Profit maximisation —oligopoly factors emphasised	Location	O.S. and G.K.†
Horst (1972a)	Profit maximisation	Location	Regression: macro
Horst (1972b)	Profit maximisation	Location	Regression: micro (Harvard project and Compustat)
Hymer (1960)	Profit maximisation oligopoly factors emphasised	Location	Marcro and micro data (company reports)
Hymer & Rowthorn (1970)	Market share and growth	Comparative growth of US and European multinationals	Micro: regressions and other tests (*Fortune Magazine*)
Johns (1967)	Profit maximisation	Flow of direct investment (financial)	Macro by industry (Australia)
Kindleberger (1969)	Profit maximisation	Location and other decisions	O.S. and G.K.†
Knickerbocker (1973)	Oligopolistic matching of investments	Location	Micro: regression and other tests (Harvard project)
Kopits (1972)	Profit maximisation	Repatriated dividends	Regression: macro
Kwack (1971)	Profit maximisation and risk minimisation	Flow of direct investment; other financial and real flows	Regression: macro
Miller & Weigel (1971)	Behavioural and profit maximisation	Location	Discriminant analysis: macro (Brazil)

Name	Theories Supported*	Decisions Studied	Type of Evidence
Moose (1968)	Profit maximisation	Plant and equipment, dividends, net capital outflow	Regression: macro
Morley (1966)	Profit maximisation	Flow of direct investment (financial)	Regression: macro
Penrose (1956)	Elements of behavioural, profit maximisation, growth	Real and financial investment	General knowledge and Australian data
Polk, Meister & Veit (1966)	Profit maximisation	Location; expansion	Interviews; macro
Popkin (1965)	Profit maximisation —under uncertainty	Location	Regression: micro (company reports)
Prachowny (1969)	Profit maximisation	Flow of direct investment (financial)	Regression: macro
Prachowny (1972)	Portfolio theory	Ratio of value of direct investment to value of US shares	Regression: macro
Reuber (1973)	Profit maximisation	Location; other decisions	Interviews; micro data
Rhomberg (1968)	Profit maximisation	Balance-of-payments flows	Regression: macro
Richardson (1971)	Profit maximisation	Location and expansion	O.S. and G.K.†
Rolfe (1969)	Profit maximisation	Location; finance, etc.	O.S. and G.K.†
Ruckdeschel (1971)	Profit maximisation	Net capital outflow	Regression: macro
Scaperlanda and Mauer (1969)	Profit maximisation	Flow of direct investment	Regression: macro
Severn (1972)	Profit maximisation	Finance: net financial flow; plant and equipment abroad and in US	Regression: macro (Office of Business Economics)
Spitäller (1971)	Profit maximisation	Financial and real investment	Relied on other Studies
Stevens (1969a)	Profit maximisation	Plant and equipment	Regression: micro (Office of Business Economics)
Stevens (1969b)	Portfolio theory and profit maximisation	Flow of direct investment	Regression: macro

Name	Theories Supported*	Decisions Studied	Type of Evidence
Stevens (1972)	Profit maximisation and risk minimisation	Plant and equipment balance-of-payments flows	Regression: macro
Stobaugh (1970)	Profit maximisation	Finance	Interview; micro data and statistical tests
Stonehill (1965)	Profit maximisation	Flow of direct investment	Interview; micro and macro data (Norway)
Stubenitsky (1970)	Growth or sales maximisation	Location; others	Interview; micro (Netherlands)
Vernon (1971)	Profit maximisation	Location	Macro; micro (Harvard project)
Wolf (1971)	Profit maximisation	Location	Regression: macro

* Appearing in the column 'Theory(ies) supported' is an interpretation of what each author claimed; if the former is not explicit, an interpretation of what his data or discussion implied is entered.
† 'O.S. and G.K.' means: relies on data provided in other studies and on general knowledge.

The evidence presented by the authors listed in Table 3.1 is of many different kinds, and directed to a variety of questions. Much of the evidence is based on interviews with the officials of multinational enterprises. Some of the interviews are supplemented with statistical data from company records;[20] but this is relatively rare.[21] An increasing number of studies rely wholly on statistical data and statistical techniques such as multiple regression analysis—therefore similar in method to the majority of studies of domestic investment. A perusal of the results shows that this type of study has been hampered by the great difficulties experienced in obtaining suitable statistical data. More will be said on this problem in the Summary and Recommendations section.

Evidence on the international firm's objective function comes from studies whose goals vary as widely as the sources of evidence they use. A very few attempted to study directly the plant and equipment expenditures of foreign subsidiaries or the multinational firm as a whole.[22] Others were interested not so much in real investment, but in financial flows such as the flow of direct investment or the net capital outflow and repatriated dividends that affect the balance of payments.[23] Still others have not concentrated on any particular dependent variables, but rather the *location* of investment.[24] As such, they have focused not so much on the determination of the firm's optimal capital stock abroad or its change through time, but on how this capital stock is to be divided between production operations at home and abroad. Of primary interest for most of these studies were differences in costs or returns, which, because of factor markets or market structure, make it more profitable to locate abroad in one form or another. The distinction between location and other studies is significant in another sense; as we saw above, the two major contending theories of the firm, profit maximisation and growth maximisation, both imply that a *given* level of output should be produced at a minimum cost. Therefore, the above locational evidence cannot be used to distinguish between these two theories—although it can be used to distinguish them from other alternatives.

The few remaining studies included in Table 3.1 cover a wide range of subjects, including the many effects of foreign direct investment on the host country. Some of these comment on the objective function of the multinational firm only in passing.

Non-Profit Maximisation Theories: Growth and Market Shares
Of those who seem to reject profit maximisation, six studies fall into a class distinguished by the hypothesis that the firm's objective function is different from that of the standard neo-classical firm. This class can be distinguished from another, similar, one where profits are maximised subject to constraints imposed by the internationalisation of production. In the first class we put theories suggested in Behrman (1969), Hymer and Rowthorn (1970), Stubenitsky (1970), Aharoni (1966), Stevens (1969a) and Prachowny (1972). The first four are based on ideas that already have been at least suggested by the growth maxi-misers and the behaviourists. The last two strike a somewhat new note by applying the theory of portfolio selection to the inter-national firm.

Behrman (1969), in his most recent study, arrives at a theory of international investment that is founded on the growth maximisa-tion hypothesis discussed in the domestic literature. He concludes: 'In sum, the primary stimulus that causes business to expand abroad is the desire for growth'.[25] Stubenitsky (1970), in a similar vein, opts for the goal of growth or sales maximization subject to a profit constraint.[26]

Both authors arrive at their conclusions by means of two types of evidence. The first is derived from interviews of business executives. The second is empirical evidence that they claim disproves the profit maximisation hypothesis: the refutation of the oft-state theory that the flow of direct investment is a function of the difference between rates of return in alternative locations.

Both of these arguments come up time after time in the literature, so their careful consideration is important.

What can be said about the impact of the interview data? The author considers it slight. First, for every corporate executive responding 'growth', there is at least one other saying 'profits': Behrman's earlier interview work (1962) demonstrates that. Second, in reaching his conclusion that growth motives pre-dominate, Behrman misinterprets the thrust of some of his responses. What several companies do, he states, is 'pay little attention to differences in potential rates of profit among domestic and foreign opportunities; if the foreign project is likely to earn above a given percentage, we consider it; if it is below, we do not'.[27] If the given percentage mentioned is equal to the firm's market-determined cost of capital, this *is* the profit-maximisation theory. Third, the motivational testimony for growth maxi-misation is unsupported by any corroborating empirical evidence. We will see below that virtually all the empirical evidence on international investment, like that on domestic investment, supports the traditional neo-classical model. Such evidence does not refute growth maximisation, but, being derived from the assumption of profit maximisation, certainly cannot be used to disprove this latter.

The second line of argument used by Behrman and Stubenitsky against the theory of profit maximisation is that there is much empirical evidence against the interest-differential theory of direct investment. This is true,[28] but it is a fact long known in inter-national research. The interest or profit-differential theory is a carry-over from the theory of portfolio capital movements[29] and is by no means identical to the profit-maximisation theory of in-vestment developed by Jorgenson and others. In this latter formulation, the flow of real or (possibly) financial investment is hypothesized to be positively related to the difference between the desired capital stock and actual capital; but it is not always or usually possible to express this as a function of the difference in observed profit rates abroad and at home. The simplest counter-example is the case where the foreign profit rate is higher than the domestic while both are less than the firm's opportunity cost of capital. The neo-classical theory would say that no investment should occur in either location, whereas the profit-differential theory would say a positive flow of foreign investment should be the result. A major reason why the profit-differential theory may fail, as the example shows, is that observed profit rates need not equal required or expected rates. This is particularly likely for international investment, where Hymer (1960), Vernon (1971) and others have argued persuasively that many investors possess technological or other monopolistic advantages which make their expected returns quite different from any observed average.[30]

In sum, it is the author's conclusion that the evidence adduced in support of growth maximisation as the primary impetus for international investment is weak. It is, in fact, much weaker than that produced by Marris (1964) and Grabowski and Mueller (1972) for domestic investment; so it is inconceivable that, as the situation stands today, the evidence from international operations could compel any change in the general theory of investment.[31]

Non-Profit Maximisation Theories: Behavioural Theories

Aharoni (1966) argues against the profit maximisation model and, further, maintains that the cause of the failure of profit maximisation is closely related to the internationalisation of the firm. More recently Weigel (1966) and Miller and Weigel (1971) have developed and tested a related model, linking it more closely to the behavioural theory of Cyert and March (1963).

Here we will argue against the proposition that the Aharoni study establishes any novel relationships between firm investment and the internationalisation of production. The position here is that (1) much of his evidence is consistent with profit maximisation under uncertainty and (2) although some evidence may not be, the behaviour uncovered is not peculiar to international operations.[32] Rather, as stated by Miller and Weigel and even Aharoni near the end of his book, the Aharoni evidence falls well within the behavioural model of Cyert and March. Under this interpretation, no *new* hypotheses are needed to explain or predict the behaviour of the multinational firm. What are needed are adequate tests of the behavioural model against the neoclassical—a problem that has faced investment theory for at least a decade.

Aharoni's hypotheses relate to the decision to make a new investment, not the expansion of existing operations. He stresses at least three phenomena in this process which he finds are contrary to profit maximisation:

(1) The search for new foreign investments seems biased. Many firms don't scan the environment, looking for profitable opportunities. Rather, they tend to investigate an opportunity only when some outside forces impels them to—e.g. an adverse action taken by a foreign government against existing export operations or an unsolicited proposal from a respected source.[33]

(2) When a search is undertaken, the result of the company's investigation is almost always that the risks are less than previously anticipated. Aharoni suggests that this happens mainly because the highest executives, lacking information about conditions in foreign countries have a tendency toward pessimism—over-estimating risks and under-estimating expected returns from foreign investment.[34]

(3) Great emphasis is put on what is called the process of commitment. By this Aharoni maintains that *past* expenditures of time and money are improperly considered in answering the question: Will it be profitable to proceed? Sunk costs are improperly considered in calculations of marginal profitability. In addition, some people push certain undesirable projects, because their goals are different from the firm's.[35]

As Aharoni himself recognises, and Miller and Weigel elaborate, much of what he says fits in nicely with the behavioural theories of Simon (1957b) and Cyert and March (1963). This is true for the first point and the last part of the third.

Further, it is possible to interpret much of the substance of these three points as consistent with the maximisation of the value of the firm under uncertainty—and thus conclude that the behavioural theory isn't really that different from profit maximisation under uncertainty. If the risk-adjusted expected returns from search are less than the costs, then it does not pay to invest in search. Costs of search may be particularly high for small companies, who do not have access to established and low-cost sources of information; this may be especially true for proposed projects in foreign countries. Also, there are likely to be decreasing costs of search per unit of investment, as the proposed scale of the investment increases. Thus, it may be profitable for all but the largest firms to eschew the search for foreign investments unless some favourable information arises without cost, such as from an unsolicited proposal. This may explain the findings of Horst (1972a, b) and Wolf (1971) that, all other things equal, firm size is strongly related to whether a firm has foreign subsidiaries. Miller and Weigel (1971) have made the only attempt to test a model incorporating the behavioural hypothesis that there are biases against search. In their study of US direct investment projects in Brazil, they found no evidence to support their biased-search hypotheses.

Finally, with respect to his third point, Aharoni may have missed the possibility that many of his interviewees were merely saying that previous fixed costs have substantially lowered the proposed investment's marginal costs, making it profitable on the margin. One of Aharoni's examples, that he claims shows an irrational commitment, is a company's decision to invest abroad to protect an export market, even though the country was a place where it would not invest 'under normal conditions'. But, assuming that the past export activities had built up a following for the company's product, an investment given this 'goodwill' might be profitable, even though an investment in the country without this prior history of exporting would be rejected as unprofitable. Throughout his discussion, Aharoni seems to forget that past costs may reduce present and future costs.

However, it would be intellectually dishonest to argue that all of Aharoni's findings are more probably than not the result of profit-maximising behaviour. His statements and examples about employee utility functions differing from the firm's sometimes seem plausible and fit in with evidence from domestic studies. His finding that management's expectations of returns and risks *before search* are biased away from investment, is hard to reconcile with a profit theory. This suggests, one might add, a theory implying *under-investment* relative to profit maximisation: the opposite to the case of growth maximisation. There might be some relation between this over-estimation of risks and the internationalisation of production; the foreign location of the proposed operation, where little prior information may be available, seems to be an important factor. This might be a fruitful line for further research. However, the finding is certainly not well enough grounded in observed fact or well enough developed theoretically to compel us to dispense with the neo-classical theory.[36] It also should be noted that bizarre behaviour in the selection of new investment projects is fairly well documented in the domestic sphere.[37] But this sort of evidence—again mainly from interviews—has not led to a reformulation of the domestic investment models, because the new models have not beaten the traditional ones in explaining and predicting investment spending.

Non-Profit Maximisation Theories: Portfolio Theory and Risk

Recently, at least two researchers, Prachowny (1972) and Stevens (1969b), have attempted to make the theory of direct investment more realistic by adopting a model which explicitly incorporates uncertainty. Both authors used the Markowitz–Tobin portfolio model to suggest the form of the firm's objective function.[38] In so doing, they assumed that the multinational firm chooses investments so as to maximise a utility function positively related to the expected return and negatively related to the variance of the firm's portfolio of investments. Such a theory leads to relationships of the following kind: in equilibrium, the optimal *ratio* of capital in any two locations (K_i/K_j) will be determined by the expected returns of the two assets (e_i, e_j), their variances or risks (v_i, v_j) and the riskless rate of interest, r^*, in the following way:[39]

$$\frac{K_i}{K_j} = \frac{(e_i - r^*)v_j}{(e_j - r^*)v_i}.$$

Both authors attempted to test the theory empirically. The results were decidedly mixed. Prachowny claimed vindication for his model, but, in fact, the significance of the crucial risk terms as explanatory variables of direct investment was questionable: when appearing alone (without being multiplied by other variables) the risk variables were always insignificant; when appearing in combination with other variables, the risk variables were occasionally part of significant products, but here it is unclear whether the risk factors contributed to this significance. In empirical work limited to direct investment to Latin America, Stevens found aggregate investment to Latin America significantly (negatively) related to the variance of past profits, as the theory implies; however, when regressions were disaggregated by country, the portfolio model was out-performed by a simple flexible accelerator model.

What neither author did was consider the relationship, if any, between their portfolio models and profit-maximisation models under uncertainty. As applied in these papers, the portfolio model represents another example of a non-profit-maximisation theory. The managers of the firm are assumed to maximise a utility function of a specific kind, but no link is forged between the managerial goals, represented by the utility function, and stock-holder desires. The natural inference is that the managers are running the firm for their own benefit. Under such an interpretation, it is natural for managers to want to avoid risk: in order to avoid bankruptcy and the loss of their jobs.[40]

It turns out, however, that a modified version of the above model can be made consistent with the maximisation of the market value of the firm. Lintner (1965) and Sharpe (1964) have shown that the behaviour of individual investors according to the portfolio model implies, through the equations for market equilibrium, an equation for the value of each firm. Managers following the neo-classical goal of maximising the value of the firm should choose their investments so as to maximise that

C

equation. The Lintner–Sharpe equation indicates that the value of every firm is an increasing function of the expected return of its assets and a negative function—via the market price of risk—of the total risk of the return; this total risk is the sum of the variances and covariances of the returns from the firm's investment *plus* the sum of the covariances between the returns of the firm's assets and all other assets in the market. This approach introduces risk explicitly into the firm's objective function, preserves all the other benefits of a direct application of portfolio theory, and maintains its consistency with the neo-classical theory of the firm.

The incorporation of risk into investment functions is in its infancy, both domestically and internationally. No conclusions, firm or tentative, can be ventured as to its importance for positive economics. However, this is an area that will see considerable work in the next few years, and, because risk seems particularly important in international operations, we might expect researchers on the international aspects of investment to be close to the theoretical and empirical frontiers.

Do International Operations Cause Constraints on the Firm's Objective Function?

Perhaps the multinational firm does try to maximise its market value, but, because of peculiarities introduced by international operations, this maximisation is subjected to constraints. A series of constraints, particularly related to sources of funds, has been hypothesised by Barlow and Wender (1955), Penrose (1956), and Behrman (1969). In general, these studies pose the important question of whether finance moves more or less without friction within the multinational firm or whether, because of psychological inertia or real costs such as taxes, certain locations are given preference over others.

On one extreme, Barlow and Wender (1955) postulated that the expansion of already-established subsidiaries is financed *exclusively* out of these subsidiaries' retained earnings.[41] Their explanation was that the foreign earnings of the multinational firm were looked at as 'gambling' earnings—you kept playing until you won big or completely lost your stake.[42]

If this hypothesis were true, it would indeed suggest that the multinationalisation of the firm's operations changes its investment behaviour. However, we do have some independent tests of the hypothesis and every one rejects the idea that a subsidiary's expansion is limited to its retained earnings. First, all empirical test of investment functions using disaggregaged or aggregated data support some form of the traditional neo-classical or flexible accelerator model and not the Barlow–Wender thesis.[43]

Further, Stevens (1969a) examined the behaviour of a sample of firms that corresponded exactly to the population for which the Barlow–Wender hypothesis is supposed to hold: a sample of 71 *well-established* subsidiaries. In no sense was it true that the expansion of these subsidiaries was financed only by retained earnings. For a large percentage of the subsidiaries in any given year (1959–62) there were large capital outflows from the US parent. Using the value of the subsidiary's plant and equipment expenditure as a rough measure of its financial needs for expansion, outflows from the United States averaged, depending on the year, from 6 to 24 per cent of total expansion requirements, an average of 14 per cent for the whole period. Moreover, for more than 20 per cent of the observations, capital outflows from the United States were greater than the reverse flow of dividends from the subsidiary to the parent.

In addition, it was not possible to detect any *tendency* for the subsidiaries' fixed investment expenditures to be determined by its own retained earnings—as, for example, Penrose (1956) has hypothesised.

Stobaugh (1970) has suggested that the type of thesis advanced by Barlow and Wender, Penrose and others may not be totally wrong: it may hold for small subsidiaries where it is presumably quite costly to have co-ordination of parent and subsidiary activities. In his detailed interviews, Stobaugh found that parent companies with total worldwide sales of $50 m or less were significantly (but not totally) less willing to invest additional funds once a subsidiary had been started. Such a distinction might save part of the gambler's earnings hypothesis, although (1) its quantitative significance is agreed to be virtually nil and (2) as revised by Stobaugh, it is perfectly compatible with profit maximisation; costs of decision-making are so high that it is optimal for the multinational firm to operate with the picturesque decision rule: 'every tub on its own bottom'.

In Behrman's book (1969) we find a different financial constraint. Foreign investment opportunities are supposedly accepted 'only if there are sufficient funds for these *and* all attractive domestic projects'.[44] This suggests a step-wise maximisation model of some kind, with total investment, foreign plus domestic, subject to some kind of a financial constraint, and domestic projects getting the first slice of the pie.

A number of empirical studies have assumed some sort of financial constraints on the international firm;[45] however, none have found that domestic investment was predetermined with respect to foreign. On the micro level, Severn (1972) came closest to testing the Behrman idea directly, including the value of domestic investment in some of his foreign plant and equipment equations; the sign of the variable was positive and significant—contrary to that hypothesised by Behrman. Stevens (1967) did not test the hypothesis directly, but rejected other 'partial' maximisation models concluding that, at the micro level, a supply constraint did exist, but that no location was given precedence.

With respect to the general question of financial constraints, a number of recent empirical studies, with data at the firm or subsidiary level, have found that variables reflecting the internal financial resources of the firm are significantly related to some form of foreign investment expenditure.[46] This suggests the existence of some sort of financial constraint or its near-equivalent: a cost-of-capital function which increases as the firm moves from internal to external sources of funds.

NEO-CLASSICAL INVESTMENT MODELS AND THE MULTINATIONAL FIRM: ALTERNATIVE ASSUMPTIONS AND VARIABLES

One conclusion of the last section must be that research on the multinational firm has not substantially supported theories of investment that reject profit maximisation. Although certain results that seem inconsistent with profit maximisation were discussed, it was argued that they certainly do not compel a reformulation of the standard neo-classical theory of investment.

What about the studies of the multinational firm that assume the traditional model, that the firm maximises its profit or market value? Do they support one particular version of neo-classical investment function, and thus throw some light on the controversies discussed in the Firm Investment section? Do they suggest a change in the set of independent variables to explain real investment? Do they suggest changes in certain assumptions, while still remaining within the class of neo-classical investment functions?

Standard Investment Functions Applied to Plant and Equipment Investment of Foreign Subsidiaries and/or the Flow of Direct Investment

The great majority of the studies that have empirically tested investment models of foreign investment have attempted to apply directly Jorgenson's neo-classical model or simpler models related to early versions of the flexible accelerator. In this category fall the works of Bandera and White (1968), Billsborrow (1968), Kopits (1972), Kwack (1971), Moose (1968), Morley (1969), Scaperlanda and Mauer (1969), Severn (1972), Stevens (1967, 1969a, 1972). Let us reiterate that, as discussed in the Firm Investment section, the important independent variables in the neo-classical model have been:

(1) A series of contemporaneous and lagged output or sales terms.
(2) The rental price of capital, composed of the price of capital goods and its rate of change, the cost of capital (some interest rate or stock yield), the rate of depreciation of the capital stock, and various tax rates.
(3) Measures of the real capital stock.
(4) More controversially, measures of internal funds, capacity utilitisation and measures of future profits.

In applying this model without conceptual alteration to international investment, most studies have adopted as the dependent variable some fairly aggregative measure of foreign plant and equipment expenditure by US subsidiaries or the financial flow, the flow of direct investment. The degree of aggregation has frequently been at the level of the country or higher—often a region or the whole world outside the United States. But there have been some studies at the micro level (see, e.g., Severn, 1972 and Stevens, 1969a.)

By far the strongest result has been the discovery that both of the above dependent variables are highly correlated with either the sales of US foreign subsidiaries or some measure of total output for the area and industry in question. Unquestionably, the importance of the first set of factors in the neo-classical model has been confirmed. The sales term has proved statistically significant in every study that has used it. (See the list at the beginning of this section.) When the models correctly incorporated the lagged capital stock term, this usually showed up with a significant (negative) coefficient, confirming the applicability of the early Chenery version of the flexible accelerator model.[47]

The independent variables which distinguish Jorgenson's neo-classical model from the early flexible accelerator are the price terms under (1) and (2) above. Some progress has been achieved in incorporating these terms into functions for foreign investment, notably by Kwack (1971) and Kopits (1972)—although no tests have been presented by these authors that conclusively establish that these price terms significantly contribute to the explanation of the dependent variable.[48] Kwack has incorporated the US long-term rate, a measure of capital gains, and the depreciation rate into the term for the rental cost of capital. The former was his measure of the US-based firm's cost of capital. And Kopits, in a study explaining subsidiary dividends but based on the neo-classical investment model, has added US and foreign corporate tax rates.

With respect to the more controversial variables in domestic investment functions, direct investment studies have frequently found that variables measuring the supply of external and internal funds are significant.[49] This is contrary to the conclusion recently reached by Jorgenson (1971), but, as mentioned above, is still a topic of debate.[50]

The conclusion to be drawn from these studies is, I think, that standard investment models and, to some extent, the neo-classical model of Jorgenson have been found to be the best explainers of plant and equipment expenditures abroad by multinational firms. As well, when linked to financial flows by simple assumptions, the standard investment models are the main part of the theory used to explain the flow of direct investment. This has been particularly true of studies done at the aggregative level. In the majority of cases, researchers have followed the developments in domestic theory and applications; because of this and data limitations, their work has been on a level more elementary than the most recent domestic studies. Below we will consider some aspects of the work of foreign investment that has been less derivative in nature.

Additional Independent Variables
The studies cited in the preceding section in the main followed a very simple, albeit fruitful, strategy: take a domestic investment function; substitute an appropriate foreign variable for the domestic one and estimate the coefficients. We will see below that there should be and, probably, is more to it than that. However, most of our statistical results have come from following the above strategy.

In the process, a number of potentially important factors have so far been neglected by the empiricists. These are all factors which can affect foreign profits via costs or returns and can be worked fairly easily into the neo-classical investment model. As such they do not change the basic profit-maximisation model, only the independent variables. No mention was made in the previous section of tariffs, exchange rates or 'investment climate'; and only brief mention was made of foreign tax systems. It is tempting to assert that these are the variables that capture the essence of the distinction between foreign and domestic investment. In some sense, by definition, the two types of investment are different only because the foreign location is under the jurisdiction of a different political authority; a different government plus the often concomitant differences in legal, commercial and cultural relations is what investors call a different 'investment climate'. In almost all cases political differences are combined with a different currency system.

All our interview evidence tells us that tariffs, the exchange-rate system (its stability and the degree of exchange control) and the investment climate are of paramount importance in the determination of foreign investment.[51] So far, however, we have very little statistical evidence of the impact on the multinational firm of exchange rates and political factors and conflicting evidence on the impact of tariffs.[52]

Given a neo-classical model, especially one incorporating uncertainty, it is quite possible to show theoretically how the expected values and risks attached to exchange rates and well-defined political factors affect the market value of the multinational firm.[53] However, it does seem difficult to relate the theoretical constructs to usable empirical data. This is partly a problem of data inadequacy, but also the old problem of capturing an *ex ante* concept with data that are necessarily *ex post*. Consider, for example, how one should go about measuring the market's assessment of the expected value and variance of a devaluation in any recent exchange crisis.

Testing for the impact of foreign tax systems, and, even, foreign wages, interest rates, and capital goods prices are similarly neglected projects. Kopits (1972) has made a start on taxes, but little has been done on the other variables.

Interactions between Domestic and Foreign Investment?
In testing their versions of profit-maximisation theories, Severn (1972) and Stevens (1969a) found that foreign plant and equipment expenditures were a function of *domestic* profits and depreciation flows. This is just one example of an empirically verified interdependence between domestic and foreign variables. If foreign investment is affected by domestic variables, then it is natural to expect the same with respect to domestic investment. So far, in domestic investment studies, no such interactions have been considered.

Under what theoretical conditions might we expect such interactions, and what evidence do we have of their significance? There are a number of theoretical possibilities—some of which cut in different directions. In general, interdependencies require that certain marginal costs or returns are affected by firm decision variables (such as investment).

On the financial side, if the firm's cost of capital is constant—independent of the sources of funds—then the interdependencies observed above cannot exist. When, however, the firm puts a lower opportunity cost on internal as opposed to external funds, or the cost of capital becomes a function of the debt–equity ratio, then an additional unit of investment in one location tends to raise the cost of capital and, thereby, lower investment in other locations.

Production interrelations can cause the opposite effect. If foreign subsidiaries use components manufactured in the United States, then increases in foreign demand stimulate both foreign investment *and* domestic investment for the production of components. However, if the increase in demand causes the establishment of a new plant abroad to produce the components, domestic investment will be lowered.

A third type of interdependence can occur when risk is introduced into the theory of the firm, as was the case in Prachowny (1972) and Stevens (1969b) above. Where variance is used as the measure of risk, each new unit of investment affects the marginal risk of *every* other unit of investment. This is because of the covariance terms which form an important part of the overall risk of the firm's portfolio of investments. A new unit of investment in one location adds to the overall variance both its own variance and the sum of its covariances with every other investment; these added covariance terms also change the marginal contribution of each other investment to the overall variance. Depending on whether the added covariances are positive or negative, the new investment will tend to decrease or increase the level of old investments.

Empirical evidence on these interdependencies is just beginning to come in. Severn and Stevens[54] have shown that foreign investment decisions are affected by the following domestic variables: domestic cash flow (both), domestic sales (Stevens), the overall debt/equity ratio (Severn) and domestic plant and equipment expenditure (Severn). Severn has gone farther and attempted to test whether *domestic* investment is indeed affected by foreign operations. He found that foreign profits definitely affected domestic investment, but foreign demand or observed investment seemed to have little effect. These interdependencies seemed to result from financial causes, and were observed using firm level data. No work has been completed that estimates the macro-economic significance, if any, of the financial interdependence. Nor has any empirical model explored the significance of production or risk interdependencies.

New versus Expansionary Investment

In lifting models from studies of domestic investment, researchers have also managed to forget or submerge important distinctions between types of foreign investment. One important distinction is between expenditures for plant and equipment for *new* subsidiaries and for the expansion of established subsidiaries.

In all empirical studies of domestic investment the firm is assumed to have one production function and one price at which it can buy each factor of production. For a significant, although not precisely known, percentage of direct investment expenditures such assumptions do not hold—expenditures on the assets of newly established subsidiaries. In many, if not all, cases of investment in new subsidiaries, the decision is the result of the maximisation of profits given the opportunity to produce in at least two locations, the United States and one or more countries abroad. Clearly, in a neo-classical model, the choice of production at home or abroad will be determined by a comparison of alternative costs of producing relevant levels of output. Depending on whether there are increasing, constant or decreasing marginal costs of production, the optimal solution may be to divide production for both markets between the two areas or produce everything in one. Given the production function, the optimal amount of capital located abroad will be a positive (non-negative) function of US costs of production, transportation costs, foreign import tariffs and a negative (non-positive) function of foreign costs of production.[55] At some point foreign production may dominate US production for all relevant levels of demand in the foreign (and/or US) market; in this case the problem simplifies to the application of the standard neo-classical model, using only the foreign production function and factor costs.[56]

So far no one has incorporated this locational choice problem into any of the empirical models meant to explain aggregate investment. Much theoretical and interview work has been done on the various determinants of this location choice.[57] A small amount of cross-sectional work by Horst (1972a, b) and Wolf (1971) and time series by Miller and Weigel (1971) has attempted to empirically verify some of the theoretical hypotheses.

Of the statical studies, both Horst and Wolf found that the choice between foreign production and exporting in an industry was affected by firm size: the larger the firm the more likely it is to produce abroad. This is probably the result of the large set-up costs necessary to start a foreign subsidiary. Wolf also found the decision to be related positively to industry profitability.

Only Horst, Miller and Weigel, and Scaperlanda and Mauer have attempted to test for factors related to costs and the production function. Horst (1972a) found that the level of tariff rates for Canada and the United Kingdom was significantly related to the share of exports in the total of US sales to those markets. However, in a separate study at the firm level (1972b), he found no relationship between tariffs and industries that are important foreign investors. Miller and Weigel (1971) found that tariff rates did not explain industry difference in the frequency of new investments for Brazil, 1956–61. Scaperlanda and Mauer (1969) found that their proxy for barriers to trade had no effect on the flow of direct investment to the EEC.

Horst (1972b) also found that the size of the market tends to encourage foreign investment relative to exports and that the average plant size tends to discourage it—both factors attempting to measure the impact of economies of scale on the choice of location.

Most economists think that cost and production function variables are important determinants of the choice of exporting from the United States or producing abroad. If the annual investment flows caused by the shift from exporting to foreign production are quantitatively important, then these variables should be included in investment functions: at least those functions explaining foreign investment and, possibly, also those explaining domestic investment.

Oligopolistic Interdependencies
Studies of domestic investment have generally ignored the market structure of the sectors, industries or firms whose investment they have sought to explain.[58] Even when the industry has had very few sellers, all empirical models have assumed no interdependence between the investment decisions of rival firms.

Monopoly and oligopoly factors have frequently been emphasised as determinants of foreign investment behaviour. Can we say that these factors should be taken into account as determinants of investment?

Following Hymer (1960), many authors have asserted that foreign investment *presupposes* some degree of monopoly advantage; firms entering a new foreign market, it is argued, must have some advantages over local firms in order to overcome the disadvantages that they have in being forced to operate in a new environment. Such advantages do not necessarily imply oligopolistic interdependencies, however. The advantages could be related to anything from the possession of technical knowledge to the services of an especially good manager, neither of which need be related to a particular market structure. However, the fact that most foreign investment is done by large firms in con-concentrated industries suggests that such interdependencies might be important.

Hymer (1960) has argued that the phenomenon of cross investment—firms in the same industry, but headquartered in different countries, investing in each other's country—can be explained as a reaction in an oligopolistic market. Further, it has been widely suggested that firms in a given industry often match each other's foreign investment decisions. Finally, Caves (1971) has argued that much foreign investment that serves to vertically integrate a firm is often the result of oligopolistic market structure.

The first two of these arguments, in particular, might be important in explaining investment over time, in addition to the equilibrium composition of investment at a moment of time.

Little work has been done to verify these hypothesis or measure their quantitative significance for foreign investment. Recently, however, in an imaginative monograph, Knickerbocker (1973) has attempted to test the importance of the second hypothesis mentioned above: that oligopolists imitate each other in entering new foreign markets. Knickerbocker found evidence that entries by US firms into foreign markets were bunched in time—more so than could be expected by chance. He found that his measures of bunching were significantly correlated with US industry concentration indices, suggesting a relation to oligopolistic interdependence. However, he also found that the bunching measures were strongly correlated with the profitability of foreign investment in the industry in question. It seems to me, there-fore, that it is too early to rule out the hypothesis that the bunching was merely the result of businesses responding—inde-pendently—to profitable opportunities.[59] Horst (1972b) pro-vides some empirical support to Cave's hypothesis about the causes of vertical integration. In his cross-section study he found that for natural resource industries, differences in foreign investment potential were positively affected by the level of concentration.

THE MULTINATIONAL FIRM AND THE FINANCIAL THEORY OF THE FIRM

The gist of the argument in the Firm Investment section was that, despite the advances sparked by Modigliani and Miller (1958), little is really known, theoretically or empirically, about the determinants of the firm's financial structure. Theoretically, work has really just begun on trying to explain the determinants of the firm's optimal financial structure, while at the same time preserving the theoretical rigor introduced by Modigliani and Miller.[60] Empirically, we have little tested knowledge. Two of the better known empirical studies are Anderson (1964) and Goldfeld (1969). Although definite steps forward, these are primitive when compared to recent work in the field of fixed investment. Theoretically, both are built on shaky, if not non-existent, foundations; neither, in fact, incorporates the prevalent belief that there exists an optimal financial structure for the profit-maximising firm.

The fact of the existence of an optimal financial plan for the neo-classical firm—if it is indeed a fact—should be good news for the students of multinational business. Many of the variables that policy-makers find most important to explain and forecast are *financial* flows: all of those that affect the balance of payments—notably the flow of direct investment and the net capital outflow—fall into this class. That these financial flows may be determined by profit-maximisation considerations is good news and, we might note, quite contrary to Modigliani and Miller's original position.

Given the importance of the above financial flows, one might have expected research on the multinational firm to have contributed much to the solution of the general problems in the theory and empirical study of corporate finance. Once again, however, the contribution has been fairly small.

There has been considerable work describing what firms do and some telling what firms should do.[61] Apparently, almost all of the descriptive work is based on interviews and anecdotes; without more, they possess the serious flaws that we have no way of telling whether the behaviour documented is widespread or isolated or whether the hypotheses suggested serve to explain the statistical data available at the macro and micro levels. The theoretical work, is apparently even less sophisticated than that in the domestic field, most of it not even showing an awareness of the problems posed by Modigliani and Miller.

A few studies have begun to appear which attempt to explain

observed data on the financial flows of the multinational corporation.[62] They have made some headway in a number of areas: (1) sorting out the relationships among the various financial and real flows that affect the multinational firm—primarily definitional ones and those caused by the firm's balance sheet identity; and (2) obtaining fairly good statistical results in explaining some financial flows. Ruckdeschel (1971) has linked total net capital outflow (for all industries) with total corporate cash flow of US corporations. Severn (1972) explores a model which makes the net financial flow to foreign subsidiaries a function of foreign and domestic variables (profits and fixed investment expenditures). Stevens (1972), indirectly, deduced an equation for the flow of direct investment from a model for foreign borrowing; it was hypothesised that foreign subsidiaries borrow funds denominated in foreign currencies primarily to minimise the risk of losses caused by exchange-rate changes. This hypotheseis was tested further by Kwack (1971) and Berlin (1971) with successful results.

Although these studies have been steps forward in the study of the multinational firm, it would be impossible to claim that they compel any changes in the general area of corporate finance. None of the above studies attacks the problem of the firm's optimal capital structure in any systematic way. Some of them do identify possibly fruitful hypotheses concerning the determinants of international financial flows, but, in all cases, it seems that the hypotheses are tentative at best and await much more extensive testing and theoretical development.

SUMMARY AND RECOMMENDATIONS

SUMMARY

My conclusion is that the growing importance of the multinational firm does not yet compel any changes in the way we now conduct the theoretical or empirical analysis of investment. Although no changes are imperative at present, in a number of areas the results of further research may require some modifications of the financial and real investment functions we now use.

In the past 20 years a number of studies have concluded that the investment behaviour of the multinational firm cannot be described by the profit-maximisation model. This paper has examined studies suggesting that the objectives and behaviour of such firms correspond to: (1) growth maximisation; (2) the realm of so-called behavioural theories; (3) profit maximisation or other behaviour subjected to financial constraints; and (4) portfolio theories of the Markowitz variety. After considering the evidence for and against these theories, my conclusion was that there was not sufficient evidence to support the jettisoning of profit maximisation; in fact, very little evidence supports the alternatives. It is my conclusion that less convincing evidence has been raised against profit maximisation in studies of the multinational firm than already has been raised in purely domestic studies; yet, we saw in the Firm Investment section, that, for a number of good reasons, profit-maximisation theories continue to be in the ascendancy in the study of domestic investment.

Most progress in the explanation of the fixed investment of foreign subsidiaries has come from applying to international operations investment functions borrowed from studies of domestic investment. It is quite possible that future research on the multinational firm will suggest the addition of new variables to these functions, variables such as exchange-rate changes and risks, that serve to capture the essence of the distinction between domestic and foreign operations. It is also possible that research on the multinational firm will suggest changes in domestic investment functions, while retaining the underlying rationale of profit maximisation; it was suggested that we may have to build in interaction effects between domestic and foreign investment, effects caused by common financial constraints and/or the shift of production from the United States to foreign subsidiaries.

In a brief discussion of studies of the financial, as opposed to the real, aspects of foreign investment, the author concluded that not enough had been done either theoretically or empirically to suggest any implications for the theory of corporate finance.

RESEARCH AND DATA REQUIREMENTS

If nothing more, the preceding discussion has established that there are innumerable questions remaining to be answered concerning the impact of the multinational firm on the theory and empirical analysis of investment. The following section will try to say what is required in the way of research to answer them. But two other questions are probably more important: Is it possible to do the required research? If so, is it a worth while thing to do?

The last question asks us to stop a moment and put this field of inquiry into perspective. It is worth while to further test hypotheses on the relationship between the multinational firm and the determinants of real and financial investment, because this is a necessary step toward the achievement of the most important goals in the study of the multinational firm. Because we are sure that the activities of multinational firms affect many of the most important goals of every nation—for example, economic growth and distribution, balance-of-payments equilibrium, national independence—we want to be able to explain, predict and control the key variables associated with these activities. As was at least adumbrated in preceding sections, some of the problems preventing this are theoretical. It is felt, however, that the *major* roadblocks will be empirical—in the realm of data availability.

Required Research

Assuming for the moment that data limitations will be overcome, what will be the most fruitful research in order to develop the required equations for the investment of multinational firms?

The evidence reviewed in the third section of this chapter seems to imply that past advances in the explanation of real investment have come primarily by applying domestic investment models, especially those related to the neoclassical theory, to international investment. It must be noted that there are special problems with international investment that cannot be solved with the application of purely domestic models; but, despite these limitations, there is much that should be done in perfecting the application of the domestic model.

For openers, we should begin to test the forecasting records of the models that seem to explain past flows well. The shortness of existing time series limited this in the past, but in the fairly near future this problem should be partly remedied as far as US data are concerned. This step should help us to rank the models that all tend to explain the past data well.

Next, within the neo-classical model, much remains to be done theoretically and empirically on testing for the impact of cost, price and tax factors. A theoretical question that has not been adequately solved is: just what should we use as the cost of capital for a multinational firm, borrowing and lending in many markets, that may be owned by shareholders residing in many different countries?

Assuming the data become available, much remains to be done in estimating the structure of the distributed lags between multinational investment flows and the independent variables causing them; this seems to have had a big pay off in explaining and predicting domestic investment.

The above, traditional questions of domestic investment analysis are fairly easy to handle conceptually, because we can follow the lead of domestic researchers. Somewhat more difficult will be the solving of problems that are unique to studies of international investment. But when the problems discussed in the Implications of Growth section are surveyed, the solution of the theoretical problem, at least, should not be impossible to come by. We have discussed the problem of incorporating factors that are peculiar to international operations. Some are just added costs, such as tariffs and transportation costs, that can be easily incorporated into the firm's profit function. Others such as exchange-rate changes and certain political factors can likewise be incorporated, but the proper consideration of these factors may also require the explicit introduction of decision-making under uncertainty. But this is no cause for gloom; much progress has been and will be made in this field.

Other important questions take us farther way from the traditional theory. The problems with the theory of corporate finance were discussed at length in the second and fourth sections of this chapter, theoretical and empirical breakthroughs are necessary if we are to properly understand the determination of the important flows that finance asset changes. But there is such interest in this area, by researchers interested in both domestic and international applications, that major progress on the questions in the next five years should be expected.

Related to both financial theory and cost theory are the questions concerning the possible interactions between domestic and foreign investment. The development of the theory of corporate finance is necessary to the explanation of those interactions that have already been detected on the financial side. A standard application of cost minimisation may provide all the theory we need to explain the shift from producing at home for export to producing abroad, another possible cause of interaction between domestic and foreign investment. If so, there may still be imposing problems in actually predicting and explaining such shifts, but they will probably be related to more empirical questions such as the timing of such shifts.

Data Problems

If our problems were only theoretical, it would be confidently predicted that the gap in the level of sophistication and predictive accuracy between studies of domestic and international investment would be eliminated in five years. In fact the author is rather pessimistic about rapid progress in explaining, predicting and controlling direct investment. The inadequacy of the data base has been the major reason for the slow progress in the past; although there have been signs of improvement, there are many reasons for continued pessimism.

There are three major types of data that can be used in studies of foreign investment: data on the foreign operations of multi-national firms; data on the domestic operations of these firms; data on conditions within the home and host countries. There are fundamental problems in the quality of the data and its availability in each of these areas. It would take and would merit an essay to do justice to this subject. What follows is only a sketch of some of the problems.

Data on Foreign Operations. For multinational firms based in the United States a fairly wide range of data is collected on the operations of US foreign subsidiaries; for the purposes of explaining real and financial investment important data are: sales by subsidiary, fixed investment spending, sources and uses of finance, trade flows, and balance sheet and income statement data. One problem is that, except for the flows that enter the balance of payments, these variables have been collected only since 1957 and only on an annual basis.

I think it was a rare act of foresight to begin collecting data such as the sources and uses of funds of foreign subsidiaries 15 years ago. However, 15 observations is just getting to be a series of decent length for any purpose. Unfortunately, some important variables, such as borrowing from foreign financial institutions, have been adequately reported only for the last few years. And some, such as accounts payable, has never been broken out.

Although we can expect improvement in our results based on these longer annual time series, it should be noted that most of the recent advances in the field of domestic investment have been made using quarterly data. Domestic studies of plant and equipment spending have usually found that from 12 to 15 or more independent variables are required to explain the dependent variable satisfactorily.[63] It is questionable if we can ever predict plant and equipment spending as well using annual data as we can using quarterly. This is due partly to the number of observations available with quarterly data and partly to the choice of a period of observation that corresponds in length to the period over which investment plans are left unchanged. The author is not now advocating a move to quarterly data collection, but the question should be seriously studied—along with the more general one of choosing the optimal period of observation for each important variable.

However, there are institutional reasons that suggest that it will be difficult to obtain important variables more frequently than at present. Except during an infrequent Census of Foreign Direct Investments, the data on plant and equipment spending and sources and uses of funds are reported on a *voluntary* basis. Such voluntary reporting probably causes unnecessary and unknown errors in the aggregates because, frequently, firms—often important ones—drop in and out of the sample. More important, it would probably be impossible to get quarterly or more often reporting, and still run the sampling on a voluntary basis. However, it is not a simple step to collect these data on a mandatory basis; the existing statutory mandate—the Bretton Woods Agreement—permits mandatory reporting for balance-of-payments purposes: some people, at least, doubt that plant and equipment spending, sources and uses of funds and the like can fit under this rubric. But without these data there will be no explaining of the balance-of-payments flows.

In addition to these problems, there are omissions in the data base that make it inferior to domestic data. All the data collected is in value terms; there is no direct way to separate real from money changes in sales, plant and equipment spending, etc. For financial decisions, we have no data on the interest rates or terms being paid by foreign subsidiaries; we have no knowledge of the currencies in which the subsidiaries' liquid balances or other assets are denominated.

Domestic Data. In order to study the interaction between foreign and domestic operations, we need data corresponding to both of these divisions of the firms activities. On the aggregative level, at the two-digit S.I.C. industry level data on purely domestic variables probably can be obtained from diverse sources, although these have never yet been used in direct investment research. But because the data are aggregates they are limited by the 15 or fewer observations obtainable for foreign activities.

Very little data on US domestic operations are available at the level of the firm. Even with the use of the confidential foreign operations data collected by the Department of Commerce, domestic data can only be obtained as a residual after a laborious process of eliminating foreign data from company consolidated figures.[64]

Thus the study of interactions is hampered on both levels: on the aggregate by the lack of observations; and on the micro level by the lack of usable domestic data.

Foreign Country Data.   Much of the discussion of the Implications of Growth section was devoted to subjects that linked
conditions in the host country to foreign investment. Prices,
factor costs, tariffs, transportation costs, taxes, exchange rates,
and political factors all affect the location of investment and its
growth. Some, but surprisingly little, of this sort of data is
available in an accurate form on a time-series basis. A few
examples from my own experience serve to show the difficulties.
Although the obvious source of data on wage rates in foreign
countries is the International Labour Office's *Yearbook of Labor
Statistics*, I have been frequently warned that such data are no
good; in fact the US Bureau of Labor Statistics has expended
considerable time and money creating what they think are
comparable time series of wage rates—for just a few European
countries and for total manufacturing alone; if you want comparable wage rate data by industry or for any non-European
countries, the problem seems insurmountable.

A second example relates to the availability of data on foreign
tax rates. As far as can be told, although a number of US accounting firms keep track of foreign tax systems, [there is no way to
easily get a *time-series* of the important characteristics of foreign
tax systems; one assumes that the countries, themselves, have
the data; but to obtain it a major data collection effort is required.
Finally, concerning the 'investment climate', as far as is known,
there is no government agency that keeps historical records on
expropriations and other official actions against US foreign
investment.

If this assessment of the situation is correct, it will take a
major effort of data collection to assemble the data required to
study the impact of conditions in the host country on the activities
of multinational firms.

For the above reasons, related exclusively to the unavailability
of relevant data, the author is pessimistic about achieving the
satisfactory explanation and prediction of foreign investment
flows in the near future. That is not to say things are not improving; they are: the time series are getting longer and some
other positive steps have been taken.[65] But all of the data problems
discussed above remain; and they are not being solved.

References

[1] My thanks go to all the participants at the Bellagio conference for their
reading and discussion of this paper; my special thanks go to George Borts
and Sune Carlson, the principal discussants at the conference, Michael Adler,

John Dunning, George Kopits, Grant Reuber, J. David Richardson, Alan Severn, Anthony Scaperlanda, Peter Tinsley, Louis Wells and Dale Weigel, all of whom shared their detailed comments with me. The errors remaining are my responsibility alone, as are the opinions expressed.

2 These figures are derived from a comparison of domestic plant and equipment spending from the OBE-SEC survey (see *Survey of Current Business,* January and February 1970, and June 1972) with the figures for 'plant and equipment expenditures by foreign affiliates of US Corporations' (see *Survey of Current Business,* September 1970 and US Department of Commerce (1960)).

3 In this chapter the words 'multinational firm' and 'international firm' are used interchangeably; 'international firm' will mean only a firm with fixed assets in more than one country. In what follows, it is not necessary to distinguish among international firms according to their outlooks or the nature of their shareholders.

4 For a detailed discussion of the definitions of these and other financial and real flows, see Stevens (1972).

5 See Chapter 2 for a more detailed discussion of the issues raised in this section.

6 See Jorgenson (1963), Jorgenson & Stephenson (1967), Jorgenson & Siebert (1968) and Bischoff (1971a, b).

7 That is to say the firm should maximise:

$$\int_0^\infty CF(t) \exp(-rt)dt.$$

A typical expression for cash flow (*CF*) at time *t*, where taxes are neglected, is: $CF(t) = pQ - wL - qI$, where pQ is total revenues, wL is labour payments, qI is payments for new capital goods; r is the firm's discount rate.

8 See, for example, Marris (1964) or Williamson (1964).

9 This theory is usually associated with the names of Simon (1957b) and Cyert & March (1963). For a good description of a representative model, see Cohen & Cyert (1965).

10 See, e.g. Baumol & Stewart (1971).

11 For example. Cohen & Cyert (1965), pp. 335–8.

12 See Fromm (1971).

13 In Jorgenson's work the lagged adjustment of actual capital to the desired level has not been justified with the same rigour as the determinants of the desired stock of capital. Jorgenson justified the lagged adjustment as the result of technologically determined lags between plans, appropriations, and construction. However, following Eisner & Strotz (1963), it has been quite possible to justify lagged adjustment within the profit-maximisation framework.

14 It is my opinion that the burden of proof should be on the advocates of the non-traditional theories; no science allows a currently accepted theory to be replaced without substantial evidence that the replacement is superior.

15 In a recent paper Gould & Waud (1970) have, with seeming success, substituted for the output term in the investment function its determinants in terms of output and factor prices. Vigorous research is also progressing on the subject of the lag structure between investment and its determinants; building on the work of Eisner & Strotz (1963), there has been considerable theoretical progress made in relating the lag structure to internal and external costs and, thus, to profit maximisation (see Nerlove, 1972). Work is also going forward on the effects of uncertainty on the lag structure (Tinsley,

1970b) as well as the general study of the incorporation of uncertainty into the theory of the firm (see Sandmo, 1971 and Stevens, 1973).

16 Related and equally important is the question of the simultaneity of the determination of fixed investment and the firm's investment in other assets: cash, inventories, receivables and so forth. For recent work in this area see Nadiri & Rosen (1969) and Craine (1971).

17 See, e.g., his Table 1.

18 See, e.g. Bischoff (1971a).

19 This is clearly demonstrated in Fromm (1971).

20 See, e.g. Brash (1966) and Reuber (1973).

21 In assessing the worth of interview studies, the author is mindful of the critical arguments made by Machlup (1946) and Eisner (1956) against this type of evidence. Although the author shares the skepticism about the usefulness of much interview evidence, no one can convincingly argue that it is always useless. In this essay the author has tried to take all evidence, from whatever source, at face value—disputing findings only on the basis of counter-evidence or logical inconsistency. This, of course, means that all conflicts will not be resolved.

22 See Berlin (1971), Billsborrow (1968), Moose (1968), Severn (1972), Stevens (1967, 1969a, 1972).

23 Before giving the list of references of those who have studied the above mentioned variables, it may be useful to reiterate what is meant by the terms 'flow of direct investment' and 'net capital outflow'. By the flow of direct is meant the change in the US ownership position—or the change in the US net worth—in US-controlled foreign branches and affiliates; the stock corresponding to this flow is called by the US Department of Commerce the value of direct investments abroad. The flow of direct investment is broken up by the US Department of Commerce into the US share of retained earnings of foreign affiliates and the net capital outflow; only the last of these enters the US balance of payments. For a more detailed discussion, see Stevens (1972).

For studies of the above and related financial flows see Aliber (1970), Bandera and White (1968), Kopits (1972), Kwack (1971), Morley (1966), Moose (1968), Prachowny (1972), Rhomberg (1968), Ruckdeschel (1971), Scaperlanda and Mauer (1969), Stevens (1972).

24 See Aliber (1970), Aharoni (1966), Barlow & Wender (1955), Brash (1966), Caves (1971), Horst (1972a, 1972b), Hymer (1960), Kindleberger (1969), Knickerbocker (1972), Vernon (1971), Wolf (1971), and Miller & Weigel (1971).

25 Behrman (1969), p. 9.

26 Stubenitsky (1970), p. 8.

27 Behrman (1969), p. 8.

28 See Hymer (1960), Morley (1966) and Spitäller (1971).

29 See, e.g., Iverson (1935).

30 I do think it would be useful to try to establish just why it is that profit-rate specifications of the investment function do not work as well as forms related to the accelerator or neoclassical model.

31 Hymer & Rowthorn (1970) suggest, probably just in passing, that the primary firm objective is the maintenance of its market share (pp. 72, 80). This does not form an important part of their argument and no empirical evidence is offered in its support. In any case, the hypothesis again is not new, being prominant in the domestic behavioural literature. (See Cohen & Cyert, 1965)

[32] One should also not forget that Aharoni is generalising from a very limited and probably unrepresentative sample—38 firms who had considered an investment in Israel. My argument in the text does not take up this point, but it also felt that it would be folly to make any decisions on the basis of this theory without much more work to formulate its testable implications and to carry out these tests on a more representative sample.

[33] See, Aharoni (1966), Chapter 3.

[34] Aharoni (1966), p. 99.

[35] See Chapter 5.

[36] Even if the lack of knowledge of *foreign* countries was an important deterrent in the past, we would expect this condition to be progressively less important in the future. On this, see Aharoni's discussion of the institutionalisation of date gathering on foreign investment opportunities caused by the wide-spread creation of international divisions.

[37] See, e.g. Cannon (1968).

[38] See Markowitz (1959) and Tobin (1958).

[39] See, e.g. Hicks (1962), Appendix. The formula in the text assumes that the covariances between returns in all areas are zero; non-zero covariances complicate the formula somewhat, but leave all principles unchanged.

[40] The avoidance of risk is not, of course, generally synonymous with the avoidance of bankruptcy; there must be a one-to-one relationship between increasing risk (say, variance) and an increasing probability of negative returns below a certain critical point; if the probability distribution of profits is normal, as is assumed by the Markowitz–Tobin model, the necessary relationship exists.

[41] At one time (Stevens 1969a), the author identified Mrs Penrose's position in her 1965 article with Barlow and Wender's thesis of *exclusive* financing by retained earnings. After talking with her on this point and rereading her article, I now see that she did not take such an extreme position. To explain the phenomena she was interested in, such as the possibility that the expansion of a foreign subsidiary will continue even after the rate of return of the affiliate falls below the rate of return in the home country, only a *tendency* to finance out of retained earnings is required, not exclusive financing out of retained earnings. Of course, it is much harder to test this sort of hypothesis than it is to test Barlow and Wender's. Up to the present time the author does not think we have established empirically whether multinational firms have a lower cost of capital for expansion out of subsidiary retained earnings than for expansion financed by capital flows from the home country.

[42] Barlow and Wender (1955), p. xxlv.

[43] See Kwack (1971), Moose (1968), Severn (1972) and Stevens (1972).

[44] Behrman (1969), p. 4.

[45] Stevens (1967) and (1969a), Severn (1972).

[46] Stevens (1969a) and Severn (1972). For aggregate evidence see Kwack (1971).

[47] Kopits (1972), Kwack (1971), Stevens (1972).

[48] This is a problem that has beset researchers applying the model to domestic investment; since price and output terms almost always appear in combination, it is difficult to test for the significance of each separately. See Eisner & Nadiri (1968).

[49] See Kwack (1971), Moose (1968), Ruckdeschel (1971), Severn (1972) and Stevens (1967, 1969a).

[50] Consider, for example the arguments of Klein & Taubman (1971).

51 See, e.g., Barlow & Wender (1955), p. 132, and Aharoni (1966), p. 93.

52 See Billsborrow (1968), Stevens (1969b), Horst (1972a, b), Miller & Weigel (1971), and Scaperlanda & Mauer (1969).

53 Stevens (1969b, 1971).

54 Severn (1972) and Stevens (1967, 1969a).

55 Here it is implicitly assuming that there will be no foreign production *for the US market*. If that is allowed then US tariffs will be an additional independent variable and the sign of the effect of transportation costs may change.

56 The distinction between the usual one-location model and the more general one can be expressed mathematically as follows: For normal investment and production decisions (without any inter-temporal effects) we maximise one-period profits ($pQ-cK-wL$) in the following framework:

Max: $pQ-cK-wL$, with respect to Q, K, L;
subject to:

$$Q = f(K, L)$$
$$Q \geqslant 0; K \geqslant 0; L \geqslant 0.$$

As usual: p = product price, Q = output, K = the input of capital services, L = labour input, c = the rental price of capital, w = the wage rate, $f( )$ = the production function. Since sales and production are in one location in the previous, normal problem, there is no need for locational subscripts. However, in the international location problem, we have i and j subscripts for each variable, to denote whether it refers to the home or foreign location. The problem becomes:

Max: $p_iQ_i + p_jQ_j - c_iK_i - w_iL_i - c_jK_j - w_jL_j$

with respect to:

$$Q_i, Q_j, K_i, K_j, L_i, L_j;$$

subject to:

$$Q_i + Q_j = f_i(K_i, L_i) + f_j(K_j, L_j)$$
$$Q_i, Q_j, f_i( ), f_j( ) \geqslant 0$$
$$L_i, L_j, K_i, K_j \geqslant 0.$$

Note: no longer must production in any area be equal to output sold in that area.

57 See Barlow & Wender (1955), Caves (1971), Horst (1972b), Richardson (1971) and Wilkins (1970).

58 For an exception see Scherer (1969).

59 In a recent conversation, Professor Knickerbocher suggests that he pretty well covers this objection on pp. 162–3 of the published version of his thesis.

60 See, e.g., Baumol & Malkiel (1967) and Tinsley (1970a).

61 See, e.g., Brash (1966), Carlson (1969), and Stobaugh (1970).

62 Berlin (1971), Hui & Hawkins (1972), Krainer (1972), Ladenson (1972), Moose (1968), Ruckdeschel (1972), Severn (1972), and Stevens (1972).

63 See, e.g., Bischoff (1971b).

64 See, on this, Stevens (1967), Appendix B. The situation has been improved somewhat by the collection in the 1966 and 1970 Censuses of Direct Investments of a limited amount of data on the US operations of the parent firms. This is a real step forward.

65 The US Bureau of Economic Analysis (formerly called the Office of

Business Economics) is in the process of establishing a computerised data system, the goal of which is to permit outside and inside researchers to have rapid access to the macro and micro-economic data on the operations of US foreign affiliates, while at the same time maintaining the confidentiality of the micro-economic data.

The Office of Foreign Direct Investments, set up within the Department of Commerce primarily to administer the US balance-of-payments programme, has collected data since its birth on a wide range of activities of U.S. multi-national firms. The Office has sought to stimulate research on the explanation and predition of the capital flows associated with the foreign operations of US firms, and has co-operated with outside researchers in providing the necessary data.

Chapter 4

THE LOCATION OF ECONOMIC ACTIVITY

Raymond Vernon[1]

INTRODUCTION

The economic theories that bear on the international location of economic activity come out of two rather distinct traditions. One body of theory, associated mainly with the names of Weber and Lösch,[2] identifies the geographical configuration of production points and markets that would represent an economic equilibrium in space. The other tradition is represented by the general body of international theory; that body of concepts can also be viewed as a theory of international location, since it specifies how the international specialisation of national economies is determined.[3] My task is to identify what effects the introduction of the multi-national enterprise may have for these bodies of theory. More precisely, does it make any difference that the decision makers on locational questions are multinational enterprises rather than independent national enterprises?

As far as the main propositions of Weber and Lösch are concerned, the introduction of the multinational enterprise in lieu of national independent factors would seem to change very little, at least on first glance. If the object is to describe a state of equilibrium in space, if the equilibrium is determined by the structure of costs, and if production technology, factor costs and transport costs are given, then the locational solution for the productive facilities of the multinational enterprise will presumably be the same as that for independent firms. But that way of stating the problem, as will shortly be evident, has the effect of assuming the real issue away. The nature of the general equilibrium in space may be substantially affected by the introduction of the multinational enterprise, albeit in ways that are at times indirect.

When international trade theory is viewed as a theory of international location, the introduction of the multinational enterprise in lieu of national firms raises more obvious questions.

The existence of the multinational enterprise bears on three key assumptions in trade theory: that the factors of production—land, labour and capital—remain fixed within their national borders;[4] that lack of information does not operate as a barrier to the exploitation of opportunities for international trade; and, finally, that the market is sufficiently atomistic in structure so that each actor can respond without having to consider the effects of his own response upon the behaviour of others.

As an international conduit *par excellence* of both capital and human skills, the multinational enterprise reduces the credibility of the assumption regarding the international immobility of the factors. On the other hand, as a relatively efficient communicator of information across boundaries, the multinational enterprise increases the credibility of the assumption regarding the availability of information. The consequences of the multinational enterprise for location theory, however, may be even more important in its bearing on the third assumption—the assumption that international markets are atomistic. The domain of multinational enterprises, as is well known, lies mainly in industries in which a few firms characteristically account for a large proportion of the output.[5] Oligopolistic behaviour is the rule, sometimes manifesting itself in various forms of product differentiation, sometimes in pricing and investing practices.

Before World War II, the oligopolies that developed in industries of this sort were usually only national in their geographic scope.[6] When the national leaders of such oligopolies found themselves in contact with one another on international markets, they were generally quick to limit that contact by means of cartel agreements. A few industries, such as oil, were organised in such a way that the oligopoly leaders were already established in one another's territories. But these were exceptional cases.

The growth of the multinational enterprise has turned the exception into the commonplace. Today, the leaders of many oligopolistically structured industries operate on a global basis. Though explicit restrictive agreements exist in some industries, any division of markets among the leaders cannot easily be defined on geographical lines. Though predatory dumping across national boundaries is not unknown, the global interests of multinational enterprises prevent them from using this tactic as readily as national enterprises. In short, the day of the global oligopoly seems closer at hand.[7]

But generalisations of this sort need refining. Some oligopolies are based on one type of entry barrier, some on another. And the differences are not unimportant to the theory of location.

THE INNOVATION-BASED OLIGOPOLIES

One basis on which multinational enterprises have built their oligopolistic strength is through the development and introduction of new products and the differentiation of existing ones. That sort of business strategy is usually indicated by relatively high expenditures for the services of scientists, engineers, and other specialists engaged in development.[8] In the present context, one need not ask the troublesome question whether the multinational character of such enterprises renders them more efficient as innovators than national enterprises. Whatever the underlying reasons may be, the facts suggest that multinational enterprises are found dominating the manufacture and trade of goods that are associated with high levels of innovational and development effort.[9]

There are two locational issues in these innovation-oriented industries which are of special interest: first, the location of the processes of research and development themselves; second, the location of the processes of production.

LOCATING RESEARCH ACTIVITIES

Activities that are directed at the formulation and test of general scientific principles are fairly distinct from those that are aimed at industrial innovation and development. A few large industrial firms, such as Bell Laboratories and Du Pont, engage in some scientific research that is not immediately related to their industrial needs and many more firms stimulate and support such research by indirect means; but, as a rule, research of this sort takes place outside of industrial enterprises. Most of the so-called R & D expenditures of business organisations go to the more mundane business of industrial innovation and its follow-on activities.[10]

The geographical location of work on industrial innovation is determined by factors that are quite different from those relating to more abstract scientific research. To be sure, some externalities and complementarities may be absolutely critical in both cases, leading to a certain amount of geographical concentration. Among the scientific researchers, a biologist may find the need for consultation with a chemist on some exotic issue of biochemistry, or a chemist with an astrophysicist; or several different types of scientists may occasionally be drawn to a common location by the presence of some specialised piece of equipment such as a particle accelerator. But as a rule, scientific researchers interact and communicate with one another through open channels such as conferences and professional journals; as a result, though geographic propinquity is often very helpful, it is not indispensable. Besides, scientists who generate abstract research output generally prefer to work in an environment where communication is among a group of science-rated peers, where interchanges in the group are relatively uninhibited, and where the final product is offered as a free good to anyone that has the capacity for using it.[11] One result is that the best scientists are not easily captured by industrial firms. Another result is that most scientific output is, in any case, available to the firm as a free good, provided that the firm has developed a receptor apparatus capable of absorbing the output. The unprofitability of developing a group of captive scientists is increased by the fact that in complex industrial operations, the sources of needed scientific knowledge are diverse, the need for any one source highly erratic, and the occasions for the need not easily predicted; accordingly, a captive facility inside the firm is likely to be under-utilised for a considerable proportion of the time.

Between abstract scientific research and applied industrial development, however, there lies a spectrum of intermediate activities. Some of these activities are quite general in character, applicable about as much to the needs of one part of a given multinational enterprise as to another. Activities of this sort often are not tied intimately to any one market of the firm; they involve no large questions of firm strategy; and they generate no pressing problems for the key decision makers of the firm. The development of testing standards is an illustration of this sort of activity; so is the investigation of the properties of materials and metals used by the firm. Research of this sort can be staked out at any of several locations from the viewpoint of the firm, without much impairment of efficiency. Such research activities may well be located, therefore, where the input costs are lowest.

But most of what is called industrial R & D is an activity that is much narrower in its objective. As a rule, the object of an industrial development process is simply to create something that responds to a specified need at an economic price.[12] Accordingly, the firm has to be in a position to recognise a need in the market, to identify and develop a possible line of response, and to test and adapt it in the market. In practice, there is a need for swift, subtle, and continuous communication among marketing specialists, production men, cost analysts, and development engineers. That kind of communication, according to various fragmentary tests, takes place more efficiently within a single firm than between firms, more efficiently face to face than in writing.[13] The errors and delays associated with incomplete communication or with misunderstanding can be very high, especially if the object of the development activity is to dominate a field by early innovation and to collect a monopoly rent.

The locational implications of these propositions for industrial innovation and development are quite strong. First, there is a powerful economic incentive to internalise the process within the firm. Second, there is a strong incentive to centralise it. The industrial innovators need to be near the marketing specialists; the marketing specialists need to be near the market; and both are better placed near the top executives of the enterprise than at more remote distances. Since the location of the top executives is probably more firmly fixed by the forces of history, inertia, and status than the location of the others in the firm, the others will tend to be moved to the executives. So grouped, they will tend to be most sensitive to the markets nearby, that is, the 'home' markets.[14] If the creative inspiration strikes in some other location such as in an overseas affiliate or subsidiary, if the inspiration is recognised as valuable by headquarters, and if it has broad applicability to the needs of the firm in many markets, there will be a strong tendency to shift the developmental activities close to headquarters. If the aberrant inspiration applies mainly to the local market in which it arises, it may be allowed to develop *in situ*, in close contact with the appropriate market; but otherwise not.[15]

To the extent that national environments differ, therefore, the expectation is that US-based multinational enterprises will tend to generate and develop innovations with special sensitivity to the conditions of the US market, European-based enterprises with sensitivity to European conditions, Japanese enterprises to Japanese conditions. Though the facts in this important point have not been arrayed with altogether satisfactory rigor, they seem impressively persuasive.[16] The US firms do appear to specialise in innovations that are responsive to high incomes and high labour costs, such as frozen foods and the drip-dry shirt; the Europeans in innovations that are land- and material-saving, including synthetic fertilisers and rayon, or that represent cheaper versions of established consumer products, such as the Volkswagen; and the Japanese in innovations that are material-saving, such as synthetic paper, or that economise on living space, such as miniaturised electronic circuitry.

The concept that businessmen react to stimuli in a limited horizon, which is inherent in generalisation of this sort, does not exclude the possibility that multinational innovators may at times respond to the conditions of markets that are far removed from the parent unit. For instance, a European or Japanese firm with a large and energetic subsidiary located in a major foreign market such as the United States may develop independent strength and may begin responding to the stimuli of the market.[17] Besides, innovations that serve the special needs of one market sometimes serve an unanticipated need in another; the sale of Volkswagens in the United States second-car market and of miniature European refrigerators in weekend homes and trailers in the United States was probably an unplanned by-product for innovators who were responding initially to the dominant features of the market in Europe. The basic propositions, however, still seem valid; the directions of innovation in the firm will be influenced by the conditions of the markets that are in the best position to stimulate it; and the industrial development activities that stem from such stimulation will tend to be located close to the prospective market.

LOCATING PRODUCTION ACTIVITIES

From the viewpoint of a locational analyst, the question of the likely locus of industrial innovation is important on two different grounds: first, in its own right; and second, because it heavily influences the choice of location of the first production facility for the new product. The first facility often comes into existence as a part of the development process itself, undertaken at a time when intimate communication between the market analysts, the engineers, the production men, and the top executives is still a matter of some importance.[18] The tendency to give only limited heed to factor costs at this early stage in the location process can be explained on economic grounds. In many cases, neither the product nor the production process is well standardised at the time of its introduction; so it is not possible with any precision to compare rival production sites. Besides, the supplier looks forward to a period of monopoly or strong oligopoly during which direct production costs may be of limited importance to survival. Moreover, it is commonly observed that first users of a new product or new process are relatively insensitive to price; unless there are very strong advantages in the innovation that require no fine figuring of the costs, the untried nature of the innovation argues strongly against its use; accordingly producers characteristically expect to confront an initial market demand that is relatively price-inelastic.

Though the first production facility of the innovator may be in the home market, additions to the firm's production capacity may well be overseas. The forces that have led US-based innovators eventually to establish production facilities overseas have been described at length and in detail, and it is not necessary to present an elaborate version of the argument here.[19] The process is usually explained as the consequence of several forces; a decline in the US innovator's control over the technology of the product or process; a standardisation of product and process, permitting a closer figuring of costs; and an increase in the cross-elasticity of demand on the part of buyers, as aggregate demand grows. The net effect is to heighten the US producer's concern for his competitive position, leading him to ask whether that position would be protected and prolonged if the firm served its foreign markets from production facilities located outside the United States.

Now observe that the answer to this question turns on various elements. First, there is the question of factor costs; in the case of US-based producers, labour-intensive products are earlier candidates for such a decision than are capital-intensive products, simply because of the high cost of labour in the United States. Then there is the question of scale; products with relatively small economies of scale in production are sooner established abroad than those with large. In addition, where transportation costs and barriers at the border are relatively high, the decision to serve foreign markets from local facilities is indicated sooner.

Though considerations of this sort may be appropriate for any firm that is trying to prolong some original innovation-based advantage, differences in the cost structures between countries may lead to different locational responses on the part of innovators, depending on where the first facility was located. Take a European firm that has developed a new papermaking machine for the European market and has established a market for the machine in the United States by way of exports of the machine from Europe. Such a firm would not necessarily reduce its costs by producing the machine in the United States, especially if the production of the machine entailed hand labour. Volkswagen's decision in the 1950s not to produce automobiles in the United States may have been quite rational at the time, while the decision of US automobile firms to expand their production in Europe may also have been rational.

One is tempted to assume that once innovational leads have disappeared in an industry, the process of location can be viewed again in terms of the classical model. At that stage, however, the period of oligopoly is not necessarily over. If scale economies in production or marketing have meanwhile become very important, they may replace the innovation factor as a major barrier to entry. In that case, the industry will have evolved to the state of what I shall call a 'mature oligopoly'.

The transition from an innovation-based oligopoly to a mature oligopoly is visible in a number of major industries. Some of the most familiar illustrations are to be found in capital-intensive industries that process raw materials, such as oil and aluminium. The transition has occurred also in various sectors of the chemicals industry, such as that of plastics, as products have aged and technology has been diffused.[20] Once the transition has occurred, some rather different locational factors begin to operate.

AGGREGATING THE INNOVATION-BASED INDUSTRIES

Before we consider the locational behaviour of firms in the mature industries, however, there is still one basic question to ponder with respect to the innovation-based industries: If the factors that affect the location of multinational enterprises in the innovation-based industries have been appropriately described, what can one say regarding the location of such industries in the aggregate? In locational terms, does it matter that multinational enterprises have come to dominate in these fields?

In addressing this intricate question, the first need is to define the alternative state of being—the situation which would exist if the multinational enterprise did not. Clearly, the alternative is not that of firms competing in an atomistic market in a homogeneous product; hence, the pure classical model is not easily available as a basis for developing a benchmark. Instead, one is led to think of alternative regimes in which innovation occurs at some point in space, to be diffused by imitation, by licensing, or by some means other than the creation of subsidiaries. There are some plausible starting assumptions that go with these alternatives: that efficiency in the transmission of information will be lower; that the skills and cerebration required at the receptor site for understanding and applying a given body of information will be greater; that these differences will shrink as a given innovation grows older; and in general, that the lag in the creation of foreign facilities which embody the innovation—the so-called 'imitation lag'—will be prolonged by some lesser or greater amount.

I do not propose to defend these propositions here; they are far too tentative to deserve an elaborate rationalisation and defence.[21] If they prove to stand up under more careful scrutiny, however, they will suggest two provocative corollaries regarding location. The first is that, as compared with the alternatives, the presence of multinational enterprises tends to concentrate industrial innovation, presumably in the country in which the main market of the innovating enterprise exists. The second is that the multinational enterprise tends to speed the dispersal of production facilities that are based upon the innovation.[22] But these propositions need substantially greater testing both at the theoretical and at the empirical level.

THE MATURE OLIGOPOLIES

In many industries where multinational enterprises predominate, the basis for the oligopoly is not the advantages of product innovation but the barriers to entry generated by scale in production, transportation or marketing. In industries such as oil, copper, aluminium, and nickel, the scale factor in production, transportation, or marketing has been supplemented by the advantages that come from the diversity of raw material sources and of markets. The diversity of production sources has given the leaders a form of insurance against the threat that one or another source might be cut off, while the diversity of markets has reduced fluctuations in levels of output and allowed exploitation of the existing resources of the enterprise at higher rates of capacity. To be sure, no oligopoly based on barriers to entry in the form of scale can hope to maintain its oligopoly structure forever. And in many oligopolistic industries, including oil, sulphur, and fertilizer, the oligopoly structure is visibly weakening. Still, industries whose entry barriers rest mainly on sheer scale are likely to be common for a very long time to come.

What has all this to do with an economic theory of location? Here, one must recall a fundamental aspect of oligopoly theory. The pricing and investment decisions of an oligopolist are taken with explicit regard for their effects on the decisions of the others in the industry. An initiative by any one can upset the existing equilibrium in the market, reduce the unit rent for all output, and turn an otherwise profitable investment into one with negative marginal yield. Accordingly, as the leaders of the oligopoly try to maximise their rent, they will be partial to a strategy that they regard as stabilising for the industry.

The reasons for the overwhelming concern with stability in these industries are clear and familiar. In each industry, some major part of the producing or marketing process is operated

D

under conditions of very high fixed cost and low marginal cost; as a result, when demand declines, the suppliers may be tempted to sell at less than full cost. If any major supplier succumbs to the temptation, however, the industry as a whole is exposed to the disconcerting consequences of competitive price-cutting. Accordingly, the leaders in these industries can be expected to pay great heed to the common interests of the oligopoly.

STABILITY THROUGH PRICING CONVENTIONS

In their effort to maintain stability, some industries have evolved fairly elaborate pricing conventions. The effect of the existence of pricing conventions upon the international location of industry has been particularly strong in a few industries, including iron ore and oil.

In the case of oil, until the 1940s, world prices were determined mainly by a basing point system whose object was to assure the leading US producers that shipments from the US Gulf ports would not be underpriced in the key markets on the US East Coast and in Europe; hence, the prevailing Gulf port price plus transportation in any given market was used as a basis for determining the delivered price in that market, irrespective of the actual source of the oil.[23] Since Gulf port oil was relatively high-cost oil, the use of the basing point protected the main sources of oil then in existence. As long as each of the leading producers limited its operations to the established sources, one potential element of instability was reduced. Exploration in new areas, which by its nature involved more uncertainty and risk than in established areas, therefore entailed added risk of another sort, namely, the risk that went with disturbing the stability of existing arrangements.

By the early 1950s, the pricing of crude oil was being determined by reference to two key basing points, one at the Gulf ports, the other in the Middle East. Without any visible formal agreement, the price of oil in the Middle East was set at levels which would be equal to that of Gulf oil when delivered to a given watershed point in Western Europe—a point at which the price for Gulf oil and Middle East oil was equalised. East of that point, Middle East oil was cheaper; west of it, Gulf oil was cheaper. Since most of the leaders had producing interests both in the Middle East and the Western Hemisphere, the new arrangements still protected their main areas of commitment.

The pricing structure for oil in world markets has gone through many more changes since the early 1950s. For example, in a period of 10 or 12 years, the watershed point gradually moved westward from Greece to Italy, then to Britain, then even to the United States. This adjustment was a reflection of the fact that the marginal cost of oil from the Middle East was much lower than that in the Western Hemisphere. Therefore, within the large multinational systems, a difference in costs found its expression in a shift in location, at least as among the areas already in production. But just as the Gulf Port basing point system had lessened the desire and the need of established producers to look for cheaper sources of oil outside of the Gulf of Mexico, so the dual basing point system probably tended to concentrate the added output of the established producers for a time in the Middle East.

The trouble with such arrangements, of course, is that new-comers who surmount the entry barriers have no incentive to adhere to the arrangements, at least not until they have captured a share of the market. Their early sales could generally be made by offering price discounts, without disturbing the stability of the price structure itself. Only after their sales have grown somewhat does the threat of instability begin to arise. When the threat becomes so great that increased sales may yield a net loss rather than a net gain, the newcomer finally has an interest in accepting the discipline of the oligopoly.

In the case of oil, newcomers have constantly threatened the stability of the oligopoly. New entrants in the multinational oil race, such as Phillips, ENI, Getty, Continental, and Occidental Oil, seem to have forced the pace in Libya, Nigeria, and other areas outside the old centres. But as the newcomers moved, the constant preoccupation of the leading firms for balance and stability has obliged them to match the newcomers' moves by developing or expanding their own output in the areas where the new arrivals were concentrating. The matching moves were needed first of all to reduce the risk that the newcomers might acquire access to a source that had a unique competitive advan-tage. Besides, once there was a good reason for expanding in another area, the decision always has the added advantage that it increased the protection of the enterprise against the pressures of government in the older areas.

None of these observations is altogether new from the view-point of economic theory. The locational logic of basing point systems and the effects of such systems on industrial location have been reasonably well explored.[24] The locational responses that any such system generates, according to the theory, depends upon its terms, as well as upon the structure of the cost curves for production and transportation and the price elasticity of demand for the product concerned. It depends also on the levels of economic risk that leaders perceive in the development of new areas. In general, however, such systems tend to slow down the response of the oligopoly leaders to shifts in geographical location that otherwise might develop.

In so far as pricing behaviour is linked to locational decisions, therefore, the growth and development of multinational enterprises in the mature oligopolies do not require much in the way of modification of existing theory. Concepts of oligopoly pricing behaviour, which heretofore have generally been treated within a single national market, must be applied in an international setting. The extension from the national level to the international level increases the importance of some of the limiting assumptions of the theory. One of these is the key assumption that cost structures are known for all alternative locations, so that relative costs can be allowed to play their role. This is an assumption which is further removed from reality in the international case than in most national situations, due to the relatively unexplored character of so much of the earth's surface. Still another limiting assumption—much more important in the mining industry than in oil—is that the applicable tax system is neutral in locational effect. Considerations of this sort reduce the relevance of existing theory which ties pricing behaviour to locational decisions, but they do not raise issues that are conceptually new in character.

STABILITY THROUGH HOSTAGES AND ALLIANCES

The location of productive facilities in the mature oligopolies is affected not only by the patterns of pricing behaviour in such industries but also by other stratagems for the maintenance of stability. Once a mature oligopoly has been plunged into a period of uncertainty, the behaviour of the leaders appears to take certain fairly well-defined forms—forms whose rationality can better be explained in game theory terms than in terms of classical economic analysis. The entry of Royal Dutch into the United States over half a century ago, for instance, was acknowledged to be a countermove to the Standard Oil's earlier entry into Sumatra. The entry of British Petroleum, Compagnie Française des Petroles, and France's Pechiney into US markets in recent years probably also can be looked on in part as a belated countermove to the US penetration of Europe. The rationale for such countermoves is fairly clear, and bears a close relation to the well-known strategies of dumping in international trade.[25]

When a leading firm has made an independent move into a rival's territory, stability is threatened. Even if the intruder produces its product inside the rival's territory, thereby operating in the same cost environment as the rival, the move may be threatening. If profit margins include a monopoly rent, the intruder's appearance may cut that rent. For the intruder, the reduction in rent may be a trivial factor because it takes place outside of the intruder's main market; even if the rent is wiped out, it may be easy for the intruder to absorb the effects in the rest of his enterprise outside the invaded territory. For the rival, however, a decline in rent in its principal market may represent a major disaster. An obvious response on the part of the rival, therefore, is to make an offsetting threat that will dampen the intruder's taste for price warfare. At times, this can be done by threatening to dump. But dumping can be blocked at the custom-house. Establishing a producing unit inside the intruder's main market is a safer response. The leaders, therefore, tend to establish a presence in the principal markets of their potential rivals, a tendency that concentrates investment more than would occur in a classically competitive market.

When the establishment of a foreign facility is intended for the exploitation of raw materials rather than for local production and marketing, some characteristic strategies for the maintenance of stability also tend to lead to the concentration of investment. One such strategy has been the development of industry-wide standards that serve as norms for enterprises in bidding on new concessions; by reducing the risks of overbidding, these conventions tend to concentrate new investments in the areas that are prepared to accept the going terms.[26] Another strategy has been the formation of joint producing subsidiaries among the leaders, or of long-term bulk purchase-and-sale contracts that amount to quasi-partnerships. Even when partnerships or other alliances do not exist, there has been a general practice among the leading firms of swapping supplies in a given market as if the producers were drawing from a common pool. In aluminium and in oil, one would be hard put to find a leading multinational enterprise that was not connected quite directly through such arrangements with every other leading enterprise.[27] The existence of these partnerships represents no ironclad guarantee of perpetual stability.[28] But their existence does strengthen the community of interest of potential rivals and increase the probability of co-operation, and it does reduce risk by allowing each of the participants to find the desired diversity of sources within the same range of countries where others in the industry are located.[29]

To be sure, the use of partnerships in the exploitation of raw materials, when taken by itself, would not necessarily affect the location of economic activity. Theoretically, one could picture a group of partner enterprises establishing their facilities in essentially the same areas as the enterprises individually might have done. Still, that does seem an improbable outcome. More likely, if the enterprises were operating individually, some of them would avoid concentrating their facilities too heavily in a single area, even if the effect was to prevent them from exploiting the full potential economies of production scale; in short, there would be a trade-off between the advantages of scale and the advantages of risk reduction. The use of partnerships avoids the need for such a trade-off and probably leads to larger undertakings than otherwise would occur. Being larger, these undertakings may well be more highly concentrated in geographical terms than those which the individual partners otherwise would have established. Once again, therefore, there is a hint in support of the proposition that the search for stability in the mature oligopolies leads to a geographical concentration of investment which could not be explained on the basis of comparative costs.

FOLLOW THE LEADER

There are added grounds for suspecting that the search for stability leads to concentration in geographical terms. A number of investigators have observed that the decision of one firm in an international oligopoly to establish a new producing facility outside its home country often seems to trigger the establishment of similar facilities in that country by others. One careful study has demonstrated that the follow-the-leader practice is a fairly systematic and pervasive phenomenon, at least among US-based enterprises operating in foreign countries; and that the strength of the phenomenon in any industry is positively correlated with the prominence of the oligopoly aspects of the industry.[30]

When the facility is intended to produce for the local market and when restrictions on imports are a probability, the reason for a follow-the-leader reaction is fairly clear. Countries that systematically use import restrictions to promote local industry commonly set those restrictions at levels which assure a profit for the producers in the country, almost irrespective of their efficiency levels.[31] This propensity accounts for the disconcertingly high number of foreign-owned automobile plants, for instance, in countries such as Argentina and Mexico.

Even when import protection is not assured, enterprises that operate in certain types of oligopolistic industries still may have a reason for following the leader. When the basis for an oligopoly is product and brand differentiation, as in food preparations and in drugs, the production facility that is in closest contact with the market generally operates at a major advantage over the others. As a result, if a leading competitor improves its contacts with the market by establishing a local production unit, others in the industry may feel threatened; hence the tendency to follow the leader.

Why should a follow-the-leader pattern exist, however, in industries engaged in the production of raw materials? Consider the state of mind of any member of an oligopoly when deciding whether to expand the production of its raw materials. No such expansion is altogether free of uncertainties. The sites that have the lowest uncertainties attaching to them in the mind of the firm are generally proven reserves located near areas that are already being worked by the firm. In these cases, the firm may feel itself able to make fairly accurate projections of the availability and cost of the materials. Beyond these cases, however, a spectrum of possibilities exists, with different degrees of uncertainty attaching to each. For each alternative, some information is available. The existing information offers the basis for an estimate of likely cost, an estimate of variance in cost, and identification of areas of ignorance. The firm finds itself obliged to confront the usual baffling problems. First, the firm has to decide whether to make investments in added knowledge in order to be able to make more informed comparisons. Second, the firm has to decide how to compare alternatives; this entails a comparison of likely outcomes, in circumstances in which different errors of estimate are attached to each outcome.[32]

In a mature oligopoly, as long as stability exists and an oligopoly rent is being earned, the willingness of the leaders to explore possibilities associated with high variance and considerable ignorance is probably relatively low. But stability, as was pointed out earlier, is far from assured in industries of this sort. Outsiders commonly upset the previous equilibrium by opening up new sources of supply in unfamiliar locations.

Assume, then, that the leaders in such an industry find the stability of their situation impaired; suppose, for example, that an outsider is developing a new source of copper production in Indonesia. Seen through the eyes of the leaders of the world copper industry, Indonesia may be one of the less attractive of the various alternative areas for expansion; the most likely outcome, when judged on the basis of facts known to them, may be poorer than some other alternatives under consideration, and the variance associated with the outcome may be larger. As we suggested earlier, however, there is nevertheless an economic reason for matching behaviour on the part of the leaders. If the outsider develops a new source of supply and if his costs of production are sufficiently low, he will represent a major threat. The capacity of the leaders to match the newcomer's source of supply reduces the newcomer's capacity to threaten, and it speeds the point at which the newcomer sees it in his interest to accept the discipline of the oligopoly.

If one aggregates the tendencies described in the past few pages, one begins to anticipate what is in fact the case—that the choice of foreign trading partners by the affiliated units of multinational enterprises is influenced by the presence of affiliation; the least cost assumptions contained in the Weber–Lösch postulates will afford a poor predictive model at times.[33] Just how poor has not been well researched, and it would be well if considerably more effort could be devoted to that purpose. In addition, there is a strong possibility that the existence of multinational enterprises in the mature industries tends to concentrate economic activity on geographical lines, to a degree that is greater than if multinational enterprises did not exist.

It could well be that oligopolies composed of national enterprises in a single national economy would tend to exhibit patterns of behaviour of a similar sort inside that economy. But when a national oligopoly is in operation, signals that are based on geographical distinctions may be somewhat ambiguous. In oligopolies that cover a number of countries, on the other hand, the very separateness of the national economies helps to sharpen some of the signals associated with the operation of the oligopoly. Lines of speculation such as these lie outside the theory of international trade in its present form.[34] Yet there are strong grounds for supposing that, in many products, propositions of this sort are needed in order to explain the location of the economic activity and the patterns of the world trade.[35]

THE SENESCENT OLIGOPOLIES

It would be wrong to assume, however, that the locational behaviour of the multinational enterprise is to be explained entirely in terms of oligopoly theory. Straightforward classical considerations—considerations based both on the general equilibrium models of Weber and Lösch and the Marshallian model of international trade theory—also contribute to an explanation of their behaviour.

Some pages back, it will be remembered, the reader was invited to consider the possibility that as a product matures, the innovational factor may decline as a basis for oligopoly and a new stage may appear. If economies of scale are very important at this stage, the mature oligopoly may prove sufficiently strong to hold down the number of competitors to the levels needed for an oligopolistic equilibrium. But scale economies may not prove all that important. What then?

In instances of this sort, the enterprises concerned may try to prolong the equilibrium, either by entering into cartels or by attempting to differentiate their trade names and their products. At times, they will succeed; but sometimes their competitive situation will become quite ambiguous. Consider the markets for many consumer durables. Though there is considerable product differentiation and brand differentiation, cross-elasticities are still uncomfortably high from the producer's viewpoint. And though the required scale presents some difficulties for new entrants, the barrier to entry is not so high as to ensure stability for the leaders.

Enterprises that are deeply involved in markets of this sort are generally aware that their future is insecure, and that their staying power will depend on costs and prices. When that fact is fully realised, some firms prefer to drop the product concerned; in the chemical industry, for instance, products of this sort are referred to pejoratively as 'commodities', to be avoided if possible. That policy presumably is followed because the firm assumes that its strength is based on some scarce rationed resource not available in the open market, such as some special organisational capability; if applied to the production of 'commodities', the scarce resource will not command a scarcity rent.[36]

There are cases, however, in which firms hang on. Sometimes they hang on because they feel that their special resource, whatever it may be, is not transferable to other products; sometimes because the sale of the item generates externalities that affect other products of the firm. Where the need to hang on is strong, the industry must resign itself to some degree of genuine price competition. In such cases, the question of costs takes on added importance. If cheaper materials or components can be secured from foreign locations, the pull to those locations is strong. In brief, Marshall takes over from Chamberlin.

This shift in perspective, however, does not explain why a

firm should feel the need to set up its own foreign producing subsidiary. Such a firm can simply buy its materials or components from foreign suppliers. That, of course, is what commonly happens in a wide variety of industries, from steel fabricating to toy making. On the other hand, manufacturing enterprises often feel uneasy about relying on independent suppliers for important components or materials, even if there are many suppliers and they are reasonably competitive. If the components or materials must be produced according to strict quality standards or close delivery schedules in order to command the highest market price, reliance on an uncontrolled supplier—especially an uncontrolled supplier in a foreign country—can be uneconomic. This is a factor that pushes enterprises to establish their own overseas producing facilities.

The propensity is even stronger if the buying enterprise is already multinational in structure. In that case, it may well be familiar with the operating conditions of some countries where the materials or components can be produced at low cost; indeed, it may already have manufacturing subsidiaries in such a country. When that is so, the parent may elect to enlarge the scale and function of the existing subsidiary so that it can supply materials or components to other parts of the system. Beginning about the middle of the 1960s, multinational enterprises farmed out the manufacture of all sorts of components to their foreign subsidiaries, components which eventually would find their way into assembled electric razors, toys, automobiles, radios, and many other products in which costs and prices were of importance.[37]

Observe that in such circumstances, the classical model provides a fairly good basis for the description of locational behaviour. The multinational enterprises that were looking for low-cost areas of production were operating under conditions that approximated the key assumptions of the model. In the products that were involved, the object was to reduce costs in the direct, conventional sense; to the extent that scale and location affected the delivered unit cost of the product, these could be taken into account in a straightforward way. Moreover, national differences in factor prices commonly had an important effect on production costs; and problems of acquiring knowledge or confronting uncertainty, always disconcerting for the classical model, were being contained within reasonable bounds. With these factors reduced to tolerable proportions, multinational enterprises could serve as the instruments for locating production facilities in low-cost areas.

There is one major respect, however, in which the activities of such multinational enterprises deviate from the assumptions of the classical model. These enterprises are not only cost-conscious scanners of the situations in different countries; they are also conduits through which the productive factors themselves are made to move from country to country. This is particularly the case with regard to finance capital and human skills. Some of the theoretical implications of that fact are examined in companion papers of this symposium. In the context of locational decisions, one important implication stands out: the structure of factor costs confronting the multinational enterprise in any given location is not necessarily based on the local market for the factor. For the lower grades of labour and of supervisory personnel, the local market may be controlling. But for other factors, the cost may depend on supply or demand in world markets.

This consideration would not distinguish the multinational enterprise if it could be assumed that all enterprises, national or multinational, have the option of importing capital or human skills from abroad. In some instances, of course, that is a realistic assumption. But more often, national enterprises run up against the very same problems that they confront in connection with international trade. Their capacity to exploit foreign markets for capital and skilled labour depends upon their willingness to invest in the knowledge necessary to scan those markets. Moreover, the terms that national enterprises can command in those foreign markets, especially the terms on which capital can be acquired, depend upon the information that the sources of capital happen to have regarding the prospective borrowers. Frictions of this sort create the basis for assuming that national enterprises will be less sensitive to factor costs that exist outside the national economy than multinational enterprises.

The differences in sensitivity to factor costs between multi-national enterprises and national enterprises may be heightened by still another consideration. At times, multinational enterprises are in a position to choose among competing production sites located in different countries in order to serve some market need; in other cases, they are foreclosed from making any such choice, by reason of import restrictions or export restrictions. When they do have room for choice, they are obliged to consider what the implications may be of future variations in exchange rates and future variations in factor prices in each of the countries. Assume that future capital inputs are expected to come from the most advantageous international source while future labour inputs are expected to come from a tied national source; then the uncertainties associated with selecting the most advantageous location in terms of future labour costs are higher *a priori* than the uncertainties associated with selecting the most advantageous location from the viewpoint of capital cost.

These ruminations are, of course, little more than starting hypotheses. The reasoning needs to be elaborated more rigorously, and has to be tested against observation. Still, it is worth while noting that if the subsidiaries of multinational enterprises are operating on the basis of a preferred factor-cost structure that differs from comparable national enterprises, that preference has numerous implications. One implication is that, even when the technologies of all firms are identical, the choice of sites will be different. For instance, if the relative cost of capital is lower for the multinational enterprise than for the national enterprise, the multinational enterprise presumably will not be as heavily handi-capped in countries in which the national cost of capital is relatively high, nor as greatly assisted by countries in which the cost of labour is low.

Another implication of the differences in factor costs is that the optimum technology from the viewpoint of a multinationational enterprise will differ from the optimum technology for the national firm. The differences will exist partly because the multi-national firm confronts a different set of factor costs from the national firm as it makes the investment decision. The differences will be strengthened by the fact that the multinational firm will have already mastered a different technology from that of the national firm as a result of past decisions. All enterprises have an economic reason to prefer the technology they have already mastered. The cost of the development of that technology is already fully sunk, so that an added application is costless to the enterprise. Of course, an unfamiliar technology may be cheaper than a technology that has already been mastered, due to subse-quent savings in capital, materials or labour. But the savings would have to be large enough to overcome the initial cost of developing and mastering the unfamiliar technology.

To the extent that the subject has been researched, it suggests that multinational enterprises behave on lines that are roughly consistent with expectations.[38] When US-based enterprises deviate from their local competitors in choice of production techniques, the deviation tends to be toward the use of techniques that reflect their access to relatively inexpensive capital and their experience with techniques that are capital intensive. On the other hand, multinational enterprises do seem to substitute labour for capital when there are no great problems for the firm in applying the labour-intensive technique and when the risks of substituting labour for capital are low.

When substitution is avoided, as it is at times, the reasons are not always economic, as measured by private or social yield. There are times when the decision is based on the desire of engineers to apply the latest techniques, or to avoid the pain and the uncertainty of adapting techniques to unfamiliar surroundings. There are other times, however, when the failure to substitute factors that seem abundant for those that seem scarce is based on more solid calculations of private cost. For example, substitution of labour for capital may involve the use of some very scarce type of labour, such as supervisory labour or maintenance men; it may entail a production process that generates a product of variable quality;[39] or it may entail a process that is incapable of increasing its output in the short run, at least as compared with a capital-intensive process.

In sum, there are various economic reasons why enterprises may appear not to be responding fully to the local pattern of factor costs. Some of these reasons apply to all enterprises, some to multinational enterprises alone. Two factors in particular distinguish the multinational enterprise, viz. the availability of factors outside the national economy and the differences in initial costs associated with the application of different techniques of production. To the extent that production costs play a role in the locational decisions of multinational enterprises, both of these factors seem to operate in the same direction. They dampen the influence of local factor costs, and they tend to concentrate production in areas whose cost configurations more nearly correspond to the environments from which the multinational enterprise draws its technologies and its productive factors.

LOCATING WITHIN A FOREIGN COUNTRY

There is one more context in which multinational enterprises may play a distinctive role in the theory of economic location. This is in connection with the choice of sites inside a national economy. The obvious question is whether a foreign-based enterprise that is establishing itself within a country would choose its site with the same locational considerations in mind as an enterprise of national origin engaged in the same type and scale of activity.

One factor that may distinguish the foreign-owned subsidiary from the national enterprise is the roles which scale and externalities are likely to play. Over the past decade or two, multinational enterprises setting up facilities in a foreign country were often beginning from scratch in that country. National enterprises that were setting up similar facilities in the oligopolistic industries, on the other hand, were generally adding to an existing nucleus of established plants. In Germany, for instance, a national chemical firm such as Badische Anilin was making its locational decisions from an established production nucleus, whereas Dow Chemical was still in process of building such a nucleus.

In cases such as these, the multinational enterprise could decide to choose a different location on economic grounds from that chosen by the national enterprise. In locational terms, the tendency might well be for national firms to expand where they were, while foreign-owned subsidiaries expanded in response to the calculations suggested by the cost of labour, by tax considerations, and the like. This may be why the subsidiaries of foreign firms are sometimes thought much more responsive than national enterprises to the subsidies and grants offered by governments to firms that are prepared to locate in backward regions of the country.[40] However, there is no need to appeal to any novel aspects of economic theory to explain these different outcomes; the difference between marginal and full costs will serve well enough.

On the other hand, another factor may well be involved in the locational decisions of foreign-owned subsidiaries. When foreign-based enterprises choose a location in some distant country, it can be presumed that their information base is thinner or is assembled at higher cost than would be the case for national enterprises, especially with regard to opportunities in remote areas of the country. Calabria, one supposes, is a more remote and distant part of Italy in the eyes of Philips Electric than in the eyes of Montedison; Philips, therefore, may be more likely to overlook the opportunities that exist in that area. In short, foreign-based multinational enterprises might be expected to settle in the more obvious and better-known areas of the country, leaving the more remote corners to national enterprises. In this case, one can explain the difference in the familiar economic terms of costs of information.

My guess is that both of the forces described in these pages are in operation—both the force that frees the subsidiaries of multinational enterprises from being pulled toward existing clusters of facilities and the force that keeps subsidiaries of multinational enterprises out of the remote corners of national economies. It may even be that one can predict which force is dominant, depending upon the objective characteristics of the firm. For instance, a firm that was operating under a strong threat of price competition, facing high demand elasticities, presumably would be ready to invest in information regarding the cost situation in remote places, whereas a firm that felt secure in its monopoly position might not count such an investment as having so high a potential payout. But this is a subject that still needs extensive investigation.

CONCLUSIONS

Perhaps the most important generalisation that emerges from this review is that the multinational enterprise which contemplates the establishment of a foreign subsidiary is engaged in measuring the marginal impact upon the enterprise as a whole. Comparative yields are measured, as they should be, by their effect on profits anywhere in the enterprise, as well as by their effect on the level of risk that the enterprise as a whole confronts.

When making its marginal calculations, unlike the economic man of classical theory, the multinational enterprise is often in a position to acquire its productive factors at the prices and costs that prevail outside the national economy where the new affiliate is to be located. In fact, the capital and the human resources to be used by the new subsidiary need not all be physically located in the economy where the subsidiary is placed.

Because the decision to establish a subsidiary is marginal to the multinational enterprise and because the existing facilities to which the subsidiary is to be added are located in other countries, optimal locational decisions generated by the multinational enterprise will differ from those generated by a group of unrelated national enterprises. The national enterprises will acquire human resources and capital at their own national prices; the multinational enterprise at the best prices available to it anywhere. The national enterprises will import goods and services at world market prices; the multinational enterprise at the marginal cost to the system.

The differences between full cost and marginal cost take on special importance as one considers the external factors likely to be provided to the subsidiaries of multinational enterprises. Among other things, the new subsidiary is likely to use the output of other subsidiaries operating under declining cost curves, as well as intangible resources such as management systems, technical information, credit guarantees, and trade names. The marginal cost to the multinational enterprise of providing those resources to another subsidiary can be expected to deviate markedly from the market price of the resource, assuming a market price existed.

One last point. The multinational enterprise, of course, is the economic man of oligopoly theory, not the economic man of classical theory. Accordingly, in its search for profits and the reduction of risk, it is obliged to take into account the effect of any given move on its part upon the behaviour of others in the oligopoly. This fact elevates the question of risk for the system to a major place in the calculation. An investment foregone or an investment undertaken can have its economic justification entirely in terms of the risk-reducing impact on the rest of the system—risk-reducing not in the portfolio sense of a reduction in variance but in the Bayesian sense of reducing the probability of a decline in an oligopoly rent. This possibility underlines even further the basic point that the rationale for the locational decision with respect to each subsidiary cannot be explained with respect to the effects upon the subsidiary alone.

References

[1] The research on which this chapter is based was financed partly by the Harvard Business School under a grant from the Ford Foundation and partly by the Harvard Center for International Affairs.

[2] A convenient summary and refinement of this body of theory is found in Hoover, 1948.

[3] The connection is seen explicitly in Ohlin (1967).

[4] Nevertheless, various models explore the theoretical implications of relaxing this assumption, notably those associated with Mundell and Samuelson. For a summary of such efforts, see Richardson (1969), especially Chapter 12.

[5] For a summary of evidence relating to US industry, see Vernon (1971a). Chapters 1, 2, 3; also Hymer and Rowthorn (1969).

[6] The phenomenon is well documented for the period before World War II. See especially Hexner (1945). For manifestations of a recent recrudescence, albeit on a more limited scale, see Mikdashi (1971), pp. 13–18.

[7] Ohlin, in the work just cited, touches on oligopoly only as an end case. He considers a situation in which scale is important and factor costs identical between locations and concludes that situations of this sort are empirically unimportant. Two other works of consequence, however, develop the theoretical implications of this situation: from the viewpoint of received theories of industrial organisation (Caves 1971), p. 1027; from a game-theoretic and Bayesian viewpoint (Vaupel 1972).

[8] See Gruber, Mehta, and Vernon (1967), p. 20; also Keesing (1969) p. 38.

[9] See Scherer (1970), pp. 352–62; also Mansfield (1968), pp. 69–98.

[10] A summary of the relevant data is provided in Pavitt (1971), p. 97. See also Caty et al. (1972), pp. 205–23.

[11] Pavitt (1971), pp. 79–103.

12 Observe the emphasis on product rather than process as the typical objective of R & D. See Scherer (1970), pp. 346–52; Mansfield *et al.* (1971), especially Chapter 3. This is an important fact which complicates the treatment of the activity from the viewpoint of economic theory.

13 For a summary of the existing evidence, see Pavitt (1971), pp. 29–75, 131; Marquis & Allen (1966), pp. 1052–60; Reiss (1969), p. 105; Mansfield (1968), pp. 80–6; Myers & Marquis (1969). That this is not a wholly culture-bound phenomenon, typical mainly of Americans, is indicated in Aigrain (1969), pp. 39–47.

14 This proposition is well developed in Linder (1961), pp. 87–91; also Wells (1966), p. 82.

15 See Conference Board (1970), pp. 2, 10. A discussion of this phenomenon, relating mainly to multinational enterprises in Canada, appears in Cordell (1971).

16 The extent to which innovations are market-oriented is, of course, widely debated in the economic literature, with important contributions especially by Schmookler (1960). See also my summary of the argument and related evidence Vernon in (1971a), pp. 65–71.

17 Illustrations of this sort are beginning to appear. For cases involving Europeans in the United States, see Franko (1971), pp. 22–3. For the Japanese as a group, Tsurumi (1972). For General Motor's Opel developments in Europe, Bannock (1971), pp. 287–90. For Shell's weed killer innovations and other illustrations in the United States, Faith (1971), p. 53 *passim.* Presumably, however, the possibility applies mainly to major subsidiaries serving large foreign markets.

18 Mansfield *et al.* (1971), pp. 145–55.

19 See Vernon (1971a), especially Chapters 2 and 3. A recent publication that presents some of the leading empirical work is Wells (ed.) (1972). See also Stobaugh (1972).

20 This is a much-researched industry that admirably illustrates many of the propositions suggested here. See, for instance, OECD (1969); Hufbauer (1965); Freeman (1963), p. 22, *et seq.*

21 Those who wish to pursue the subject further will find especially useful Hufbauer (1965); Stobaugh (1968).

22 In more nearly classical terms, one might view these shifts as an alteration in comparative advantage based on the exploitation of latent scale economies in research in the home country of the multinational enterprise.

23 For background, see Adelman (1972), Penrose (1968); US Federal Trade Commission (1952), Mikdashi (1966).

24 See, for instance, Kaysen (1958), pp. 163–8; also Machlup (1949), pp. 233–7.

25 For a classical treatise, see Viner (1966), p. 27.

26 Mikdashi (1972), Chapter VI.

27 For aluminium: Mikdashi (1971), pp. 8–34. For oil: Adelman (1972); Penrose (1968), pp. 150–72.

28 Note, for instance, the antidumping suit brought in the United States by Aluminum Co. of America against ALCAN of Canada. These two giants are prevented from engaging in direct alliances by court judgments in a previous antitrust case.

29 The importance of achieving such diversification as a business objective is elaborated in Penrose (1968), p. 237.

30 Knickerbocker (1973).

31 For evidence on this point, see Balassa, *et al.* (1971), pp. 71–88.

[32] For a systematic approach, see Grayson (1960), especially part 2.

[33] Compare Tilton (1966), pp. 419–74.

[34] At least that is the conclusion to be drawn from such standard surveys as Corden (1965), and Bhagwati (1969).

[35] For explanations of trade patterns which draw on considerations of this sort, see Hufbauer (1970), pp. 145–231.

[36] See Vernon (1971a), pp. 47–66.

[37] For a careful compilation of such cases, see Adam (1971), pp. 349–67.

[38] Some significant pieces of research bearing on the issue are Mason (1971); Clague (1970), pp. 188–205; Yeoman (1968); Steel (1971). See also Strassmann (1968), pp. 171–81, 200.

[39] Baranson (1967).

[40] Evidence on this point is actually superficial and the indications so far are unclear. See Hellman (1970), p. 284; also Holland (ed.) (1972), p. 27. The propensity for the US subsidiaries of European firms to settle in the relatively underdeveloped areas of the United States, including areas in the southern states and Appalachia, is developed in Faith (1971), pp. 119–36.

Chapter 5

INDUSTRIAL ORGANISATION

Richard E. Caves

INTRODUCTION

Industrial organisation deals primarily with the structures of markets and their effect on economic welfare. As a branch of economic analysis, it applies the theory of markets to actual product markets. It draws criteria from welfare economics for how a market should best perform, and hypotheses from the theory of markets about what structural traits yield good or bad performance.

We might take two approaches to integrating the multinational enterprise into this frame:

1. Jettison the conventional practice of accepting the nation's boundaries as the (outer) geographic limit of the market and recognise that the chain of substitution potentially girds the globe. The multinational corporation and international commodity trade then become the principal channels of arbitrage among the national subsectors of the world market.

2. Accept the national market as the basic unit of analysis and modify the concepts and hypotheses ordinarily applied to it, in order to allow for the fact that some players (actual or potential) are multinational enterprises.

The second approach lacks generality, but its operational efficiency more than offsets the fault. Theorists have tended to study markets in a two-stage process, first defining the market and then contemplating the higgling and bartering that transpire within. Applied economists requiring an operational approach find this separation largely pointless.[1] They find no difficulty incorporating extra-market rivalries and opportunities as constraints on the behaviour of individual transactors parallel to those imposed by intra-market rivals. The fact that the national market contains regional submarkets, or itself comprises a subsector of a larger market, then becomes one of the salient aspects of 'market structure'. This approach comports well with the data available, which typically pertain to the national market. It also enjoys a negative justification in the lack of specific guidance from the muse of economic theory on how to handle the inter-dependences between national markets.

This essay first outlines the changes indicated for our standard concepts of national market analysis when the multinational enterprise is present. We then couple these adjusted concepts with models of markets to predict some consequences of the multi-national firm.[2]

ELEMENTS OF MARKET STRUCTURE, CONDUCT AND PERFORMANCE

The most effective approach to the study of industrial markets employs a taxonomic structure of concepts, derived as operational tools from the theory of markets and designed to embody many hypotheses about the determinants of welfare. Elements of market *structure* constrain the behaviour of sellers and buyers in the market. *Conduct* comprises a systematic description of the ways sellers form their individual strategies and reconcile them in the market place; it includes actions tending in the long run to modify the constraints—the elements of market structure. Finally, market *performance* refers to our normative appraisal of the resource allocations effected by market conduct subject to the constraints of market structure.[3] Theory suggests, and empirical research has to a degree confirmed, the importance of a short list of components of structure, conduct, and performance. Let us consider those components affected by the multinational enter-prise.

MARKET STRUCTURE

Our decision to stick with the national market as the first-approximation unit of analysis lets us put aside a principal element of market structure: the number and size distribution of rivals. We proceed on the view that concentration in the national market is measured in the usual ways, whether or not multi-national enterprises are among the sellers. Seller concentration, however, interacts with other elements of market structure; furthermore, in the long run, concentration itself appears to depend on other structural variables.

The condition of entry, a principal element of market structure, is sharply affected by the multinational enterprise. Statistical studies of US manufacturing industries have found an important source of excess profits and thus allocative inefficiency both in overall barriers to entry (measured in the fashion pioneered by J. S. Bain) and in their individual component sources (scale economies, absolute-cost disadvantages, and product differentiation).[4] The theory of entry barriers, as originally set forth, assumes that the prototypical entrant is a firm created *de novo*, and only casual attention has been given to constraints on entry by going firms located in other product markets. The establishment of a subsidiary by a multinational enterprise amounts to entry into one national market by a going enterprise based in another geographic market. It may or may not be based in a different product market, however. Most entries by multinational firms seem to fall into two classes. The firm may make a *horizontal* expansion, its subsidiary producing the same product (or product line) as the parent. Or it may undertake *vertical* expansion across national boundaries either backward to produce raw materials or intermediate products used in its 'home' operations or forward to provide a distribution channel for its export sales. Forward vertical expansion is usually a routine adjunct to export sales promotion; after noting that it sometimes proves to be an intermediate step to a horizontal expansion, we put it aside. Vertical integration backward poses quite a different set of issues from a horizontal direct investment, and will receive only passing attention in the discussion that follows.

The multinational enterprise establishing a subsidiary holds several clear advantages over the *de novo* firm. It retains certain disadvantages as against going firms: the barriers to entry do not tumble entirely, but their relative significance changes. Consider their three principal sources:

1. *Scale economics* might seem to affect the multinationa entrant the same way as the new firm, since they are inherent (broadly speaking) in technical properties of the production function. However, they may not affect equally all physical stages of fabrication commonly carried out by a given industry, or all lines of output typically produced and sold together. In such cases, the multinational entrant enjoys the option of undertaking the processes or products afflicted by scale economies at its home (or other central) location, exporting them to its subsidiary. The subsidiary thus may be able to avoid small-scale diseconomies which would disadvantage the *de novo* firm. The advantage should not be overstressed, however; if the products or processes

are physically separable, the independent entrant also enjoys the potential flexibility of a make-or-buy decision.

2. *Absolute-cost* entry barriers adhere in the control of scarce specialised resources by going firms (e.g. raw materials, patents or process technology, skilled personnel)[5] or in the elevation by lender's risk of the cost of financing a large initial investment. The subsidiary certainly enjoys an advantage in the access to capital via the parent's retained earnings. The horizontal subsidiary should also be able to command know-how and patents from its parent that provide it with an advantage over the *de novo* firm (if not necessarily parity with its extant rivals).[6]

3. *Production differentiation* barriers represent a special case of absolute-cost disadvantages and arise because the entrant firm must either incur higher selling outlays or accept a lower unit price than its established rivals.[7] The multinational's relative advantage in coping with this hindrance might stem from two sources. The firm first establishing a differentiated brand has to acquire marketing skills. Once in hand, these become 'public goods' to the firm and reduce the expected cost of a goodwill investment elsewhere, if they are not entirely culture-specific to the parent firm's national home. The second possible advantage over the *de novo* firm stems from any spillovers of advertising messages or brand identification from the parent's home market (or the domains of its other subsidiaries) to the national market where entry occurs. How much the multinational enterprise benefits from such public-good aspects of sales-promotion outlays is difficult to say. If advertising media capture all rents from the messages they deliver, the firm buying advertising services gains no benefit from spillovers or public-good attributes of advertising. International spillovers may be small, but the corresponding rents probably do accrue to the multinational enterprise and provide a product-differentiation advantage to its subsidiary over the *de novo* entrant.

Notice that the multinational enterprise's advantages with regard to the various sources of entry barriers may interact in multiplicative fashion. Its access to capital (and thus relative freedom from a principal source of absolute-cost barriers) places it in a stronger position for exploiting any economies of scale which may exist in nationwide sales promotion.[8]

Against these advantages over entry barriers of the multinational enterprise we must weigh a potential disadvantage in its exposure to risk. The firm establishing a foreign subsidiary faces a systematic disadvantage in its 'foreign-ness', meaning that it must make costly investments in knowledge about market conditions, laws, and institutions that would come more cheaply to a firm native to the foreign market. Because this information is more costly, the multinational enterprise rationally makes do with less of it, and perforce incurs a higher level of risk. It is also exposed to risk from an obvious source of hostile regulation or discriminatory treatment—the foreign government—against which it may have little leverage once its initial investment is made. These sources of risk to the new subsidiary do not easily fall under the standard classes of entry barriers; one may count them an absolute-cost barrier consisting of a higher risk-adjusted cost of capital for entry into foreign markets. Even this barrier may be turned to advantage by the multinational, however. The international firm may make not one but a number of risky investments in several countries. Negative covariances among their expected returns are quite possible. Hence the multinational could find any one investment more risky than would a *de novo* domestic entrant, yet still derive a greater marginal yield from adding it to its portfolio.[9]

Our conclusion about entry barriers facing the multinational enterprise must be stated with care. Its subsidiary does possess potential advantages against a *de novo* entrant in regard to each source of barrier to entry. But it is not exempt from all disadvantages relative to going firms—whether nationally owned or other subsidiaries. Thus, when we evaluate the height of barriers to entry for some country's industries in a given country, we expect that taking account of potential subsidiary entrants will change our conclusions in two ways: (1) the barriers to entry in the average industry will appear lower than otherwise; (2) the ranking of industries by height of entry barriers may be changed, because the proportional advantage of subsidiaries over *de novo* firms differs from industry to industry. The change is probably least where scale economies are the principal source of barriers to entry, greatest where they rest principally on product differentiation. This hypothesis is important in light of the evidence that the highest entry barriers surrounding US manufacturing industries are usually due to product differentiation rather than other sources.[10] If the same holds for other countries—which it need not—the potential importance of the multinational firm as a competitive force is elevated. In any case, the variation from industry to industry of the multinational firm's advantage over the *de novo* entrant matters for the multivariate statistical analysis customarily used to test hypotheses about the influence of elements of market structure on performance.

Product differentiation makes two appearances in the standard list of elements of market structure—once as a source of barriers to entry, once on its own as an influence on price competition and other forms of rivalry among sellers. In the latter guise, we ask whether the extent of differentiation will be the same in a given industry (*cet. par.*) when a substantial portion of the sellers are multinational as when all are national firms. The conceptually appropriate test is whether the presence of multinationals elevates the cross-elasticity of demand between pairs of randomly drawn sellers. The easy answer is that the presence of subsidiaries should raise the level of differentiation, for two reasons. First, success in differentiation is important for making the firm go multinational, at the outset. Second, a subsidiary's product is often marked at least somewhat by the national traits of its parent's homeland, and thus may differ more from the output of a domestic-owned firm than would that of another domestic enterprise. We predict relatively low substitutability between the outputs of subsidiaries and home-owned firms, or between subsidiaries whose parents differ in nationality. This analysis can be related to the concept of a chain of substitutes, popular in early contributions to the theory of monopolistic competition. A firm locating itself somewhere along the chain tends to raise cross-elasticities in that neighbourhood of product-space; a seller whose product is 'very different' finds himself on the end of the chain and generally fails to raise average cross-elasticities. The subsidiary probably tends toward the latter type.

The assumption that product differentiation bears the marks of the national culture of the parent's country of origin has more implications. Differentiation might be moderate between the products of firms sired in relatively similar cultures, or in countries with similar levels of income *per capita*. High degrees of differentiation might prevail between firms of dissimilar origin. Thus, the degree of product differentiation in a market is influenced not only by the subsidiaries' proportion of sales but also by the diversity of their national origins.[11]

MARKET CONDUCT

Market conduct comprises the processes by which firms first form their strategies regarding the price and the attributes of the product they offer, and then reconcile these preferences when they collide in the market place. The distinction between these two phases of collective decision-making is, of course, artificial in an ongoing market. Nonetheless, it helps to separate the influence of the internal characteristics of the firm—its motives and perceptions—from those of the external data to which it applies its sensory and adaptive apparatus. The multinational enterprise could differ from the national firm in either its motivation or its mode of interacting with its rivals. The following remarks pertain to the horizontal direct investment, since the subsidiary that transfers output to its corporate relatives for further processing puts itself outside the market.

There seems no reason to assign the multinational enterprise a primary motivation different from that of the national firm. The debate over profit maximisation versus competing hypotheses about entrepreneurial motives has convinced few students of industrial organisation that they should found their theoretical predictions about market behaviour on some rock other than the profit motive. Whether or not one chooses to regard this issue as settled, no evidence seems to suggest that multinational and national firms dance to different tunes. On the contrary, the available research supports the view that the multinational enterprise maximises profits from its activities as a whole,[12] rather than (say) telling each subsidiary to maximise independently and ignoring the profit interdependences among them.[13]

Nonetheless, the subsidiary of a profit-maximising multinational enterprise could behave toward a given national market differently from an identical but independent firm. An action that maximises the subsidiary's own profits might not maximise those of the total enterprise. In particular a conflict could arise over the rate of earnings retention or remittance; a subsidiary might rationally pass up an otherwise profitable local use of funds if they could be employed for a higher expected yield elsewhere within the enterprise. The subsidiary's range of reaction strategies might differ from that of a competing national firm, because of its parent's inventory of proprietary knowledge assets. As a result, any given disturbance might prompt different changes in the resource bundles committed to the market by a multinational enterprise and an otherwise (initially) identical national firm.

This difference stemming from global instead of local profit maximisation is amplified by a difference in the cognitive resources, and hence the stock of information possessed by the multinational enterprise. Its corporate family relations give it access to more information about markets located in other countries—or (what is equivalent in its effect) information to which it can attach a higher degree of certainty. This information is not necessarily unavailable to the national firm, and indeed need not cost it any more. The point is that *at any given time* the multi-national enterprise by its nature already has the superior information-stock in hand, whereas its national rival may or may not.[14]

These potential differences in motivation and information sets can affect a multinational member's market conduct in important ways. Its more elastic range of alternatives to its current price–quantity offer can affect its preference among the possible group or market outcomes for the oligopoly in which it sells. We customarily view these group outcomes as running along a scale from full recognition of mutual interdependence (which would by definition yield the monopoly outcome if the group's cost conditions are those of a single-firm monopolist) to independent behaviour that conduces at the limit to a purely competitive outcome, and covers the possibility of short-run price warfare and equivalent struggles over market share or other market parameter values. The multinational enterprise's distinctive traits make it no foe of monopoly profits, but they do colour its view of actions that might increase its share (and its own profits) at the expense of the shares of other firms (and total industry profits). On the one hand, it holds better information about the opportunity cost of committing more resources to the market in question (not to mention a potentially more elastic supply of capital resources). On the other, it also holds better alternatives outside the market in question, so that the threats to the enterprise's total rate of return and organisational survival from an outbreak of warfare are less than they would be for a national firm.[15] In short, both the motivation and the information characteristics of the multinational enterprise dispose it toward strategies yielding a larger profit (but with a higher variance) than those an equivalent national enterprise would prefer. Notice that this argument should apply to the parent in its home market as well as its subsidiary abroad.

The outcome in an oligopoly market depends not only on the preferences of the various rival firms but also the mode of co-ordination and reconciliation adopted among them. The processes range in formality from overt collusion (enforced or adhered to in varying degrees) down through informal co-ordination procedures involving heavy reliance on 'focal points'[16] and commonly shared perceptions. The casual evidence available suggests that, in most industrial countries, fully enforced cartels are the exception rather than the rule, so that the forces determining the extent of informal and incomplete co-ordination take on particular importance. Would the multinational enterprise pick different strategies in this co-ordination game? Its subsidiary might, especially in the early years of its life in a foreign market. The young subsidiary, even if formed through the acquisition of a going national firm, stands outside the network of tacit understandings and rules of the game developed by the previous market occupants. Its foreign status implies less ability to read correctly the signals transmitted by its rivals and to anticipate their reactions to its own signals. Thus it would be more apt to rock the collusive boat—even inadvertantly—than a national firm in the same situation. Furthermore, a multinational unit may find its price preferences influenced by factors that would not affect a national firm, such as the need to align its price with that charged in other national markets for the identical product sold by it corporate siblings—plus or minus appropriate tariffs and transport costs.[17] The effective recognition of mutual dependence among market rivals should thus be less when subsidiaries are present than when only nationals are involved. This suggestion needs two qualifications, however. The subsidiary eventually loses its *parvenu* status; a good deal of survey evidence suggests that it grows more to resemble a national firm in behaviour as it ages. Second, in some cases the subsidiary may be vulnerable to the greater political influence of its national rivals, and hence exert great caution about the extent of its rivalrous impact.[18]

Patterns of market conduct encompass the determination of both price and the quality and variety of the product offered. Product rivalry can occur where the outputs of competing sellers are (in equilibrium) homogeneous and indistinguishable from one another (for instance, in lengthening or shortening the lifespans of homogeneous lightbulbs). It takes on special importance as a mode of oligopolistic rivalry, however, where product differentiation is a structural trait of the market. Where active rivalry can take the form of improving or diversifying the characteristics of the product, or increasing sales-promotion outlays, these forms of conduct offer alternatives to price competition. The casual evidence of industry studies suggests that non-price competition in oligopoly is less tempered by recognised mutual dependence than is price competition. The chief reason is that any fool can cut his price, but rivalrous non-price moves cannot always be matched successfully, or without a delay.

We argued above that subsidiaries' products are apt to be 'more different' from the modal output of national firms than would be the output of any randomly chosen national firm. With its *raison d'être* resting on intangible skills in marketing and tailoring its product,[19] the subsidiary becomes particularly likely to slant its market conduct toward non-price (and away from price) competition. The oligopolist gains from his rivals not only by a winning game in any one aspect of market conduct, but also by slanting rivalry toward the game he is most likely to win. Thus, holding other traits of market structure constant, the presence of subsidiaries disposes an industry toward venting its competitive animal spirits through non-price rather than price competition. This conclusion should not be read as an unqualified statement that 'the multinational firm biases rivalry away from price and toward product variation'. When the *ceteris paribus* clause is removed, it could make itself an oligopolistic irritant on both scores. The reasons why the international firm might wish to disturb the prevailing price level are largely independent of the reasons why it might benefit from tilting the typical pattern of rivalry away from price and toward product strategies.

The concept of market conduct includes behaviour designed to react upon and alter the elements of market structure. The obvious example is predatory or exclusionary conduct, designed to weaken or crush rivals and thus raise the level of seller concentration. Structure-changing behaviour can, however, include much more, notably actions to raise the barriers to entry and the level of product differentiation. We first consider predatory conduct in its traditional guise—that aimed at extant rather than potential rivals.

In the absence of legal restraint, it could pay a firm to invest in destroying its rivals if the entry of new ones were unlikely or even merely delayed; even then, the use of the threat of predatory actions to induce co-operative behaviour might be more rational for the potential aggressor.[20] Are multinational enterprises particularly prone to predatory actions? This question is made interesting less by *a priori* considerations than by the outcries of host-country national firms facing rivalry from subsidiaries of large international firms, especially United States corporations. More important, such measures as merger among national firms are widely viewed as natural and necessary to permit competition with the multinationals. Perhaps these actions reflect no more than, say, the normal concern of a dachshund first meeting a St Bernard that the beast might prove unfriendly. The mere fact that the fear is widely voiced and acted upon makes it worthy of analysis. That entrants with important potential advantages in efficiency should be feared provides no surprise. The puzzle is that the threat might lie in the multinational's total size *per se*—not its efficiency, or its size in the particular national market. Only two explanations of this attitude prove at all satisfying. First, disparities in size impair the counter-threat capacity of the smaller firm in an oligopoly game. It need not be harder to enter a big market than a small one, but it may be harder to attain a given share of a big market.[21] Assume that the same share of income is spent on product A in the United States and France. A firm holding 30 per cent of the US market establishes a subsidiary with a capacity to serve 10 per cent of the French market. A threatened French producer holding 30 per cent of his own smaller domestic market cannot mount a parallel counter-invasion without a much greater proportional drain on his corporate funds.[22] Thus, if the corporation's total stock of liquid assets governs its counter-threat capacity, the prevailing concern of national market rivals for the aggregate size of the multinational corporation makes sense even if the subsidiaries display no overt predatory behaviour.

The second explanation lies in a possible effect of the breadth of a firm's product line on the relation between size and unit costs. Most studies find that scale economies in manufacturing are typically exhausted well short of the sizes of the larger industrial countries' national markets. However, the firm's minimum efficient scale of production depends on the heterogeneity of its output. The diversity of competing firms' outputs may differ enormously, even when their product lines are confined to the same relatively narrow statistical category. And the presence of *some* fixed costs associated with each variant produced implies that, of two firms with aggregate outputs of equal value, the one with the more homogenous output is more apt to exhaust the economies of scale. Casual observation suggests that output heterogeneity increases with relative size, or market share; broad-line dominant firms often compete with smaller narrow-line sellers. The two groups may attain available scale economies in about the same measure. Such market structures appear to be stable, with no marked changes in either relative sizes or the lengths of product lines.

Now, inject into such an industry the subsidiary of a large multinational firm. It may choose a more homogeneous output-mix than similar-size national firms, for several reasons; chief of these is the possibility it enjoys of purchasing from its parent (or other relative) any outputs that would complement its line but cannot be produced at efficient scale in the host country. This option increases the subsidiary's threat capacity against national firms of comparable size, and impels them to consider either narrowing their product lines or increasing their total outputs by merger (to reduce plant output heterogeneity without losing market share). This model may seem to rest on quite restrictive assumptions, but its central proposition about the effect of increased rivalry on the heterogeneity of output lines is well documented.[23]

MARKET PERFORMANCE

Several dimensions of market performance require amendment in consideration of the multinational enterprise. In the case of allocative efficiency, the problems it raises are statistical rather than conceptual. In the case of progressiveness and product performance, however, the standard concepts are called into question.

Pareto-optimality generally demands that resources be allocated among constant-cost economic activities so that risk-adjusted internal rates of return on capital are equalised. Book or accounting rates of return, averaged over a few years, serve in statistical studies as the dubious but expedient proxy for the analytically correct measure. The presence in an industry of multinational enterprises (either parents or subsidiaries) creates new sources of slippage between accounting and economic rates of return. Principal among these is arbitrary transfer pricing in intra firm but international transactions, undertaken with the objective of minimising the enterprise's worldwide tax bill. Lurking behind discretionary transfer prices, however, is the deeper problem of the role of proprietary knowledge as intangible capital to the multinational enterprise. In general it represents a costly wasting asset to the firm, and the research, shake-down losses, or other costs of its production must be compensated.[24]

The need to allow a return on that capital in some market, however, does not necessarily translate into the need to allow every subsidiary to earn a normal (or better) return on the dowry of intangible capital bestowed by its parent. Empirical evidence on the determinants of direct investment strongly suggests that the multinational establishes its subsidiary in order to maximise the quasi-rents obtainable from foreign markets on intangible capital whose worth is already proven (i.e. rewarded) in the home market. The general argument for a social reward to investments in the creation of proprietary knowledge (e.g. through extending the privilege of patent protection) holds for a closed economy, or the world as a whole. But the small country (like any consumer of public goods) maximises its own welfare by concealing its willingness to pay, and denying a return to intangible capital produced elsewhere. The weakness of the case for the privilege of patenting foreign innovations in small and developing countries has been noted;[25] it extends to the proprietary intangible capital of the multinational enterprise.

Another problem for assessing the allocative performance of subsidiaries also arises as a statistical dilemma cloaking a substantive issue. What is the opportunity cost of capital, to which a sector's marginal rate of return should be equal? This issue causes trouble enough for appraising the allocative efficiency of an ordinary domestic industry; in the United States and other industrial countries with reasonably well-integrated capital markets a single opportunity-cost of capital is elusive but not evanescent. The subsidiary, however, raises a complicating substantive issue in its access to world capital markets, whereas national rivals may be tied to a national capital market with a higher prevailing opportunity cost. In appraising the allocative efficiency of national firm and subsidiary together, do we concede the subsidiary the arbitrage profits on the cheaper capital it brings from abroad? The problem is, admittedly, no different from that of capital-market discrimination against small (relative to large) national firms—a problem acknowledged with notable infrequency in industrial-organisation research.

'Progressiveness' comprises another dimension of market performance. It subsumes questions of optimal investment in research and development, optimal timing of innovations, and optimal diffusion of innovations once tested. The problem raised here by the multinational enterprise is closely related to that of appraising the quasi-rents earned by its intangible capital. Evidence from various sources suggests that the multi-plant corporation typically gains some economies from centralising its research in one location. If the subsidiary is viewed as principally a conduit to transmit research, the criteria for innovative performance in the host-country market should be modified accordingly. Local research then matters principally for adapting innovative knowledge to the needs of the local market or local production conditions.[26] Imitation and diffusion take on relatively greater importance, and the incidence of research activity in subsidiaries and national firms alike should be valued partly for its 'listening post' function of making productive use of the continuing international flow of knowledge. The American habit of judging a sector's research output by its research inputs makes clear economic sense for other countries only if the inputs yield a return that can be appropriated within the nation, or if sufficient externalities from research activities can be shown (rather than assumed) to exist. These suggestions about priorities for innovative performance of course contrast sharply to the familiar tendency of nationalists to judge research performance by the local inputs utilised rather than by the local availability of output.

An unfortunately vague dimension of market performance is the appropriate extent of product differentiation and sales promotion. There should not be 'too much' advertising, 'too frequent' model changes, etc. One would avoid this shadowy corner of welfare economics except for the fact that horizontal direct investment tends to concentrate in industries marked by product differentiation, and any pervasive objection to commercially successful differentiation would give it a near-automatic bad mark. Because the multinational enterprise tends to be better at differentiating its product than the national firm, it is apt to devote more resources profitably to advertising and product promotion. Thus, the presumption of fault does to some extent apply. Furthermore, the evidence grows increasingly strong (for the United States, at least) that high levels of advertising expenditures serve to elevate the barriers to entry and thus contribute in the long run to excess profits and probably increased seller concentration. Even if we concluded, though, that some limitation of advertising outlays would improve market performance, it would not follow that heavier restrictions are appropriate for the multinational enterprise because it is better at product promotion (and possibly advertises more) than its single-country rivals. In many instances the subsidiary's differentiated product offers buyers a real expansion of their set of choices. The product differentiation and the advertising that gives notice of its availability then cannot be condemned out of hand.

MODELS OF MARKET STRUCTURES AND THEIR CONSEQUENCES

We have shown how the elements of market structure, conduct, and performance as defined for the closed economy should be modified to take account of the multinational enterprise. These concepts serve as working tools in the field of industrial organisation. They are used to express operational hypotheses derived from the theory of markets. These hypotheses seek to identify the effects on economic welfare of various alternative forms of economic organisation or patterns of enterprise behaviour. Most of the empirical research on industrial organisation aims to detect the influence of market conduct or (especially) market structure on performance. Popular methodologies include the historical study of a particular industry and the statistical analysis of a sample of manufacturing industries drawn from some industrial country. A less developed but important line of inquiry explores the interdependence among the elements of market structure, and the ability of conduct to feed back and alter the structural environment surrounding rival firms.

Most research of these types has been carried out on the United States economy. It has had moderate success in confirming some major hypotheses about the theory of markets and—in the process—pointing out some ways to redirect oligopoly theory along more useful lines. Still, the hypotheses remain rough-hewn, and the unexplained variance is considerable. Study of the multinational corporation should tighten the specification of these hypotheses and help improve our empirical understanding of the subject as a whole.

Furthermore, as research in industrial organisation spreads to other countries more open to both international trade and foreign investment, the need to take these forces into account is increased. In this section we ask how the hypotheses of industrial organisation should be changed or re-specified to accommodate the multinational corporation.

MARKET STRUCTURES AND THE MULTINATIONAL ENTERPRISE

To proceed efficiently, we explore the effects and implications of direct investment only within a selected range of market structures. Fortunately, both theory and empirical evidence confine the range of structures that typically shelter the multinational corporation. We deduce the possible conduct patterns of the multinationals within these markets and their implications both for market performance and the long-run stability of market structure.

Markets populated by international firms are typically marked by product differentiation and a relatively small number of sellers—differentiated oligopoly. The affinity of multinational enterprise for product differentiation was explained above; in the absence of differentiation, it is difficult to see what rent-yielding asset of the firm could be exploited through direct investment (more efficiently than by other techniques), in the face of the systematic disadvantages of 'foreignness'. The 'oligopoly' prediction results from the relatively high fixed costs of information and search associated with undertaking a direct investment (and possibly also minimum efficient scale in the investment itself). Direct investment thus becomes an attractive strategy only for firms able to generate a large volume of internal funds to meet these costs. Large firms are, on a probabilistic basis, relatively

E

dominant in at least some of the product markets in which they sell, and so oligopoly becomes likely.[27]

Another structural generalisation that will help confine our inquiry is that the larger firms in a given source-country industry are more likely to have foreign subsidiaries than their smaller rivals. This hypothesis also rests on both theory and empirical evidence. Multinational status is probably more common among larger firms for at least two reasons: (1) firms holding larger shares of the domestic market are likely to have founded them on some rent-yielding asset of intangible capital that would also tend to render foreign investment profitable; (2) because information costs associated with undertaking a foreign investment are both heavy and relatively fixed, small but rising firms that might some-day find direct investment profitable may rationally postpone it until their penetration of the home market is more advanced. A statistical study of US firms investing abroad has found size (measured by firm sales) an overwhelmingly important discrimi-nant between US firms with and without subsidiaries.[28]

A similar pattern should appear in countries that are primarily hosts rather than sources of direct investment: subsidiaries should be concentrated in markets of differentiated oligopoly, and they should on balance hold larger than average shares in those markets. The theory of multiplant enterprises, which applies to the decision process of the potential multinational enterprise planning investment in a subsidiary, suggests that the multi-national should be if anything less likely to open a subsidiary establishment of suboptimal scale than would the *de novo* domestic firm. The multinational always enjoys the potential option of supplying a market through imports, whereas the domestic firm by definition does not. Thus, in industries where scale economies are of relatively great importance, one would expect (*cet. par.*) to find larger shares of host-country markets held by subsidiaries, but a relatively smaller number of subsidiaries present. Horst has confirmed this finding for Canadian markets and the portion of US firms having subsidiaries in Canada.[29]

Our analysis holds that direct investment and high seller concentration tend to result from common causes. Product differentiation and large size of plant and firm are favourable to both. One can hold little hope of a reasonable test for the popular notion that direct investment causes increased seller concentra-tion—at least on the basis of cross-industry observations at a given time.[30] We return below to the question of a causal link running from direct investment to high seller concentration.

A third structural trait of multinational firms is that neither theory nor observation leads us to expect that the parents will all fly the same national flag. The multinational firm gets its successful start in the national market of *some* industrial country, but that country need not be the largest or the wealthiest. True, winning a significant share in a large national market encourages multi-national status, because of the fixed costs of going abroad; a larger domestic market implies relatively more ample internal funds for meeting these costs. So does establishment in the country with the highest income *per capita* and relative cost of labour inputs, since both aspects of affluence encourage the quest for innovations that can subsequently be exploited via foreign direct investment. Thus it is no surprise that the United States is a major but not predominant sire of multinational enterprises, or that European-based firms typically produce only small fractions of their total sales through their United States subsidiaries.[31] Hence, we should expect multinational firms to be domiciled here and there; national markets will seldom be purely sources or purely hosts.

INTERDEPENDENCE ACROSS NATIONAL MARKETS

The consequences of the multinational enterprise depend on the way it modifies oligopoly behaviour. As we noted above, the strategy of industrial organisation is to divide market conduct into two phases: each firm selects its preferred market outcome (e.g. price or product quality); and the rivals reconcile their conflicts in the market place. The multinational enterprise raises the possibility that this reconciliation—the games oligopolists play—may reflect the interdependence of firms in more than one national market. The accord worked out by multinational firms A and B in country X may reflect their relations in country Y—a going agreement there, or one seller's capacity to threaten or reward the other in Y's market. Specifically, we define two limiting cases;

1. Multinational status (parent or subsidiary) makes no difference to the conduct patterns preferred or chosen by firms in a national market. This pattern implies that the member units of a multinational firm serve as independent profit centres with full autonomy over national price and product decisions. It suggests that the multinational enterprise could affect conduct in a given national market because it differs from a national firm, but that cross-national links in market conduct would not be involved.

2. Multinational enterprises might recognise their inter-

dependence comprehensively wherever seller concentration is high enough and their perceptions sharp enough to permit it. That is to say, firm A sets its actions in market X taking account of B's reactions not only in X but also in any other market Y where both operate.

Between these extremes of cross-national independence and full cross-national interdependence, a variety of patterns could permit some dependence across boundaries but also maintain cordons along others. National origin might tell: firms domiciled in country X might recognise their interdependence there and in host countries $Y, Z, \ldots$ Interdependence might be recognised among those units (whether parents or subsidiaries) producing in the largest single national market and also with parallel operations in other national markets. Interdependence might run outward from a national market where law and custom smile most kindly on overt collusion. It might transcend national boundaries for those multinational enterprises facing each other in most of their national markets, but not those colliding in only a minor portion of their markets.

EFFECTS ON STRUCTURE AND PERFORMANCE

Having mapped the market structures in which multinational enterprises appear and the patterns of recognised mutual dependence that may emerge among them, we derive some predictions for patterns of market conduct and qualities of performance.

Entry and Oligopoly Behaviour
The founding of a subsidiary itself can be a rivalrous move. Even if its output only substitutes for exports a firm previously sent to the market, local production allows more effective servicing of the product and styling it for the local market, and removes for customers some risks of impeded delivery. Hence it makes the seller (*cet. par.*) a more formidable rival in terms of the potential price–product package he can offer. Entering a market thus becomes an important form dimension of rivalry among multinational enterprises. Entry threatens not only the going local enterprises but others as well. Exporters selling in that market are menaced directly, and the multinational's rivals in other markets face a secondary threat because the new subsidiary might uncover some product or process that the parent can profitably exploit in its other markets as well.[32] If mutual dependence is recognised beyond the single national market, collusive behaviour naturally

takes the form of spheres of influence and mutual non-aggression pacts, such as the divisions of geographic and product space featured by the cartel agreements in the period between World Wars I and II. On the other hand, rivalrous or independent conduct can appear as parallel acts of entry. Firms domiciled in different nations might invade each other's home markets, or parents in country X might simultaneously start subsidiaries in country Y.[33]

A familiar generalisation from industry studies is that oligopolists recognise their independence much less fully in product rivalry than in price rivalry. Starting a new subsidiary resembles rivalry of the product type, and so we might expect rivalrous foundation of subsidiaries even where multinational firms face each other in tight-knit oligopolies. A recent study by Knickerbocker tested for parallel action by US corporations in founding subsidiaries abroad. Their dates of establishment during the years 1948–67 indeed proved to be bunched in individual countries more than one would expect on a chance basis (note that scale economies cut against such bunching). Furthermore, the effect was more marked in industries with higher seller concentration, and in industries where foreign investment had been uncommon before World War II (so that imitative behaviour would be rational to avoid risks in a fluid situation). Knickerbocker also found a weak tendency for tighter parallel action by firms not highly diversified in the US market, and thus exposed to greater risk if rivals should successfully steal a march via foreign investment.[34]

Price and Product Adjustments
The patterns of price and product rivalry likely to result from the influence of multilateral enterprises were indicated in the first section of this paper. Product differentiation is a fundamental skill of the multinational firm, and the effect of its presence (*cet. par.*) is naturally to channel rivalrous conduct away from price and toward product strategies. Furthermore, the differing national origins of foreign subsidiaries may make their products 'more different' than if domestic managements controlled the same enterprises. By lowering cross-elasticities of demand between firms, this effect reinforces the bias toward product and away from price rivalry. This impact of subsidiaries' presence is apt to erode, however, as they age and assume increasingly the colouration of domestic firms. As we noted above, the welfare significance of this bias is unclear: on the one hand, resources are diverted towards advertising and other modes of differentiating the

product; on the other, the set of choices open to consumers may undergo a significant expansion.

Where mutual dependence is recognised among multinational corporations across national boundaries, price discrimination among national markets may result. Consider an industry in which money costs of production (at the going exchange rates) are the same everywhere, and scale economics not an important consideration. Demand elasticities differ from country to country, and hence so do the rates of maximum monopoly profit. Tariffs and transport costs are unimportant. Finally, suppose that the number of domestic producers in each national market is relatively small. If mutual dependence were not recognised beyond national boundaries, price differentials between national markets could hardly persist (even if arbitrage by independent traders were impractical). Entry by foreign firms (through foreign investment, or simply through exporting) would tend to erode differential rates of excess profit in those markets where high price–cost margins would maximise monopoly gains. With interdependence recognised across national boundaries, however, among firms with parallel structures of subsidiaries, collusive maintenance of jointly profitable discrimination becomes more likely. The rewards can be shared in roughly equal proportion by all sellers without any actual profit-sharing or other intricate arrangements. Preliminary research suggests that the international farm tractor industry may supply an example of this pattern of pricing.

Market Performance: Technical Efficiency

The term 'technical efficiency' refers to the degree to which an industry's output is produced at minimum attainable cost. Technical inefficiency can result when firms are of unsuitably small scales, or produce their chosen outputs at higher than the minimum attainable levels of real cost. It can also stem from excessive delay in adopting the best production or distribution techniques used by producers in other countries.

The predicted effects of multinational enterprise on technical efficiency are both positive and negative, although the positive effects may be the more important. The multinational is a conduit for the transfer of technical knowledge from one country to another. It should accelerate this transfer and raise productivity levels in countries that are consumers rather than producers of new technology, under certain plausible conditions. The first of these conditions is that the multinational enterprise has no perfect substitute as a conduit for technical knowledge; in its absence transfer through other channels (the flow of non-proprietary scientific knowledge, the process of imitation, the embodiment of knowledge in traded capital goods) must be slower, or use up more resources. The second is that domestic firms in a given market are quicker to imitate the innovations of an adjacent subsidiary than they are those of a firm located abroad.[35] This transfer mechanism of course implies a positive effect of the multinational firm on technical efficiency.

A conceptually separate positive effect might occur if the multi-national firm, as an entrant into a tranquil domestic oligopoly, presses home-owned firms to a higher level of (static) technical efficiency. Such a (one-shot) gain might occur if collusive arrangements have sheltered firms that were inefficiently small, or simply inefficient. The instances of merger activity among European firms, as they face either increased rivalry from foreign subsidiaries or increased international competition over reduced tariff walls, might be explainable partly as a process of squeezing out inefficient units. As we noted above, however, other explanations of these defensive mergers and consolidations are possible. The foreign subsidiary must score reasonably high in technical efficiency in order to press its rivals to lower unit costs. The theory of multiplant enterprise suggests that the international firm is less likely to countenance units of inefficient scale than the single-plant firm, and research on Canadian manufacturing has found a larger share of sales to be held by foreign firms in industries where scale economies appear relatively important.[36] On the other hand, where product differentiation occurs, exhausting the economies of scale is not a necessary condition for maximum profit. Consider a model that has been proposed to explain the structure and behaviour of subsidiary-dominated industries in Canada, where manufacturing is largely an import-competing activity carried on behind substantial tariff barriers. The world price plus the tariff provides a convenient focal point for price collusion among oligopolists in the domestic market. If this price would allow substantial excess profits for efficient-scale producers, the multi-national firms may crowd in with subsidiaries of inefficiently small scale, their numbers and average unit costs increasing as profits are pressed down—not to a competitive level, but to a level reflecting the opportunity cost of capital for these international oligopolists and the degree of recognised interdependence. Because of product differentiation (and perhaps expected oligopoly reaction), it does not pay any one seller to cut price and seek to expand to an efficient scale.[37] An entrant subsidiary might eschew an efficient scale in order to avoid excessive offence to domestic rivals having political influence with the host-country government.

Going subsidiaries in tacit or open collusion over market shares might add capacity in inefficiently small increments, to avoid disrupting their mutual understanding. Thus, the favourable effect of multinational enterprises on technical efficiency is subject to serious qualifications.[38]

Market Performance: Allocative Efficiency

'Allocative efficiency' refers to the appropriateness of an industry's level of output, normally inferred from the presence of other than 'normal' profits. We neglect here the problems of reported profits as an indicator of ideal output noted above, and of the interdependence between technical and allocative efficiency. The impact of the multinational corporation on allocative efficiency, as on technical efficiency, is probably favourable but subject to some questions.

A critical issue is the importance of the multinational as an actual and potential market entrant. As we noted above, the multinational enjoys systematic advantages in establishing a foreign subsidiary over the *de novo* entrant to the same foreign market. This is of particular importance, because the multinational making horizontal direct investments tends to flourish in just those industries afflicted with strong product differentiation, and perhaps other sources of high entry barriers as well. In industries where the deck is stacked most adversely against the *de novo* entrant, the multinational corporation is most likely to be present as an actual or potential entrant to the national market.[39] As such, it tends to limit the departure of allocative performance from the competitive norm. Oligopoly is still oligopoly: one expects that entry by multinationals will curb the departures of national markets from ideal output, but that mutual dependence will remain sufficient to sustain some excess profits. The point is, these departures should be smaller than if foreign subsidiaries were forbidden.

The doubts one may have about this generalisation turn on the stability of market structures when multilateral firms are present. Just as some economists (and others) have always voiced fear about the ability of small domestic firms to compete with large ones, now the same concerns are heard over the ability of one-country firms (large or small) to compete with multinationals.[40] What are the principal issues?

1. Does entry by the multinational firm into a new national market occur through merger, or through starting a subsidiary afresh? From the viewpoint of the market entered, the latter

process creates a new decision-making centre; the former may change a going firm's behaviour pattern, but does not launch a new entity. Entry via acquisition may improve the performance of the national industry affected, but expansion through merger certainly qualifies the virtues of the multinational as an actual and potential entrant. Furthermore, it raises an international issue of antitrust that is little recognised: when a firm in country X acquires a firm in country Y, antitrust authorities of both countries will see seller concentration remaining unchanged; however, it has increased for that industry worldwide, with obvious consequences if mutual dependence is recognised beyond national boundaries.

2. Can large multinational and smaller domestic firms coexist for sustained periods of time? The tendency of defensive mergers to occur among European domestic firms following an influx of subsidiaries was discussed above. One would not be surprised at some reactive consolidation among domestic firms, possibly enough to offset the multinational entry and leave the market more concentrated than before. To put this concern in perspective, however, one must note a broader comparative question: do firms with differing sizes and scopes of operation coexist in domestic markets? The evidence from the United States is partially reassuring, but no more. On the one hand, seller concentration is fairly stable in most industries, and on the average has not changed much in this century; the same seems to hold, from casual inspection, for many industries containing a mixture of national and regional firms—the intranational analogue of the 'world' industry populated by multinational and national firms. On the other hand, there is evidence that US seller concentration has been increasing in those industries where product differentiation (measured by advertising) is important—the very industries where multinational operations flourish.[41] The question of the long-term stability of market structures populated by multinational firms must be viewed as an open one.

3. Does the expansion of shares held by multinational firms in the average national market raise the extent of mutual dependence recognised across national boundaries? The question as put demands a positive answer: the sign of the relation could hardly be negative. But what really matters is the extent of cross-national oligopoly behaviour in the market structures we now observe in the industrial countries, and its relation to the structure of cross-national corporate links. Our evidence on these patterns aspires to the epithet 'fragmentary'; one can only hope for some international industry studies[42] and, perhaps, some pertinent cross-industry statistical research.[43]

4. Has the rapid expansion of multinational firms in the past two decades shown any tendency to drive down their rates of return, or the rates generally prevailing in the markets they have entered? Evidence from a number of sources is consistent with multinational enterprises having earned substantial innovation rents in the 1950s and early 1960s, but suffering some decline in average profit rates since then, both absolutely and relative to their domestic rivals.[44] The multinationals appear on most showings to earn more than their smaller domestic rivals, but profit differentials between competing firms are not necessarily inconsistent with stable market structures when the product is differentiated. Thus, the actual profit record of the multinationals is not broadly inconsistent with their having a long-run favourable effect on allocative efficiency. One must interpret these profit figures with care, however. It is well established that young subsidiaries on the average earn substantially lower rates of return than older ones which have survived;[45] hence the decline in the aggregate profit rate of subsidiaries during a period when their number has increased rapidly could simply reflect the shake-down losses of novices.

To conclude, horizontal direct investment is important as a source of entry to national industries otherwise afflicted by substantial entry barriers. It is not clear, however, that in all cases or even on the average the multinational entrant reduces seller concentration and oligopolistic joint conduct after all effects are taken into account. The evidence needs to be collected, and carefully weighed.

VERTICAL DIRECT INVESTMENT, STRUCTURE, AND PERFORMANCE

The market models and concepts that appear useful for explaining vertical direct investment differ from those set forth for horizontal expansion by the multinational enterprise. This duality is inelegant but necessary: the causes and consequences of vertical expansion in terms of the parent's market environment are simply quite different from those relating to horizontal expansion.[46] Vertical expansion via foreign direct investment, of course, amounts to vertical integration, and is naturally compared to an arm's-length buyer–seller relation between identical but independent units. In this section we briefly sketch an industrial-organisation model useful for exploring at least a certain class of vertical direct investments.

Once again, theory and empirical evidence help in narrowing

the range of applicable models. Vertical investments appear to fall broadly into the following two classes:

1. The production of intermediate inputs to production processes of the parent (or its other subsidiaries) for which the worldwide number of suitable production sites or primary-input deposits is small. In practice, this class of cases is confined to natural-resource extraction, and the production processes are frequently large-scale and capital-intensive.

2. The production of intermediate inputs to production processes of the parent (or its other subsidiaries) for which the worldwide number of potentially feasible production sites is great, and scale economies and capital-intensity relatively modest. In practice this class of cases includes mostly manufactured labour-intensive inputs or components, where the governing locational pull is low efficiency wages. Natural resources could fall into this class, however, if the production function lacks the traits noted in the first case above.

It is clear that many aspects of these vertical investments lie in the domain of location economics, and are thus discussed by Raymond Vernon in Chapter 4 of this volume. The firm making the second type of investment simply seeks a cost-minimising location for the production of inputs, and thereby raised few significant issues for industrial organisation. The locational explanation for such investments, which have become common in such countries as Ireland and Taiwan,[47] rides on a combination of relatively low efficiency wages and a shortage of native entrepreneurship capable of organising the necessary activities in an independent firm. (Without the latter shortcoming, it is difficult to see the foreign investor would choose to face the intrinsic disadvantages of foreign entrepreneurship and international administrative co-ordination.) They would not tend to affect the national or world market for the intermediate good in question, if entry barriers are absent or minor and national markets are not sharply segmented by product differentiation. Like other small disturbances in purely competitive markets, no important consequences for welfare emerge. As Vernon suggests, the principal point of juncture between such investments and industrial-organisation models is the possibility that some disturbance tending to decrease profits among oligopolists in a national market might bestir a search for cost-reducing techniques, including investment in lower-cost inputs sources abroad.

The consequences for industrial organisation are greater, however, when vertical investments fall into the first group noted above. Entrepreneurial scarcities and capital rationing in the resource-owning nation can explain the exploitation of large-scale and lumpy resource deposits through direct investment. But it may also result because arm's-length bilateral oligopoly would bring high uncertainty with an independent seller needing to make a large and durable investment in resource extraction without assurance about the price–quantity offers he can later command in an imperfect market. Vertical integration then provides potential arm's-length buyers and sellers with a device for reducing private uncertainty. This beneficial reduction in uncertainty, however, may have its cost in several adverse effects on market structure:

1. When direct investment decreases the portion of the intermediate good passing through an arm's-length market, the level of risk afflicting the remaining independent sellers and buyers rises. Removal of one buyer–seller pair from the open market by an international vertical merger cuts the number of arm's-length traders available to the remaining independent firms. They have an incentive to shrink the open market further through collusion or integration.

2. Barriers to entry rise at both the raw-materials and finished-good stages of the production process. The potential entrant *either* must start out vertically integrated and incur the (assumed) high capital costs, *or* enter at one stage only and face the greater risk of transacting in a shrivelled spot market. This elevated entry barrier of course raises the expected long-run level of concentration for these vertically related activities.

3. Increased vertical integration through direct investment can change patterns of market conduct at either stage. At the raw-materials stage one expects increased resort to long-term contracts and related uncertainty-reducing devices by remaining arm's-length sellers (although no definite prediction about the direction of change in price or profits can be made). The vertically integrated multinational firms may themselves undertake joint ventures at the extractive end to minimise the risk of disturbances to their oligopolistic relations, and possibly to provide through common raw-materials ventures an avenue to collusion in markets for fabricated products. (Product market collusion might otherwise be difficult because of antitrust laws or other reasons.) Vernon discusses these possibilities in connection with their impact on the location of foreign investments.[49]

4. The effects of the multinational enterprise on overall market performance once again are indeterminate. We have noted a

potential gain in performance through the reduction of uncertainty (*cet. par.*). A complementary gain might arise in technical efficiency if, in the absence of vertical integration, independent firms would produce at inefficiently small scales. They might do so either because of capital constraints (absolute-cost entry barriers) or from risk avoidance (where a larger share means greater transactions uncertainty without any increase in shared monopoly–monopsony power). However, the prospect is for a long-run decline of allocative efficiency because of augmented barriers to entry.

IMPLICATIONS FOR RESEARCH IN INDUSTRIAL ORGANISATION

We noted that industrial organisation has been largely a closed-economy subject, due to its development in the large and relatively closed United States economy. Indeed, neglect of the international side of the subject has been greater in the more analytical and statistical lines of research which have otherwise provided the intellectual motive power for the subject in the past two decades. Such international phenomena as cartels and 'import discipline' has been left for more descriptive and intuitive treatment. Indeed, the multinational corporation has been studied almost exclusively as a problem of business management or the theory of the firm rather than a phenomenon of industrial organisation. Yet this paper has shown that the basic concepts and hypotheses of the subject can and should embrace the multinational corporation. And our refurbishing has indeed gone only part of the distance, because foreign trade as well as foreign investment cries out for incorporation in the standard research concepts and techniques. The two are interrelated—not just casually because both are 'international', but fundamentally because exporting and foreign investment are alternatives for the potential multinational firm.

Let me close with some suggestions about how the proven research techniques of industrial organisation might serve to approach these issues. First, take the technique of multivariate analysis of the determinants of performance, using a sample of manufacturing industries drawn from a particular country. This approach has enjoyed a fair measure of success in finding the determinants of allocative efficiency in US manufacturing, but applications to other countries have yielded mostly negative results. That fact itself may put a price on the folly of omitting the international linkages. The cost in US-based research may be simply some mis-specification and a generous measure of unexplained variance, whereas for other countries the mis-specification due to a closed-economy approach may prove fatal to the hypotheses under test. Hence, the changes in concepts and hypotheses implied by the multinational corporation (and international trade) might first be applied to countries where they matter the most.

The same propositions largely hold for statistical research on the determinants of technical efficiency—in particular, the scale of establishments and the extent of suboptimal capacity. In recent years, research has uncovered an overwhelmingly persuasive link between the size of establishments and the size of the market they serve[50]—a link not generally predicted by economic theory, though it makes sense if we assume product differentiation and elements of oligopoly. If 'the division of labour is limited by the extent of the market' in this fashion, foreign investment and trade variables bearing on market size and the alternatives available to the market's participants become leading candidates for inclusion in the analysis.

Logically prior to these modifications and extensions of our statistical techniques is the job of testing some of the assumptions and predictions set forth here concerning the multinational corporation itself. The asserted affinity of horizontal direct investment for market structures of differentiated oligopoly, the prevalence of size differences between member units of multinational and domestic firms, the disturbance to market understandings following a multinational entry—these and many other facets of the multinational's behaviour and consequences are supported by theory and some evidence, but cleaner tests (feasible with the rapidly improving data base) would receive a warm welcome.

Last but not least, these extensions of the framework of industrial organisation open major opportunities for that homely technique—the industry study. Easily spurned by sophisticated computer buffs, the detailed analysis of the structure and behaviour of individual national industries has nonetheless made an invaluable contribution to our understanding of how the elements of market structure interact with one another, how special or rare traits of market structure can affect performance in particular industries, and what significance (if any) we can give to the various patterns of conduct that emerge among firms. It is not likely that we can uncover the long-run effect of the multinational corporation on entry barriers and seller concentration, its impact on price and product competition, or its innovative performance except through the patient assembly of information on individual industries over time. Furthermore, the issues raised by the multi-national corporation invite a new cut at the industry study—defining the industry to include sellers in more than one country, or exploiting a comparative analysis of the same industry in different countries. One hopes that the necessary skills have not become entirely *passe* among economists: a flexible command of simple theoretical tools; resourcefulness in using simple statistical techniques; knowledge of foreign languages; and a willingness to grub for obscure and diffuse kinds of information.

References

1 For example, Worcester (1967), Chapters 2 and 3.

2 This chapter develops and extends an analysis first presented in Caves (1971). That paper contains fuller citations to the copious descriptive literature on the multinational enterprise.

3 The principal treatise setting forth this framework is Bain (1968). Also see Scherer (1970).

4 Mann (1966), Comanor & Wilson (1967).

5 A common criticism of the theory of entry barriers has been that, in a competitive (if thin) market for specialised inputs, the entrant would pay more than the pre-entry going price, but also drive up the price for going firms. This criticism disposes of the source of entry barriers only if the potential entrant is certain that his extant rivals' costs will promptly rise to the level he expects for his own. Such certainty is empirically improbable and indeed unwarranted if the going firms own the potential rent-yielding input and bought it at prices which did not capitalise the probability of his entry.

6 Survey studies of foreign subsidiaries regularly show that they have free access to the parent's technology and in most cases consider it of vital importance to their success. See Brash (1966), Chapter 6; Safarian (1966), pp. 196–8. Safarian found that dependence on the parent's technology did not decline for older subsidiaries or those having their own research facilities.

7 The disadvantage of the new producer of a differentiated product can also be looked at as the capital cost of building an investment in good will comparable to those of going firms. It then becomes strictly a component of absolute-cost barriers.

8 The existence of such advantages is controversial. Strong positive evidence appears in Comanor & Wilson (1972).

9 This possibility has been noted by Shearer (1964), and Dunning & Steuer (1969).

10 This was the conclusion of Bain (1956).

11 A similar analysis has been applied to patterns of trade by Linder (1961). Also see Caves (1971), pp. 19–22.

12 Paradoxically, a number of the complaints about behaviour of subsidiaries in host countries refer to alleged behaviour contrary to global profit maximisation by the multinational enterprise. For instance, the parent is said to forbid its subsidiaries to develop export markets. The evidence from survey studies generally fails to confirm such charges; see, for instance, Safarian (1966), Chapter 4.

13 Stevens (1969a).

14 A paradoxical confirmation of this trait of the multinational firm appears in the attacks on it by governments and private interest groups for its ability to make international substitutions and resist lump-sum extractions. For instance, governments wishing to use 'suasion' and quantitive controls rather than price adjustments for balance-of-payments purposes may get better co-operation from domestic firms than from multinationals because the latter hold better information about the profitable opportunities they are being asked to forgo. Some economists have concluded that the multinational firm's evasive capability is a serious threat to national sovereignty. Another interpretation is that the multinational's access to alternatives increases the relevant elasticities of international trade and capital flows and points up the consequences of inefficient choices of national policies.

15 The effect is the obverse of that, noted in the literature of industrial organisation, of high fixed costs on patterns of market conduct. High fixed costs create a large penalty for price warfare in an oligopoly industry and, hence, a stronger inclination of sellers to enter into collusive arrangements. The multinational firm's situation allows reduced penalties or uncertainties from market warfare. On the (adverse) effects of high fixed costs on market performance, see Scherer, pp. 192–8; and Sherman & Tollison (1972).

16 Schelling (1960).

17 The implications of this arbitrage constraint on the multinational firm's pricing in different national markets are explored by Horst (1971).

18 The range of behaviour patterns suggested in this paragraph seems to match what Brash observed in Australia: disturbance of collusive arrangements and oligopolistic tranquillity by some new subsidiaries, participation in going collusive arrangements by others. See Brash (1966), pp. 182–92; Stonehill (1965).

19 The theory and evidence behind this assertion are noted below.

20 See Telser (1966).

21 The evidence on entry by foreign firms to the United States market suggests that they face the same sort of motives and problems as multinational entrants in other industrial countries. See Daniels (1971). They take actions to stretch the resources that they can commit to the market (pp. 78–81), but such strategies are also used in other national markets.

22 Hymer & Rowthorn (1970), pp. 71–4; Behrman (1969), pp. 9–10.

23 The reduction of tariff barriers in the European Economic Community has tended to lead not to competing down of producers exposed to cheaper imports but to increased intra-industry specialisation and interpenetration of trade. This has occurred not only in differentiated products, where one would expect it, but also in industries producing homogeneous products such as steel. See Balassa (1966); Grubel (1967), Adler (1970).

24 For a study of the influence of these factors on the relation between accounting and economic (internal) rates of return, see Stauffer (1971).

25 Johnson (1970), Chapter 2.

26 Surveys of foreign subsidiaries show that multinational corporations tend strongly to centralise their basic research activities in a single location—usually the parent's home—and use the subsidiaries' research organisations to adapt the firm's products to the local market and to serve a listening post function. A few large multinationals divide basic research projects among their subsidiaries, however. See Professor Mansfield's discussion in Chapter 6 of this volume.

27 A fuller statement of this argument and a summary of the evidence supporting it appears in Caves (1971), pp. 2–10.

28 Horst (1972).

29 *Ibid.*

30 The simple correlation between concentration and foreign investment has often been documented. See Steuer *et al.* (1973), Chapter 4; and McManus (1972), p. 87.

31 There is also an argument from general-equilibrium theory to explain the 'cross-hauling' of direct investment; see Caves (1971), pp. 17–22. Related empirical evidence appears in Hymer & Rowthorn (1970), pp. 76–9.

32 The Reddaway Report suggests that useful feedback from subsidiaries in industrial countries occurs in a majority of cases. Reddaway *et al* (1968), pp. 322–4.

33 Learning effects may also be involved, of course. Some foreign firms report that they took courage to enter the United States market from the discovery that they could compete successfully with American subsidiaries in their home market. See Daniels (1971), p. 47.

34 Knickerbocker (1973).

35 This second condition is not necessary for the multinational firm to serve as an efficient technology transfer mechanism among its own member units, but is required for the transfer mechanism to spill over to recipient-country producers as a group.

36 Horst (1972).

37 English (1964), Chapters 4–5. English notes that, if the subsidiaries all belong to US-based firms, each Canadian industry then tends to become a miniature replica of its US counterpart.

38 Safarian's study of foreign investment in Canada uncovers clear evidence of small-scale inefficiency in subsidiaries. The subsidiaries of small absolute size (measured by assets) reported higher unit production costs relative to their parents than did large subsidiaries. Also, he found that subsidiaries' product lines were typically about as broad as their parents' despite the smaller size of the Canadian market. See Safarian (1966), pp. 201–3, 211–13.

39 Product differentiation probably also weakens international trade as a force limiting departures of a given national market from a competitive outcome. Thus, the multinational firm probably has no close substitutes as a discipline to the national market in those industries where it flourishes.

40 See, for example Hymer (1970).

41 Multinational operations and increased seller concentration might be due to a common cause—the effects of advertising—rather than reflecting direct causation. This conclusion would alter but not remove the policy problem of setting policies toward the international firm to secure satisfactory performance. It does point to the difficulty of designing a satisfactory statistical test of the influence of foreign investment on concentration.

42 It has been argued that the world automobile industry is in a process of both increasing concentration and increasing recognition of mutual interdependence among international oligopolists. See Sundelson (1970), Chapter 10.

43 In one systematic statistical test of the relation between concentration and direct investment, Rosenbluth found that the share of foreign subsidiaries in Canadian manufacturing industries was not related to seller concentration once one took account of the larger average size of subsidiaries than of domestic firms. This does not settle the issue of the multinational

firm's effects on allocative efficiency, however, unless the subsidiaries' larger average size can be shown to rest on technical (scale) determinants. See Rosenbluth (1970).

[44] e.g. Dunning (1969); Johns (1967).

[45] e.g. Reddaway (1968), pp. 225–31.

[46] Theories of the multinational enterprise that claim to bridge the horizontal–vertical distinction dwell on administrative or portfolio-balancing considerations that are themselves largely without content for predicting a firm's market behaviour and its consequences. See Aliber (1970), Chapter 1; and McManus (1972).

[47] See Andrews (1972); Schreiber (1970).

[48] This analysis is set forth more fully in Caves (1971), pp. 10–11.

[49] Chapter 4 of this volume. Another possible channel for increased collusion arises when the integration proceeds forward from the raw-material to the fabrication stage—admittedly not the common pattern of foreign investment. Students of extractive oligopolies in the United States have noted that integration forward to the fabricating stage may improve the changes for collusion and market control, even when seller concentration in fabricated output is no higher than at the raw-material stage. The difference lies in the impossibility of product differentiation at the primary stage of production, and perhaps also in the presence of a competitive fringe producing a recycled output (e.g. reclaimed copper or aluminium ingot) and subject to significant demand/supply disturbances. See Comanor (1967) esp. p. 263.

[50] e.g., Bain (1966), Saving (1961), Chapter 3; Eastman & Stykolt (1967) Chapter 3; Pryor (1972).

Chapter 6

TECHNOLOGY AND TECHNOLOGICAL CHANGE[1]

Edwin Mansfield

INTRODUCTION

One of the most remarkable economic phenomena of the last 20 years has been the growth of the multinational firms. According to various estimates, direct foreign investment now totals over $100 billion. As the number and power of the multinational enterprises have grown, economists have devoted increasing amounts of attention to the reasons for this growth and to the effects of the multinational enterprise on the world economy. It is perfectly clear that technology and the multinational corporation are often inextricably bound together, both because firms often become multinational to exploit their technological superiority on a wider scale and because the multinational firm is an important agent in the production and diffusion of technology. And it is equally clear that more information is needed, both for public policy and private decision-making, concerning the technological activities of the multinational firms.[2]

This paper attempts to do the following three things. First, to describe very briefly the present state of knowledge concerning the processes by which industrial organisations produce, apply, and transfer technology.[3] Since research in this area has been expanding at a rapid rate, it must be selective. Second, describe and examine the role of the multinational firm in transferring technology, in producing new technology, and in pioneering in the application of new technology and in so doing, to try to summarise briefly the results of the studies which have been carried out regarding the technological activities of the multinational firm. Third, to suggest various types of research which, in the author's opinion, are badly needed if we are to achieve a more satisfactory understanding of the actual and potential technological role of the multinational firm in the present-day world economy.

THE PRODUCTION OF NEW TECHNOLOGY

During the past 20 years, economists—in league with other social scientists and some technologists and natural scientists—have begun to study systematically the factors underlying the production of new technology. On *a priori* grounds, one would expect the rate of technological change in a particular area to depend, to a considerable extent, on the amount of resources devoted by firms, by independent inventors, and by government agencies to the advancement of technology in that area. The amount of resources devoted by the government depends on how closely the area in question is related to the defence, public health and other social needs for which the government assumes major responsibility; on the extent of the external economies generated by the relevant research and development; and on more purely political factors. The amount of resources devoted by industry and independent inventors depends heavily on the profitability of their use. Econometric studies indicate that the total amount that a firm spends on research and development is determined in large degree by the expected profitability of the R & D projects under consideration, and that the probability of its accepting a particular R & D project depends heavily on the project's expected returns. Case studies of particular inventions, detailed studies of decision-making in particular laboratories, and studies of patent statistics all seem to support this view.[4]

From the proposition that the amount invested by private sources in improving technology in a particular area is influenced by the anticipated profitability of the investment, it follows that the rate of technological change in a particular area is influenced by the same kinds of factors that determine the output of any good or service. On the one hand, there are demand factors which influence the rewards from particular kinds of technological change. For example, if a prospective change in technology reduces the cost of a particular product, increases in the demand for the product are likely to increase the returns from effecting this technological change. Similarly, a growing shortage and a rising price of the inputs saved by the technological change are likely to increase the returns from effecting it.

On the other hand, there are also supply factors which influence the cost of making various types of technological change.[5] Obviously, whether people try to solve a given problem depends on whether they think it can be solved, and on how costly they think it will be as well as on the expected payoff if they are successful. The cost of making science-based technological changes depends on the number of scientists and engineers in relevant fields and on advances in basic science. In addition, the rate of technological change depends on the amount of effort devoted to making modest improvements that lean heavily on practical experience. Although there is a tendency to focus attention on the major, spectacular inventions, it is by no means certain that technological change in many industries is due chiefly to these inventions, rather than to a succession of minor improvements. In recent years, Arrow and Hollander, among others, have stressed the importance of minor improvements and of learning by doing.[6]

Due in large part to the activities of the National Science Foundation, the postwar period has seen the development of statistics concerning expenditures on research and development. Although these statistics are not without their shortcomings, they are an important step towards a fuller understanding of the factors determining the rate of technological change. Many studies have been made of the factors determining the amount spent by a firm on research and development. Also, studies have been made of the relationship between the amount spent on R & D and various measures of inventive output, the results of which suggest that this relationship is reasonably close. In addition, studies have been made of the composition and characteristics of the R & D expenditures in various industries. Studies of this latter sort are needed because R & D includes work of quite different kinds, and for many purposes, it is important to disaggregate total R & D expenditures. For example, it is often important to separate research aimed at major advances from routine product development.[7]

R & D is, of course, a risky business. In recent years, a number of studies have been carried out which shed light on the nature and extent of these risks. For example, a series of studies done at the RAND Corporation indicate that the risks involved in weapons development are large indeed. However, there is a vast difference between military R & D and civilian R & D. In civilian R & D, the technical risks—the risks that the technical objectives of the project cannot be met—tend to be quite modest, due largely to the fact that the bulk of the civilian R & D projects are aimed at fairly modest advances in the state of the art. The commercial risks—the risks that the new product will not be profitable in the market—tend to be much larger than the technical risks in civilian R & D. In other words, it is much more likely that an industrial laboratory can solve the technical problems involved in developing a new or improved product or process than that it will be economically worth while to solve these problems.[8]

To help reduce these risks and to help make industrial and government R & D more efficient, a large number of studies have been made of the decision-making process concerning R & D. We know a good deal about the ways in which firms and government agencies choose R & D projects, the accuracy of the estimates of cost and benefits that are made, the ways in which R & D organisations are organised, the sorts of managerial concepts and rules of thumb that are often adopted, the information flows and communication patterns in research and development, and the ways in which R & D organisations interact with the rest of the firm or agency. Also, some progress has been made in devising mathematical techniques to aid decision making. For example, models indicating the optimal number of parallel development efforts and network models to help schedule development tasks have proved useful under certain circumstances.[9]

TECHNOLOGICAL INNOVATION

Research and development is only a part of the process leading to successful technological innovation. In recent years, economists have tended to abandon the traditional two-step model of invention and innovation in favour of a richer model of the process that, if successful, leads to the first commercial introduction of a new product or process. The first part of this process takes place in the interval between the establishment of technical feasibility and the beginning of commercial development of the new product or process. This time interval may be substantial. For example, it averaged about a decade for important postwar innovations. (Note, however, that this time interval is much shorter than it was 50 years ago.) The second part of this process takes place in the time interval between the beginning of commercial development and the first commercial application of the new process or product. This time interval contains a number of distinct stages—applied research, preparation of product specification, prototype or pilot plant construction, tooling and construction of manufacturing facilities, and manufacturing and marketing start-up. In all this time interval has averaged about five years for important post-war innovations. Studies have also been carried out to determine the relative importance, in terms of cost and time, of the various stages contained in this latter time interval.[10]

In recent years, economists and businessmen have come to recognise that the management of innovation entails a great deal more than the establishment of an R & D laboratory that turns out a lot of good technical output. In many industries, the bulk of the innovations are not based to any significant extent on the firm's R & D. For example, Myers and Marquis found that only a minority of the recent innovations in housing, railroads, and computers were based directly on R & D. They also found that technological innovations are more often stimulated by perceived production and marketing problems and needs, than by technological opportunities. That is, in the bulk of the cases, it takes a market-related stimulus to trigger work on a successful innovation. However, it is quite likely that the innovations based on technological opportunities—and on R & D—are the more important ones.[11]

It is important to recognise that many innovations rely on little in the way of science. But it is is also important not to push this idea too far. In more and more areas of the economy, innovations have come to depend on a strong scientific base. Merely to be able to imitate or adapt what others have developed, it is necessary for a firm in the aircraft, electronics, or chemical industries to have access to high-quality scientists. Of course, this does not mean that leadership in basic science is a prerequisite for leadership in technology. Unless a country is able to exploit its leadership in basic science, this leadership may not have a great effect on its technology. Moreover, it is not at all accurate to assume that innovations, when they are science-based, must rely on or exploit new science. According to recent studies, industrial innovations generally are based very largely on relatively old science.[12]

One of the most important problems facing a firm that attempts to be innovative is to effect a proper coupling between R & D, on the one hand, and marketing and production, on the other. The great importance of this problem is emphasised by recent work of Freeman, and of my co-workers and myself.[13] Many R & D projects are designed without sufficient understanding of market and production realities. Many marketing and production people are unnecessarily impervious to the good ideas produced by R & D people. To try to reduce these problems, some firms promote frequent contacts between R & D people and people in other parts of the firm, there being considerable evidence that person-to-person contacts are the most effective way of transferring ideas and technology. Firms also try to break down resistance—in the R & D department and elsewhere—to ideas stemming from outside the firm. Even in R & D-intensive industries like chemicals and pharmaceuticals, recent studies indicate that a large proportion of the innovations are based on inventions made outside the innovating firm.[14]

Many studies stress the difficulties of carrying out radical innovations in the large, established firm, the evidence indicating that such innovations often have to be spearheaded by new firms and 'invaders' from other industries. Also, there is some evidence that firms where problems and tasks are broken down into specialities and where there is a strict vertical chain of command are less likely to be innovative than firms where there is no strictly-defined hierarchy, where communication resembles consultation rather than command, and where individuals have to perform tasks in the light of their knowledge of the tasks of the whole firm. Some large firms, like DuPont and ICI, are trying to get some of the advantages of the small firm by creating a number of teams in their development department that operate somewhat like small firms.[15]

THE DIFFUSION OF INNOVATIONS

Once a new process or product is introduced, the diffusion process begins. The diffusion of a new technique is often a slow process. For example, measuring from the date of first commercial application, it generally took more than 10 years for all of the major American firms in the bituminous coal, steel, railroad, and brewing industries to begin using a sample of important new techniques I studied a decade or so ago. More recently, similar results have been obtained for the chemical and other industries as well. Also, the rate of diffusion varies widely. Sometimes it took decades for firms to install a new technique, but in other cases they imitated the innovator very quickly. To some extent, these differences may reflect a tendency for the diffusion process to go on more rapidly in more recent times than in the past. But according to the available evidence, this tendency is not as clear-cut as one might expect.[16]

A fair amount of evidence concerning the determinants of the rate of diffusion has been amassed in recent years. It is clear at this point that the rate of diffusion of an innovation depends on the average profitability of the innovation, the variation among firms in the profitability of the innovation, the size of the investment required to introduce the innovation, the number of firms in the industry, their average size, the inequality in their sizes, and the amount that they spend on research and development.

Using these variables, it is possible to explain a large proportion of the variation among innovations in the rate of diffusion. Moreover, this seems to be the case in a wide variety of industries and in other countries as well as in the United States. Econometric models using these variables seem to be useful devices for technological forecasting.[17]

Recent studies have also been made of the characteristics of the firms that are relatively quick—or relatively slow—to introduce new techniques. Based on studies of a number of industries, it is clear that firms where the expected returns from the innovation are highest tend to be quickest to introduce an innovation. Also, holding constant the profitability of the innovation, big firms tend to introduce an innovation before small firms. In some industries, this may be due to the fact that larger firms—although not necessarily the largest ones—are more progressive than small firms. But even if the larger firms were not more progressive, one would expect them to be quicker, on the average, to begin using a new technique—for reasons indicated elsewhere. Also, holding other factors constant, firms with younger and better educated managers tend to be quicker to introduce new techniques—or at least, this seems to be the case in industries where firms are small.[18]

Studies have also been made of the rate at which individual firms substituted new techniques for old ones. The results indicate that firms differ greatly with regard to the intra-firm rate of diffusion—the rate at which, once it has begun to use the new technique, a firm substitutes it for older methods. A considerable amount of this variation can be explained by differences among firms in the profitability of the innovation, the size of the firm, and its liquidity. Also, there is a tendency for late starters to 'catch up'. That is, firms that are slow to begin using an innovation tend to substitute it for older techniques more rapidly than those that are quick to begin using it. It is also relevant to note that the same sort of process occurs on the international scene: countries that are slow to begin using an innovation tend to substitute it for older techniques more rapidly than countries that are quick to begin using it. The reasons for this tendency, both at the firm and national levels, seem clear enough.[19]

Sociologists and economists have studied the nature and sources of information obtained by managers concerning new techniques. Judging from the available evidence, firms, once they hear of the existence of an innovation, may wait a considerable period of time before beginning to use it. In many cases, this is quite rational. But to some extent this may also be due to incomplete or erroneous information, prejudice, and resistance to change. The sources of information sometimes vary depending on how close the manager is to adopting the innovation. For example, in agriculture, mass media are most important sources at the very early stages of a manager's awareness of the innovation, but friends and neighbours are most important sources when a manager is ready to try the innovation. Also, there is evidence of a 'two-step flow of communication'. The early users of an innovation tend to rely on sources of information beyond their peer group's experience; after they have begun using the innovation, they become a model for their less expert peers, who can imitate their performance.[20]

Finally, a number of other factors also influence the rate of diffusion of an innovation. For example, the diffusion process may be slowed by bottlenecks in the production of the innovation —as in the case of the Boeing 707. Also, the extent of advertising and other promotional activities used by producers of the new product or equipment will also have an effect. So too will the innovation's requirements with respect to knowledge and co-ordination, the diffusion process being impeded if the innovation requires new kinds of knowledge on the part of the user, new types of behaviour, and the co-ordinated efforts of a number of organisations. If an innovation requires few changes in socio-cultural values and behaviour patterns, it is likely to spread more rapidly. Also, the policies adopted by relevant labour unions influence the rate of diffusion. There is, of course, a considerable literature on the effect of collective bargaining on the rate of adoption of new techniques.[21]

THREE MAJOR ROLES OF THE MULTINATIONAL ENTERPRISE

As noted at the outset of this paper, multinational firms have grown substantially in power and size in the postwar period. The reasons why firms have become multinational are varied. In some cases, firms have established overseas branches to control foreign sources of raw materials. In other cases, firms have invested overseas for defensive reasons. But in a great many cases, firms have established foreign branches to exploit a technological lead. After exporting a new product (or a cheaper version of an existing product) to foreign markets, firms have decided to establish plants overseas to supply these markets. Once the foreign market was big enough to accommodate a plant of minimum efficient size, this decision did not conflict with scale economies. Moreover, freight costs and tariffs often hastened such a decision. Also, in some cases, the only way that a firm could introduce its innovation into a foreign market was through the establishment of overseas production facilities.[22]

By carrying its technology overseas, the multinational firm has played a very important role in the international diffusion of innovations. For reasons that will be elaborated in subsequent sections, a firm with a technological edge over its competitors often prefers to exploit its technology in foreign markets through wholly-owned subsidiaries rather than through licensing or other means. To some extent, this is because of the well-known difficulties in using ordinary market mechanisms to buy and sell information. To some extent, it is due to the difficulties in transferring technology across organisational, as well as national, boundaries. For these and other reasons, there are advantages to the innovating firm in transferring its technology to other countries by establishing subsidiaries abroad. Since it is advisable to build on existing trade, labour, and other relationships, firms sometimes merge with or buy existing foreign firms rather than establish entirely new branches.

Multinational firms transfer technology to foreign countries in a variety of ways. In those countries where they have plants, they train people as operatives and managers. Also, they sometimes stimulate suppliers to upgrade their technology. For example, pharmaceutical companies have helped local firms in developing countries with the fabrication of dosage forms. In addition, multinational firms sometimes set standards for their competitors. For example, American electronics firms seemed to apply considerable competitive pressure on European firms in the 1960s. Also, they sometimes establish overseas R & D facilities, which aid in the transfer of technology. Beyond this, they often train users and provide service for customers. For example, in the computer area, IBM has transferred a considerable amount of important technology by training potential users, providing software, and servicing computer installations in various countries. Also, whether or not a firm has a plant in a particular country, the availability of its product in that country may be a form of technology transfer.[23]

Besides being an important vehicle for the transfer of new technology from one country to another, the multinational firm is also an important producer of new technology. The bulk of the R & D carried out in the United States is performed by large—and thus probably multinational—firms. And this is true in other advanced countries as well. For example, in eight industrially advanced OECD countries, eight firms account for at least 30 per cent of all industrial R & D in each country.[24] Of course, this does not mean that multinational firms contribute practically all of the new technology that arises. On the contrary, as we shall see in the section on the Multinational Firm and Production of New Technology, small firms contribute a very significant share of the important new ideas and concepts that underlie major technological advances. But recognising this fact, it is nonetheless true that the multinational firm is an important producer of new technology.

In addition, the multinational firm is an important vehicle for the initial application of new technology. In other words, the multinational firm is an important source of innovations, as well as inventions. The innovator—the firm that is first to apply a new process or introduce a new or modified product—must be willing to take the risks involved in introducing an untried process or product. These risks often are high. Although R & D can supply much of the data regarding the performance and costs of production of the new process or product, and market research can supply considerable data regarding the demand for it, there are many areas of uncertainty that can be resolved only by actually introducing or using the innovation. The innovator plays a vital social role by obtaining information concerning the actual performance of the new process or product. The multinational firms are responsible for a great many significant innovations, as we shall see in the section on Multinational Firm and Technological Innovation.

Thus, as stated in the previous paragraphs, the multinational firm has played three major roles in the process of technological change—as a vehicle for the international diffusion of technology, as a producer of new technology, and as an innovator. The next five sections of this paper describe in more detail the nature, extent, and importance of each of these roles; and in so doing, will try to summarise the results of the research which has been carried out concerning the technological activities of the multinational firm, as well as to extend these results by providing some new empirical results.

GAPS IN TECHNOLOGY

To understand the role of the multinational firm as a vehicle for the international diffusion of technology, one must know something about the nature and extent of the technological gaps among nations. In recent years, there has been considerable interest in such gaps, particular attention being centred on the technology gap between the United States and Western Europe. A number of studies have been made, and a flurry of papers has appeared. These papers generally measure the technology gap in two ways—by making international comparisons of total factor productivity and by looking at which countries develop and export new and improved products. Based on these measures, there appears to be a considerable amount of evidence indicating the existence of a gap between European and American technology. For example, Denison concludes that productivity differences between America and Europe cannot be totally explained by differences in capital per worker, education, or other such factors.[25] Vernon and Hufbauer have shown that, to a large extent, American exports are in new products which other countries are not yet producing.[26]

The available evidence, which is fragmentary at best, suggests that the existence of this technology gap is by no means new. For example, Nelson points out that scattered impressionistic evidence prior to 1850 suggests the existence of such a gap in many fields. And after 1850, the available quantitative evidence indicates that total factor productivity was higher in the United States than in Europe, that the United States had a strong export position in technically progressive industries, and that Europeans tended to imitate American techniques. The existence of such a gap in the nineteenth century would not be surprising, since this was a heyday of American invention. (Among the key American inventions of the period was the system of interchangeable parts.) Needless to say, the United States did not lead in all fields, but it appears that they held a technological lead in many important parts of manufacturing.[27]

In the 1960s, Europeans expressed considerable concern over the technology gap. They asserted that superior know-how stemming from scientific and technical achievements in the United States had allowed American companies to obtain large shares of European markets in fields like aircraft, space equipment, computers, and other electronic products. In 1966, Italy's Foreign Minister Amintore Fanfani went so far as to call for a 'technological Marshall Plan' to speed the flow of American technology across the Atlantic. In response to this concern, the OECD made a large study of the nature and causes of the technology gap. It concluded that a large gap existed in computers and some electronic components, but that no general or fundamental gap existed in pharmaceuticals, bulk plastics, iron and steel, machine tools (other than numerically controlled machine tools), non-ferrous metals (other than tantalum and titanium), and scientific instruments (other than electronic test and measuring instruments). Thus, the OECD studies indicated that the American technological lead was greatest in relatively research-intensive sectors of the economy.[28]

The factors responsible for these technological gaps are difficult to sort out and measure. A host of factors—the social climate, the educational system, the scientific community, the amount and quality of industrial research, the nature of domestic markets, the quality of management, and government policies, among others—influence a country's technological position. According to the OECD studies, the size and homogeneity of the American market is an important factor, but not a decisive one. Also, the large size of American firms is another factor, but not a decisive one. In addition, the large government expenditures on R & D in the United States have played an important role. Also, according to the OECD studies, a very important factor is that American firms have a significant lead in the techniques of management, including the management of R & D and the coupling of R & D with marketing and production. Needless to say, much more research is needed in this area.

Thus far, we have been concerned only with the technology gap between the United States and Europe. In addition, there is a much wider technology gap—between the industrialised nations and the developing nations. Much has been written about the nature and importance of this technology gap. Unfortunately, much of the new science and technology being produced today is largely irrelevant to the needs of the developing countries. What is needed in many of the developing countries is relatively old technology—i.e. old from the point of view of the industrialised nations—which does not require relatively sophisticated skills or much capital. Of course, this is not to deny that the 'green revolution', the birth-control programmes and the other programmes built on relatively new science and technology have been important. But the major point to bear in mind is that the technology gap between the industrialised and developing countries is essentially very different from that between the United States and Europe: it is both wider and more difficult to close.

THE INTERNATIONAL DIFFUSION OF TECHNOLOGY AND THE MULTINATIONAL FIRM

Because of the differences among nations in technological capabilities, there is a continual process of international diffusion

Table 6.1. Payments for Patents, Licences and Technological Know-how, 1964 (1963 for France, Italy and Japan)

Payments by:	US	UK	Germany	France	Italy	Japan	Switzerland	Canada	Holland
				Payments to (millions of dollars)					
United States	—	21·0	10·8	11·7	2·3	5·0	n.a.*	37·0	n.a.
United Kingdom	81·8	—	3·4	11·7	2·2	0·3	8·4	n.a.	—
Germany	65·3	17·2	—	5·3	1·7	0·2	42·8	2·0	11·2
France	59·7	11·9	7·5	—	2·0	—	27·0	0·7	4·6
Italy	57·2	15·0	15·2	14·6	—	0·4	22·3	0·7	5·6
Japan	84·7	11·0	12·5	3·0	1·7	—	9·5	0·8	4·6
Total	348·7	76·1	49·4	46·3	9·9	5·9	110·0	41·2	26·0

* n.a. = not available.
Source: OECD (1970), p. 201.

of technology. Knowledge can be transmitted in various ways—by emigration of engineers and skilled workers, by export of goods and services, by licensing, and by direct investment, among others. Data are available concerning national receipts and payments for patents, manufacturing licences and technological know-how between parent firms and their subsidiaries

Table 6.2. Ratio of Receipts to Payments on Patents and Licences, by Industry, Selected Countries.‡

Industry	United States	France	Germany	Italy	United Kingdom
Non-electric machinery⎫	12·4	0·2⎫			0·2
Transport equipment ⎭		0·6⎪			1·0
Other transport (aircraft)	6·1	0·9⎬	0·4⎫	0·3	
Basic metals and metal products	5·1	0·3⎭	⎭		n.a.† n.a.
Electrical machinery	30·0	0·1	0·4	0·2	1·2
Chemical and allied products	3·3	0·8	0·6	0·3	1·7
Food, drink, and tobacco	6·0	0·1	*	0·3	3·7
Others	4·0	0·4	0·3	0·2	1·0
Total	5·9	0·4	0·4	0·2	1·1

* Less than 0·05.   *Source:* OECD (1970), p. 203.
† n.a. = not available.
‡ The US data are for 1956, the French and Italian data are for 1963, and the German and British data are for 1964.

as well as between independent firms.[29] Taken at face value, these data seem to indicate that very substantial payments are involved, that the United States was the single most important supplier of technology to other major Western nations, and that a large proportion of these payments for the international transfer of technology represents the transactions between American parent firms and foreign subsidiaries. However, many experts regard these figures as extremely unreliable. Although good data do not exist, it seems clear that the multinational firm has played an important role in the international diffusion of technology. For example, the OECD studies concluded that: 'The concept of imitation is probably apposite in the Japanese case where still the major part of technological agreements appear to be made between . . . US companies and companies under Japanese ownership. But in the case of Europe and Canada, the large inflow of United States technology appears to be much more

Table 6.3. Percentage of US Receipts for Licences, Patents, Royalties and Management Fees derived from Transactions between Parent Companies and Subsidiaries

Year	United Kingdom	Source OECD Europe (*percentage*)	Canada	Japan
1957	44·4	43·1	75·4	15·4
1965	72·3	70·8	89·5	24·5

Source: OECD (1970), p. 262.

a reflection of the rapid increase in United States investment in Europe than of such imitative behaviour on the part of European companies.'[30]

Many case studies of particular industries attest to the important role played by the multinational firm in the international diffusion of technology. For example, Tilton's study of the diffusion of semi-conductors shows that, of the major innovations in semi-conductors in the 1960s, American subsidiaries were the first to produce about one-third of them in Britain and about one-fifth of them in France.[31] In particular, subsidiaries of American (and other foreign) firms were relatively quick to use silicon and planar techniques, and, by competing strongly with established European firms, they were able to capture large shares of the market. For example, in 1968, foreign subsidiaries had 44 per cent of the market for semi-conductors in Britain, 33 per cent in France, and 22 per cent in Germany. As described by the OECD study of electronic components, 'the old patterns of moderate competition have been disrupted in a relatively short time by the development of American direct investment. The change, which occurred around 1962, has been continuing at a rapid pace since and is closely linked with the technological revolutions which took place in the industry, and the failure of many European companies to make the transition to the new technologies early enough.'[32]

Many case studies also describe the role played by the multinational firm in the transfer of technology to the developing countries. For example, Baranson has described the transfer of diesel technology to India.[33] It is important to recognise, however, that these firms face much more difficult problems in transmitting technology to developing countries than to industrialised countries. Many of the techniques of the multi-

F

national firms may not be suited very well to the less developed countries, with their plentiful unskilled labour, few skills, and little capital. Moreover, there may be little incentive for multinational firms to adapt their products, production techniques, and marketing methods to the conditions present in developing economies, and (unfortunately) developing economies lack the technical capability to effect the necessary adaptations themselves. The technological gap is so wide that multinational firms find it exceedingly difficult to transfer many technologies to developing countries; and when they manage to effect a technological transplant, its effects often are restricted to narrow segments of the local economy.[34]

Finally, two additional points should be noted. First, the multinational firm is not always an American firm taking American technology abroad. Some case studies have been made of the transfer of technology from other countries to the United States. For example, information is available concerning Olivetti's take-over of Underwood, and its subsequent infusion of new concepts and technologies into Olivetti Underwood.[35] This is an interesting case, because it serves to remind us that, although the multinational firm generally has taken American technology abroad, the international diffusion of technology works in both directions. Second, the rate of international diffusion of technology seems to be increasing. Because of the activities of the multinational firm, as well as a host of other factors, it is commonly believed that technology spreads from nation to nation more rapidly than in the past. For example, Richard Cooper has presented some fragmentary evidence to support this view. Also, the OECD studies of the technology gap seem to come to this same conclusion.[36]

DIRECT INVESTMENT VERSUS ALTERNATIVE MEANS OF DIFFUSION

Clearly, direct investment is not the only way that technology can be transferred abroad. A firm with a significant new product or process may engage in licensing agreements with foreigners covering patents, trade-marks, franchise, technical assistance, and so on. Licensing agreements often call for the licensee to pay a certain percentage of its sales to the licenser, plus, in some cases, a flat fee for technical help. Some licensing agreements also require the licensee to buy certain inputs from the licensor. Still another way in which technology can be transferred is through the formation of a joint venture, an operation owned jointly by the firm with the technology and a firm or agency of the host country. Joint venture agreements are often made by smaller firms which need capital to complement their technology.[37]

A number of factors determine which of these means of transferring its technology is preferable to the innovating firm. According to the available evidence, firms seem to prefer direct investment if they can obtain the necessary resources, and if they believe that licensing will give away valuable know-how to foreign producers who are likely to become competitors in the future. Of course, the longer the estimated life of the innovation, the less inclined a firm is to enter into a licensing agreement. Also, firms prefer direct investment over licensing when the technology is sophisticated and foreigners lack the know-how to assimilate it or when a firm is concerned about protecting quality standards. On the other hand, licensing is often preferred when the foreign market is too small to warrant direct investment, when the firm lacks the resources required for direct investment, or when advantages accrue through cross-licensing. Also, in some countries, like Japan, direct investment has been discouraged by the government. As for joint ventures, they have advantages with respect to forging good relations with host countries, but they have disadvantages and problems in operation, personnel matters, and the division of profits.[38]

To the government of the host country, the choice between these alternative means of obtaining technology looks quite different than it does to the firm with the technology. To the host government, direct investment creates many problems because the wholly-owned subsidiary of a foreign firm is partly outside its control. The direct investor is only partly responsive to the host nation's economic policies. The investor can draw on funds and resources outside the host country. Moreover, the investor has a global strategy which may be at odds with the optimal operation of the subsidiary from the viewpoint of the host government. Also, the host government cannot be certain of the effect of direct investment on its balance of payments. Joint ventures may overcome some of these disadvantages of direct investment, but they have the disadvantage that the host country must invest more capital. Licensing arrangements eliminate many of the problems of control, but they have the disadvantage that the foreign firm with the technology has little commitment or incentive to help the licensee with managerial and technical problems.[39]

According to the available evidence, there is considerable variation among industries in the extent to which the international transfer of technology takes place via direct investment rather than by other means. For example, the OECD studies indicate that in computers and advanced electronic components (where nearly all of the transferred technology is of American origin), the technology was transferred to Europe by direct investment in about half of the cases and by licensing in about half of the cases. However, in value terms, direct investment was considerably more important than licensing. On the other hand, in plastics and pharmaceuticals (where much of the transferred technology originated in Europe as well as the United States), the situation has been quite different. In pharmaceuticals, direct investment seems to have been the major means of transferring technology within the OECD countries. In plastics, on the other hand, the principal means of transferring technology has been through licensing agreements and joint ventures. According to Pavitt, these differences among industries seem to be due to differences in the extent of the technological lead enjoyed by innovating firms, the extent of competition in the industry, and the extent of specialisation of firms in different product areas.[40]

Recent studies also indicate that, with regard to a particular new product, the relative importance of direct investment as a means of transferring technology seems to depend on the stage of the new product's life cycle. For example, consider the case of petrochemicals. Stobaugh has shown that, when various important petrochemicals were relatively new, direct investment was the dominant form of technology transfer, but that as they became mature, licensing became dominant. One reason for this sort of pattern lies in the changes over time in the relative bargaining positions of the innovating firm and the country wanting the technology. When the technology is quite new, it is closely held, and countries wanting the technology are under pressure to accept the firm's conditions, which often are a wholly-owned subsidiary. But as time goes on, the technology becomes more widely known, and the host country can take advantage of competition among technologically capable firms to obtain joint ventures or sometimes licenses. Eventually, the technology may become available in plants that can be acquired by the host country on a turn-key basis from independent engineering firms.[41]

THE MULTINATIONAL FIRM AND THE PRODUCTION OF NEW TECHNOLOGY

Besides being an important factor in the diffusion of technology, the multinational firm is also an important producer of new technology. About 90 per cent of the R & D expenditures in the United States are made by firms with more than 5000 employees; and many of these large firms are multinational. However, it is easy to exaggerate the importance of the multinational firm by looking at statistics concerning R & D expenditures. There is a considerable amount of evidence that the really major inventions seldom stem from the laboratories of the large firms, which are principally contributors of minor 'improvement' inventions. Studies by Jewkes, Hamberg, and others show the importance of small firms and independent inventors in originating major new concepts and inventions. The large firms play a more important role in the development of major concepts and inventions than in originating them. It is important to note, however, that giant firms, as distinct from merely large ones, are seldom required to carry out the development work. In very few cases are the development costs so high that only the biggest American firms in a particular industry are needed to do the development work.[42]

As part of their inventive and development work, some multi-national firms carry out R & D in overseas laboratories. Until very recently, statistics concerning these overseas R & D activities have been almost non-existent. In recent months, the Department of Commerce has released figures concerning the overseas R & D operations of American multinational corporations in 1966.[43] Table 6.4 shows the amounts spent by various industries and in various locations. About two-thirds of these expeditures were in Europe. Comparing the amount spent abroad with the amount spent at home, my calculations indicate that R & D expenditures by foreign affiliates equal about 4 per cent of R & D expenditures in the US. Table 6.5 shows that this percentage was somewhat higher for food products, machinery, and transportation equipment than for other industries. Comparing the ratio of R & D to sales of foreign affiliates with that at home, we find that foreign affiliates devoted a much smaller percentage of their sales to R & D than did the parent American firms. As shown in Table 6.4, the industries where the difference is smallest are the electrical equipment and food industries.

There are many reasons why multinational firms establish R & D laboratories abroad. In some cases, it is advantageous to have development people in close contact with the local market requirements. (Recall the discussion in the Technological Innovation section of the importance of coupling R & D with marketing.) In other cases, there are environmental conditions abroad that cannot easily be matched at home. For example, research on equatorial plants can best be performed near the equator. In

Table 6.4. Research and Development Expenditures of Foreign Affiliates of US Manufacturing Firms, by Industry and Area, 1966.

(Note that some R & D expenditures were made in areas and industries not listed below. For this reason, the individual items will not equal the total.)

Area or Industry	Foreign Affiliate R & D Expenditures (Millions of $)	Foreign Affiliate R & D as per cent of US R & D	Foreign Affiliate R & D as per cent of sales	US Private R & D as per cent of sales
Total	566	4	1·1	2·0
Area:				
Canada	157	n.a.	1·0	—
United Kingdom	145	n.a.	1·9	—
Common Market	196	n.a.	1·7	—
Rest of Europe	21	n.a.	0·6	—
Japan	3	n.a.	0·4	—
Latin America	17	n.a.	0·3	—
Industry:				
Food	17	10	0·3	0·4
Paper	3	4	0·2	0·7
Chemicals	71	5	1·1	3·5
Rubber	4	2	0·2	1·7
Primary metals	5	2	0·2	0·7
Fabricated metals	4	2	0·3	1·2
Machinery (exc. electrical)	90	7	1·8	3·0
Electrical machinery	103	3	2·6	3·4
Transportation equipment	133	10	1·4	2·6
Stone, clay and glass	4	3	0·5	1·6
Instruments	21	5	1·6	4·0

Source: US Department of Commerce, *US Direct Investments Abroad, 1966*, Part II: Investment Position, Financial and Operating Data, Group 2: Preliminary Report on Foreign Affiliates of US Manufacturing Industries. US R & D expenditures and US R & D as a per cent of sales are from National Science Foundation, *Research and Development in Industry*, 1966 (Washington, 1968), as quoted in Scherer (1970), p. 349.

still other cases, firms want to make use of skills and talents that are not readily available at home, or they want to take advantage of lower salaries for scientists and engineers abroad. According to many accounts, firms also use their overseas laboratories to monitor what is going on in relevant scientific and technical fields abroad.[44]

There are problems as well as advantages in operating a

multinational network of R & D laboratories. Cultural differences among countries sometimes make life difficult. Co-ordination of R & D work in multinational laboratories is a major problem, particularly in firms where there is a uniform and compatible product line. The 'not-invented-here' syndrome, which is such a headache in transferring ideas within a single country, is even more of a problem in transferring ideas from one country to another. Nationalistic pride can interfere with the effective transfer of technology. Sometimes the prevailing attitude is: 'It's done this way in the US and we can't believe it won't work for you.' Sometimes the prevailing attitude is: 'We never heard of this before, so it can't be good.' Achieving the proper communications and understanding among groups in various locations is of great importance and often requires a great deal of travel and personal contacts. Attention must be devoted to transferring ideas and technology across the interfaces.[45]

Unfortunately, there have been no detailed case studies of the international R & D operations of individual multinational firms. However, some information has been published concerning the multinational R & D activities of IBM, Eastman Kodak, and Farbenfabricken Bayer, among others.[46] Perhaps IBM has gone furthest in integrating its R & D activities on a world-wide basis. Until 1961, IBM used its overseas laboratories to support the local market. But finding it difficult to make optimal use of these laboratories when their mission was limited in this way, the firm decided, when it developed the 360 line of computers, to bring the European laboratories into the world-wide development programme. In the case of the 360 line, which consisted of six basic computers, each laboratory, whether American or European, was given a specific mission. For example, the smaller machine came from Germany, and the medium-sized machine was designed in England. The need to maintain constant liaison between laboratories was obvious. Using modern communications technology, engineers in Poughkeepsie were able to talk with and transmit circuit designs back and forth with engineers in Europe. Here, as in many other areas, innovations in communication and transportation have made economical many of the activities of the multinational firm.[47]

THE MULTINATIONAL FIRM AND TECHNOLOGICAL INNOVATION

The multinational firm has been an important source of innovations, as well as an important producer of new technology. In other words, the multinational firm has often been the first to introduce various new products and processes to the commercial market. To a considerable extent, this has been due to the fact that multinational firms tend to be fairly large. There is plenty of evidence indicating that firms must attain a certain minimum size before they do any appreciable innovating. That is, there is a threshold effect. But the threshold in many industries is not very high, and the evidence indicates that, in practically all industries for which we have data, the biggest firms do proportionately less innovating than firms that are a fraction of their size. Consequently, although there is a threshold effect, there is no evidence that giant firms—by American standards—are required to carry out innovations.[48]

Nonetheless, because innovation generally requires much more resources than the origination, or even the development, of the basic concept, the role played by the bigger firms is certainly more important than their role in the inventive process. There are substantial costs involved in constructing the manufacturing facilities and in the manufacturing start-up and marketing start-up associated with a new product. On the average, such costs seem to be higher than the R & D costs.[49] But, as noted in the Technological Innovation section, the advantages of the large firm derived from its greater resources are often offset by its bureaucracy and sluggishness. Particularly where radical innovations are concerned, the larger firms have often been slow to recognise their potential. Small firms and 'invaders' from other industries, to use Don Schon's phrase, have often been first to introduce radical innovations.

For a handful of important industries, it is possible to quantify the importance of the innovative role of multinational firms, at least roughly. In previous publications, my co-workers and I have formulated lists of innovations in the petroleum, steel, bituminous coal, pharmaceutical and chemical industries. In Table 6.5, the author has computed the percentages of these innovations carried out by firms with subsidiaries or other productive facilities outside the United States. (Of course, in some cases, these foreign activities accounted for only a small share of the firm's business.) In all industries—other than coal—the result exceeds 50 per cent. Indeed, in the chemical, pharmaceutical, and petroleum industries, the vast majority of the innovations carried out in recent years were introduced by firms with foreign operations. Needless to say, these results are very rough, and should be interpreted with caution. For one thing, some of these innovators had relatively small foreign operations, and would not be con-

Table 6.5. Percentage of Innovations Introduced in the United States by Firms with Productive Facilities Outside the United States

Industry	Time Interval	Percentage
Iron and steel	1950–58	51
Bituminous coal preparation	1950–58	33*
Petroleum	1950–58	85
Pharmaceutical	1950–62	94
Chemicals	1960–69	100

* This percentage is non-zero due entirely to the fact that a single firm, which carried out 33 per cent of the innovations, was owned by another firm with a very small proportion of its productive facilities in Canada.
Source: See Note 49. In the case of the pharmaceutical innovations, only the 20 most important innovations during 1950–62 were included. See Mansfield, *et al.* (1971).

sidered multinational, according to many definitions. For another thing, any percentage of this sort is a very crude measure. Also, it should be recognised that, since multinational firms control a large share of the sales and assets of many of these industries, it is by no means surprising that they should account for the bulk of the innovations. For example, according to Vernon's estimates, multinational firms account for *at least* about 80 per cent of pharmaceutical sales, 70 per cent of petroleum sales, and 60 per cent of chemical sales in the United States. Finally, it should be noted that the results do not contradict the assertion that many radical innovations seem to come from small firms and 'invaders'. Most of the innovations included in Table 6.5 could not be described as radical.[50]

Given the increased costs of R & D in many areas and the reduced lead time that, according to many observers, an innovator is likely to enjoy, it is clear that a potential innovator, whether or not it is a multinational firm, is sometimes forced to exploit its innovation on an international scale. National markets in some countries are just too small to repay the costs of innovation.[51] However, this does not mean that firms in small countries cannot be innovators. Witness the case of the Swiss pharmaceutical firms, among others. What it does mean is that firms are pressed to exploit their temporary technological edge in international markets as quickly as possible. For example, it has been reported that some small science-based European firms have introduced their new products in the American market before their own domestic market.[52]

FEARS OF THE MULTINATIONAL CORPORATION IN HOST COUNTRIES

To the host countries, the technological activities of multi-national firms are often viewed with suspicion and fear. Multi-national firms are often viewed as instruments of their parent country's policies. Because of military, political, or economic events, the parent country may induce the multinational firm to withhold its product, reduce its investment in foreign subsidiaries, or alter its policies in other ways which are contrary to the interests of the host country. Also, the host country sometimes fears that the multinational firm, in pursuit of its own profits, may engage in activities that are contrary to the host country's interests and policies. Before granting a licence or charter to a firm, host countries generally negotiate with the firm about taxes, amounts of capital to be raised locally, repatriation of profits, and other financial matters. In addition, they sometimes offer incentives for firms to establish R & D laboratories in the country, and apply pressure to get the firms to set up fully integrated plants to upgrade local skills. Also, they often force firms to hire and train local workers, and encourage firms to purchase components from local suppliers.[53]

In Western Europe (and Canada), many observers have expressed serious concern in recent years regarding the technological activities of the multinational firms. They are worried about a number of aspects of these activities. First, they express considerable concern over American firms taking over European firms, since they fear that, in cases where the European firm is about to make an important innovation, the benefits of the innovation will accrue to the United States rather than Europe. Whether or not this is the case depends, of course, on the amount that the American firm pays for the European firm. Dunning has described the conditions under which one might expect that the price would not reflect the firm's true social worth. As he points out, many of the reasons commonly given for expecting the price to be below the firm's true worth are fallacious.[54]

Second, they fear that American firms, once they take over European firms, will reduce or eliminate existing R & D efforts carried out in Europe. These activities will be transferred to the firm's central headquarters in the United States. It is difficult to tell whether this is true. As pointed out in the ninth section of this chapter, American foreign subsidiaries seem to spend a much smaller percentage of sales on R & D than do their parents in the United States. But according to Dunning, American subsidiaries in Britain spend more on R & D, as a per cent of sales, than their British competitors.[55] Moreover, even if it were true, its implications would not be obvious. As Dunning and others have pointed out, it is not obvious that European countries would be hurt appreciably if European engineers and scientists were to work for European firms rather than American subsidiaries—particularly if, as some have claimed, there is a shortage of qualified scientists and engineers in some European countries.[56]

Third, they fear that they will become technologically dependent on the United States. For example, the president of the Canadian National Research Council has said that, because many Canadian enterprises are 'branch plants' and 'research is normally done by the parent organisation' outside Canada, 'Canadian industry has been largely dependent on research in the United States and in Britain. The result of this is that, by comparison with the United States or Britain, relatively little industrial research has been done in Canada by industrial organisation. . . .'[57] However, it is by no means obvious that direct investment really results in a decrease in the host country's inventive and innovative efforts. Moreover, in technology as elsewhere, there are a great many advantages in international specialisation and trade, particularly as the cost of product development in certain areas increases. For example, Pavitt and Quinn have argued that such specialisation should form an important part of an enlightened public policy toward science and technology.[58]

Fourth, in contrast to the prevalent view in Canada and many parts of Europe, some countries do not want foreign-owned firms to conduct research and development on their soil. For example, Japan has not favoured the creation of R & D laboratories by multinational firms. Apparently, one reason for this attitude is that foreign-controlled R & D is considered a subtler type of 'brain drain', since the host country's scientists and engineers are being used by foreigners, even though they do not move abroad. However, one obvious difference is that by staying in the country, they continue to create various externalities that may be important. Of course, an important consideration here—as elsewhere in this section—is control. Host countries do not feel comfortable about foreign control of much of their technological resources and capability.[59]

AMERICAN FEARS OF THE MULTINATIONAL CORPORATION

In the past few years, there has also been considerable concern expressed in the United States regarding the multinational firm. During the past 10 years or so, many observers feel that our technological lead over Western Europe and Japan has shrunk considerably. Unfortunately, we really have little hard evidence as to the extent to which the 'technology gap' has narrowed in various fields, but fragmentary data seem to indicate some reduction of the gap in particular areas. For example, according to studies we are currently doing for the National Science Foundation, about 30 per cent of the important process innovations in the chemical industry in the 1960s came from abroad, whereas about one-tenth came from abroad in the 1950s. To some extent, such a reduction in the technology gap was to be expected as the war-torn economies of Europe and Asia got back on their feet. But in addition, there are other factors. For example, it has probably been due in part to the considerable increase in recent years in the amount spent by Germany, Japan, and other countries on research and development.[60]

Many observers attribute the deterioration of the US balance of trade to the narrowing of our technological lead. They point out that domestic producers seem to be having a harder time maintaining the technological edge over foreign producers that enabled us to sell effectively abroad and to hold our own against foreign competition. To some extent, this certainly is true, but we lack data indicating the extent to which a narrowing of our technological lead is responsible for the deterioration of our balance of trade. Obviously, lots of other factors were also at work. For example, during the late 1960s and early 1970s, our price level increased substantially. Also, there was the Common Market which eliminated tariffs among members but retained them on American goods. In addition, there were other factors.

Some groups, feeling that the narrowing of our technological lead is due in considerable part to the technological activities of multinational firms, argue that the activities of such firms should be subject to various new kinds of regulations. They point out that multinational firms have been an important factor in transmitting American technology to our foreign competition, thus narrowing our technological lead. Among the most vocal critics of the multinational corporation are the American labour unions. For example, representatives of the AFL–CIO testified in 1971 that 'While we share the concern of those who talk about the decline of America's trade balance . . ., we are equally concerned about the export of technology itself'.[60] Needless to say, the unions are concerned about the effect of the export of technology on jobs. In their view, the multinational firm is a 'runaway' corporation, which takes jobs away from the American economy.

More specifically, the AFL–CIO made the following proposals in 1971:

'Clear legislative direction is necessary to give the President authority to regulate, supervise, and curb the outflows of US capital . . . Authority within the President's hands should include consideration for the kind of investment that would be made abroad, the product involved, the country where the investment would be made, the linkage of the investment to the flow of trade and its effect on US employment and the national economy . . . US government policy has encouraged the export of technology in recent years. . . . This policy should be reversed by giving the President clear authority to regulate, supervise, and curb licensing and patent agreements on the basis of Congressionally determined standards. These would include the kind of investment, the product involved, the country of investment, the linkage to trade flows from such transfers and the effect on US employment and the economy.'[62]

Subsequently, legislation has been introduced in Congress to create a federal agency to stem the outflow of technology, jobs, capital, and production.

In general, economists seem to be much less inclined to favour such interference with the international diffusion of technology. However, some economists, notably Richard Cooper, have suggested that, if international monetary arrangements cannot be worked out to permit American firms to compete fairly in world markets, 'it may be necessary to restrict the activities of American firms abroad, that is, to exploit what remaining immobility of technical knowledge there is'.[63] But he hastens to add that this 'is distinctly a second-best solution'.[64] This seems to me to be the case, both because it would be difficult to accomplish and because it would invite retaliation. After all, technology flows in both directions across the Atlantic—as evidenced, for example, by the fact that about 30 per cent of the significant new chemical processes in the 1960s came from abroad, and that over

30 per cent of the significant new pharmaceuticals marketed here since 1950 came from abroad.[65]

NEEDED RESEARCH CONCERNING THE MULTINATIONAL FIRM AND THE DIFFUSION PROCESS

Although economists have devoted a considerable amount of attention in recent years to the multinational firm, we really know very little about the technological activities of these firms. In the next three sections, the author lists some areas where, in his opinion, research is badly needed.[66] Of course, the choice of topics will reflect the author's interests and biases. With regard to the role of the multinational enterprise in the diffusion process, it seems to me that studies of the following kind are needed. First, we need to know much more about the decision-making process within firms with regard to the transfer of technology abroad. What sorts of factors are most important in determining the sorts of technologies that are transferred to foreign subsidiaries? What sorts of adaptations are made to meet local conditions? What is the nature of the decision-making process and how does this process vary from industry to industry and from firm to firm? Although Aharoni and others have made studies of the decision-making process with regard to the general aspects of foreign investment, little information is available concerning the decision-making process with regard to the transfer of technology.[67]

Second, how do multinational firms go about transplanting their technologies to a new environment? What are the costs involved in transferring technologies? How do these costs depend on the characteristics of the technology, the characteristics of the organisation and country to which the technology is to be transferred, and the characteristics of the organisation and country from which the technology is to be transferred? How do the 'learning curves' abroad compare with those in the United States? How do firms go about reducing the costs of transferring technology? What sorts of transfer mechanisms seem to have been most successful? Do the same sorts of transfer mechanisms work best for various technologies, industries, or countries? If not, what sorts of differences are there? Again, there have been a number of useful case studies, including those by Baranson and Hall and Johnson.[68] But much more information is needed to answer these questions.

Third, can we characterise and measure more precisely the effects of foreign subsidiaries on the technological capabilities of local firms? As emphasised in the section on Three Major Roles of Multinational Firms, foreign subsidiaries are generally regarded as important forces in raising the technological capabilities of local suppliers, local customers, and local competitors. Is it possible to document, describe, and measure these effects in particular cases? Can we say anything about the circumstances under which foreign subsidiaries have a large impact, and the circumstances under which they have a small impact? Also, can we say anything about the relative costliness of this means of transferring technological and managerial techniques to local industry, as compared with other means of doing the same thing? There has been some work in this area. For example, Dunning has found that, in Britain, in industries where American subsidiaries and British firms compete, the British firms have tended to increase their productivity and profitability relative to the American subsidiaries in recent years.[69] But much more work is needed.

Fourth, can we measure and explain the productivity differences among the various foreign and domestic plants of a multinational firm? To what extent are these differences much the same for various firms in a particular industry? What factors account for interfirm and interindustry variation in these international differences? Also, can we measure and explain productivity differences between foreign subsidiaries of a multinational firm and their local competitors? How do these productivity differences vary from industry to industry and from country to country? These questions are obviously of basic importance. Some work has been carried out concerning them. For example, Dunning has compared the productivity of American subsidiaries in Britain with their British competitors.[70] But much more work is needed.

Fifth, much more information and analysis is needed concerning the costs to the host country associated with its receipt of technology via the multinational firm. Clearly, as Canada's Watkins Committee suggests, these costs—as well as the benefits of new technology—must be considered. If the foreign firm captures all of the return on its superior technology and leaves product prices and input prices undisturbed, there is no net benefit to the host country—other than the right to tax these profits. Tax considerations aside, the costs swallow up the benefits. To what extent have multinational firms been able to appropriate the benefits? To what extent have competition, host governments, and other factors reduced these costs to the host country? Johnson and others have provided theoretical analyses of the benefits and costs of direct investment to the host country.[71] Despite the great difficulties involved, perhaps more empirical or econometric analyses may be feasible.

Sixth, it is extremely important that we learn more about the ways in which various devices, including the multinational corporation, can be used to transfer technology to the developing countries. This, of course, is one of the crucial—and most difficult—problems of our time. As noted in the International Diffusion of Technology section, the multinational firms have experienced great difficulties in transferring technology to developing economies, because of low levels of skill, small markets, government policies insisting on the hiring of nationals, and many other factors. Research is badly needed to help make the multinational corporation into a more effective transmitter of technology, and to help guide public policy in a direction that will encourage the transmission of the proper technology. Obviously, technology transfer is not enough: the right sorts of technology must be transferred. Also, research is needed concerning the extent to which the multinational corporations can be induced to adapt techniques and products to meet the needs of the developing countries.[12]

NEEDED RESEARCH CONCERNING THE MULTINATIONAL FIRM'S ROLE AS A PRODUCER OF NEW TECHNOLOGY

With regard to the multinational firm's role as a producer of new technology, it seems to me that studies of the following kind are needed. First, we need more information concerning economies of scale in particular types of R & D. There are numerous reasons for thinking that there are economies of scale in R & D up to some point—'lumpiness' of capital equipment used in R & D, advantages from specialisation of labour, reduction of risks due to the law of large numbers, and so forth. However, we know very little, industry by industry, about the extent of these economies of scale for particular kinds of work or about the size of R & D establishment beyond which further increases in size bring little or nothing in the way of further efficiencies for the type of work in question. This is unfortunate, since it is often alleged that the advantages of the multinational firm are bound up with such economies of scale. Moreover, the socially optimal organisation of R & D will depend on these economies of scale.

Second, we need more information concerning the size and function of the overseas R & D operations of multinational firms. What determines the proportion of a firm's engineering and R & D expenditures that it spends abroad? When cutbacks occur in total R & D expenditures, how are they allocated between domestic and overseas laboratories? What determines the function or mission of overseas laboratories? To what extent is it still true, as a 1963 report of the Stanford Research Institute concluded, that many American firms view their European R & D as a way of monitoring R & D in Europe and of obtaining entry into the European scientific community? On the other hand, to what extent is the IBM concept of internationally integrated development programmes spreading? In various industries and in various countries, how does the ratio of R & D expenditures to sales of foreign subsidiaries compare with that of their local competitors? Clearly, all of these questions are of importance. Yet we have very little information to answer any of them.

Third, we need more information concerning the management of overseas R & D laboratories by multinational firms. How great are the costs of co-ordinating an international network of laboratories? What devices seem most useful in reducing these costs? What are the extent of the international differences in salary scales in R & D? How great are the international differences in the productivity of R & D scientists and engineers, in the eyes of the multinational firms that hire them? To what extent and under what circumstances do the R & D laboratories of foreign subsidiaries enter joint research relationships with other local laboratories and participate in programmes with local universities? To what extent have the overseas R & D laboratories of multinational firms hastened the diffusion of various analytical R & D management techniques—for example, PERT—among local laboratories? Only fragmentary and largely anecdotal information seems to be available concerning these questions.

Fourth, more information is needed concerning the extent to which the presence of foreign-owned R & D laboratories benefits the host country. To what extent are local R & D resources, particularly scientists and engineers, used more efficiently by the multinational firm than they would be by local firms? To what extent are they used by multinational firms to attain objectives that are less beneficial to the host country than would be the case if they were used by local firms? To what extent can the multinational firm siphon off the benefits from the local R & D resources it uses? As pointed out in previous sections, although these questions have been the subject of some discussion and controversy, we really know very little about their answers.

NEEDED RESEARCH CONCERNING THE MULTINATIONAL FIRM'S ROLE AS INNOVATOR

With regard to the multinational firm's role as an innovator, it seems to me that studies of the following kinds are needed. First, we need more information concerning the sources of significant innovations in various industries. Similar information is also needed regarding inventions. With regard to innovations, what has been the relative importance of firms of various kinds—large, small, conglomerate, single product, multinational, single-nation, and so on—in particular industries? The author and his co-workers have tried to provide data for a handful of industries—petroleum, steel, coal, pharmaceuticals, chemicals.[73] Attempts should be made to identify the firms that pioneered in the introduction of important new processes and products in other industries. Such information is needed if we are to obtain a better understanding of the factors and conditions conducive to innovation and invention and the relative efficiency and creativity of various kinds of organisations.

Second, we need to know much more about the costs of technological innovation in various industries. A number of recent studies have focused attention on 'technological thresholds'—i.e. minimum sizes of firm—that must be achieved before a firm can be a successful innovator. For example, in the electrical equipment industry, Freeman has presented evidence indicating that these thresholds are very high.[74] It seems obvious that they are lower in many other industries, but we know little about their size or rates of change. According to Pavitt's recent OECD report, 'few generalisations can be made about the thresholds necessary for effective industrial innovation'.[75] In considerable part this is because we have so little data concerning the costs of innovation in various industries. Clearly, such costs are greatly in excess of R & D costs alone, but beyond this, little is really known. This question is important in connection with the multinational firm, since one reason why firms may become multinational is that domestic markets alone may be too small to support an innovation.

Third, studies are needed concerning the conditions and mechanisms leading to the application of basic science and its translation into new products and processes. Also, studies are needed of the conditions that promote or thwart the rapid conversion of an invention into an innovation, given that market and technical factors make such a conversion socially desirable. According to OECD studies, American firms seem to be more adept at applying basic science and converting inventions into innovations than are European firms.[76] This factor seems to be an important part of the advantage that American multinational firms have over their European competitors. But what are the reasons for the superiority, if indeed it exists? A number of studies have been directed to this question, but their authors would be the first to say that they have only scratched the surface.

Fourth, more study is needed of the optimal extent and pattern of international specialisation with respect to technology. Most countries cannot hope to have strong capabilities for technological change in most areas of technology, because of their limited R & D resources. To what extent should these countries specialise in particular areas of science and technology? What determines the particular areas that a country should specialise in? As Pavitt, Quinn, and others have pointed out, a certain amount of specialisation seems essential, even for a big country. But the optimal strategy—for a single country or for broader groups— has not been studied in any real depth. It is, of course, a much more difficult problem than the relatively simple, static problem regarding specialisation and trade with respect to goods. Obviously, it involves a great deal more than the activities of the multinational firm. This question is of fundamental importance, and it deserves much more attention than it has received.[77]

In conclusion, it might be noted that the importance of obtaining a more adequate understanding of the technological activities of the multinational firm has been emphasised recently by the OECD's group on New Concepts of Science Policy. Recognising the important role of the multinational firm, the OECD group recommends strongly that an intensive study be made 'of multinational firms in relation to their research programmes, national science policies, and their effects on the total course of innovation'.[78] It is hoped that this recommendation will be accepted and acted on, since we know much less than we should about the scientific and technological activities of the multinational firm.

References

[1] This paper was written while the author was a Fellow at the Center for Advanced Study in the Behavioral Sciences at Stanford, California. Much

of the research underlying this paper was supported by grants to him from the National Science Foundation. Parts of two sections of this paper—those on the international diffusion of technology and American fears of the multinational firm—were included in a speech given at the 1973 annual meeting of the Industrial Research Institute. The speech appeared in *Research Management*, January, 1974.

2 For excellent general discussions of the multinational firm, see Kindleberger (1969a), Vernon (1971a), Dunning (1970a, 1971), Rolfe (1969), and Behrman (1970).

3 No attempt is made to summarise, or comment on, other aspects of the economics of technological change. However, the references provided in subsequent footnotes provide discussions of other important aspects of the subject.

4 For some of the case studies, see National Bureau of Economic Research (1962). For some of the studies of individual laboratories, see Mansfield (1968). For some studies of patent statistics, see Schmookler (1966).

5 In addition, the rate of technological change in an industry is affected by the quantity of resources devoted by other industries to the improvement of capital goods and other inputs it uses. Also, it is affected by 'spill-over' from other industries, the industry's market structure, the legal arrangements under which it operates, the attitudes toward technological change of management, workers, and the public, and many other factors. Finally, there is a large stochastic element: many inventions occur largely by chance. See Mansfield (1968).

6 Arrow (1962) and Hollander (1965).

7 For descriptions of some of these studies, see Mansfield (1968b), Nelson, *et al.*, (1967), and Mansfield *et al.* (1971).

8 For the RAND studies, see Marschak *et al.* (1967). For studies of risks in civilian R & D, see Mansfield *et al.* (1971).

9 For a discussion of these studies and techniques, see Mansfield (1968a).

10 For data concerning the two parts of this process, see Lynn (1966). For an analysis of the cost and time involved in the various stages of the second part, see Mansfield *et al.* (1971).

11 See Myers & Marquis (1969) and National Science Foundation (1967). Also, the National Science Foundation's *TRACES* study and the Defense Department's *Project Hindsight*.

12 Freeman (1971) and Mansfield, *et al.* (1971).

14 See Price & Bass (1969), Tannenbaum, *et al.* (1966), and Brooks, *et al.* (1967).

15 For discussions of the difficulties in carrying out radical innovations in big firms, see Schon (1967) and Pavitt (1971). For evidence concerning the effects of organisational factors on a firm's innovativeness, see Burns & Stalker (1966).

16 See Mansfield (1971). The author is referring here to the diffusion process within the United States. For discussion of the changes over time in the rate of international diffusion, see Gaps in Technology section.

17 For an excellent early study of the diffusion process, see Griliches (1957). For the basic models referred to in the text, see E. Mansfield (1961). For the results for other countries, see Hsia (1971) and Nasbeth (1971). Studies of a number of other industries in the United States are being carried out by Husic and Romeo in their doctoral dissertations, which are being directed by the author.

18 Mansfield (1971). The reasons why big firms would be expected to be quicker to begin using new techniques are spelled out in Mansfield (1968b).

[19] *Ibid*. For the international data, see Ray (1969).

[20] See Rogers (1962); Bohlew *et al*. (1961); Katz (1961).

[21] See Mansfield (1968a).

[22] For a brief discussion of the reasons for 'multinationality', see Vernon (1970).

[23] See Quinn (1969), Baldwin (1970), and Wortzel (1971).

[24] Pavitt (1970).

[25] Denison (1967).

[26] Vernon (1966) and Hufbauer (1966). Also, see Keesing (1967).

[27] Nelson (1971).

[28] Organisation for Economic Co-operation and Development (1968). Also, separate studies were published for electronic components, electronic computers, pharmaceuticals, non-ferrous metals, scientific instruments and plastics.

[29] For further description and discussion of these data, see OECD (1970). Also see 'Knowhow Jumps the Language Barrier', *Business Week*, 19 December 1970. The OECD report indicates that in 1964 the United States received about \$550 m from other countries for patents, licences, and technological knowhow, exclusive of management fees and service charges.

With regard to the results concerning the chemical industry, it is interesting to note that these results agree with the opinions of other observers. See Layton (1969).

[30] OECD (1970), pp. 262–3.

[31] Tilton (1971)

[32] OECD (1968a), p. 115.

[33] Baranson (1966). Also, see the reference cited, and the discussion by Hymer and Johnson. In addition, see Baranson (1969) and Svennilson (1964).

[34] See Pavitt (1970) and Freeman's comments on his paper.

[35] For example, see Peccei's paper (1967).

[36] Cooper (1971) and OECD (1970), pp. 259 and 262.

[37] See Dunning (1970b) and Behrman (1970).

[38] See Baranson (1970) and Wells (1969).

[39] *Ibid*.

[40] Pavitt (1970).

[41] Stobaugh (1970); United Nations Institute for Training and Research (1971); and 'Where in the World Should We Put that Plant?', *Harvard Business Review*, January–February 1969.

[42] For a good summary of the evidence, see Scherer (1970), Chapter 15. The figure in the second sentence of the paragraph comes from NSF data, cited by Scherer on p. 358.

[42] US Department of Commerce, US Direct Investments Abroad, 1966, Part II: Investment Position, Financial and Operating Data, Group 2: Preliminary Report on Foreign Affiliates of US Manufacturing Industries. The author is indebted to Norman Friedman of the National Science Foundation for making him aware of these figures, and for obtaining information concerning the nature of these data.

[44] According to a 1963 report of the Stanford Research Institute, this is one of the most important reasons for establishing R & D labs abroad. See the section on Research Concerning Multinational Firm's Role. Also see Papo (1971).

[45] Potter (1971).

46 See Papo (1971), Hanson & van Rumker (1971), the paper by Groo (1967), and Maisonrouge (1971).

47 *Ibid.*

48 See Mansfield (1968) and Mansfield *et al.* (1971).

49 See Mansfield *et al.* (1971); and US Department of Commerce, (1967).

50 For the sources of Table 6, see the references in note 49, as well as Husic's work on his doctoral dissertation at the University of Pennsylvania. To find out whether, at the time when the innovation occurred, the innovator had any foreign operations, we consulted *Moody's Industrials*. Note that a firm was regarded as having foreign operations if it was owned by a firm with foreign operations. In six out of 79 innovations, we could not determine whether the firm had any foreign operations. Thus, these innovations had to be omitted.

For Vernon's data, see Vernon (1972a), pp. 14–15. Note that he only includes firms as multinational if they are on *Fortune's* list of 500, and if they have manufacturing subsidiaries in six or more countries. Clearly, the percentages he gives are lower than the percentage of sales accounted for by firms with productive facilities outside the United States, the criterion underlying Table 6.

51 Freeman (1965).

52 Pavitt (1970).

53 Quinn (1969).

54 Dunning (1970a), Chapter 8.

55 Dunning (1966). Also, see Brash (1966) and Safarian (1966).

56 Peck (1968).

57 *Canadian Research Expenditure*, submitted to the Royal Commission on Canada's Economic Prospects, Ottawa, 8 March 1956.

58 Pavitt (1970) and Quinn (1969).

50 Of course, the crucial importance of control has been stressed elsewhere. In particular, see Vernon (1971a) and Kindleberger (1969).

60 See my testimony before the Subcommittee on Science, Research, and Development of the House of Representatives, 13 April 1972. Note that we are concerned in this section with only one kind of American fear regarding the multinational firm. In addition, there are others based on antitrust, balance of payments, and other considerations. See Kindleberger (1969a).

61 See the testimony by Biemiller before the Subcommittee on Science, Research, and Development of the House of Representatives, 28 July 1971.

62 *Ibid.*

63 Cooper (1971), p. 16.

64 *Ibid.*

65 The figure for chemical processes comes from our study cited in note 50. The figure for pharmaceuticals comes from OECD (1969).

66 This is not to imply that studies of the multinational firm are more badly needed than studies of some other aspects of technological change. The activities of the multinational corporation are only one of a number of areas that badly need further study. For other areas that, in my opinion, need further study, see Mansfield (1972).

67 See Aharoni (1966).

68 Baranson (1967) and Hall & Johnson (1970).

69 Dunning (1970a), pp. 336–7. Also see Brash (1966).

70 *Ibid.*, Chapter 9.

71 Johnson (1970). Also, more information is needed concerning the effects of the multinational firm on competition. For example, see Hymer (1970).

72 See Cooper (1968), Maddison (1965) and Freeman *et al.* (1971), for discussion of some of the issues involved. Also, see Baranson (1967), and the discussion of his 1970 paper.

73 See note 48.

74 Freeman (1971). Freeman defines the threshold as the minimum R & D expenditure per year, rather than the minimum size of firm. Clearly both measures are useful.

74 Pavitt (1971).

76 OECD (1968).

77 For example, see Pavitt (1971) for some discussion of this question.

78 OECD (1971), p. 101.

Chapter 7

THE THEORY OF INTERNATIONAL TRADE

W. M. Corden

The purpose of this paper is to consider the implications of the multinational enterprise for international trade theory. The emphasis is constructive. The aim is to show that international trade theory can be adapted to analyse the location decisions of multinational firms and their welfare implications for host countries. But one should not understate the difficulties which the multinational enterprises create for a rather simple-minded body of theory.

WHAT IS TRADE THEORY?

The first problem is to define what one means by international trade theory for the purpose of the present discussion.

It is not difficult to list the main questions, positive and normative, with which trade theory is concerned. Why do countries export and import the sorts of products they do and how are these trade flows related to the domestic characteristics of a country? How does trade affect domestic factor prices? What are the effects of trade interventions, such as tariffs, on output and demand patterns and on factor allocations and factor prices? What are the gains from trade (a closed economy compared with free trade)? What are valid arguments for trade intervention, and what are the principles of optimal trade intervention?

One could define trade theory narrowly to include only the central body of rigorous general equilibrium theory which is devoted to answering these questions. This central body of theory—to be called the 'orthodox theory' here—is usually (though not necessarily) presented geometrically in terms of two goods, and has the characteristic that each part fits explicitly into the main theoretical system and, hence, is clearly related to every other part. It is hardly necessary to survey or expound it since so many surveys and expositions are available.[1] Here it will only be observed that while there is some problem in precisely delimiting trade theory so defined, it is this body of theory which students are systematically taught and which is very influential. But the definition is not meant to be so narrow that it includes only the Heckscher–Ohlin–Samuelson (H–O–S) theory. Thus James Meade (1952) expounded orthodox theory in its pre-H–O–S phase. This body of theory takes some account of international capital movements, but certainly not of the multinational enterprise. We will return to this point shortly.

Alternatively, one could include in trade theory the whole vast literature which is concerned in one way or another with answering the questions listed above. One would include, then, a peripheral literature that has not been integrated in the orthodox theory. In this peripheral literature there are many articles and some books that refer extensively to international capital movements and some that refer specifically to the international movement of technology and management and to the multinational firm. Some discuss these matters in relation to trade, notably articles and books by Posner (1961), Hufbauer (1965a), Vernon (1966, 1971a) and (Dunning 1970a, 1973b). Perhaps the most systematic model seeking to explain trade and investment flows together, and giving a prominent role to the multinational enterprise, is the celebrated article by Vernon (1966).

This chapter is concerned only with the orthodox theory. This does not mean that the peripheral literature is not important. But most of the papers concerned have already been referred to by other contributors in this volume. Furthermore, they do not easily lend themselves to summarising, simplicity of argument being generally sacrificed to the search for realism.[2]

In addition, the paper is concerned only with *real* or *pure* trade theory. It will always be assumed that balance of payments equilibrium is maintained by appropriate exchange rate adjustments, and internal balance by appropriate monetary and fiscal policies. The effects of the multinational enterprise on a country's balance of payments, on the appropriateness of exchange rate variations, and on the ability of monetary policy to regulate the internal economy are of course also of great interest. But these are large topics that will not be discussed here.

CHARACTERISTICS OF TRADE THEORY

Let us now look at five aspects of trade theory which are likely to be relevant if one wishes to allow for the multinational enterprise.

CAPITAL MOVEMENTS

The multinational enterprise is a conduit of international capital movements. It is, of course, much more than this, but this is certainly one of its aspects. Therefore one needs to know whether trade theory takes some account of such movements.

The answer is that the very simplest body of theory—the *core* theory—does not. It assumes that each country has a given stock of factors of production. This does not mean that all the conclusions obtained from this simple theory turn out to be wrong when capital movements are allowed for. More important, at a more complex level, capital movements have been allowed for, and there is in fact an extensive literature within the broad framework of orthodox trade theory that takes into account capital movements both from a positive and a normative point of view. Trade theorists would, indeed, have been excessively naive if they had failed to allow for such an obvious feature of the world. This literature will be summarised in the next section.

TRANSFER OF KNOWLEDGE

A crucial role of the multinational enterprise is to transfer knowledge or technology—including managerial know-how—between countries. Some writers, notably Johnson (1970a), regard this as its main role. Orthodox theory has not explicitly incorporated such knowledge transfers.

Sometimes theorists have assumed that production functions for any given product are the same in all countries. This is one of the simplifying assumptions of the H–O–S model at its basic level, and is one of the assumptions required if trade is to equalise factor prices. It implies that knowledge is, in fact, costlessly and perfectly mobile between countries, but does not concern itself with the *process* of knowledge transfer. In any case, this assumption cannot be regarded as a central assumption of orthodox theory. It can be, and has been, removed within the framework of the H–O–S model, since various implications of production functions differing between countries have been explored (for example in Jones, 1970). Furthermore the H–O–S model is not the whole of orthodox trade theory.

More generally, orthodox theory assumes only that there are given production functions for each product in each country. These may differ between countries, and among the causes of international trade and the sources of the gains from trade are international differences in production functions. The original

Ricardian exposition of comparative costs can be interpreted in these terms. Furthermore, production functions may be altered by exogenously-determined technical progress, and the trade theory literature has exhaustively explored the implications of various types of bias in such technical progress on countries' production structures and their terms of trade. But the important point here is that technical progress is always conceived of as exogenous to each country, with no necessary connection between progress in one country and another.

CONNECTIONS BETWEEN FIRMS

The multinational enterprise generally involves some kind of international integration so that a good deal of international trade is intrafirm trade. This has numerous implications, to some of which we shall refer below. The main point is that the apparent international trading partners may not be independent of each other. The transfer prices they record for international transactions may not be 'arm's-length' market prices. Each partner may not be concerned with maximising his own profits; rather, the interest may be in maximising joint profits.

None of this is provided for by orthodox trade theory. It is always assumed that the trading firms in one country are entirely distinct from the trading firms in another country or, if there are any connections, these play no role in the analysis.

MONOPOLY AND OLIGOPOLY

It is generally said that the multinational firms compete in international markets as oligopolists. Furthermore, in many countries they are so large that they are also monopsonistic buyers of factors or of produced inputs.

General equilibrium trade theory does not allow for oligopoly or monopoly. There are, of course, piecemeal analyses of monopolistic situations, notably in connection with dumping, but these are all partial equilibrium. An important point (stressed by Johnson, 1967) is that orthodox trade theory is essentially general equilibrium, and no one—whether in or out of trade theory—has yet succeeded in adequately incorporating monopolistic or oligopolistic considerations in a general equilibrium framework. The result is that orthodox trade theory assumes perfect competition. Through the theory of the optimum tariff, it takes into account the possibility that a nation can exploit its monopoly or monopsony power in international trade; but this theory assumes that the nation will only do so if governments intervene, private enterprise being perfectly competitive.

On the face of it, the perfect competition assumption seems a crippling limitation. Yet perhaps it is not so serious. It is not necessary to have all the conditions of perfect competition for a situation to exist where, taking a longer period into account, firms cannot significantly affect the prices of the goods they sell or the factors they buy—and this is the crucial implication of the perfect competition assumption. Sometimes, an oligopolistic situation leads to much the same result. Furthermore, the assumption does not appear to be essential to some of the results of orthodox trade theory. Finally, it is sometimes possible to modify orthodox theory in a partial equilibrium way to allow for monopoly in particular markets. All of this does not, of course, resolve the problems completely.

Closely connected with the problem of monopoly is that of economies of scale. These are clearly very important in the case of the multinational corporation. Economies of scale have been discussed in trade theory over a long period, especially in connection with the infant-industry argument for protection. But internal economies of scale are not compatible with perfect competition, so that, following the method of Marshall, orthodox trade theory has allowed for economies of scale by assuming them to be external to firms and internal to the industry. There is an intricate literature exploring the implications of scale economies, so defined (Kemp, 1969, Chapter 8). It is probable that the conclusions derived from it would still be roughly applicable if the scale economies were internal to firms—as is more realistic—but this is not certain.

WHOSE WELFARE IS BEING MAXIMISED?

The interests of the multinational enterprise may not coincide with the interests of the populations of the host countries in which it operates or with the interests of large sections of the population in its own home country. If one is concerned with normative questions, one cannot just focus on the maximisation of gross national product produced within the geographical boundaries of a particular country nor on the total income received by the population as a whole. In the case of the host country one must, at the minimum, distinguish income received by the local population from income earned and retained after tax by the foreign enterprises, and one must really go further and distinguish the interests of different sections of the community. The latter distinction must also be made in the case of the home country.

Some simple theorems in orthodox trade theory focus on Pareto-efficiency, hence ignoring income distribution. This applies, for example, to the simple but influential gains-from-trade argument. It is also true of the literature on optimal trade intervention in the presence of domestic distortions, which argues that in general divergences between social and private costs or benefits which are domestic in nature should be dealt with by domestic and not trade interventions. Indeed it is true of a large body of the literature which assumes that government policy brings about costlessly a desired income distribution. Nevertheless, trade theory cannot really be accused of ignoring the income distribution effects of trade policies. The Stolper–Samuelson (1941) theorem shows how factor prices and hence income distribution are affected by trade and trade restrictions within the context of the H–O–S model. Meade (1955) has developed a comprehensive approach for assessing trade policies while taking into account income distribution effects by attaching 'distributional weights' to the various effects of a particular policy.

CAPITAL MOVEMENTS IN INTERNATIONAL TRADE THEORY

Let us now look, in somewhat more detail, at the role that international trade theory has given to international capital movements. This is certainly relevant for studying the implications of the multinational enterprise for trade theory. First of all, multinational enterprises have increased international capital mobility. It is true that sometimes a corporation may establish a subsidiary in a particular country and draw mainly on domestic capital. Nevertheless it always has the potentiality of importing capital and presumably finds domestic capital cheaper in such cases. Second, the transfer of technology and managerial know-how which is so central to the purpose of the multinational corporation is essentially the transfer of a form of capital—human capital—and hence the theory of international capital movements should be applicable in analysing it.

The problem is how international capital movements and international trade are related. We must distinguish positive from normative theory here.

POSITIVE THEORY

One approach has been to study the effects of a given factor movement from one country to another, considering the effects on the terms of trade and on factor prices, and taking both supply and demand repercussions into account (Meade, 1955, Chapter 27). One can also draw out of these models rather obvious effects on trade flows. If capital flows from A to B, production in the former will fall and the latter rise; and if the comparative advantage pattern is given, there will be a relative rise in output and fall in the price of the product that is mainly produced in B, at least if one focuses only on the supply side. If owners of the transferred capital do not move out of country A, there will be an increase of exports from B to A, necessary to transfer the returns on the capital. In addition there will be demand effects, which can be quite complex. If demand patterns of people in A and B are identical but the capital movement raises aggregate world income, the relative price of the income-elastic good will tend to rise on that account, and so the terms of trade of the country that exports that product will tend to improve.

The other approach is more interesting. Capital is assumed to move internationally in response to relative returns, the tendency being for capital movements to equalise the returns to capital in different countries. There is an extensive literature, mainly continental European, which has explored the nature and consequences of such induced capital movements. This has been surveyed in Caves (1960, Chapter 5). But as early as 1906, Pigou (1935) made the further and crucial point which has become a central proposition of the Heckscher–Ohlin model that factor movements are, at least to some extent, a substitute for trade, and vice versa. Ohlin (1933) developed this theme at length. The point is, by now, most familiar. A country relatively well-endowed with capital (and which, in isolation, would thus have low returns to capital) will tend both to export capital-intensive goods and to export capital. Both trade and factor movement will raise the returns to capital in that country and tend to bring closer together its factor prices and the factor prices in the country that is well-endowed with labour, which will be exporting labour-intensive goods and importing capital. Ohlin stressed that trade on its own would only *tend* to equalise factor prices; because of transport costs and differences in production functions, trade and factor movements are not perfect substitutes.

Modern theorists have built the H–O–S model upon Ohlin's work. Mundell (1957) has explored the special case where trade and factor movements are perfect substitutes. There are no transport costs, production functions for each good are identical in the two countries, and the same product is relatively labour- or capital-intensive in each country (no factor reversals), so that free trade on its own will completely equalise factor prices. This extreme model leads him to various extreme results: starting with free trade, the imposition of a tariff, however small, will create factor price differences which will then be eliminated by a capital movement that will restore factor price equalisation and equalise commodity prices. With commodity prices equalised by the capital movement, all trade will cease. If the tariff is then removed, there will still be no inducement for any trade, so a temporary tariff has become prohibitive of trade. The virtue of Mundell's analysis is to bring out the logic of an extreme model. Its danger is that such a fantastic result makes the model look ridiculous. In fact, as soon as one introduces differences in production functions between countries or transport costs, the extreme result disappears.

A number of authors, notably Kemp (1969, Chapter 9), Jones (1970) and Chipman (1971), have recently explored this general type of model further. They have two products, two countries and two factors, labour being immobile in each country and capital perfectly mobile, so that its reward is equalised between countries. There are no transport costs, but they allow technology to be different in the two countries. The latter assumption is necessary because otherwise, in the absence of factor reversals, they would simply have the Mundell (1957) model. They have explored such questions as whether in either or both countries production would be specialised in one product, and how changes in demand would affect capital movements and also commodity and factor prices.

In general, all things seem possible, and the refinements of these sophisticated articles cannot be spelt out here. But two results are worth noting. Chipman has shown that over a range a shift in demand in either country will lead to a movement of capital between countries rather than to a change in relative commodity or factor prices. Jones has explored the important question of which country will have a comparative advantage in which good. When capital is perfectly mobile, one can no longer apply the simple H–O–S factor-endowment approach, arguing that the country that is relatively well endowed with capital must export the capital-intensive good. For it may export its capital instead, to the point where it ceases to be relatively well endowed with capital. If country A is more efficient (has a more favourable production function) in product I compared with country B, and if either the two countries are equally efficient in the case of product II, or if country B is more efficient in producing that product, one would expect that A would export I and B would export II (unless demand effects were offsetting). But Jones has brought out another consideration. Suppose that country A is more efficient to the same extent in both products compared with country B. Capital will then tend to flow to country A to exploit this efficient environment, so that the capital–labour ratio finally will be higher in A than in B. Thus the more efficient country, A, will export the capital-intensive product and import the labour-intensive one. This will be so even if initially, before any capital movements are allowed, country B is the country relatively well endowed with capital. Of course, if the higher efficiency of country A is itself the fruits of investment in human capital, which is assumed here to be immobile, or imperfectly mobile, we must say that while B may be initially well endowed with potentially mobile capital, country A is well endowed with immobile (human) capital.

The models of Kemp, Chipman and Jones operate within the traditional framework by having only two factors and two products, but at least they allow for different production functions between countries. Furthermore, it would be possible to allow for economies of scale, and perhaps additional immobile factors could also be added without too much difficulty. One could also allow for factor reversals, in which case trade might widen the wedges between factor prices internationally and so actually stimulate capital movements. A general framework of analysis which lends itself to the exploration of many cases and to the addition of various complications is certainly available. It is to be hoped that theorists will devote themselves to those elaborations that are likely to be of some practical relevance. For this purpose complete rigour may sometimes have to be foregone.

NORMATIVE THEORY

The normative theory of international capital movements is a very recent development, and its integration with the normative theory of trade even more recent. At a rigorous level, the theory really began with the well-known article by McDougall (1960a), who used simple neo-classical methods to show in which circumstances a capital-receiving country would gain or lose from a capital inflow. The main point that emerged was the crucial role of taxation: a gain is likely when, as is usual, the profits are taxed by the government of the capital-receiving country, and provided this is not offset by subsidies.

Subsequently Kemp (1962b) extended this analysis by applying the standard optimum tariff argument to capital imports and exports. From a national point of view, and assuming no retaliation, a capital-importing country may be able to exploit its monopsony power or a capital-exporting country its monopoly power by imposing a tax on the import or export of capital, respectively. These will improve the terms of foreign borrowing or lending, and along familiar lines derived from elementary monopoly theory there will be an optimum rate of tax which will depend on the foreign capital supply or demand elasticities. The object of this approach, it must be stressed, is not to maximise tax revenue but rather to arrive at a Pareto-efficient position from a national point of view.

Recently this theory of the optimum tax on capital inflow or outflow has been integrated with the theory of the optimum tariff by Kemp (1966), Jones (1967) and Gehrels (1971). The following exposition assumes that the concern is with a single country's national welfare, no foreign retaliation, and that the country can affect both its terms of trade and its terms of foreign borrowing or lending. We shall refer to the case of a capital importer, though the analysis is fully applicable to capital-exporting countries. The relevant literature is quite intricate, and it is only possible to sketch out some of the main results and arguments here. One must distinguish the first-best policy from second-best policies. The first-best policy is to use two instruments of policy—the tariff (or export tax) and the tax on the import of capital; essentially the first is directed to optimally improving the terms of trade and the second to improving the terms of borrowing. In addition, there are two second-best situations that have been considered: the only instrument of policy might be the tariff (or export tax), or alternatively the only policy instrument might be the tax on capital imports.

Let us begin with the first-best situation. The complication here is that a tariff may not only affect the terms of trade but may also affect the terms of borrowing. What is relevant here is the effect that the tariff has on the foreign capital supply curve facing the country. Suppose that the foreign country (which is the capital-exporting country) exports its capital-intensive product. This, of course, would be so if the simple assumptions of the H–O–S model applied. A tariff by the home country will then reduce the foreign country's exports, hence will lower the price of capital there, and thus will shift its capital-export supply

G

curve downwards, so improving the home country's terms of borrowing. In this case a tariff has more than just improved the home country's terms of trade; it has also improved its terms of borrowing. Similarly, a tax on capital imports would not only improve the home country's terms of borrowing but would also improve its terms of trade. It is quite useful to draw attention to these indirect repercussions, and the authors referred to show that the optimal rates of tariff and tax will be higher than otherwise because of them. In the anti-Heckscher–Ohlin case, where the capital-exporting country exports its labour-intensive product, the optimal rates of tariff and tax will be lower than otherwise, and indeed one of them could be negative.

Next consider the second-best cases. Since the two cases of a tariff as the only instrument of policy and the tax on the import of capital as the only instrument are completely symmetrical, we need only consider one case, and shall take the case where the only policy variable available is the tariff. One could assume more realistically that there is some given rate of tax on profits of capital inflow, but that it cannot be changed, and is below the optimum. To simplify, let us ignore the foreign repercussion, supposing that the foreign capital supply curve is not affected by a tariff.

We can suppose that, initially, a tariff is imposed which improves the terms of trade optimally. Next we must ask whether the tariff encourages or discourages capital inflow. If the import-competing product is capital-intensive and the exportable labour-intensive, a tariff will raise the return to capital and so encourage capital inflow. This is undesirable. The first-best way of bringing about the appropriate restriction of capital inflow would be through the optimal tax on capital inflow, but in the absence of such a tax the tariff should then be lower than otherwise, the aim being to improve rather than worsen the terms of foreign borrowing. The extent to which the second-best optimum tariff is below the level it would be in the absence of any effect on capital inflow represents the role of the tariff in taking the place of the first-best optimum capital tax. Essentially the tariff is reduced in order to squeeze foreign capital. It is even possible that the second-best optimum tariff is negative in such a case. There is a lot more to be drawn out of these models, even though their ingredients are very simple. One could introduce the foreign repercussion into the second-best case, and one could play through the case where the tax on capital inflow or outflow is the only policy instrument.

A more comprehensive but less rigorous analysis of the relationship between optimum trade intervention and foreign investment has been provided in Corden (1967). The simple assumptions of the H–O–S model are dropped. Capital is assumed to be 'sector-specific', externalities are allowed for, as well as monopoly and distorting taxes on domestic capital. The general argument is that tariffs can act as second-best taxes or subsidies on foreign capital. Furthermore, if there is a given non-optimal tariff system the gains or losses from foreign investment will be affected. Foreign capital that is attracted by tariffs may inflict a loss on the economy when it might have yielded a gain if it had come without protection.

This completes a brief review of how trade theorists have taken into account capital movements. It is, of course, not complete. While the literature on capital movements is very old, especially in continental Europe, the emphasis on the relationship with trade really stems from Ohlin's great work. Much formal theory has indeed assumed that factors are immobile between countries, but it can no longer be said that orthodox international trade theory in general neglects capital movements.

THE LOCATION DECISIONS OF MULTINATIONAL ENTERPRISES

Can one use the basic methods and concepts of trade theory to set out a framework for analysing the location decisions of multi-national corporations? A general approach will be sketched out here. It will be assumed that the corporations aim to maximise profits. From the point of view of the corporations the analysis is normative but from the point of view of individual countries it is positive. Only those considerations which trade theory can handle easily will be introduced; this means that we must ignore peculiarly oligopolistic behaviour which is discussed in the stimulating paper by Vernon (see Chapter 4). The present discussion and that of Vernon might be regarded as complementary. Essentially we are concerned with what determines costs of production and marketing in different locations, including the costs of bringing products to particular markets. When we concern ourselves with the international location of production we are also concerned, as a by-product, with the international pattern of trade. Taking demands in various countries as given (which may not always be a justified assumption), flows of exports and imports fall naturally out of the production location decisions.

We consider a firm which produces a number of different

products that it expects to sell in the world's markets. In each market it faces demand curves which take into account the state of competition there, or its absence. The corporation can produce in any country. We make eight assumptions, and then remove all but the first.

(1) In each country the corporation faces production functions for each of its products which allow for inputs of at least three factors. The factors are capital, knowledge and the immobile factor(s), which we can call labour. Since knowledge is a special type of capital, one could say, alternatively, that there are two types of mobile capital, namely conventional capital which finances waiting and physical capital-goods, and human capital, taking the form of knowledge.

(2) Capital and knowledge are perfectly mobile internationally within the corporation.

(3) The production functions and the factor endowments facing the corporation do not change over time.

(4) There are constant returns to scale in all production functions.

(5) Government restrictions and taxes, such as tariffs and profit taxes, are absent, or, at least, do not affect the corporation's location decisions.

(6) There are no transport costs.

(7) Production functions for any given product in all locations are identical.

(8) In each location, there is only one immobile factor, namely labour, which is also identical between countries.

These assumptions yield a Mundell-type result. The returns to capital and knowledge will be equalised throughout the corporation's empire, and given the constant returns to scale assumption, this will also equalise the marginal products of labour. The tendency will then be for costs of production to be the same in all locations. It will not matter where any product is produced. Trade could, though need not, cease; it will be a matter of indifference.

Now remove assumption (8). Let there be at least two immobile factors, say skilled and unskilled labour, or alternatively labour and land, and let the endowment ratios vary between countries, some countries being relatively well endowed with skilled and some with unskilled labour. Immediately, we are back in the familiar H–O–S world. Skilled-labour-intensive products will be produced in the countries relatively well endowed with skilled labour and unskilled-labour-intensive products in countries relatively well endowed with unskilled labour. Note that only the relative intensities of the *immobile* factors are relevant. It does not matter at this stage whether a product is capital- or knowledge-intensive.

Now remove assumption (7) and allow production functions to differ. It must be remembered that knowledge is mobile so production functions must differ for other reasons. Interpreting the concept 'production function' broadly, the physical infrastructure provided by governments, or political conditions, including security, may differ. Furthermore, there may be some types of knowledge that are immobile and can be treated as influencing production functions. In any case, we now obtain further familiar guides to locations decisions with obvious consequences. The Jones point is relevant here: countries which are generally more efficient, not just in some but in most or all products, will attract more of the mobile factors, and hence will tend to produce and export the products intensive in these mobile factors. This appears to be confirmed by casual observation.

Now remove assumption (6) and allow for transport costs. If transport costs were very high there would be no trade and the corporation would have to satisfy demand in each country from local production. In the absence of such an extreme situation one can only say that there will be a tendency for production to be near markets. If tastes differ between countries the location decisions will be influenced by these differences; furthermore, production will tend to take place in the large markets. Of course, all this may be over-ridden by significant cost differences, owing to different factor endowments or production functions.

Now remove assumption (5). Tariffs and import restrictions as well as export taxes will have the same effects as transport costs, encouraging import substitution rather than exporting, and so being trade-restricting. International trade theory has certainly laboured this effect. Furthermore, the location decisions may be affected by differences in taxation. The general point is well known, but the subject of differential taxation is too large and complex to be discussed here.

Now remove assumption (4) and allow for increasing returns to scale. If we had not removed assumptions (5) to (8) the corporation would then locate each product in one country only. If the increasing returns are to some extent external to its various products though internal to the corporation, and if locational proximity is required for the external effects to be reaped, then the corporation will locate all its activities in one country only. Once we allow for different production functions and different immobile-factor endowment ratios, cost curves will differ between countries for each product and the considerations discussed earlier will come back into the story. Because of increasing returns, the tendency will be to avoid locating production of any product in more than one or a few locations.

When we allow for transport costs and trade restrictions, the sizes of domestic markets for various products will become relevant. In the absence of economies of scale, one could say that, because of transport costs, countries will tend to produce for home markets, and so their production patterns will be biased towards goods for which there is a domestic demand, up to the point where domestic demand is satisfied; the tendency will be for trade to be restricted. But when there are economies of scale, transport costs will have a further effect: they will give countries with large domestic markets for particular products a comparative advantage in these goods if the latter are economy-of-scale intensive, and will cause them to export these products.

Now remove assumption (3) and allow production functions and factor endowments to change over time. For example, one country's educational system or the extent of its educational effort may change over time, or alternatively it may 'learn-by-doing' more rapidly than other countries so that its endowment of immobile human capital may change: unskilled may turn into skilled labour or the production functions facing the corporation may change. At a theoretical level it may be somewhat arbitrary whether one regards a certain change as increasing the factor endowment or improving the production function. In any case, this will then require the corporation to reallocate its resources.

Finally, remove assumption (2) and allow knowledge (techniques and managerial know-how) to be imperfectly mobile within the corporation. Knowledge may be generated as a form of investment in the corporation's home country and may spread outside at a cost and with lags. Thus over a period of time, knowledge in the outer provinces of the corporate empire improves and so, again, comparative advantage changes. This is one element in the 'product-cycle' approach of Vernon (1966).

The general conclusion is that it is possible to use various bits of analysis derived from trade theory to study the location decisions of multinational corporations and their effects on trade flows. Perhaps the main point is that one must use models which allow for some mobile and some immobile factors, and once one allows for more than one immobile factor or allows production functions to differ between countries one arrives at results generally familiar from trade theory.

MULTINATIONAL ENTERPRISES AND THE THEORY OF TARIFFS

Let us now see how tariff theory may be affected if one takes into account trade by multinational enterprises. We shall look briefly at three familiar arguments for protection or intervention of some kind: the terms of trade argument, the income distribution argument and the antimonopoly argument. Finally, we look at the problem of transfer pricing.

TERMS OF TRADE

The familiar terms of trade argument for tariffs or export taxes rests, among other things, on two assumptions. First, it assumes that while the country has potential monopoly or monopsony power, this is not exploited by private producers or traders. If exports were already controlled by monopolists, there would be no need to induce them to restrict exports so that marginal costs would be equal to marginal revenue of the industry. Second, the concern is with maximising total real income produced in the country (in the potential Pareto sense), normally with no regard to internal distribution effects.

The first assumption is unlikely to be valid when trade is in the hands of multinational enterprises. One might imagine a continuum of possibilities. At one end the exporting and importing firms are quite competitive, extra exports by one firm lowering the profits of other firms, and this effect not being taken into account at all in any one firm's decisions. In that case the usual optimum tariff and export tax formulae apply. At the other end there is a complete monopoly, hence no need for government intervention to induce monopolistic behaviour, and the optimum tariff or export tax is zero. In between there may be some degree of competition and some degree of collusion, and the optimum tariff or export tax will be positive but less than indicated by the usual formulae.

The second assumption is also unlikely to be valid. The concern is likely to be to maximise the real incomes of residents, perhaps excluding those managers of the multinationals who are foreign in origin or permanent residence. If profits tax rates on foreign corporations are given, there are then two considerations to take into account.

First, the greater the profits of the corporations the bigger the revenue gain to the country, the taxpayers or the Treasury of the country, in effect, being shareholders in the corporation. If tariffs increase the profitability of foreign-owned import-competing industries, some part of this benefit will thus be returned to the people or government of the country.

Second, tariffs and export taxes shift real incomes away from factors intensive in export industries towards factors intensive in import-competing industries, and there will be some net redistributive effect even allowing for taxation. The familiar optimum tariff-export tax structure will maximise the combined income of residents and subsidiaries of the corporations, but not the income of residents on their own. We have here, in fact, the second-best problem which we discussed earlier. First-best policy would be to apply the optimum tariff-export tax structure (taking into account the existing degree of monopoly or collusion) and combine this with the optimum structure of taxes on foreign capital. But if taxes on foreign capital are given, being either too low or too high, it may be necessary to vary the tariff-export tax structure so as to squeeze foreign capital appropriately.

INTERNAL INCOME DISTRIBUTION

Let us now consider the income distribution argument for protection. We have already referred to income distribution in our discussion of terms of trade effects; and in order to isolate income distribution considerations, let us now assume that the country concerned is small and cannot affect its terms of trade. But we assume that it can still affect the cost of capital and knowledge that it obtains through the multinational corporations. Suppose it is desired to shift income distribution towards workers in certain import-competing industries, and that foreign corporations operate in these industries. A tariff will have the desired effect of raising the wages of the relevant labour; but it will also shift income distribution towards foreign profits, which is presumably not desired.

We have here the usual complications created when inappropriate instruments are used to pursue particular targets. If it is desired to shift income distribution of residents towards particular types of labour, first-best policy is to raise taxes from the general population in a minimum-distortion way (probably by income tax), and then subsidise or remit taxes to the sections of the population which it is desired to favour. At the same time foreign enterprises should be taxed so as to optimally exploit the country's monopsony power in relation to them, as indicated by the approach discussed earlier. Taxes on trade are second- or third-best methods of bringing about desired income redistribution effects. Not only are they likely to be imprecise in bringing about the desired income distribution effects, but they also create distortions in the production and consumption patterns which could be avoided, or at least reduced, if more direct methods were used.

MONOPOLY AND MARKET STRUCTURE

Next, let us consider the role of tariffs when there is actual or potential monopoly in domestic markets, or at least when the market structure is not perfectly competitive. International trade theory is notoriously inadequate in this area, mainly—as Johnson (1967b) has pointed out—because of its concern with general equilibrium. Hence one cannot really draw on any adequate existing analysis. All that will be done here is to draw attention to a few points.

First of all, consider the question of how tariffs affect market structure. Suppose that a particular product market is supplied by a number of firms, some producing domestically and some producing abroad and selling in the domestic market as well as to their own markets. The product may be differentiated. The number of firms and their behaviour may be influenced by various barriers to entry, and various kinds of oligopolistic behaviour patterns may operate. Given the market as we find it before tariffs, we want to know what effect the injection of a tariff will have primarily on the number of sellers, but also on the intensity of competition between them, determining the extent to which the group will exploit its joint monopoly power. A tariff is a discriminatory tax on producers, taxing only the products of foreign producers not domestic producers. How does such a discriminatory tax affect market structure?

One approach is to focus on the *dominant firm effect*. If the dominant firms are domestic while the smaller firms and potential entrants are foreign, a tariff will increase concentration and monopoly power. On the other hand, if the dominant firms are foreign while the smaller firms and potential entrants are domestic, a tariff will have the opposite effect. The same results could be brought about not by an actual tariff, but by the threat of a tariff designed in the first case to preserve a domestic dominant firm and in the second case to preserve domestic competition and protect small producers.

Now let us introduce foreign investment and the multinational enterprise into this story. The relevant point is that a firm producing abroad and handicapped by a tariff can leap the tariff wall by setting up a domestic production facility. Yet our basic argument is not affected. Suppose there is a foreign dominant supplier, and a tariff is imposed to handicap him, the aim being to increase competition. So he responds by setting up his factories behind the tariff wall. If his original success was based on low costs of production in his own country, the geographic transfer of his production may be a very imperfect substitute for producing in his own country and then exporting; but if his success was based on brand goodwill, connections with distributors, patents and know-how, these can all be carried with him. Nevertheless, any tariff imposes some handicap on him even if he can manage to stay in the market by moving his enterprise, or part of it, geographically. If in the absence of the tariff he chose to produce in his own country and export, then presumably that was more profitable. The tariff forces him to choose a less economic location and to raise his prices or reduce his profits, or both.

Let us now consider another problem. A multinational firm is the only actual and potential foreign supplier of a product and is also the only potential domestic producer. Thus there is complete monopoly. This, of course, is an extreme case but is a simple way of posing an important problem. A tariff is imposed to encourage it to cease exporting the product from overseas and to establish domestic production. How would one analyse the gains or losses to the tariff-imposing country?

In the absence of the tariff, the corporation exports and there is no domestic production. This maximises its profits. The tariff forces it to shift the location of some of its production. It may yield the corporation good profits from its new subsidiary, but its world-wide profits will fall, for otherwise it would have set up in the country without the tariff. The corporation's costs of supplying the market of the tariff-imposing country will have gone up. If this is true of marginal costs, it will then charge a higher price. Hence some of the burden of the tariff will be borne by the company itself, and part will be borne by consumers of the tariff-imposing country. This consumer cost might be described as the gross cost of protection to the country. But there may be gains to set against these, notably profits tax collected from the company. Furthermore, the establishment of its subsidiary will increase the demand for labour in the country and raise the wage-rate. If the effect is more than marginal and if labour is paid its marginal product in alternative uses (and even more so, if it is paid *more* than its marginal social product, as is likely in less developed countries) there will be a further gain on this account. On balance a net gain to the country is thus possible even though consumers will lose.

TRANSFER PRICING

Finally we come to the problem of transfer pricing. When the subsidiary of a multinational firm imports from or exports to another part of the firm, the nominal prices at which goods are transferred may not be equal to true marginal costs or to world market ('arm's-length') prices but may be adjusted so as to minimise tax or tariff payments.

One implication of this is for the calculation of effective protective rates. A subsidiary may import components from another subsidiary, and the transfer prices may deliberately over-price these components so as to shift taxable profits away from the component-importing country which may have the relatively higher tax rates or which may restrict the remittance of profits. The components may even be priced so high that it appears that they cost more than the value of the final product when the latter is valued at world market prices. In this latter case there appears then to be *negative value added* at world prices, the rate of effective protection being infinite (though arithmetically negative) (see Corden, 1971, pp. 50–5). In any case, even if such an extreme result does not come about, an impression is conveyed of very high protection for the activity of producing or assembling the final product. Yet this may not convey a true impression since the calculation is based on component prices that are in excess of the prices that the corporation must be using for its own resource allocation decisions.

It is well known that a vertically-integrated multinational enterprise can use transfer prices to shift profits between countries and so reduce its tax payments, at least if tax rates differ significantly between the various countries in which it operates. It can shift profits away from a country by raising transfer prices on imported components or lower transfer prices on goods that it exports. A country may thus impose a high rate of profits tax, higher than that payable by the corporation in its home country or other bases of operation, and yet the net result may be for the country to lose revenue compared to a situation with a lower profits tax. Where then do tariffs come in?

A firm can reduce the incidence of *ad valorem* tariffs by *under*-valuing imported components. But it is not sufficient to look at the amount of customs revenue that the corporation avoids paying in order to assess its gains from the undervaluation. Recorded profits will be shifted away from the supplying country towards the importing country; and if the profit tax rate is higher in the latter than in the former, there will be a net loss to the corporation on this account, which must be set against the gain from saving tariff payments.

If the aim of the tariff is to protect domestic producers of the components, a government can counter such partial evasion of tariffs by fixing component prices for duty purposes which are closer to market prices, by imposing anti-dumping duties, by converting *ad valorem* into specific tariffs or by replacing tariffs with import quotas. But if the aim is to raise revenue, the tariff-imposing country is actually likely to gain from the understatement of import values induced by an *ad valorem* tariff. Its loss in customs revenue is likely to be more than offset by a gain in profits taxes. This suggests a simple remedy to profits tax evasion through overstatement of import values. Governments should impose tariffs on those imported components believed to be *over*-priced through tax-evasive transfer pricing, and hence encourage the corporation to *under*-price them instead.[3]

THE GAINS AND LOSSES FROM MULTINATIONAL ENTERPRISES AND THE ENCLAVE APPROACH

The discussion so far of normative issues has been piecemeal. Clearly one requires a systematic framework for analysing the effects on economic welfare of multinational corporations. An approach will be sketched out here which makes use of trade theory, which focuses on the interests of the residents of the countries in which the corporations operate, but which involves a departure from the usual approach. The Kemp–Jones–Gehrels theory of optimal trade and capital taxes conceives of a country buying and selling both goods and factors from and to the outside world; it concerns itself only with goods and factors that pass across the country's borders, but it does not allow for the multinational corporation as an agency which is apparently both a foreign supplier and buyer and a domestic supplier and buyer of these goods and factors. Furthermore, it does not integrate into the analysis the numerous possible divergences between private and social costs and benefits—that is, *domestic distortions* of all kinds. The *enclave approach* can perhaps deal with these matters more easily.[5]

We can think of the multinational enterprise as an enclave cutting across national boundaries that is rather like an independent country. This enclave (*a*) buys and sells factors, (*b*) buys and sells goods, (*c*) makes and receives transfers, and (*d*) creates various external effects. We are interested in the effects of these four types of operations on Our Country—which we should think of as any country in which the corporation operates other than its home country. There will be *linkages* with Our Country, namely (*a*) the corporation raises some capital locally and employs local workers, (*b*) it buys raw materials locally and sells some of its final products to local consumers, (*c*) it pays taxes to the local Ministry of Finance, and possibly also receives some subsidies, and (*d*) it creates a variety of external effects—that is, effects that by-pass the market—for example through labour and managerial training, and through spreading modern techniques of various kinds, and through pollution. The problem is to analyse each of these linkages between the corporation and Our Country.

One can then ask two questions. First, does Our Country gain from the presence of the corporation on our soil, the alternative being the complete absence of the corporation and of the package of factors, technology, and know-how that it brings with it? Second, can taxes, subsidies or restrictions maximise Our Country's gain from the presence of the corporation? The first question is the equivalent of the familiar 'gains from trade' question: does a country gain from trade compared with no-trade, and the second is the equivalent of the optimal-trade-intervention question: given various constraints and domestic distortions, what is the optimal structure of tariffs, export taxes, subsidies and so on?

It is not proposed to spell out this model, and put it through its paces, in full detail here. We begin by considering the first question. It is important to stress that if one accepts this approach, one is only interested in trade between the corporation and Our Country; thus the corporation's sales to domestic consumers of import-competing products are of interest, but its sales to foreign consumers of export products are not. This is a complete reversal of the normal approach in international trade theory. Similarly, the corporation's import of capital and knowledge from its mother country is not of interest, but its use of locally-raised capital and labour is.

Consider first linkages (*a*) and (*b*) (factor and trade movements). Let us just take two of them. Our Country sells labour to the corporation. If the labour supply curve is upward-sloping and the wage-rate is equal to the marginal opportunity cost of labour in Our Country, there will be no gain on the last man employed, but there will be an intra-marginal gain. If the wage-rate exceeds the marginal opportunity cost of labour—as it may well do in many less developed countries, especially but not only if the labour would otherwise be unemployed—there will be a gain even on the last man employed, and an even greater intra-marginal gain.

Next, Our Country buys products produced by the corporation. If these are non-tradeable goods, there may well be a gain: the corporation will have increased the supply of these goods, this will have brought down their prices, and this will yield an intra-marginal gain to consumers (consumers' surplus). But the corporation's products are more likely to be traded goods, replacing goods that would otherwise have been imported. If they are sold at the same price as the imports replaced, there will be no gain or loss because of this linkage. But if tariffs or import restrictions make it possible for the price to be higher, there will be a consumer loss on this account. Indeed, this may often be the main source of loss in the case of corporations operating in countries where high rates of protection are prevalent. This loss would have to be set against the two main sources of gain: the gain through employment of labour and the gain through tax revenue. One could analyse in a similar way all the other linkages. When the corporation issues shares to local investors, are they paying a price which is equal to or departs from the marginal social product of capital when invested locally? Furthermore, what is the marginal cost to Our Country of the demands that the corporation makes on local infra-structure, and how does this compare with the corporation's payments, if any?

The corporation may be highly efficient and make use of the latest and best technology. It may make big profits and export vast amounts of goods from its local subsidiary to other countries. But all of this is of no interest in this approach, other than as an indication of the taxable potential of the corporation and hence the opportunity it presents of being squeezed. We are not interested in growth of geographical GNP or in the flow of trade as usually understood, especially as trade flows may be valued by transfer prices designed to minimise tax payments. We are interested only in the taxes paid by the corporation and in the valuation of the various linkages, including those that by-pass the market completely. We may also wish to take into account the income distribution effects in Our Country by attaching *distributional* weights to the income gains and losses of different sections of the population, as suggested by the method of Meade (1955).

Finally, let us consider briefly our second question. What would be the optimal intervention by the government of Our Country in the latter's goods and factor trade with the corporation so as to maximise Our Country's benefits? This is quite an intricate subject, and it is only possible here to indicate lines of approach, ignoring numerous necessary qualifications. We shall consider three possible cases.

First, suppose the corporation cannot be taxed directly through profits tax. This is equivalent to the situation between independent countries, where one country cannot tax another country directly. Our Country should then exercise any monopsony or monopoly power it has in its purchase or sale of goods and factors from (to) the corporation. This is the equivalent of the usual optimum tariff-export tax argument. The corporation's elasticities of demand for or supply of goods and factors will be relevant in determining appropriate rates of tax, as well as the degree of private monopoly already existing among Our Country's suppliers and buyers.

Next, at the other extreme, suppose that it is possible to charge and collect any rate of profits tax desired. The previous policy, which was designed to redistribute income from the corporation to Our Country by manipulating trading prices, will then be second-best. First-best policy will be to aim at maximising geographic product (which may involve taxes and subsidies designed to correct domestic distortions but not designed to improve the terms of trade of Our Country relative to the corporation) and then impose the optimum profits tax. If one thinks of the corporation as an indivisible operation that either stays in the country or does not, the optimum profits tax will be the highest rate of tax compatible with the corporation not going away as a result.

A third possibility is that there is a positive rate of profits tax which cannot be varied. It may be equal to the rate of tax in the corporation's home country since a lower rate would simply cause the home country's Treasury to scoop up the difference (given the usual arrangements whereby host-country tax paid by a subsidiary is deducted from tax payable in the home country), and since a higher rate would lead to evasion of Our Country's tax through transfer pricing. In that case it will again be optimal for Our Country to seek to improve its terms of trade through restricting or taxing the demand for or supply of goods and factors by (to) the corporation. But the optimal rates of tax will be lower than in the first of our three cases where the profits tax was assumed zero.

CONCLUSIONS

One might ask whether international trade theory should be radically reconstructed or perhaps abandoned completely because a significant part of world trade is carried on by and within multinational corporations.

It is clear that some reconstruction and development along the lines of the fourth and sixth sections of this chapter are needed. In particular, the main body of the theory should allow for some internationally mobile factors as well as for immobile factors. While capital mobility has not been ignored there has, perhaps, been too much emphasis on models where all factors are internationally immobile.

In assessing the usefulness of trade theory, one needs to bear in mind its limited objective. It can hardly be expected to give a precise and detailed description of the real world; and the fact that countries produce more than two products, and industries are not generally perfectly competitive, does not necessarily mean that the theory as usually taught is useless. One cannot do better than quote Johnson here:

'In the broader context of economics as a systematic approach to the understanding of economic phenomena and as the organisation of disciplined thinking about these phenomena and about policies relating to them, however, the purpose of theory is to abstract from the complexity of the real world a simplified model of the key relationships between dependent and independent variables, and to explore the positive and normative implications of changes in the "givens" of this hypothetical system. For this purpose, the validity of the empirical foundations of a theory is, obviously within limits, not of such crucial importance, in the sense that the principles of interrelatedness, of systematic response to change, and of optimisation remain valid in the face of wide variations in assumed economic structure.' (Johnson, 1970b, p. 10.)

Nevertheless, there is a deeper question that one needs to face. The multinational corporation cuts across national boundaries and makes a good deal of international trade into intra-firm trade. Financial capital is quite mobile within the corporation, as are senior managerial talent and the technical and managerial know-how which possibly provide the main rationale for the existence of the corporation. A model which assumes factor immobility between nations and which places primary importance upon national boundaries would seem to be utterly irrelevant. One could then argue that trade theory should be abandoned altogether, at least for the analysis of the activities of the multinational corporations. One should treat the world—perhaps the non-communist world—as a single market in which large corporations compete and collude in various ways. The theory of market structure and performance elaborated for the study of the large United States market would then be appropriate. One would think of all factors of production with the exception of natural resources as mobile. There would still be questions of location to discuss, but these questions would be of interest only to land-owners, property developers, and those concerned with land-use planning. The central economic questions would have to do with productivity in particular industries throughout the vast market and with competitiveness and oligopolistic behaviour.

Yet this approach, in spite of a superficial appeal, is not satisfactory. The main reason is that all factors are not mobile. In general, labour is fairly immobile between countries, and this is the factor with which policy is primarily concerned. Financial capital and certain types of knowledge may be mobile, but human capital embodied in the labour-force of different countries is not mobile. Furthermore, the capital embodied in the infrastructure of different countries must be regarded as more or less immobile except over a very long period. With labour somewhat immobile, governments are attached to different areas, exercising controls of various kinds, taxing, and seeking to maximise the welfare of the mainly immobile population living in the area. Hence it is still important to know how individual countries (or regions) are affected by the operations of the multinational corporations, whether they locate in one area or another, and whether they raise or lower the welfare of people in particular countries. As long as separate countries (or regions) matter in this sense, the basic concepts of trade theory will continue to be of some relevance.

References

1 See Caves (1960), Bhagwati (1964), and for a simple recent exposition, the text by Heller (1973).

2 The papers which come closest to dealing with the issues of the present paper are Robertson (1971), Caves (1971), Johnson (1970a, 1972), and

Dunning (1973a). Robertson deals specifically with trade aspects, Johnson with normative aspects, and Dunning with the location problem.

3 See also a recent paper by Dunning (1973b).

4 After completing this paper, the author came across an important article by Horst (1971), which gives the most rigorous and systematic analysis available of the effects of tariffs on transfer pricing and the location of production of the multinational firm. It considers both the increasing and the decreasing cost case. The method is partial equilibrium (as is some of the discussion of the present paper), but shows a useful direction in which rigorous analysis can go. It confirms some of the propositions in the Capital Movements section and the Theory of Tariffs (Terms of Trade) section, but also goes much beyond the argument there.

5 The enclave concept is not new in discussions of foreign investment in the export industries of less-developed countries. The principal normative analysis of the multinational enterprise is by Johnson (1970a), and in certain respects the approach here is implicit in his paper.

Chapter 8

LONG-RUN CAPITAL MOVEMENTS

George H. Borts

INTRODUCTION

Investigations of the role of the multinational firm have been mainly exercises in microeconomics. A growing body of scholars has examined the multinational firm's financial and entrepreneurial behaviour in the face of a myriad of intercountry differences in laws, regulations, economic and geographic conditions. Detailed empirical investigations have been undertaken to identify and explain the conditions under which the firm raises capital in different markets, transfers funds between currencies, and engages in production in different localities. Some writers have suggested the notion of stages of development which describe, albeit imprecisely, when the firm begins to establish branch plants in a country instead of exporting to that market from some other country. Among the factors influencing the location of production are economies of scale, the technological lag between countries in the production of new products, and the role of tariffs and quotas in protecting firms which could not otherwise survive foreign competition. As a result of these empirical studies, (e.g. Horst, 1972a and Klein, 1973), we have been led to accept the idea that the multinational firm is indeed a vehicle for the transfer of capital and technology between countries.

Superficial evidence supporting this conclusion also comes from a casual inspection of foreign investment in the European Economic Community (EEC) dating from the time when internal tariffs were lowered, after the signing of the Treaty of Rome. Again we see that foreign firms, particularly American, presumably in response to the erection of a common outside tariff and the elimination of an inside tariff, have established branch plants inside the EEC, as an alternative to exporting over the tariff wall. Not all of the empirical evidence is in, however, and some observers claim that it is the growth of EEC as much as the tariff inducements which has stimulated branch plant construction (Scaperlanda and Mauer, 1969 and Goldberg, 1972). But most investigators would agree that tariff inducements are at least theoretically capable of stimulating relocation, and that tariffs may be employed to increase the number of foreign-controlled branch plants a country enjoys.

These conclusions derived from microeconomics, run up against some possible contradictions in a macroeconomic context. It is not obvious or clear that the stimulation of branch plant investment implies a movement of capital. Is it true at the macro level, for example, that country A can increase the flow of borrowed capital from country B by levying tariffs on B's exports? Suppose country A were an international lender rather than borrower: could it reduce the volume of its lending by levying tariffs on B exports? Some of the evidence at the macro-economic level tends to stimulate such doubts. Many of the EEC countries were traditionally international lenders in the nineteenth and twentieth centuries, and had returned to that posture by the end of the decade of the 1950s. The formation of EEC and the creation of a common external tariff did not appear to change the long-term pattern of foreign asset accumulation by these countries.

The following tabulation shows (a) the cumulated current account balance of payments surplus and (b) the increase in foreign assets held by the official agencies (Central Banks plus exchange funds). The time span is 1957–63 inclusive, except for France where it is 1958–63. Data are from *International Financial Statistics*.

	(a)	(b)	
Belgium–Luxembourg	33·4	43·8	billion francs
France	3,253	3,858	million dollars
Germany	47·7	9·8	billion DM
Italy	104·1	1,560	billion Lire
Netherlands	1,552	1,123	million dollars

The figures for Germany also show a cumulated sum on transfer account of 24·9 billion DM. These observations indicate that the five countries in question enjoyed a net current account surplus, largely used to accumulate official reserves, or in the case of Germany, pay external obligations. In the longer run such surpluses will be used to balance private accumulation of foreign obligations and equities.

These observations hardly constitute final evidence, and a careful aggregate study of the balance of payments of EEC countries may reveal that the common external tariff of EEC did attenuate long-term lending. But I think that it is safe to say on the basis of casual observation that the common tariff, in the period of the late 1950s and early 1960s, while stimulating branch plant location with tariffs, did not turn the EEC into a net foreign borrower. Thus the empirical evidence at the macro-economic level does not resolve the puzzle, and I think it is up to the theorist to provide a framework within which the logical possibilities may be explored.

DEFINITIONS OF TERMS AND A CONCEPTUAL MODEL

A SAVINGS-INVESTMENT FRAMEWORK

In what follows the author will assume that a country's balance of payments is in equilibrium, with the balance on current account (equal to the balance of trade plus the net flow of dividend and interest payments) plus the balance on private capital account summing to zero. Thus a country which is an international lender will show a positive balance on current account (representing a net transfer of currently produced goods and services) and a negative balance on capital account (representing the net purchase of foreign securities). If all of the markets of this country are in equilibrium, then its balance on current account will equal the excess of savings (private + government) over investment (ditto); and the excess of savings over investment will represent a net excess demand for securities to be satisfied by the purchase of foreign securities.[1]

With these definitions in mind, it is possible to specify a conceptual model of capital movements, which identifies the major economic parameters. Recall that the balance on current account contains the net flow of dividend and interest payments earned on overseas investment. For a borrowing country, this entry is negative. Write the interest and dividend payments as the sum of all past loans, multiplied by their respective interest yields. Assume that all loans bore the same rate of interest. Then we may write:

$$D_t = \sum^{t} r_\tau B_\tau, \tag{1}$$

where D is the flow of dividend and interest payments, and B is the balance on current account, which measures, under my assumptions, the net borrowing or lending. The rate of change of D over time may then be written

$$\dot{D} = r_t B_t, \tag{2}$$

under the assumption that the same interest rate prevails. From national income accounting definitions, we also know that D is the difference between a country's gross national product (GNP) and gross domestic product (GDP).

$$GNP = GDP + D. \qquad (3)$$

We may then write the rate of change of this accounting definition with respect to time as

$$G\dot{N}P = G\dot{D}P + \dot{D} = G\dot{D}P + rB_t. \qquad (4)$$

Assuming that all markets are in equilibrium, we also know that the balance on current account equals the excess of savings (S) over investment (I) Thus

$$G\dot{N}P = G\dot{D}P + r[S - I]. \qquad (5)$$

Assume that GNP and GDP grow at a constant rate k: that savings are a given proportions **s** of GNP, and that investment is a given proportion **i** of GDP. We then have

$$k \cdot GNP = kGDP + rsGNP - riGDP, \qquad (6)$$

$$GNP = GDP \left[\frac{k - ri}{k - rs} \right]. \qquad (7)$$

Thus working back to the flow of capital, measured by the balance on current account, we see the share of GDP lent overseas:

$$B = GDP \left[\frac{k(s - i)}{k - rs} \right] \qquad (8)$$

Assuming that the denominator is positive, as it must be for the stability of models of this type, the flow of lending by a country is determined by the difference between **s**, the share of GNP saved, and **i** the share of GDP invested. Any policies which alter the balance of payments and its components, can only have a permanent effect on the flow of lending if they alter **s** or **i** (Borts and Kopecky, 1972).

Within this framework, it is not reasonable to look at the balance of trade or its components to see if international lending is altered by a government policy or a change in the economic environment. In particular, if we wish to examine the impact of the multinational firm on long-term borrowing or lending, we must determine what impact it has on the savings or investment ratios, **s** or **i**. This framework suggests that the microeconomic analysis may mislead us into believing that branch plant activity constitutes long-run borrowing or lending. What we may be seeing is the cross-hauling of establishments because of technological or name-brand advantages (Johnson, 1970), with no net change in long-term borrowing or lending at all.

A DIGRESSION ON PORTFOLIO THEORY

A number of empirical investigations of capital movements have been based on a framework of analysis different from that presented above (Branson and Hill, 1971). Such studies focus on changes in the long- and short-term capital accounts, but ignore the requirement that the financial flow be accompanied by a transfer of goods and services. The investigations are based on models of portfolio selection in which the investor is assumed to allocate his wealth among a group of assets, some of which originate abroad. The allocation will depend on the level and variance of return on each asset. Since they are not assumed to be perfect substitutes, the investor may hold positive amounts of each asset, even if the returns or variances differ. Such a framework will generate financial flows in two ways:

(a) If the level of return on a particular asset rises, then individuals will seek to increase the share of that asset in their portfolio. If that asset originates in a particular country, then its capital account will reflect the equilibrating transactions. In this view, capital flows respond to changes in interest rates, and disappear once the individual portfolio holders are again in equilibrium.

(b) As the wealth of individuals grows over time, they will devote given shares of their portfolio to assets originating in different firms and countries. At the same time, firms in these countries will be issuing new securities to finance acquisition of capital goods. An equilibrating process will occur to match and equalise the firms' issuance of new securities with the individuals' acquisition of new securities. These transactions will be reflected in a country's capital account and current account. In this view, capital movements could occur with unchanged interest rates. In fact this second view of the portfolio acquisition process is virtually identical with the theoretical framework sketched out earlier. It is the first view, however, which has been employed in empirical studies of capital movements.

There is no contradiction between portfolio studies of capital movements and the savings-investment process specified earlier. Portfolio studies are concerned with variations in financial flows as they are reflected in the country's private capital account, and empirical research using such a framework has been reasonably successful in explaining the short-run variations in capital flows. Portfolio studies do not assume the overall balance of payments is in equilibrium, and do not require or attempt to explain how the real transfer process occurs. Thus the portfolio theory may be regarded as a description of the short-run adjustment of international financial markets to changes in the data (interest rates, monetary policy). The portfolio theory will not be useful in describing the long run, or, to be more accurate, it will not be more useful than the savings-investment theory. For in the long run both current and capital accounts must be consistent with each other.

THE ROLE OF THE MULTINATIONAL FIRM

What effect does the multinational firm have on the long-run flow of investment? That is, what can be said about the magnitude and direction of international capital movements with and without multinational firms? As we have seen the presence of such a form of business enterprise can only influence capital movements if it affects the level of savings and investment in a country. There are three possible directions the influence might take.

(*a*) *Savings:* The level of savings in a country is generally considered to be a function of the level of income and the level and variance of the rate of return on wealth. The multinational firm is likely to affect saving by influencing the second factor, the level and variance of the rate of return on wealth. Note, however, that it is more likely to have this effect in the host country where it invests than in the originating country where its equities are held. One would expect this influence in the long run to reduce the host country's dependence on foreign capital for development. One would expect savings levels to rise in the host country as a consequence of development.

(*b*) *Investment:* The level of investment in a country is considered to be a function of costs of raising funds, the level of technology, the quality and growth of co-operating factors of production, and the level and growth of demand for the products of capital-using processes. Here the international firm is likely to have an energising effect on investment levels in a host country. Again the effects in the originating country are likely to be small.

(*c*) *Arbitraging of Prices:* The flow of international capital depends on the degree to which resources flow from capital-rich to capital-poor areas. In the absence of such flows, rates of return would be lower in the capital-rich than capital-poor areas. To the extent that lenders attach risk premia to investment opportunities in capital-poor areas, they will require a higher return in compensation and the flow will be attenuated. The international firm will reduce such risk premia, for three reasons: First, by holding a mixed portfolio of investments in different industries, localities, and countries, the variance of such outcomes will be reduced. In principle, any single investor may do the same with his wealth, but the opportunities may not be as readily available, and the information very expensive to acquire. This last remark suggests the second method by which the international firm will reduce risks of investment. The costs of gathering information about investment possibilities are centralised, and consequently reduced. The third reason is the application of a specific and uniform technology to a wide variety of investment opportunities. When GM builds an auto assembly plant in a host country, the investor has no doubt that GM knows how to manufacture and market autos. Thus the multinational firm reduces the risks of foreign investment. By doing so, it also acts to increase the market liquidity of its liabilities. On balance, therefore, the multinational firm is likely to increase the flow of international investment.

A MODEL OF TRADE AND INVESTMENT

The central problem to be investigated in this paper is whether the factors which stimulate the location of foreign-owned branch plants will also stimulate international borrowing. As a specific case a model will be examined in which the government policy in question is the protective tariff. It will be assumed that the tariff is effective in inducing a transfer of branch plant production to the country imposing the tariff. The question to be investigated is whether the tariff also or through the same adjustment process stimulates a change in foreign borrowing.[2]

As we have seen, foreign borrowing will be stimulated if the tariff raises the share of GNP invested or lowers the share of GNP saved. The connection between a tariff and the savings rate is too distant to bear theoretical investigation.[3] But a connection can be drawn between the tariff and the rate of investment.

In what follows, I shall assume that investment goods are exclusively produced at home, and that the hypothetical economy operates subject to full employment of its factors of production.

The purpose of these conditions is to get at the most general possible cases, and to avoid providing answers which are based on special assumptions and circumstances.

If, for example, investment goods were imports, then it would not be difficult to show that tariff protection to capital-intensive industries would, other things being the same, raise the level of investment and foreign borrowing. In similar vein, if we assumed the existence of unemployment, then tariff protection would have an employment effect which very likely would induce an increase of the level of investment. Thus the most general case to investigate would appear to be the one in which investment goods are exclusively produced at home and not transported in international trade. Moreover, I shall assume the existence of full employment.

The model employed for this purpose is adapted from the one used by Samuelson (1965) in his paper on the equalisation of interest rates through commodity trade. His model contained three commodities, each produced subject to constant returns to scale in the two factors of production, labour and capital. The investment good X_0 was assumed to be produced subject to fixed proportions in labour and capital, and this assumption will be retained, although it is a simplification which does not influence the major results. The other two commodities, X_1 and X_2, are produced under a neo-classical production function, allowing substitution subject to diminishing returns. Samuelson assumed that capital depreciated. This is a nicety which will be discarded for ease of presentation. Capital is assumed to have permanent life, so that gross and net income to capital are identical. Moreover, the interest rate can be expressed as the ratio of the annual income earned by the capital good divided by its purchase price. The Samuelson model may then be written in terms of the constraints that price equal average cost in each industry:

$$P_0 = wA_0 + RB_0, \qquad (9)$$

$$P_1 = wA_1 + RB_1, \qquad (10)$$

$$1 = wA_2 + RB_2. \qquad (11)$$

The terms w and R denote the wage and rental rate of capital, assumed the same for all industries. The prices of the three goods are P_0, P_1, and 1, respectively. The term A_0 denotes L_0/X_0, the ratio of employment to output in the investment goods industry; and a corresponding interpretation attaches to A_1 and A_2. The term B_0 denotes K_0/X_0, the ratio of capital to output in the investment goods industry, with corresponding interpretations for B_1 and B_2.

Under the assumption of perfect competition, the factor input–output coefficients A_1, A_2, B_1, B_2, are functions of the wage–rental ratio, while by assumption A_0 and B_0 are technologically fixed.

Samuelson's proof of the equalisation of interest rates proceeds from the assumption that X_0 is not traded internationally, while X_1 and X_2 are traded. For a given pair of international prices, $(P_1, 1)$ a pair w, R is determined. In turn, this pair w, R determine the cost of producing investment goods, and thus determine their price P_0. Thus the interest rate $r = R/P_0$ is determined. The interest rate equalisation theorem, like the factor price equalisation theorem depends on

(a) The existence of a one-to-one mapping from $(P_1, 1)$ to (w, R).

(b) Identical factor input–output functions A_0, B_0, A_1, B_1, A_2, B_2 in this country and the rest of the world.

(c) The absence of tariffs or other barriers to trade.

(d) The existence of perfect competition.

In his proof of interest-rate equalisation, Samuelson does not have to indicate (nor did he) what determines the level of output of the three industries, nor need he indicate whether the open economy being modelled is constrained to a zero balance on current account. Neither of these details are needed for the proof of his proposition, but both must be specified if the model is to illuminate the effect of tariffs on the output of investment goods.

It is clear that merely adding a full employment constraint on the utilisation of labour and capital is not sufficient to determine the output levels of the three sectors as functions of the prices P_0, P_1, 1. The reason may be seen by an intuitive argument. Precise arguments are found in recent articles by Melvin (1968) and Travis (1972).

Fix a level of X_0. This determines the input quantities L_0 and K_0 (remember, fixed proportions are assumed for X_0), and therefore the dimensions of an Edgeworth–Bowley box in $L_1 + L_2$ and $K_1 + K_2$. For a given pair of prices $(P_1, 1)$ of the goods X_1 and X_2, there will be a determinate pair of factor input ratios L_1/K_1, and L_2/K_2, and a determinate pair of outputs X_1 and X_2. Now fix a different level of X_0, and repeat the process. A new pair of outputs X_1 and X_2 will emerge with the same prices. Note that this indeterminacy does not depend on the assumption of fixed proportions in X_0, since we could have started the demonstration by assuming an initial value of w/R, fixed X_0 and found determinate values of $L_1 + L_2$ and $K_1 + K_2$.

There is one easy way to solve the double problem of establishing the values of the outputs X_0, X_1, and X_2, and of determining a balance of payments equilibrium condition. This way out is to assume a determinate savings function (e.g. savings are a function of income and the interest rate), and to assume that international lending does not take place. Under this assumption, the level of X_0 is determined by the condition that savings equal X_0P_0. We then know the dimensions of the box $L_1 + L_2$ and $K_1 + K_2$. Knowledge of consumer choices of the two final goods X_1 and X_2 would then permit derivation of an offer curve as a function of the prices $(P_1, 1)$; and the unknowns would then become known. But this way out prevents us from analysing capital movements, since the assumed equality of savings and investment implies no long-run borrowing or lending.

Another route, and the one employed in this paper, is to determine the output of the investment goods industry for different values of the interest rate, assuming that the prices of the traded goods X_1 and X_2 are given in the rest of the world. This investment function, in conjunction with an assumed savings function, determines the volume of long-term international borrowing (or lending) which the country wishes to undertake. The investment function (and thus desired borrowing) will be shown to shift as a result of tariffs which alter the relative prices of the internationally traded goods. The nature of the shift will depend on the relative factor intensity of the protected industry. In the remainder of this section the investment function will be derived. In the section on Tariffs and Investment Function the assumptions necessary for investment to be dependent on tariffs will be indicated.

We have already seen that a certain value of the interest rate (call it $\bar{r}$) is implied by a particular set of values of world prices (call them $\bar{P}_1$ and 1). We have also seen that at $r = \bar{r}$, the outputs X_0, X_1, and X_2 are indeterminate. But what happens at $r > \bar{r}$ while still keeping the same world prices? It is clear then that one of the two traded goods becomes too expensive to produce, because its costs of production exceed the world price. The commodity which becomes too expensive is relatively capital intensive to the other. If this is commodity X_2, then it will cease production, and only commodities X_0 and X_1 will be produced, with X_1 exported to pay for whatever imports the country demands. In similar vein, if $r < \bar{r}$, then the labour-intensive traded commodity will become too expensive relative to the capital-intensive traded commodity. Let this be commodity X_1. It will cease production and only commodities X_0 and X_2 will be produced, with X_2 exported to pay for whatever imports are demanded. What happens to the production of X_0 under these circumstances?

We may answer the question by constructing the Edgeworth–Bowley diagram as shown in Fig. 6. It will be assumed that the

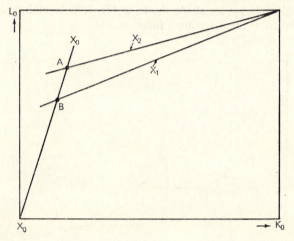

Figure 6.

investment goods industry produces subject to fixed proportions, and is relatively labour-intensive compared to the two internationally traded goods. Inputs into X_0 will be measured from the Southwest origin, while inputs into X_1 and X_2 will be measured from the Northeast origin. The factor input rays with slope L/K are drawn for X_1 and X_2 under the assumption that the interest rate is $\bar{r}$. Moreover, X_2 is assumed capital intensive relative to X_1. It is immediately apparent that the scale of production of X_0 will depend on the relative outputs of X_2 and X_1. If only X_2 is produced then X_0 scale is shown at point A, while if only X_1 is produced the X_0 scale is at point B. Thus for the prices $(\bar{P}_1, 1)$ and the interest rate $\bar{r}$, the scale of X_0 production will be somewhere between points A and B. Suppose now that the interest rate falls just below $\bar{r}$, so that the labour intensive traded good X_1 goes out of business. Ignoring for the moment the induced change in L_2/K_2, we see that production of X_0 shifts to A. Similarly when the interest rate rises just above $\bar{r}$, so that X_2

goes out of business, production of X_0 shifts to B. Thus there is a negative but discontinuous relation between the production of X_0 and the interest rate at point $\bar{r}$. What about other values of r, farther away and on either side of $\bar{r}$? Here the relation between the scale of X_0 and the level of r is continuous. As r continues to fall below $\bar{r}$, L_2/K_2 would continue to decline and production of X_0 would continue to expand. Similarly, with $r > \bar{r}$, as r continued to rise, L_1/K_1 would rise, and production of X_0 would continue to contract. The relation between the production of X_0 and r thus has the shape shown in Fig. 7. This relation will be referred to as the investment function.

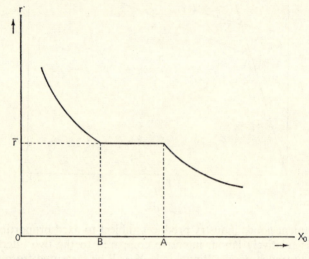

Figure 7.

It is interesting to note that the analysis would not change substantially if another international commodity (say X_3) were brought into the picture. Suppose X_3 has a fixed international price of P_3, and further suppose that X_3 is even more capital intensive than X_2. We would then have two critical interest rates.

$$\bar{r} = \bar{r}(\bar{P}_1, 1, \mid P_3^D > \bar{P}3), \tag{12}$$

and either

$$\bar{\bar{r}} = \bar{\bar{r}}(1, \bar{P}_3 \mid P_1^D > \bar{P}_1), \tag{13}$$

or

$$\bar{\bar{r}} = \bar{\bar{r}}(\bar{P}_1, \bar{P}_3 \mid P_2^D > 1). \tag{14}$$

The notation P_3^D, P_2^D, and P_1^D refers to the domestic unit cost of production of the respective commodity compared to the world price. For example, at $\bar{r}$, we know that $P_1{}^D = \bar{P}_1$ and $P_2{}^D = 1$, but that $P_3{}^D$ may exceed $\bar{P}_3$, and if so X_3 will not be produced. However, if at $\bar{r}$, $P_3{}^D < \bar{P}_3$, then one of the other two commodities will not be produced, and the reallocation of output will shift the interest rate to either $\bar{\bar{r}}$ or $\bar{r}$. The relation between r and X_0 will display flat segments for each of the critical interest rates.

We are not yet at the point where it is meaningful to examine the effect of tariffs on investment. For while a tariff can change the composition of output, driving out one international commodity and replacing it with another, this will also change the interest rate. What we will be looking for are shifts of the investment function relating X_0 and r, rather than movements along it. The reason is explained in the next section.

TARIFFS AND THE INVESTMENT FUNCTION

In order to see how tariffs might affect the level of investment, it is necessary to derive the investment function and then show how it shifts as tariff levels change. Thus assuming the country in question faces an infinitely elastic supply of capital funds at some interest rate $\bar{r}$, the tariff will induce an increase in borrowing, if it induces an outward shift in the investment function, and conversely, if it induces an inward shift.

Let us for the moment assume that the interest rate is fixed by infinitely elastic supply, and inquire into the effect of tariff changes. With a fixed interest rate, the capital–labour ratios are determinate in all industries producing subject to constant returns to scale. Suppose we return to the example of X_0, X_1, and X_2. With a price ratio of $\bar{P}_1$, 1, the interest rate would be $\bar{r}$. Were a tariff imposed on the import-competing good (either X_1 or X_2), it would change the price ratio to $(P_1{}^1, 1)$ and the resulting interest rate r^1, would differ from $\bar{r}$. The only way that the interest rate $\bar{r}$ could survive in the face of a tariff is for one of the two commodities to cease production. With r fixed at $\bar{r}$, the unprotected commodity would cease production, leading to the anomaly that the country had eliminated its exports and was borrowing to pay for its imports. This case has no empirical content, and indicates that a less restrictive set of assumptions must be investigated. Under less restrictive assumptions the tariff would reduce the output of exports, but not drive out the industry entirely.

One way to accomplish this result is to depart from the strict homogeneity assumptions made with regard to production functions. If there are decreasing returns to scale in the production of one internationally traded good, then the output of that industry will be dependent on the level of its product price and input prices. The introduction of tariffs will then alter the scale of its output, and thus alter the levels of resources available for production of the other international good and of the investment goods industry.[4] Later on the extent to which the same results hold for increasing returns to scale of the external economies variety will also be indicated.

ONE GOOD IS PRODUCED SUBJECT TO DECREASING RETURNS TO SCALE[5]

Let us then assume that there are three industries producing the three goods: X_0, the investment good, and X_1 and X_2, the two internationally traded goods. The assumptions will be retained that X_0 is produced subject to fixed proportions and constant returns to scale, and that X_1 is produced with a neo-classical production function with constant returns to scale. Now, however, it will be assumed that X_2 is produced with a neo-classical production function, subject to constant returns to scale in labour, capital, and land, *but* decreasing returns to scale in labour and capital. The author also continues to assume that X_0 is labour intensive relative to the two international goods, and that X_1 is labour intensive relative to X_2, that is for w/R, $L_0/K_0 > L_1/K_1 > L_2/K_2$.

Write the condition that price equal average cost of production for the three industries

$$\frac{1}{r} = P_0/R = \omega A_0 + B_0, \tag{15}$$

$$P_1 = R[\omega A_1 + B_1], \tag{16}$$

$$1 = R[\omega A_2 + B_2 + vC_2]. \tag{17}$$

The notation is as follows:

r, P_0, P_1, R, A, B are defined earlier,
ω = wage–rental ratio, w/R,
v = ratio of land rent to rent on capital,
C_2 = ratio of land to output in X_2.

It assumed there is a fixed amount of land, used exclusively in the production of X_2, and that X_2 is produced subject to *constant* returns to scale in its three inputs. But due to the fixed land supply it is produced subject to decreasing returns to scale in the two transferable inputs, labour and capital.

We may now derive the investment function for this three good economy and show how it shifts with a tariff. For a given level of the interest rate, $\bar{r}$, there is a corresponding value of the wage–rental ratio $\bar{\omega}$, which determines the value of $\omega A_1 + B_1$. The international price, P_1, then determines R, the rent on capital. Thus we know $\bar{w}$ and $\bar{R}$. The marginal cost function for X_2 depends solely on $\bar{w}$ and $\bar{R}$, since the return to land is a price-determined residual. The intersection of the marginal cost function for X_2 with the normalised price $P_2 = 1$ then determines the level of output X_2, and the level of the inputs L_2 and K_2 used to produce X_2 at minimum cost. We then know the dimensions of the Edgeworth box $(L_0 + L_1,\ K_0 + K_1)$, from which the industries X_0 and X_1 will choose their inputs. The input ratio L_1/K_1 is determined by $\bar{\omega}$, thus the scale of X_0 and X_1 is determined. Whether X_1 or X_2 is exported or imported will then be determined by the composition of internal demand within the country. By assumption overall balance-of-payments equilibrium is assured by the condition that any current account surplus or deficit is matched by a corresponding outflow or inflow of long-run capital at the given interest rate. Thus the level of investment (the production of X_0) is a function of r, and the two international prices $(P_1, 1)$.

Now introduce a tariff on the import-competing good. There are then two cases:

(a) X_2 is the import-competing good. The tariff is imposed on X_2. The effect of the tariff is to raise the price of X_2, and thus to raise its level of production. This has the effect of shifting labour and capital from X_0 and X_1, reducing the dimensions of the Edgeworth box $(L_0 + L_1,\ K_0 + K_1)$. Labour and capital will move to X_2 in the proportion L_2/K_2, which by assumption is less than the initial ratio $(L_0 + L_1)/(K_0 + K_1)$. Thus not only does the box shrink, but its ratio of labour to capital expands, since more capital is withdrawn from the box relative to the amount of labour withdrawn. At the same time, the ratios L_0/K_0 and L_1/K_1 will remain fixed, the first due to fixed proportions and the second due to the unchanging value of ω. Thus we have a problem of the type first analysed by Rybczynski (1955). The result is that the production of X_0 expands and X_1 contracts. These changes are depicted in Fig. 8 below as the movement from points A to B. Thus the tariff on the import-competing good has raised the level of investment. This was done because in the new

H

equilibrium resulting from the tariff, the production of X_0 expanded and the production of X_1 contracted, at the given interest rate $\bar{r}$.

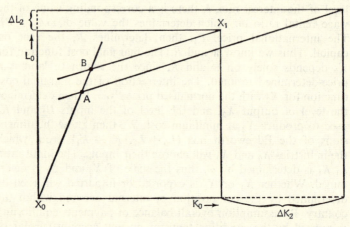

Figure 8.

(b) In the second case, X_1 is the import-competing good. The tariff is imposed on X_1. This raises the domestic price of X_1 above the world price P_1. The effect is to raise R, the rental to capital, since $\omega A_1 + B_1$ is determined by ω. The increase of R also implies an increase of w, the cost of labour. This implies a leftward shift of the marginal cost function of X_2, and a reduction in the output of X_2, the export good. The reduction in the output of X_2 releases labour and capital to the production of X_0 and X_1. Thus the Edgeworth box expands its dimensions, $L_0 + L_1$, $K_0 + K_1$; but under the assumption that $L_2/K_2 < L_1/K_1 < L_0/K_0$, the box increases by a greater proportion in the capital dimension than the labour dimension. Since ω is unchanged, L_1/K_1 is unchanged, while L_0/K_0 is fixed by assumption. In this case the production of X_0 will contract. As shown in Fig. 8, we have a movement from B to A. Note that the conclusions of this case are symmetric to that of the previous case, in the sense that both effects depend on the capital intensity of the industry releasing or absorbing resources. In case (a) when X_2 expanded, it raised the labour–capital ratio of the box available for X_0 and X_1. In case (b) when X_2 contracted, it lowered the labour–capital ratio of the box available for X_0 and X_1. Suppose that we had a different ordering of capital intensities from that assumed in case (b).

Suppose we had the following: $L_0/K_0 > L_2/K_2 > L_1/K_1$. Would a tariff on X_1 then lead to an increase in X_0? The answer is maybe. The answer will be yes when $L_2/K_2 > (L_0 + L_1)/(K_0 + K_1)$. In this event, when X_2 contracts it raises the labour–capital ratio of the box and thus induces X_0 to expand. Note however, that the inequality requirement on L_2/K_2 then depends on the initial composition of output between X_0 and X_1, and on the initial scale of X_2 output. Finally, if we have the ordering $L_2/K_2 > L_0/K_0 > L_1/K_1$, there is a clear conclusion that a tariff on X_1, which causes X_2 to contract will raise the labour–capital ratio of the box and cause X_0 to expand. We can then derive the general conclusion: A tariff on the import-competing good will cause the production of investment goods to increase if the resources released or absorbed by X_2 (the non-constant returns good) cause an increase in the labour–capital ratio of the box ($L_0 + L_1$, $K_0 + K_1$).

While these conditions appear quite restrictive they do give us an indication of what to look for when investigating the effects of tariffs on investment levels. Note that the analysis hinges on the existence of one industry which experiences non-constant returns to scale. In the cases considered above we were dealing with decreasing returns.

ONE GOOD PRODUCED SUBJECT TO INCREASING RETURNS TO SCALE

Can the analysis be extended to increasing returns? Ordinarily increasing returns lead to monopoly, and the problem would change quite dramatically. But what about external economies? Suppose firms in the X_2 industry faced a production function of the form:

$$X_{2i} = f[L_1, K_i, N], \tag{18}$$

where X_{2i} is the output of the ith firm, L_i the amount of labour it uses, K_i the amount of capital, N the number of firms. Further, suppose f is homogeneous of the first degree in L_i and K_i and $f_3 > 0$. In that case we could have stable competition, in the sense that we could specify $K_1 = 1$, i.e. all firms would be of identical size, and the competitive equilibrium would be a solution for X_i, L_i, and N, all dependent on the industry demand function for final output and on the supply functions for the inputs purchased by the industry. The stability of the competitive solution would of course require that the long-run supply function of the industry (long-run in the sense that N is variable) have a smaller slope than the demand function, as shown in Fig. 9. For in this case an increase in the demand function would ultimately (as N increased) lead to greater output at lower price. Presumably this is one of the cases considered to be a rationale for a tariff, since the unfettered operation of the free market would not lead to a point on the utility possibility function. If the externality is non-reversible the tariff would be of the infant-industry variety, or the industry could be subsidised directly. Either policy would lead to an increase in the value of the country's output, because

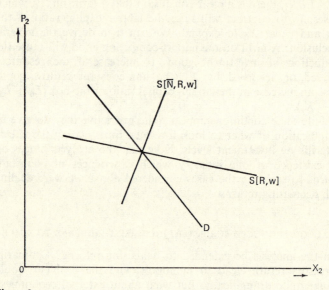

Figure 9.

by limiting imports and transferring the demand to the domestic industry it can be satisfied at lower cost. Economists have always been wary of the existence of external economies and have distrusted arguments for infant industry tariffs (see Baldwin, 1969). Indeed, there does appear to be a certain amount of magic in the production function described above. However, without claiming that such cases are widespread, there is no question they are possible and that they suggest another way in which tariffs might affect the level of investment.

Consider then an economy of three industries, X_0, X_1 and X_2, in which X_0 is the investment good, X_1 and X_2 are internationally traded. X_0 is produced subject to fixed proportions and constant returns to scale; X_1 produced subject to constant returns in labour and capital, with a neo-classical production function;

X_2 has the production function described above in equation (18). Again we can show that the level of investment is a function for the interest rate r, and of the international prices $(P_1, 1)$, and that the investment function will be shifted by the tariff.

First note the determination of the investment level. For a given interest rate, we have a given wage rental ratio ω. With a given P_1, this determines the level R of rentals to capital and w the wage rate. The levels of w and R determine the long-run supply function of X_2. The international price $P_2 = 1$ determines the output level of X_2, and thus the levels of L_2 and K_2 needed for its production. As noted below, we really cannot assume a perfectly elastic international demand or supply of X_2, but must assume instead a negatively sloped demand function or a positively sloped supply function. The box $L_0 + L_1$, $K_0 + K_1$ is thus determined and the levels of X_0 and X_1 determined as described previously.

What happens now if a tariff is imposed on the import competing industry?

(a) Suppose that X_2 is import competing: A tariff will as previously, stimulate its output and draw resources away from X_0 and X_1. The effect on the level of X_0 depends as before on the change in the labour–capital ratio of the Edgeworth box ($L_0 + L_1$, $K_0 + K_1$) as labour and capital move to X_2. What is unusual about this case is that we require more information than previously to determine the scale of output in the X_2 industry. Earlier, we could get by with the knowledge that the world price was normalised at $P_2 = 1$ and that it was increased by the tariff. Now we need to know in addition the home demand for X_2 as a function of P_2, and the world supply of X_2 as a function of P_2. The extra information is required due to the downward sloping home supply function for X_2, and the fact that an increase in the demand for domestically produced X_2 will lead to a price lower than the original price. Moreover, this price reduction could drive out imports of X_2 entirely if the world supply were completely elastic at $P_2 = 1$.

Perhaps the reason economists distrust the case for external economies and infant industry tariffs is that it contains the logical possibility of events not likely to be observed.

(b) Suppose that X_1 is import competing and X_2 the export industry: Before analysing the tariff on X_1, we again must specify a downward sloping world demand for X_2. For otherwise we can generate unstable solutions. Provided that the combination of home and foreign demand for X_2 has the shape of the demand curve shown in Fig. 9, we can work with the case where X_2 is the export. It will also be assumed that the externality is reversible, to avoid any kinks in the long-run supply function for X_2. The tariff on X_1 will then raise the price P_1, raise R and w, and shift the long-run supply function for X_2. The output of X_2 will contract, it will release labour and capital, expanding the dimensions of the box $(L_0 + L_1, K_0 + K_1)$, thus yielding to the same analysis as earlier.

CONCLUSIONS AND POTENTIAL EMPIRICAL APPLICATIONS

We have seen that the imposition of tariffs is capable of stimulating an increase in a country's foreign borrowing under the following assumptions:[6]

(a) Capital goods are not transportable in international trade.
(b) The production of capital goods is labour-intensive relative to other products.
(c) The import-competing industry, which is protected by the tariff, is capital-intensive relative to other products.

The empirical validity of the first two assumptions is, of course, open to question.

(a) Some capital goods are directly imported. If they are, however, then it is not difficult to see that protection of capital-intensive industries will increase the demand for capital goods, as the capital-intensive industries expand under the tariff stimulant. There is thus both a short- and long-run increase in investment. Investment increases in the short-run to satisfy the newly desired amounts of capital used for current production. Investment increases in the long-run because a larger capital stock implies a greater absolute amount of investment to maintain appropriate capital–output and capital–labour ratios as the economy grows. This case is not investigated in depth, because it leads to a consideration of the effects of long-run growth on the demand for investment. The previous analysis has been restricted to the static effects of resource allocation resulting from the imposition of the tariff in a full employment economy.

(b) The assumption that capital-goods production is relatively labour intensive has both theoretical and empirical justification. In theoretical growth models which allow for a capital-goods sector, the factor-intensity assumption is needed to give the model stability. The possibility of instability can be seen by considering briefly the implications of the contrary assumption, namely that capital-goods are capital-intensive. In that case, a shift of resources to capital-goods production raises the labour–capital ratio in all production sectors which allow factor substitution, lowers the wage–rental ratio and thus raises the interest rate. The investment function is then a positively sloping function of the interest rate. The possibility of unstable equilibria then arises in closed economic models, for an interest rate above the level for which investment equals total saving could lead to an excess of investment over savings, with still higher interest rates. While this event is unlikely to occur in an open economy which permits foreign borrowing, it is still the kind of assumption one is unhappy to make.

The empirical justification for the factor intensity assumption is based mainly on the casual observation that a substantial fraction of investment activity is construction, which is one of the most labour-intensive industries in any developed economy. It is true, of course, that many types of business, personal and governmental services are even more labour-intensive than construction, so the assumption may still be open to some question.

The third assumption is a matter of historical accident in the sense that empirical investigations of tariffs are not likely to uncover any particular pattern of factor-intensity among protected industries. But this is a matter of conjecture which can only be answered through empirical investigation. Investigation of the relative capital-intensity of import-competing industries has up until now been stimulated by the desire to provide empirical verification of the Hechscher–Ohlin model. The results are well known, particularly the papers which have attempted to defuse the famous Leontief paradox. Apparently, none of the writers in this area have investigated the capital intensity of protected industries. However, Travis (1972) has recently set a challenge in the form of a conjecture that trade in Heckscher–Ohlin goods is effectively eliminated by tariffs. If the surmise by Travis is correct, then the industries protected by US tariffs would be labour intensive, while those protected by non-US tariffs would be capital intensive.[7]

Returning for the moment to the EEC, it does represent the most wide ranging example of structural change produced by tariff change in recent years. However, in order to test the conjectures of this paper, it would be necessary to discover first which industries have received protection, on balance, and which have had protection reduced. This is not an easy question to answer since tariffs may have gone up and down for the same industry in one country, in the sense that tariffs on intra-EEC trade have been lowered while in some cases they have been raised on extra-EEC trade. Moreover, the combination of tariff changes on industrial products and the introduction of a price support programme for agricultural commodities makes it difficult to determine which way resources will be pulled by the package of policies pursued inside the EEC.

What is clear from the models discussed is that tariffs may attract branch plants, but a much more restrictive set of conditions must be met before we can be sure they will lead to overseas borrowing.

References

[1] With the use of Walras's law, this framework can be adapted to the case where the balance of payments is not in equilibrium, and the balance on current and capital accounts sum to a non-zero value which is offset by some type of official financing, either gold or reserve flow or central bank borrowing or lending. The official financing can be regarded as a simultaneous set of central bank transactions in the money and foreign exchange markets. Thus if a country runs a surplus, we can regard the central bank as issuing liabilities to households and firms and acquiring an equal amount of foreign exchange. Assume for simplicity that all excesses and shortfalls between the private demand and the supply of money are met by the sale or purchase of securities by households and firms. Also assume that the markets for commodities and bonds are cleared. Then a balance of payments surplus may be regarded as the consequence of private demand for money being in excess of the supply of money. The households attempt to restore their cash balances to a desired level by the sale of securities. This reduces the net purchases of foreign securities, and thus yields a larger balance on capital account than consistent with equilibrium. The surplus in the overall balance of payments then results from the failure of the central bank to purchase the securities sold off by households and firms. This behaviour may be the result of the conscious desire of the central bank to avoid expansion of the money supply, or to increase the stock of international reserves. Such an interpretation may be applicable to those EEC countries which ran current account surpluses in the 1960s but did not engage in an equivalent amount of long-term international leading.

[2] As I indicated earlier, tariffs are only one of several factors which stimulate foreign branch plant location. The model will be applicable to these other cases, but the analysis is not presented here.

[3] In their famous paper, Laursen & Metzler (1950) assumed that the savings ratio was an increasing function of real income, and consequently influenced by the terms of trade. Were this assumption correct, the savings ratio would also be influenced by imposition of a tariff. I have not followed this lead for two reasons: First, the empirical basis of the assumption has been substantially weakened by later work on savings behaviour. Second, a protective tariff designed to stimulate output in a particular sector may have

different effects on real income (positive and negative) at different points in time.

4 An alternative approach is to start with the case of three international goods, where $r = \bar{r}$, $P_1 = \bar{P}_1$, $P_2 = 1$, and $P_3^D > \bar{P}_3$. That is begun with the case where it is too expensive to produce X_3, which is assumed to be more capital intensive than X_0, X_1, X_2. Now holding r at $\bar{r}$, impose a tariff on X_3 which makes $P_3^D = P_3 + $ tariff. There is no resulting change in w and R; all that has happened is that producers of X_3 can now buy labour and capital at the previous prices and sell X_3 domestically. There is however a rightward shift of the investment function. This may be seen in Fig. 6 by the fact that production of X_3 is more capital intensive than X_1 or X_2. This case is of less interest than the one analysed in the text because it fails to resolve the indeterminancy of output; that is, we don't have enough information to determine the levels of X_1, X_2 and X_3.

5 A similar model, applied to questions of economic development, is employed by Teubal (1972).

6 Some of the discussants of this paper also objected to the competitive framework used in the analysis, pointing out that in many cases branch plant location is induced by government grant of a monopoly to the international firm. The details of the analysis would have to be altered in such cases, but this should not alter the main conclusions. Any disturbance to the allocative equilibrium will influence investment by its effects on the factor availabilities and factor proportions.

7 A 1965 article by Balassa (1965) is somewhat discouraging on this point. He failed to find any relation between effective rate of protection and labour intensiveness for a large group of traded manufactures. He did find a weak negative relation for Japan.

Chapter 9

MONETARY POLICY

Geoffrey W. Maynard

INTRODUCTION

Monetary theory is concerned with the influence, broadly viewed, of money in the economic system. Monetary economists are therefore concerned with formulating and testing propositions and theories about such matters as the nature and fundamental properties of money itself, the factors determining the demand for and supply of it, and the effect of changes in the latter on the economic system in general, and on the price level and output of commodities in particular. Monetary policy is a policy of employing the central bank's control over the money supply to achieve stated economic objectives; and clearly, it has its basis in monetary theory itself, since without knowledge of how changes in money supply can be brought about and how they affect the economy, it would not be possible to relate in any rational way monetary means and economic ends.

It is not obvious why the existence and growing influence of multinational enterprises should affect monetary *theory*. There seems no good reason why the essential nature and properties of money itself should be changed, or why, in principle, at least, the factors determining demand for and supply of money should be affected. Nor does there seem need to re-think in any radical way the *channels* through which changes in the quantity of money affect economic activity. But this lack of need to re-think monetary theory does not mean that the growth of multinational enterprises in the world economy has not had, and will not continue to have, important monetary consequences—consequences which have implications for the conduct and effectiveness of monetary policy and economic policy in general as practised by sovereign national states.

Some of these consequences are already with us; others can be expected to emerge as the world economy and its economic institutions adjust to the growing influence of multinational enterprise. As far as the future is concerned, we are clearly involved in some crystal gazing; but crystal gazing is not without merit and usefulness provided it is based on reasonable inference from and extrapolation of developments already becoming apparent.

In part, at any rate, this paper is such an exercise in crystal gazing, its aim being no more than to provide a broad speculative framework for continuing analysis and observation of the monetary consequences of multinational enterprise. Its argument and conclusions can be summarised in terms of the following propositions:

(a) The activities of the multinational enterprises and the existence of the international capital market, which in practice, if not in theory, are intimately related, substantially weaken the effectiveness of domestic monetary policy, complicate the task of managing national balances of payments and exchange rates, and by contributing to wage inflation, increase the difficulties facing national governments of reconciling a high level of employment with reasonable price stability.

(b) Although a move towards a floating, or at any rate, a more flexible exchange rate system could be resorted to enable countries to get more control over their domestic money supply, the problem of monetary management would still be complicated by the fact that the growth and spread of multinational enterprises has already reduced, and can be expected to continue to reduce to an increasing extent, the possibility of individual nations remaining feasible currency areas.

(c) As a consequence of these trends, control over the operations of multinational enterprises may well require the formation of larger monetary areas subject to supranational political and economic control.

It will not be possible to support these propositions, in their totality at any rate, by recourse to empirical evidence, and they are clearly open to argument; but in so far as they represent a true description of what is both already happening and likely to come about, it is evident that the monetary impact of multinational enterprise will be substantial.

MULTINATIONAL ENTERPRISES AND
DOMESTIC MONETARY POLICY

It is now established doctrine that a system of fixed exchange rates and a fully developed international capital market virtually preclude a country from having full control over its domestic money supply and from pursuing an effective domestic monetary policy; moreover, although advantage can be taken of international capital flows, triggered off by appropriate interest rate differentials, at any rate to finance, in the short run, balance of payments deficits, fixed exchange rates complicate the task of reconciling long-term balance of payments equilibrium with other domestic economic objectives, such as a high and stable level of employment and faster economic growth.

The manner in which the existence of the international capital market, which facilitates the transfer of huge volumes of short-term funds from one national capital market to another, inhibits national control over the money supply under a system of fixed exchange rates is well known and requires only brief summary here (Cooper, 1972; McKinnon and Oates, 1966). For instance, a central bank may employ open market operations with the aim of reducing the domestic money supply; these operations will tend to cause domestic interest rates to rise, but in a situation where international capital is highly mobile and sensitive to interest rate differentials, foreign capital will be attracted into the country, thereby maintaining the liquidity of the banking and financial system and offsetting the reduction in the money supply which it is the central bank's intention to bring about. Conversely, if the intention of the central bank is to lower interest rates and increase money supply, capital may shift to countries where interest rates are now relatively higher.

The international mobility of capital is not, of course, perfectly elastic with respect to interest rate differentials. Even in a fixed exchange rate system, exchange rates are normally allowed to fluctuate within narrow margins either side of parity. Operators in the market may therefore have to cover themselves for the exchange risk by selling in the forward exchange market, at a discount, the currency they have bought on interest arbitrage grounds. Interest rate differentials can persist therefore, depending on the cost of forward cover. Moreover, the *covered* interest arbitrage schedule itself is not perfectly elastic over all of its relevant range so that significant *covered* interest rate differentials can also exist between national markets. The basic reason for this is that in large part international movements of capital take place as a result of once for all adjustments of capital stocks in response to relative interest rate movements. Once the size of these stocks have been adjusted to the covered or uncovered interest differentials, *flows* of capital dry up, except to the extent that portfolio stocks grow over time (Grubel, 1968; Leamer and Stern, 1970).

Despite these qualifications, it is evident that the mobility of international capital, facilitated by an efficient capital market, must make it more difficult for national governments to bring about changes in interest rates, relatively to levels ruling in other countries, and to bring about changes in their domestic money supply. In these circumstances economic policy has to rely heavily on fiscal measures, whose influence on the economy is admittedly strengthened by the international mobility of capital, to control the level of aggregate demand, employment and the price level.

In theory, the evolution of the international capital market and the growth of multilateral enterprise can be distinguished from each other; in practice, they have been closely and intimately related. Foreign investment by United States' firms in affiliates abroad throughout the 1960s contributed in no small measure to the United States balance of payments deficit; and this, in turn, underlay the growth of the Euro-dollar and Euro-bond markets. This market now provides a source of funds on a massive scale to international companies which are in the main the final borrowers in the market. These companies also invest their surplus funds in this market rather than in the domestic capital markets of individual countries. Without access to the Euro-dollar market, many of the activities of the multinational enterprises would not be possible; on the other hand, without the multinational enterprises, the international capital market, and the Euro-dollar market, in particular, would operate on a much smaller scale,[1] and the integration of national capital markets would be carried less far.

Given the existence of the international capital market, the operations of multinational enterprises tend to raise the interest rate sensitivity of capital flows facilitated by it. By virtue of the fact that they typically dispose of large stocks of potentially mobile funds, denominated in different currencies, and also have widespread banking connections which give them access to credit lines and other borrowing facilities in the countries in which they operate, multinational enterprises are able to act as large scale arbitragers in the market, shifting funds from one national capital to another in response to emerging 'covered' and 'uncovered' interest rate differentials. The flow of funds which results tends to iron out such differentials and limits the degree to which any one country can fix its own domestic rate of interest at a level of its own choosing. In acting in this way, multinational enterprises have the advantage that their subsidiaries provide them with a stream of relevant information concerning local credit conditions and currency risks. Because of this advantage, they are probably more willing than are purely domestic firms to incur the risks associated with foreign investment and more able to protect themselves against them.

Quite apart from their arbitrage activities in the international capital market, multinational enterprises are able to avoid much of the impact of local credit squeezes (which governments may attempt to impose by selective credit means even when they cannot control money supply) and evade a scarcity of local equity finance. This is because they have ready access to souces of funds external to the national economy.

These sources are of two kinds: first, there are the funds internal to the international firm itself, in the form of profits and other income generated by the firm's trading operations; and second, as had been said, multinational enterprises have ready access to the international capital market. Like all large firms, multinational enterprises tend to finance a large part of their investment with funds obtained from their own earnings. Multinational enterprises tend, however, to be larger than purely domestic concerns and, therefore, tend to generate larger flows of funds than do the former; moreover, operating, as they tend to do, in many countries simultaneously, there is a presumption that their total income is less subject to fluctuations than are the profits of purely national firms catering largely for domestic markets and whose income will be subject to the cyclical upswings and downswings affecting individual economies.

As a consequence of being able to exert centralised control over the use of funds arising from the activities of many subsidiaries, multinational enterprises are able to shift funds from one affiliate to another, thereby avoiding credit stringencies appearing in one or other country. Various methods for shifting funds from one country to another, including centralised control over flows of dividends, royalties, and similar remittances from one subsidiary to another, are employed, as well as the practice of transfer pricing, i.e. the process of internal costing and accounting designed to realise profit flows in one country rather than another. Transfer pricing is usually aimed at minimising the total tax burden of the multinational enterprise, but it can also be used as a means of directing financial flows through the network of subsidiaries comprising the company.

Multinational enterprises also have privileged access to the international long-term capital market. They find it much easier to borrow in the Euro-dollar currency and bond markets than do national firms, partly because they have better and more acceptable credit standing for international capital market borrowing, partly because, as a result of being multinational, they have extensive relationships with international banks and international banking consortia which take a leading part in arranging and underwriting international issues, and partly because, owing to their very great size, they are able to borrow in amounts that the international capital market is best able to handle.

Since they have this access to funds external to the national economy, multinational enterprises are enabled to avoid the full impact of credit stringency which may be imposed by national governments in the interests, for example, of controlling inflation or putting the balance of payments into equilibrium; the consequence is that the burden of credit squeezes falls increasingly on national firms whose growth and development may thereby be inhibited and restricted as compared to the multinational enterprises. The influence of the multinational firm is accordingly and progressively increased and the impact of domestic monetary policy further weakened and localised.[2]

Although not strictly relevant to the subject of this paper, it may be noted that multinational enterprises are also probably less affected by fiscal policy than are national firms. Although the integration of national capital markets, to which the operations of multinational enterprises have provided a major spur, tend in general to strengthen the impact of fiscal policy on the domestic economy (owing to the fact that a high international mobility of capital tends to stabilise interest rates in the face of expansionary or contractionary national budgets), paradoxically the multinational enterprise is able to escape fiscal restraint. Exports tend to form a larger proportion of the total sales of multinational firms than they do of the sales of domestic firms, and export markets are clearly less affected by domestic fiscal policy than are domestic markets. Moreover, as a consequence of their ability to draw on many sources of funds, multinational enterprises have access to finance much less affected by fiscal measures operating, for example, through changes in profits tax and in depreciation and investment allowances, and similar measures, than is the case with purely domestic firms.[2]

BALANCE OF PAYMENTS AND THE EXCHANGE RATE

The fact that multinational enterprises are in control of substantial volumes of funds arising from many different sources implies that their operations have a significant impact on the foreign exchange market. Their ability to shift large volumes of funds from one domestic capital market to another is sometimes welcome, for instance, when interest rate policy is being employed to attract or repel funds on balance of payments grounds; on the other hand, they can often put severe upward pressure on some currencies and downward pressure on others, thereby disturbing exchange rate alignments. But, while there is no doubt that opportunities are offered to them by the adjustable peg exchange rate system, it would be a simplification to assume that speculative profits have provided the major motive. Clearly, since multinational enterprises operate in many countries and are involved in large capital investment projects requiring financing, they must necessarily take into account the likely behaviour of the exchange rate in choosing the most appropriate source and form of finance. They will, for instance, have strong incentive to finance investment in countries whose currencies appear weak, by borrowing as much as possible in local currency, while building up assets denominated in currencies whose value is likely to appreciate. In order to do this they will vary intra-company transfers and flows of funds as much as possible and, like domestic firms, resort to 'leading and lagging' in their normal trading operations. Of course, all companies, whether national or international, will do their best to protect themselves against exchange loss arising from exchange rate changes; but, as indicated earlier, multinational enterprises can do this more effectively since they can take advantage of centralised control over funds which arise, at source, in many currencies. But while, because of the very large volume of funds which they have under their control and their access to local sources of borrowing, multinational enterprises can clearly exert massive pressure on exchange rates, they do not determine these exchange rates in the long run. They are simply in a good position to take advantage of exchange rates which because, for instance, of different relative rates of inflation and the stubbornness of governments have become seriously out of line. While they can exacerbate the exchange rate difficulties of individual countries they cannot, at bottom, cause them.

WAGE INFLATION

The impact which the multinational enterprise can have on the price level and on the trade-off between inflation and employment is perhaps less well recognised and certainly less documented.

Quite apart from the weakening effect which the operations of multinational enterprises and the existence of the international capital market have on the operation of domestic monetary policy, multinational enterprises have probably already contributed significantly, and are likely to contribute much more in the future, to inflation through the so-called wage transfer mechanism. This mechanism involves the transmission of wage pressure from sectors of the economy in which labour productivity is high and increasing rapidly to other sectors of the economy in which it is much lower and increasing much less quickly.

If the rate at which *average* money wages in the economy as a whole are increasing is determined very largely by the rate at which they are increasing in those sectors of the economy in which productivity is growing relatively fast, then the fact that money wages will then be rising at a much faster rate than productivity in other sectors of the economy imposes serious upward cost pressures in these latter sectors; as a result the price level in these sectors will also rise and thus contribute to general inflation, even if the price level in the high productivity growth sector is not itself rising.[4] High productivity growth tends to be associated with capital intensiveness and the employment of modern technology, labour costs usually being a rather small proportion of the total costs of production.

Trade unions operating in industries with these characteristics are in a favourable position to get substantial wage increases which are closely geared to the rate at which labour productivity is rising. Capital intensive firms are reluctant to face up to strikes which can be very costly for them; indeed, they may see great advantage in buying labour peace and trade union acquiescence to changes in technology by offering substantial wage increases and fringe benefits. Such increases in wages which can be afforded by the high productivity industries lead to parity wage demands elsewhere in the economy which cannot be afforded by more labour intensive industries without raising their prices, but which, nonetheless, must be yielded to, to some extent at least, in order to maintain reasonable industrial peace.

It is obvious that the rise in the price level produced by the wage transfer process operating in a situation of differential sector productivity growth (often described as structural or productivity inflation) must be validated by an expansion of the money supply; and this fact causes some economists to deny the inflationary consequences of the process just described and to attribute inflation more directly to what happens to the money supply itself. Against this view, however, it must be recognised, first, that strong social pressures exist in advanced political democracies for rough equality in wage increases (not necessarily wage levels) in all sectors of the economy irrespective of sector productivity growth, and second, that the strong oligopolistic characteristics of much of modern industry, reflected in, among other things, a disposition of firms to compete with each other on the basis of advertising and other promotional campaigns rather than on the basis of price, tend to produce a widespread downward inflexibility of industrial good prices.

These two facts tend to ensure that the benefits of rising productivity accrue in the form of rising money incomes rather than in the form of a falling price level while the change in relative costs and prices necessitated by differential sector productivity growth tends to be more easily achieved in the context of a rising price level than in terms of a stable one. The attempt by government to restrain the rise in price level (which clearly has a structural rather than an excessive aggregate demand or excessive money supply character) by measures operating on aggregate demand could succeed in the short run (which may in fact be quite long) only by imposing a severe constraint on output and employment, and in the long run, only if radical changes occurred in the nature of industry such that price competition and downward price flexibility became more common. Understandably, governments prefer to give greater priority to maintaining growth and employment in the short run, while attempting to increase price competition in industry in the long run by appropriate anti-monopoly measures.

Multinational enterprises have probably contributed significantly to structural or productivity inflation in recent years, particularly in the UK. There are a number of reasons for this. In the first place, the typical multinational enterprise tends to be more capital intensive (particularly if human capital is included with physical capital), and more advanced technology based than is the typical national firm; and output per head of the labour force employed tends to be higher in the former and to increase at a faster rate. Its ability to pay higher money wages and to grant larger annual increases is therefore correspondingly greater.

Second, the typical affiliate of a multinational enterprise often tends to be one link in an integrated international production complex in which components of a finished product are produced in a number of different countries and assembled in yet another. This fact, plus the fact of capital intensity, human and physical, and relatively low marginal labour costs per unit of output, may make it costly in terms of its total activities for multinational enterprises to face up to strikes in a country facing particular labour difficulties, and more willing to ensure labour peace by conceding substantial wage increases and other fringe benefits. They are less concerned with the possible repercussions on wages elsewhere in the economy than are national firms which have to take into account the impact of a wage concession in a particular plant on wages they have to pay in other plants in the same country.[5]

Third, it is an important fact that the majority of multinational enterprises operating in the UK and in Europe generally are US owned and operate extensively in the US as well as abroad. These companies tend to bring US technology, which is based on relatively high US labour costs, and wage bargaining practices into the host countries in which their subsidiaries operate. As a consequence, existing wage patterns and relativities are disturbed with widespread repercussions in the economy generally.

In the UK, and to a significant extent in other European countries as well, wages are determined by the process of industry wide collective bargaining between, on the one hand, officials of national trade unions and, on the other, representatives of national employers' associations belonging to the industry or industries involved. The wage agreements that result are industry wide agreements expected to be applied nationally, although modifications may be made at the workplace as a result of discussions between shop stewards and company management. In general, the factors taken into account in arriving at the wage agreement relate very largely to matters external to the individual firms comprising the industry; thus the parties to the bargaining process are largely concerned with such things as profitability of the industry as a whole, labour supply to the industry, past and expected changes in the cost of living, and movements in wages and earnings of labour with comparable skills and conditions in other industries. The wage that will be arrived at is likely to be acceptable to most of the least efficient of the firms comprising the industry rather than be geared to capacity to pay of the most efficient firms.

The situation is quite different in the US where company wage bargaining is the accepted rule and where plant productivity is the major factor determining the size of the wage award gained by the workers employed by the firm. Trade unions may or may not be directly involved; but even where they are involved, wage agreements arrived at with individual firms are not necessarily nor even generally applied over the industry to which the firm belongs, although, of course, a favourable wage agreement arrived at with one firm will provide the basis of bargaining with another. With this type of bargaining practice, wage increases tend to be more tied to the ability to pay of the most efficient and productive firms comprising the industry, in contrast to the outcome of industry wide collective bargaining.

A major innovation in UK industrial relations in the 1960s has been the spread of plant and firm bargaining based on plant productivity. The prices and incomes policy pursued by the Labour government in the mid 1960s provided a strong 'fillip' to this development, but undoubtedly US owned multinational enterprises took a leading part (Gennard, 1972; Steuer and Gennard, 1971). These enterprises were anxious to obtain the acquiescence of British labour to changes in working practices which would increase plant efficiency and bring it closer to that typical of US based plants: indeed, it is clear that US owned subsidiaries operating in the UK with US technology have been expected to raise labour productivity closer to levels ruling in the US. Thus productivity agreements have been sought in return for substantial increases in wage rates and other fringe benefits which, provided the productivity gains were in fact achieved, would be self financing on the basis of existing prices. US trade unions have been more than interested spectators. Fearing that low wages abroad would attract US investment and threaten employment opportunities in the US, they have applied pressure on US firms operating subsidiaries abroad to pay wages nearer to those ruling in the US.

While the increase in labour productivity which such wage bargaining practices tend to encourage is clearly to be welcomed, the spread of plant bargaining in the UK and possibly in Europe has had unwelcome inflationary repercussions as well. There is evidence to suggest that the wage increases paid by foreign multinationals have set the pace and size of wage settlements elsewhere in the economy (Gennard, 1972, p. 33). These settlements have not always been matched by willingness or opportunity to raise labour productivity and the result has been pressure on costs and prices in many industries in which multinational firms are not involved. Unemployment has also resulted, and this has made governments less willing to take the necessary monetary and other measures which would help contain the spread of inflation. The transmission of wage pressure and inflation has probably been more severe in the UK than elsewhere owing to the high degree of unionisation of British labour (40 per cent of the UK labour force are members of trade unions as compared with only 20 per cent in the US), and to the strong centralisation of the movement and the political influences and power which it is able to exert.

There may be disagreement as to the actual contribution of the multinational enterprise to the spread of wage inflation in the UK and in Europe so far, although it is noteworthy that the acceleration of inflation in the international economy in the late 1960s followed the rapid extension of the activities of such enterprises in the early and middle years of the decade, and the extraordinary growth of the international capital market. No doubt other factors, such as the major realignment of currencies in 1967, also played a part. But whatever has been the contribution in the past it seems very likely that the influence of multinational enterprises in this respect will become increasingly important in the future.

One development which seems likely to contribute to this, is the appearance of the 'international trade union', the antecedents of which are beginning to make themselves apparent in response to the growth of the multinational enterprise itself. Trade unions everywhere are beginning to become aware of the bargaining power available to the international firm and are girding themselves to meet it. So far, trade unions in host countries have largely concerned themselves with obtaining parity of earnings between multinational firms and domestic firms operating in the same country; but it will surely not be long before parity of earnings between subsidiaries of international enterprises operating in different countries will become a major objective (Levinson, 1970). Given that one of the major impacts of the multinational enterprise is to standardise technologies and production functions in use, at least in the developed industrial countries, the companies themselves are not likely to oppose this development.

The long-term aim of international trade unionism, at any rate in the advanced developed countries, would seem likely to be to compel all subsidiaries of an enterprise to pay the same money wage (after conversion into a common currency unit at current exchange rates) to all workers of comparable skill, grading and performance, irrespective of country of employment. The wage rate paid by the best practice country is likely to be the standard. Some evidence for this can be seen in a resolution passed at a recent conference of the World Automobile Council (in the setting up of which the United Automobile Workers' Union of the US took a leading part) the substance of which was that all workers employed by a given multinational automobile firm should have parity of real wages.

The parity that would be achieved by a policy of demanding equal money wages converted at currency exchange rates into the currencies of the countries in which the subsidiaries are located would of course be parity of 'own product' wages rather than parity of real wages since the latter depends on the prices of the wide range of goods entering into workers' consumption, including many, perhaps a majority of, non-traded goods, the composition and relative price of which would differ from country to country. Moreover, it is clear that unions are as yet far from achieving parity of 'own product' wages for all workers, irrespective of country, employed by a multinational firm. There are obvious formidable difficulties of a linguistic, religious and cultural character in the way of the full internationalisation of trade unionism; but it would be surprising if these were not eventually overcome (Warner and Turner, 1971).

If and when international wage bargaining has developed, wage rates in important sectors of the economy will be determined largely independently of the *average* level of labour productivity in the particular host economy. Wage pressure will have become internationalised and the wage transfer process will operate internationally. Until the non-multinationalised sectors of European and other economies become geared to the high productivity of the multinational firms (or the operations of the multinational firm penetrate more widely in the economy as a whole), wage pressures and consequent inflation are therefore likely to be exacerbated. Even more serious consequences for the domestic economic management of individual economies might also result, and these are discussed in the remainder of this paper.

MULTINATIONAL ENTERPRISES AND FEASIBLE CURRENCY AREAS

It could be argued that if exchange rates were allowed to float, an independent monetary policy would then become possible for national government despite the existence of the international capital market and the operations of the multinational firm. Moreover, currency speculation by multinational enterprises and others would become inhibited and less profitable since speculators would no longer be offered a one-way option which is available to them under the present exchange rate system. For well-known reasons, fiscal policy *per se* would become less effective but this would not matter greatly since the combination of varying the fiscal deficit plus appropriate changes in the money supply could still be relied upon to obtain significant control over the domestic economy. The questions arise, however, whether, in a world in which multinational companies play a large and probably increasing role in international trade, national economies can remain independent currency areas, and whether changes in exchange rates can be relied upon to produce appropriate changes in relative prices and domestic absorbtion which would make balance of payments equilibrium possible. This leads us into a discussion of the concept of *feasible* currency areas (Corden, 1972).

The classical argument for relying on changes in the exchange rate to maintain or restore balance of payment equilibrium is essentially based on two assumptions: first, that money wages are not flexible in a downward direction while, second, real wages are. If, in the case of a balance of payments deficit, money wages were flexible in the downward direction, devaluation of the exchange rate would not be required; the fall in money wages could be relied upon to bring about the change in relative prices and real absorbtion required to correct the situation. On the other hand, if a devaluation is resorted to and real wages are not flexible in the downward direction, the devaluation *per se* would be virtually useless in restoring balance of payments equilibrium.

In the absence of changes in money wages, devaluation tends to raise the price level of international traded goods relative to non-traded goods and therefore tends to lower real wages relatively to what they would have been in the absence of the devaluation. Thus, if money illusion exists or wage and other incomes are fixed in domestic money terms, the devaluation will lead to a reduction in the demand for imports in real terms and/or an increase in exports without a decline in employment and real output being required. But if money illusion does not exist and/or income contracts are not fixed, at least in the short run, in domestic money terms then money wages throughout the economy will adjust to the new exchange rate. In these circumstances, devaluation can only produce an improvement in the balance of trade by causing a decline in real output and employment. The more open the economy is (that is to say the higher the proportion of domestic expenditure which falls on internationally traded goods), the less likely is money illusion to exist and the more likely are money wages and other incomes to be fixed directly or indirectly in foreign currency terms. In other words, a small open economy is not likely to be a feasible currency area since it cannot, by varying the rate of exchange of its currency for units of other countries' currencies, bring about changes in relative prices and real absorbtion.

It can be expected, however, that most large industrial countries even those relying quite extensively on international trade, are feasible currency areas. Money wage contracts and other income contracts are largely determined independently of what is happening in other countries; and, provided the exchange rate change is not excessively large and/or inflation has not been continuing for some time at a high rate, money illusion will be prevalent at least to some extent. In these circumstances, changes in the exchange rate can be relied upon to maintain balance of payments equilibrium or restore it in the case of structural shifts in demand or supply, without employment and output having to suffer.

However, the growth and spread of the multinational enterprise may begin to change this. There are two developments that seem likely to operate in the future. The first we have already discussed, namely, the increasing tendency for the wage transfer process to operate internationally. The significance of this for the existence of a feasible currency area is that in the event of a country's exchange rate being devalued, there will be pressure from unions in that country to raise the money wages of its workers in proportion to the depreciation of the exchange rate; and this pressure will be supported by unions in other countries whose currencies have not been devalued. In so far as it is conceded to and leads through the wage transfer mechanism to successful parity claims for higher money wages across the devaluing economy as a whole, the depreciation of the exchange rate will be offset partly if not wholly by a general rise in money wages: the essential conditions for a feasible currency area and a successful outcome of a change in the exchange rate—namely, widespread money illusion and/or money wage rate contracts fixed in domestic money terms—would be violated.[6]

The second development that would bear on the existence of feasible currency areas would be a policy of the multinational enterprises themselves to price the output of their affiliates on the basis of market sharing arrangements rather than on the basis of allowing subsidiaries to compete against each other, at any rate on the basis of price. Thus, it could be that, given a devaluation of the exchange rate of a country in which it has a subsidiary, the multinational enterprise would prefer to keep the foreign currency price of its subsidiary's local output sold abroad unchanged rather than expose another subsidiary operating in a non-devaluing country to greater competition from the first.

Such a policy would reinforce the wage pressures on the subsidiary operating in the devaluing country referred to earlier. The presence of national competitors in the developing country would, of course, impose a constraint on the ability of the multinational enterprise to maintain market sharing arrangements between subsidiaries. But assuming that the wage transfer process operates strongly in the devaluing country, the constraining influence of national competitors on market sharing arrangements employed by multinational enterprises in managing their subsidiaries would be rapidly diminished, and the price and money income level in the devaluing country would quickly rise to offset the devaluation of the currency.[7] Only a fixed money supply in nominal terms could then make the exchange rate change effective in improving the balance of payments, and then, as indicated earlier, only at the expense of falling output and employment.

Thus, as a consequence of the spread and growing influence of multinational enterprises, accompanied, as seems likely, by the growth of multinational trade unions and the internationalisation of wage bargaining goals and practices, fewer and fewer countries seem likely to remain feasible currency areas, and more and more countries will find it increasingly difficult to maintain balance of payments equilibrium without bringing about significant changes in the levels of their employment. This means, that although a floating exchange rate would permit national governments to obtain control over their domestic money supply, at any rate in nominal terms, the problem of using it to maintain high employment with reasonable price stability would become increasingly more difficult. The problem would be particularly acute for countries in which the *average* level of productivity was low and increasing slowly, for in these countries the wage transfer process (both national and international) would be putting considerable upward pressure on the price level, and the attempt to offset this by employing a restrictive monetary policy would result in more unemployment.

CONCLUSIONS

The conclusion of the preceding paragraphs is that nation states could well be faced with important policy dilemmas. The internationalisation of the capital market is likely to become more and more incompatible with the operation of an autonomous domestic monetary policy in a fixed exchange rate system while the growth and spread of the operations of the multinational enterprises is likely to make a system of flexible exchange rates less effective in combining balance of payments equilibrium with high and stable employment. Moreover, the inflation-employment trade-off dilemma is likely to become more acute, complicating the task of monetary management. It is, therefore, not certain that the nation state can survive in its present form in the face of the growth of international capitalism and putative international trade unionism. The probability is that it will have to give way to some supranational organisation.

At the very least, in order to retain some control over their economies, countries may find it necessary to group together to form economic unions which can exist as feasible currency areas. From the economic point of view, countries will more easily integrate, the more alike they are in technicological advancement, and in productivity and real income levels; and uniformity in cultural patterns and mores may also be important since these will bear on real income and wealth aspirations. Even so, such economic groupings would probably have to exert control over the operations and spread of multinational firms based in their own economies and owned by residents of other feasible currency areas.

Perhaps in the very long run, even such powerful groupings as the European Economic Community may not be able to remain autonomously managed areas. Eventually, perhaps, the growing strength of international capitalism and spread of ever advancing technology will make a world state and world government inevitable. But this chapter contains crystal gazing enough. The trends and developments we have been discussing are by no means definitely established; and until they have been it is hardly worth while to explore the problems with respect to international capitalism. In the meantime, however, the considerations discussed in this chapter may well provide a useful frame of reference for observing the growing impact of multinational enterprise in the world economy.

References

[1] This was written before the appearance of the massive financial surpluses of the oil producing countries.

[2] On the other hand, there is a growing tendency for national governments to discriminate against multinational enterprises in the implementation of credit squeeze policies.

3 Although it does not contradict the argument concerning the impact of fiscal policy, it should be recognised that firms which export a substantial proportion of their output are more vulnerable to over-valued exchange rates. For a general examination of the sensitivity of the capital formation of multinational enterprises to macroeconomic policies of host governments see Dunning (1973c).

4 For an empirical study of Swedish inflation based on this approach to the theory of inflation see Edgren, *et al.* (1971).

5 A counter argument is that the power of local trade unions to bargain for wage increases is effectively constrained by the threat of multinational enterprises to shift their operations to other countries. A statement to this effect made by Henry Ford Jnr, in England a year or two back is now notorious. However, when much capital has already been invested, the force of the threat must be in some doubt; moreover, in the case cited, labour discipline rather than excessive wage demands seems to have been the main point at issue.

6 In this situation trade unions are clearly 'trading off' the maintenance of the real wages of their members against unemployment, but this policy is not irrational given the acceptance by governments of responsibility for maintaining at least a minimum standard of living for the unemployed.

7 If the combined influence of multinational enterprises and international trade unionism is to integrate factor markets, international exchange would then be increasingly based on absolute instead of comparative advantage.

Chapter 10

THE THEORY OF
DEVELOPMENT POLICY[1]

Paul Streeten

INTRODUCTION

In the early phase of the theory of development policy in the
Fifties it was capital that was stressed as the strategic factor in
development. Foreign investment by the multinational enterprise
(MNE) was therefore regarded mainly as a source of foreign
funds which supplemented domestic savings efforts. Nurkse's
thesis that countries are poor because they are poor and needed
large injections of foreign capital became widely accepted.[2]
According to this view, a poor country could not raise its low
ratio of savings to national income very quickly or very easily. A
low savings and investment rate led to a low rate of capital
accumulation. This, in turn, implied that workers were endowed
with relatively little capital: this kept their productivity low. Low
productivity per worker perpetuated low income per head. The
low investment ratio was both cause and effect of poverty. In
order to break out of this vicious circle of poverty, massive
injections of capital from abroad would be necessary. Foreign
investment could contribute to pulling poor countries out of this
low equilibrium trap.

The experience of the last 20 years has shown that capital was
considerably less scarce, and that capital/output ratios were
lower, than this doctrine had postulated. Capital was more
abundant, partly because more foreign aid and private foreign
capital were available, and partly because, in spite of their low
incomes, many countries achieved quite high domestic savings
ratios. During the Sixties, the share of gross investment in the
GNP of developing countries was nearly 20 per cent and the share
of savings in GNP over 15 per cent, substantially higher than
either the early writers had anticipated or countries industrialising
earlier had achieved at a corresponding stage. Rostow had

reasoned that the ratio of investment to income would have to rise from 5 to 10 per cent in order to achieve 'take-off'. England had a savings ratio of only 5 per cent in the eighteenth century, during her industrial revolution, and achieved 10 per cent not until the 1840s.[3] It is, of course, true that the savings ratio of 16·6 per cent in 1970 for all developing countries is lower than the 22·9 per cent achieved by the industrialised countries in the same year. But by historical standards domestic savings ratios were unprecedently high and by the standards of the early writers they were unexpectedly high. In addition, there is now much evidence that the capital in existence was underutilised. The underutilisation of labour had, of course, been a common theme from the beginning of the study of development policy, but the emphasis on capital underutilisation, often substantially greater than in developed countries, is relatively recent.[4]

The absence of a severe bottleneck in capital was confirmed by certain *a priori* considerations. It was found that there was no reason why the savings ratio out of low incomes should be smaller than that out of high incomes. It was also argued that savings and capital are not so much a factor of production with which countries are 'endowed' and which causes development to proceed, as the *result* of the adoption of new technologies and of development. The identification of investment opportunities tends to generate the necessary savings.

High growth rates were associated with relatively high savings ratios and low capital/output ratios. Capital/output ratios were low, partly because the adoption of existing Western techniques of production economised in the use of capital to invent new techniques, thus avoiding the waste of trials and errors, partly because some countries spent relatively little on capital-intensive overhead facilities, and partly because in countries where land was abundant a high rate of growth of the labour force yielded considerable extra agricultural output with relatively little extra capital, even if non-monetary investment, such as land-clearing, is properly accounted for. For these reasons capital turned out to be not such a severe constraint as had been thought.[5]

Another strand of thinking stressed the contribution that foreign capital could make to scarce foreign exchange. Foreign exchange scarcity was derived from the trade pessimism that prevailed in the Fifties and from doctrines of structural imbalance. While foreign exchange clearly was a serious bottleneck in the progress of many countries, others achieved remarkably high growth rates of exports in the Sixties.

The contribution of private overseas investment tended to be seen in the framework of a Harrod–Domar model, linking growth rates with either savings or foreign exchange receipts. But it soon became evident that many activities of the MNE brought with them relatively little capital or foreign exchange, but a good many other things instead.[6] Direct foreign investment in developing countries, including reinvested earnings, rose to $4000 m annually at the end of the Sixties, compared with total capital formation in the developing countries of about $40 000 m and the total external flow of financial resources of nearly $16 000 m.

Later writers stressed training and the transfer and local creation of skills (investment in human capital), management, entrepreneurship (i.e. innovative rather than administrative management), science and technology, and research and development (R & D). As it became increasingly clear that development involves also social, cultural and political change, interacting in a complex manner with economic factors, and as the definition and objectives of development shifted from accelerated aggregate economic growth to social objectives such as equality and, above all, jobs, livelihoods and generally meeting the needs of the masses of poor people, the contribution of the MNE came to be judged by its effects upon these objectives rather than by the contribution of savings or foreign exchange to economic growth.

The relation between the MNE and these social objectives will, to a large extent, depend upon the ability and willingness of the host government to pursue the 'right' policies. A view focusing only on the contribution of the MNE to resources generally available for development is justified if the government pursues appropriate policies with respect to distribution and employment, through science policy, land reform, foreign exchange rates, etc. If, on the other hand, such policies are absent or defective, the MNE may be judged by its impact on variables normally regarded as proper direct objectives of government policies.

Thus, with an efficient fiscal system and an honest administrative service, the MNE can be encouraged to pursue efficiency and high profits. Through tax collection, these profits will then make a contribution to the attainment of the social objectives. But if the fiscal and administrative system is defective, the direct contribution of the MNE towards the social objectives will have to be taken into account. Efficiency and profit criteria will then have to be supplemented by criteria of social justice, regional development, employment creation, environmental protection, etc.

The change in thinking reflected earlier changes in the nature of private overseas investment. The most important of these is the shift from nineteenth century portfolio to direct foreign investment, often accompanied by the MNE's efforts to raise capital locally. There was also the growing importance of new technologies, some of them embodied in capital equipment, others independent of specific pieces of equipment but related to organisation, marketing and the commercial use of scientific knowledge. The growing size of the multinational firm and the tendency to horizontal, vertical and, much more rarely, lateral integration of the operations of the firm meant that monopoly or oligopoly power played an increasing role. The shift of analytical emphasis from capital goods and financial flows to technology, advertising and bargaining reflects these changes in the system of international production.

THE OPERATIONS OF THE MNE AND THEIR IMPLICATIONS FOR POLICY OBJECTIVES

The difference between targets, needs or requirements and domestically mobilisable resources has been identified or measured by a variety of 'gaps'—gaps in savings, foreign exchange, skills. While such aggregation has serious weaknesses and has recently been replaced by much greater emphasis on detailed project by project appraisal, it can serve as a very rough first approximation. The impact of MNEs on national development policies can then be listed under their contribution to filling these various gaps and by their effects on other variables relevant to the development objectives.

(1) The contribution to filling the resource gap between desired investment and locally mobilised savings.
(2) The contribution to filling the foreign exchange or trade gap between foreign exchange requirements and foreign exchange earnings plus official net aid. While this gap is *ex post* always identical with the savings gap, requirements or targets for foreign exchange are not identical with those for savings if there is a structural balance of payments problem.
(3) The contribution to filling the budgetary gap between target revenue and locally raised taxes.
(4) The contribution to filling the management and skill gap by providing foreign management and training local managers and workers.

The analytical value of looking at the contribution in terms of one or more of these gaps is that the value to the economy may exceed the value accruing from a particular project. Gap analysis brings out the multiplier effect of the foreign contribution. If domestic resources are underutilised because some crucial component is missing (e.g. foreign exchange or a particular kind of skill), the breaking of this bottleneck has a magnifying effect upon resource mobilisation in the rest of the economy. Unless such externalities are properly allowed for in project appraisal, they will get left out.

In addition, the contribution of the MNE may be judged by the following criteria.

(5) Technology is very poorly developed in many developing countries. The MNE may either transfer foreign and often inappropriate technology or, by adaptation or new invention, generate a more appropriate technology. It is in the market for knowledge that some of the most interesting problems arise.

(6) Entrepreneurship is something different from a skill that can be taught and learned. The MNE may contribute to the growth of indigenous entrepreneurs by subcontracting to ancillary industries, repair shops, component makers, etc. It may be in its interest to stimulate such growth among its suppliers or buyers or those performing intermediate tasks between inputs and outputs of the firm.

(7) The MNE may, through its own actions, shift the balance of bargaining power in negotiating and renegotiating contracts. Most obviously, the balance of power will be quite different at the time before an investment is made and after money has been sunk. Less obviously, negotiation will itself improve the skills in negotiation and will contribute to the stock of useful knowledge for later negotiations.

(8) An important contribution often quoted is the ability of the MNE to establish contact with overseas banks, market outlets, sources of supply and other institutions, which would otherwise remain unknown to the indigenous firms.

Finally, there are the contributions to macroeconomic policy objectives. Among these the following may be singled out.

(9) The MNE may make a contribution to creating jobs and thereby raising employment.

(10) It may improve a country's income terms of trade either by lowering costs more than export prices or by reducing dependence on foreign products.

(11) It may contribute to a more efficient market structure or

reduce the type of monopoly profits that are enjoyed in the form of inefficiency and a 'quite life'.

A major difficulty in assessing these contributions is that far from being able to quantify precisely these effects, we do not even know, in general, their direction. MNEs provide capital, but also may reduce domestic savings (e.g. if saving is limited by investment opportunities and these themselves are limited, or foreign investment leads to a shift to wages with a lower savings propensity) and impose capital servicing costs upon the host country. They may improve its foreign exchange position but equally may reduce foreign exchange earnings and may impose a primary and secondary foreign exchange burden, depending on the relation between retained profits and new investment on the one hand and remittances on the other.[7] They may contribute to public revenue, but frequently tax concessions, investment grants, the provision of factory sites and tariff policy erode this contribution. They may transfer and adapt technology, but it may be inappropriate for the available factors or social and physical conditions of the country, not just in some abstract, irrelevant sense but inappropriate in relation to the cost that the country has to pay for it. They may provide foreign management and train local managers, but, like engineering technology, the management techniques may be inappropriate, because they economise in the use of uneducated, diseased, ill-nourished and undisciplined labour, the employment of which would yield social but not equivalent private benefits. They may encourage local entrepreneurs, but again they may stifle the growth of indigenous entrepreneurship in weak and rudimentary markets. They may provide training in the skills of negotiation by producing managers and officials who put their experience to work in negotiating for their countries, but they may also reinforce the uneven initial balance of power.

They open up a society to world influences and thereby enable it to draw on resources and skills on a world-wide scale, but they also destroy local activities by exposing them to these influences. They may reduce unemployment or they may raise it by increasing wage costs and destroying traditional crafts. They may improve or worsen the terms of trade according to the direction of their activities and their foreign trade bias. They may make local industry more competitive or more monopolistic. Politically, they may introduce benefits by wider contacts, but may also create unrest and, by buying up politicians and officials who should be controlling them, spread corruption. Socially and culturally, they may increase inequalities between income groups,

I

sectors and regions, may Westernise attitudes, on the one hand imposing a sophisticated, high income, consumption pattern, on the other, possibly leading to high turnover, low-mark-up methods of business. They often use capital-intensive techniques to produce capital-intensive products for a small, relatively well-off élite, including the aristocracy of workers fortunate enough to hold jobs. On the other hand, they may identify processes or components in a set of vertically integrated operations which are labour-intensive and locate these in low-income countries, exporting the semi-finished products and then reimporting them to the parent country. They may bring traditional societies into the twentieth century or they may reduce them to 'dependence', imposing technical, managerial and cultural subservience on the host country.

Another theoretical difficulty in analysing the contribution to development of the MNE is the problem of attribution. The MNE may, in particular circumstances, do things that (a) are not essential attributes of the MNE but might be peculiar to particular individuals responsible for its affairs, or to the policies of host governments,[8] or to a specific locality or to history; or (b) could have been done equally well or better in other ways than through the MNE. Ideally one would wish to identify those features that are peculiar to *all* (or a group of) MNEs and *only* to MNEs.

Amongst the most common charges raised by developing host countries against the MNE are the following. Some of them raise the problem of attribution, especially to government policy. Some of them were mentioned as the reverse side of the positive effects but it is worth bringing them together.

(i) Its impact on development is very uneven and it therefore creates or reinforces dualism and inequality. This inequality may apply to income by size (employed workers *versus* the rest), by sector (manufacturing, mining, plantation *versus* food for domestic consumption) and by region (urban, industrial *versus* rural).

(ii) It introduces inappropriate products, which are normally closely linked to the technology and inappropriate consumption patterns. This point is related to the previous one, for inequality of income distribution gives rise to a fragmented consumption pattern and to a small market for sophisticated consumer goods.[9] These are the goods produced by the sophisticated technology in the rich industrial countries for their high-income markets, in which the monopolistic advantage of the MNE lies.

(iii) A consequence of the previous two points is that the *local* investment funds on which the MNE draws and which have an opportunity cost are wrongly allocated and not in accordance with the social priorities of the country.

(iv) The MNE is also charged with influencing government policy in directions unfavourable to development. It may secure excessive protection, tax concessions, subsidies to inputs or provision of factory sites or other services of infrastructure. As a result substantial private profits may be consistent with low or negative social returns.

(v) It is said to stifle private enterprise, because its superior know-how and management prevent indigenous entrepreneurs from initiating enterprises.

(vi) Finally it is accused of causing political friction by the suspicion that foreign interests control assets and jobs.

The above approach of listing under various headings the merits and drawbacks of the MNE (which might be described as the laundry list approach) is common but unsatisfactory. What would be more satisfactory is an analytical framework in which these various possibilities are accommodated, possibly classified according to relevant criteria, and then filled with empirical, quantitative content.

In the first place, one would seek criteria by which the importance of the different headings can be distinguished. These might be found in the nature of the MNE's operations: are they conducting vertically integrated activities, beginning with extraaction and ending with the final processed product? Or are they market-orientated manufacturing subsidiaries drawing on the brand name or the research of the parent company? Distinctions by type of product or by type of process may be useful here.

Next, it is important to identify the causes leading to the various possible outcomes: are they government policies and, if so, are these themselves autonomous or exogenous variables or are they the result of the firms' pressure, persuasion or bribery? Are they the result of the transfer of existing but inappropriate technologies? Are they the result of the use of bargaining power by large, well-informed companies confronting small, weak, ignorant, fragmented and competing governments?

RESEARCH ON THE MNE

Much of the research on the MNE has been in the neo-classical tradition. Sir Donald MacDougall analysed foreign investment as a flow of additional capital into a country, while everything else is held constant. The static effects of marginal investments can be analysed according to marginal productivity theory.[10] This approach can then be enlarged by gradually relaxing the restrictive assumptions and tracing the implications of increasing returns, indivisibilities, imperfect competition, learning by doing, etc. Much of this was done by Sir Donald MacDougall. It is also possible to assume that the foreign firms shift or twist the production function in various ways with varying results on marginal returns, intra-marginal returns and the distribution of profits between domestic and foreign capitalists and workers. As restrictive assumptions are relaxed, the range of possible conclusions is enlarged and it is then quite possible to construct cases where the introduction or enlargement of privately profitable foreign investment detracts from the host country's real income. MacDougall concluded that the most important direct gains from more rather than less foreign private investment 'seem likely to come through higher tax revenue from foreign profits (at least if the higher investment is not induced by lower tax rates), through economies of scale and through external economies generally, especially where . . . firms acquire "know-how" or are forced by foreign competition to adopt more efficient methods.[11]

Some of the limitations of this approach were pointed out by Balogh and Streeten,[12] although not with specific reference to developing countries. MacDougall himself had reasoned that the host country might lose if the foreign investment used strongly labour-saving techniques or if the foreign firms used their mono-poly power to exploit local buyers.[13] These objections were elaborated by subsequent writers.

Most of the writings on the MNE had, of course, to abandon the assumption of perfect competition on which much of MacDougall's analysis was based. Kindleberger, Caves and Diaz-Alejandro[14] specifically build their analysis on the assump-tions of imperfect competition, oligopoly with interdependence recognised or monopoly power.

Even in the case of developed countries, where markets are less imperfect, the widely observed fact of two-way investment in the same industry is inconsistent with the assumption of perfect competition. In developing countries competition is notoriously imperfect or absent in sectors and industries in which the MNE operates.

Awareness that oligopoly is in the nature of the MNE has led to an approach that has combined the theory of industrial organisation as applied to the relations between oligopolies and the theory of international trade and investment.[15] This approach identifies a special advantage of the firm (e.g. superior knowledge or goodwill acquired by the use of a brand name) that enables it to produce abroad in spite of the inferiority of local knowledge and connections, combined with an advantage in producing near the place of sales or the source of supply. In this way the superiority of producing abroad over exporting from a home base or licensing the right to make use of the special advantage, are explained. Tariffs and other protectionist devices, often cited as the main cause of the establishment of local subsidiaries, will tend to raise profits of the subsidiary but are neither a necessary nor a sufficient condition; not necessary, because even without protection the special advantage may be exploited; not sufficient, because where the special advantage is absent, no amount of protection will lead to the establishment of a subsidiary.[16] The proprietary knowledge or the goodwill possessed by the firm is an indivisibility, so that its use abroad involves low costs to the firm, and it tries, through patents or advertising, to prevent others from appropriating this advantage. The local knowledge acquired in the process, also, is indivisible and this will tend to make for a few large firms carrying out investment and setting up an oligopolistic structure.

A related approach, without, however, the rigorous framework of a theory, has become known as the doctrine of the product cycle. This doctrine[17] has emphasised *monopolistic* elements in investment, *technological innovation* with special rights in new discoveries and *uncertainty* about costs, demand and rival behaviour. The new theory (or 'model' or 'concept' or 'hypothesis', as Raymond Vernon prefers to call it) also emphasises the need for experiment and reconnaissance, the economies of scale to be reaped from research, marketing and management and the ability to routinise novel processes after a time. It is essentially a model of a succession of temporary monopolistic advantages, which are gradually eroded through diffusion and imitation. It is a model of a know-how treadmill.

According to this model, new products are first introduced by large firms with extensive research programmes in their established, wealthy domestic markets. Consumers' tastes are better known there, incomes are high and demand for the new product is price inelastic. If the product proves successful, output expands, costs per unit fall and the firm begins to export. In markets where exports are successful, they are backed at first by small foreign investments aimed at marketing and servicing the product. These are followed by assembly and local purchase of some components. If conditions are favourable or if exports are threatened by rivals, more processes are located abroad and foreign subsidiaries are established to make use of lower labour costs and proximity to the market. Ultimately, the product may be exported from the foreign subsidiary to the parent home market or to other markets abroad. This particular product cycle is closed, though new ones will meanwhile have started. On this view, exports serve as a feeler, a form of reconnaissance. They establish whether a market exists and whether it should be backed by investment. Diffusion may, however, take other forms than foreign investment. There may be licensing or imitation.

The model of the product cycle does not, however, account fully for a recent trend in foreign investment to which attention has now turned, viz. the location in low-income countries of low-skill, labour-intensive processes or the production or assembly of components or spare parts in a vertically integrated multinational firm. Above all, in electronics and electrical components, but also in the making of gloves, leather goods, luggage, baseballs, watches, motor car parts and other consumer goods, and in electrical machinery, machine tools, accounting machines, typewriters, cameras, etc., processes that require much labour and limited capital and skills (sewing, boring holes, assembling) have been located in South Korea, Taiwan, Mexico, Hong Kong, Singapore and the West Indian islands.[18]

In one sense, the doctrine of comparative advantage seems to be vindicated, though in a manner quite different from that normally envisaged. It is foreign, not domestic, capital, know-how and management that are highly mobile internationally and that are combined with plentiful, immobile, domestic, semi-skilled labour. Specialisation between countries is not by commodities according to relative factor endowments, but by factors of production: the poor countries specialising in low-skilled labour, leaving the rewards for capital, management and know-how to the foreign owners of these scarce but internationally mobile factors. The situation is equivalent to one in which *labour itself* rather than the *product of labour* is exported. For the surplus of the product of labour over the wage, resulting from the co-operation of other factors in less elastic supply, accrues abroad. The differential international and internal elasticities of supply in response to differential rewards, and the differences in monopoly rents entering the rewards of these factors have important implications for the international distributions of gains from investment and trade.

Since the firms operate in oligopolistic and oligopsonistic

markets, cost advantages are not necessarily passed on to consumers in lower prices or to workers in higher wages, and the
profits then accrue to the parent firms. The continued operation
of this type of international specialisation depends upon the
continuation of substantial wage differentials (hence there must
be weakness of trade union action to push up wages), continuing
access to the markets of the parent companies (hence stronger
pressure from importing interests than from domestic producers
displaced by the low cost processes and components, including
trade unions in the rich importing countries) and continuing
permission or encouragement by host countries to operate with
minimum taxes, tariffs and bureaucratic regulations.

The packaged nature of the contribution of the MNE, usually
claimed as its characteristic blessing, is in this context the cause
of the unequal international distribution of the gains from trade
and investment. If the package broke or leaked, some of the rents
and monopoly rewards would spill over into the host country.
But if it is secured tightly, only the least scarce and weakest
factor in the host country derives an income from the operations
of the MNE, unless bargaining power is used to extract a share
of these other incomes.[19]

The situation is aggravated if there is technical progress, so
that the labour-intensive activity in the underdeveloped host
country might be knocked out by an innovation using capital or
technology in the parent country. Other processes or components
will still be left to which the labour force could be switched. But
such switching has its costs. Skills acquired are wasted and the
bargaining power of the host country and its labour force is
further reduced, unless retraining is short and its costs are carried
by the MNE.

The bargaining power of host countries and of the plentiful
factor—semi-skilled labour—in such a situation is likely to be
weak and the question is whether such a division of gains between
parent and host, between the foreign investment 'package' and
domestic labour, remains acceptable. The gains to the host
country are confined to the wages of those employed if the alternative is unemployment. The fact that these earnings are in
foreign exchange may put them at a premium. There may, in
addition, be linkages, but these may be positive or negative.
While such investment has attractions for some countries faced
with labour surpluses and foreign exchange shortages and poorly
endowed with natural resources, the potential gains may not be
considered worth the social risks and social costs, including a
form of dependence and dualistic development of a new kind,

different from that of the colonial mines or plantations economy, but similar in its distributional impact.

TRANSFER PRICING

One important reason why the MNE does not fit easily into the theory of comparative advantage and its normative conclusions is the phenomenon of transfer pricing. A large and growing volume of international trade today is conducted within the firm —between affiliates, subsidiaries, branches located in different countries—and not between independent firms. It has been estimated that one quarter to one third of world trade in manufactures (and possibly more) is intra-firm trade and therefore not at arm's-length. This proportion is likely to be even larger for LDCs. This fact has very important implications of which existing trade and investment theory has hardly begun to take note.

The reason why intra-firm trade raises entirely different issues from inter-firm trade is that the items entering such trade will be valued according to other considerations than those determining competitive market prices. The chief considerations relevant to the pricing of intra-firm transactions will be taxation (including allowances and loss offset provisions), tariffs, exchange rates (expected changes, multiple rates, restrictions on remissions), political and social pressures (trade unions, fear of potential competitors) and joint ventures with local share holders.[20] The phenomenon goes much deeper than 'fiddling' prices to evade tax payments. The allocation of the large overhead and joint costs, that give the MNE its special advantage, between firms, products and components is bound to be arbitrary within wide limits and a policy of maximising global post-tax profits from the world-wide system of operations of the firm will greatly reduce the significance of declared prices, capital values and rates of return for purposes of national policy.

It may, of course, remain true that the actual quantities traded will obey the principle of comparative advantage. Firms will presumably be guided by money costs and, to the extent that these reflect comparative costs, the principle will remain applicable. Those looking for the appropriate competitive prices would find them in the hypothetical or real second set of books kept by the companies for their accounting purposes. Indeed, the theory of transfer pricing presupposes that the firm has some idea of what it would charge in a competitive market. Other forces, such as oligopolistic market structures, bilateral monopoly and subjective risk premia will, of course, qualify or suspend the application of the doctrine of comparative advantage, but the transfer pricing mechanism by itself need not interfere with it as far as quantities traded are concerned.

But this is of little use to ignorant and weak host governments, concerned with framing policies with respect to taxation, tariffs, foreign exchange rates, foreign exchange restrictions and local participation in shareholding. Neither existing theory nor practice are equipped to deal with this new phenomenon and it presents an important agenda for future research.[21]

The implications for the theory of economic policy will become clearer only after considerably more work has been done on the range, scope and limits of transfer pricing. But it is plain that there are important implications for tax policy, tariff policy and setting other incentives for MNEs. The incentive and opportunity to overprice inputs in order to reduce declared profits can be mitigated or reversed by a state trading corporation trading in all imports or by local participation and control (though participation without control based on full information creates an incentive to over-invoice). These corrective measures, however, may create new difficulties.

Ultimately, the only proper response to an organisation that takes a global view will be global control. Thus, if companies had to be incorporated internationally and pay uniform internationally determined tax rates, one important incentive for transfer pricing would be removed. But until such de-nationalisation and internationalisation, national governments will have to find ways of counteracting some of the potential damage done to them by transfer pricing.

PROBLEMS OF BARGAINING

The oligopolistic structure and certain other features peculiar to the market for advanced technology limit the use of analysis in terms of smooth and continuous marginal productivity and demand functions and of project evaluation by means of shadow prices. The location of subsidiaries in developing countries normally draws on the R & D expenditure of the parent firm and on its technical know-how generally, or on exploration costs or on heavy advertising expenditure or on other overhead or joint costs. These expenditures precede and do not enter into the operating costs of the enterprises but they bestow a 'special advantage' on the enterprise. (Whether the advantage is real, because based on scientific knowledge, or imagined and 'artificial', because based on the exploitation of created fears and wants, is not relevant here, except in so far as the 'advantage' cannot be used to justify the activity.) The 'special advantage' of the MNE is an indivisibility of this type. Since the activities in low-income countries do not enter into the calculations when R & D expenditure (the Philips research centre near Eindhoven is an exception), exploration costs or administrative costs are decided upon at headquarters, the cost of using the results of these expenditures in LDCs is small, not only *ex post*, when only variable costs count, but also *ex ante* in relation to expected returns. In the extreme case, this cost is zero or even negative. Normally, there will be positive costs of administration and adaptation. There may also be opportunity costs of using the technology in low-income countries. Operations there may reduce profits on established lines in other countries. Asking for favourable terms by one country may also set a precedent for quotations in other countries, where the opportunity costs may be higher.

On the other hand, such opportunity costs may be negative. Operation by the subsidiary may raise profits, or may prevent a fall in profits, elsewhere. The possibility of such 'organic' interaction makes the bargaining process even more difficult for the host country, for it implies that entirely properly calculated local profits may be low, yet be of greater value to the company than is reflected in these profits, because of their contribution to the profits, or to the reduction of losses, of the whole system of the company's world-wide operations. The use of bargaining power in this situation would require knowledge of the world-wide operations, including the threats from competitors, not just of those in the country. So much for the cost to the MNE.

To the host country desiring to acquire the technology (or any other of the 'special advantages') on the other hand, the cost can be high. It is the cost of embarking itself on the research and independently evolving the know-how or of duplicating exploration. The existence of such large fixed and joint costs means that there is a large gap between the minimum 'returns' a MNE will accept and still find it worth while investing, and the maximum 'returns' the enterprise can enjoy and make it still worth while for the host to permit operations. In principle, it would be possible to determine this range for different acts of investment both by different firms and for different sizes of investment and different contracts of the same firm.

This large gap between marginal and average costs of the

technology is only one of several factors making for monopoly power. Another arises from the fact that knowledge to buy knowledge is often the knowledge to be bought itself and from the fact that tie-in agreements make it possible to make the transfer of technical knowledge conditional on the purchase of certain pieces of equipment or other inputs. In these ways the MNE can extract a yield substantially above the marginal costs incurred by the transfer.[22] The only mitigating factor is the competition between several oligopolies in possession of competing know-how.

One source of monopoly power of the MNE therefore derives from the technological dependence of the developing host country. But there is a second quite distinct source, which also leads to a divergence between private profits and social benefits and establishes a range within which bargaining can take place. This source is the policy pursued by the government of the host country. Tariffs and non-tariff barriers on competing imports, taxes on the exports of necessary inputs, subsidies to inputs, overvaluation of exchange rates and tax concessions can lead to social losses. If imported inputs are overvalued, costs overstated and profits understated, an appearance of greater need for protection is created than is warranted.[23] While apparently no or low real profits are repatriated, repatriation takes place through transfer pricing or charges such as management fees, royalties or interest which accrue to the parent firm. The point is well made by Diaz-Alejandro: 'if foreign investors can borrow from host country's credit resources at interest rates which are often negative in real terms, make profits sheltered behind effective rates of protection which reach 100 per cent and above, benefit from holidays and exemptions from import duties on their raw materials, and remit profits abroad at overvalued exchange rates, there may be doubts as to the net benefits which the host country receives from such an activity.'[24]

It is often argued that governments have the remedy in their own hands. Let them reduce protection, liberalise trade, establish 'realistic' exchange rates, raise the price of capital, lower the cost of labour and thus align private costs to social costs. There is some evidence that, where the incentives are right (e.g. the relative price of capital is high), the MNE *does* adapt its techniques of production to local factor availabilities, using more capital-saving methods of production than domestic enterprises. But assuming the government believes that the investment is useful for the country, it is often the MNE that uses pressure on the government to introduce the 'distortions'. Ignorance about the value of the technology and the accounting methods induce the country to accept the terms of the MNE.

Policies themselves are influenced by the MNEs, both when negotiations are conducted about their establishment and, later, by their operations. The link between unequal distribution of income and wealth and the tendency of the MNE to cater for the needs of a relatively rich élite illustrates the point. While it is true that the MNE caters for the needs of an unequal income distribution, the profits and wages it generates reinforce this distribution. It is just as true to say that the income distribution elicits the product range and the processes employed by the MNE, as it is to say that the product range and the processes reinforce the income distribution.[25]

Similarly, protection is often treated as if it were autonomously determined by government policy. In fact, governments yield to the pressures of foreign companies documented by transfer prices. This is not to say that foreign companies welcome the complicated system of import controls, delays, red tape and corruption. But such a system is partly the result of the pressures of interest groups, including those of foreign companies.

The author has argued that continuous, smooth, marginal productivity curves are inappropriate in analysing the relations between host government and MNE. For the transfer of a certain 'package' of know-how, capital, management and inputs there is a range of values which would be acceptable to both sides but which both sides have an interest in concealing. The ability to conceal the relevant values is however much greater for the MNE than for the host country.

In settling the bargain and in drawing up the contract, a large number of items may be for negotiation, in addition to tax concessions and tariff and non-tariff protection of the product.[26] Among these are:

> Specific allowances against tax liabilities, such as initial or investment allowance, depletion allowances, tax reporting techniques, loss offset provisions, etc.
>
> Royalty payments, management fees and other fees.
>
> Duty drawbacks on imported inputs for exports.
>
> Content of local inputs.
>
> Profit and capital repatriation.
>
> Structure of ownership and degree and timing of local participation.
>
> Local participation in management at board level.
>
> Obligations to train local labour.

Transfer pricing.
Rules and requirements relating to exporting.
Degree of competition and forms of competition.
Credit policies (e.g. subsidised interest rates).
Extent of capitalisation of intangibles.
Revalorisation of assets due to currency devaluation.
Subsidies, e.g. to energy, rent, transport.
Place and party of jurisdiction and arbitration.
Time and right of termination or renegotiation.

A contract between the MNE and the host government will contain provisions under some of these headings.[27] Such possible contracts can be ranked in an order of preference by the MNE and by the government. If both the MNE and the government prefer a certain contract to another, the latter can be eliminated. The only complication here is that either party has an interest in concealing the fact that its interest coincides with that of the other party. For by appearing to make a concession, when in fact no concession is made, it may be spared having to make a concession on another front where interests conflict.

But leaving this complication aside, amongst the contracts that remain when those dominated by others have been eliminated, the order of preference for the MNE will be the reverse of that for the government. If the least attractive contract from the point of view of the MNE is outside the range of contracts acceptable to the government, no contract will be concluded. But if there is some overlap, there is scope for bargaining. The precise contract on which the two partners will settle will be determined by relative bargaining strength.

Ranking of contracts in order of preference

MNE	Government	
	F	
A	C	↑
B	(E)	
C	(D)	Range of bargaining
(D)	B	
(E)	A	↓
(F)		

E and D are ruled out because both the MNE and the Government prefer C; F is ruled out because it is unacceptable to the MNE.

At the same time, in determining the relative value of the different contracts, the host government will find cost-benefit analysis useful. By comparing the present value of the stream of benefits with that of the costs the disparate components in the bargain can, at least in principle, be made commensurable. Cost-benefit analysis and bargaining power analysis are not alternative methods of approach but are complementary. Cost-benefit analysis will not tell a government whether a particular project is acceptable or not, i.e. whether it falls within the bargaining range, but it will help it to rank those that are acceptable.

It has sometimes been argued that host countries are well advised to accept any project and contract that shows a rate of 'return'[28] to the foreign firm lower than the maximum that the country would find acceptable. (In terms of the table: the Government should accept A.) But this is clearly one-sided pleading. Vaitsos has compared this with advice given to workers to settle for a subsistence wage. It could equally well be said that the foreign company should be content with any 'returns' higher than the minimum acceptable to it (i.e. C).

A particular form of this argument is the often repeated attack on those who compare the inflow of new investment and retained profits with the profits remitted abroad and use the difference as an index of the gain to the host country. The attack usually takes the form that the effects of the foreign investment on real incomes in the economy and on exports and import substitution must be taken into account. The fault of this argument is that it neglects to compare the impact of the foreign investment with the best feasible alternative, such as domestic investment or borrowing and hiring the necessary factors. If the social opportunity costs of foreign investment were to include the benefits to be derived from the forgone next-best alternative, there would, for any specific project, be only one way of doing it that shows positive returns. The maximum returns forgone by choosing the foreign investment project must appear as a cost of this project. The appropriate shadow price is the benefit lost as a result of not adopting the best of the alternative projects rejected.

In cases where good, other-foreign, non-foreign or less-foreign feasible alternatives exist, the analysis should compare profit outflows with the opportunity cost of providing the same package from alternative sources. Only in cases where no alternative exists is the analysis that takes full credit for the foreign investment for all its indirect effects correct.[29]

The main forces determining where within this bargaining range a settlement is made are information, skill in negotiation and competition from other countries that have similar attractions for the MNE and from other firms wishing to enter. Information about some important aspects of cost and price determination is secret. Information about other aspects is hard to get. The market price of some imported component produced by the vertically integrated firm and not normally bought and sold is not easy to verify. As Vaitsos puts it, 'there is no price for Volkswagen doors'. Such transactions are essentially different from market transactions.

Another aspect of bargaining power arises from the threat that the firm will go to some other developing country if the terms of the contract are too hard. This raises the possibility of joint action by several LDCs, such as that displayed by OPEC. Such agreements suffer from the drawbacks of all cartel agreements: they face the Prisoner's Dilemma. The more successful the ring, the stronger the incentive for any member to break away and to underbid the ring. On the other hand, if others were to break away, the losses to those who adhere might be greater than if they had never joined an agreement. The situation is therefore highly unstable unless solidarity is strong or effective deterrents are applied. Cartel-like agreements on taxation also encourage the search for substitutes that reduce dependence on the host country.

There is almost universal evidence that foreign investors say that tax concessions and pioneer status play no or only an insignificant part in bringing them to the country.[30] This is entirely consistent with the rejection of a continuously downward-sloping marginal revenue function and the presence of a range of outcomes (a substantial element of rent or quasi-rent), all acceptable to the firm, which would induce the specific investment.

Since there are possibilities of trade-off between various items on the list on pp. 268–9, a proper evaluation would have to consider the whole set of conditions. Thus it might be possible to recoup some of the taxes lost by an understatement of profits resulting from transfer pricing by putting a tariff on intermediate inputs or capital goods. Or, for the firm, the removal of protection may be compensated by the provision of public services such as transport, power or training.

From the point of view of the host country, it is important to evolve a strategy that maximises the impact on domestic policy objectives subject to not deterring the company, assuming at least one contract has positive benefits. There may be a number of items on which negotiation will benefit both sides. There will be others, where changes in conditions will alter the types

of MNEs attracted but not the total of foreign investment.

A specific choice arises as to whether to make *markets* more
attractive by tariff and non-tariff barriers against competing
products or whether to improve *resources* and *inputs* by providing
better physical and social overhead facilities. The firms attracted
will be those catering for import substitutes for the domestic
market in the first case and those producing exports and re-
exports in the second.

The second strategy of making resources and inputs more
attractive implies:

    (i) Fewer controls and greater administrative efficiency.
    (ii) Greater security and less political uncertainty.
    (iii) More investment in education, training, transport facilities
        and utilities.

PECULIARITIES IN THE TRANSFER OF TECHNOLOGY

If, then, one of the specific contributions of the MNE is technical knowledge and if this knowledge bestows bargaining
power, why has competition in the market not eroded this power?
Why has the market system not provided incentives for the
appropriate direction and utilisation of science and technology?
Though underdeveloped countries are poor, they are potentially
large and growing markets. Why have there been so few inventions
of low-cost, simple, agricultural or industrial machinery? Why has
there not been more progress in low-cost construction or transport? Why do those industrial countries that have a comparative
advantage in manufacturing industry, protect, often at high cost
to themselves, their agriculture, instead of exchanging low-cost
machinery and durable consumer goods (say a £10 refrigerator)
for the agricultural exports of underdeveloped countries? Henry
Ford announced in 1909 that his aim was to produce and sell a
cheap, reliable model 'for the great multitude' so that every man
'making a good salary' could 'enjoy with his family the blessing
of hours of pleasure in God's great open space'. The mass
production of the model T Ford ushered in a major industrial
and social revolution, the products of which have, incidentally,
destroyed the 'great open space'. Why has no one initiated a
corresponding revolution to raise and tap the purchasing power
of the world's teeming millions? Insufficient foresight in the face
of still small markets (small in terms of purchasing power) and

overestimation of risks or a divergence between private (including political) and social risks may be part of explanation. Another part follows from the concept of the product cycle. The multinational enterprise is aware of its vulnerability. Concentration on sophisticated, high-income, high-technology products rather than simpler products is the result of wishing to maintain its monopoly advantages in technology. Simplicity is easier to imitate than complexity and the profits of the MNE derive from maintaining superiority in technology.

It is easier to see why the market in complex, specialised, often secret or patented, modern technology is different from the market for turnips or even for land. Technical and managerial knowledge and its commercial and industrial application cannot easily be assimilated to the treatment of the conventional factors of production: land, labour and capital, for at least five reasons.

In the first place, knowledge, although clearly not available in superabundance, is not scarce in the sense that the more it is used in one direction, the less is left over for use in another, or the more I use it, the less is left for you. The stock of knowledge is like an indivisible investment and average costs diverge widely from marginal costs. The result of this is that it is much cheaper for the MNE to use what it already has: the existing but 'inappropriate' technology developed in high-income, labour-scarce countries than to spend money on developing a new technology, more appropriate for the conditions of the developing countries.

Second, there is the well-known difficulty of appropriating the fruits of efforts devoted to increasing knowledge and the need either to treat it as a public good or to erect legal barriers to appropriation by others, in order to create and maintain incentives for research and invention. This leads to the divergence of social from private benefits and costs.

Third, knowledge is, in a sense, substitutable for other productive factors, so that an improvement in technical knowledge makes it possible to produce the same product with less land, labour or capital, or with more capital but a more than proportionate decrease of labour or land, or a better product with the same amount of other factors. But its costs fall under those of either labour (especially trained employees) or capital (purchase of patents or research laboratories or equipment or intermediate products or other assets embodying the knowledge). As a result, the market for knowledge is normally part of the market for these inputs. If the owners of the inputs that embody knowledge command monopoly power, they can exercise this power over the sale of the knowledge component of the whole package.

Fourth, the accumulation of knowledge is only tenuously related to expenditure on its acquisition. Indeed, useful knowledge can be accumulated without any identifiable allocation of resources for this purpose and, conversely and more obviously, large resources can be devoted to research without any productive results. There is, in the nature of discovery, uncertainty about the outcome of efforts devoted to inventions. This uncertainty cannot be removed by insurance, for insurance would also remove the incentive for research. A common way of reducing it is through diversification of research activities. Only large corporations are capable of this. In a private enterprise system the large MNE has an enormous advantage in reducing the risks attached to research.[31]

A fifth and even more fundamental difference lies in the absence of the justification of the common assumption about the 'informed' buyer. Where technology is bought and sold, as it often is, through the purchase of an asset (or through admitting direct private foreign investment), the underdeveloped recipient country as 'buyer' of the technology is, in the nature of things, very imperfectly informed about many features of the product that it buys. The common assumption about an informed buyer choosing what suits him best is even less justified here than is usual. In some case, if the country knew precisely what it was buying, there would be no need—or considerably less need—to buy it. Knowledge about knowledge is often the knowledge itself.[32] Part of what it buys is the information on which an informed purchase would be based. As a result, the recipient government will be in a weak position *vis-à-vis* the investing firm when it comes to laying down terms and conditions. Excessive 'prices' paid by recipient governments for capital equipment or imported components and technologies inappropriate from the country's point of view, or acceptance of excessively onerous conditions must therefore be the rule rather than the exception in a market where information embodied in equipment is bought by ignorant buyers.

The five features characteristic of the market for technical knowledge—(i) indivisibility, (ii) inappropriability, (iii) embodiment in other factors, (iv) uncertainty and (v) impossibility to know the value until the purchase is made—go some way towards explaining the absence of a free market in which the low-income countries could buy knowledge.

The situation is quite different from that of an 'equilibrium price' reached in a competitive market. It is more like that of a bilateral monopoly or oligopoly where bargaining theory applies.

There is a gap between the incremental cost to the owner of the technology of parting with it and the value to the country or firm wishing to acquire it. The cost to the seller is either zero, since the investment has already taken place, or the small amount required to adapt it to the circumstances of the developing country. The value to the buyer is the large amount that he would have to spend to start inventing and developing from scratch and to 'go it alone'. The final figure in the range between these two limits is determined by bargaining strength, which is very unequally distributed.

International inequality and internal inequality in the poor countries reinforce one another. Unequal income distribution is both effect and cause of inappropriate technologies and products. It is an effect because capital-intensive methods and products raise the share of profits and of rewards for skills and reduce that of unskilled labour; and markets for sophisticated, differentiated products require a small élite with high incomes. And it is a cause, because the existence of a market for differentiated luxuries deprives enterprises of any incentive to produce for a mass market of low-cost, more appropriate products.[33] Henry Ford had the advantage not only of imagination but also of relatively high real wages.

REGIONAL INTEGRATION AND THE MNE

Many developing countries are eager to promote regional integration and one of the questions they ask is what contribution the MNE can make to this. According to traditional theory, tariff reductions between a group of countries which maintain a common external tariff afford higher protection to investment within the protected area. The export opportunities of foreign firms to the region are reduced and therefore, if they wish to continue selling, their incentive to invest in the region is raised. We have seen that such tariff protection is neither a sufficient nor a necessary condition for the establishment of local subsidiaries by the MNE. It is not sufficient because, without the special advantage over indigenous enterprises discussed on p. 261, investment cannot take place; and it is not necessary because with that advantage investment may take place even without tariff protection, though protection may lead to establishment of a local subsidiary instead of exports to the country. But given the necessary and sufficient conditions, regional protection will raise the returns and strengthen the incentive to invest.

This incentive is further reinforced if, as a result of tariff reductions, the market is enlarged or its rate of growth accelerated, and if some firms, wishing to maintain market shares, fear that unless they invest, others will anticipate them, or if some firms see themselves forced to follow those that have gone ahead, in order to maintain their shares of the market.

It is, of course, true that such regional arrangements will tend to reduce profits and hence investment incentives for industries which are now prevented from purchasing lower-cost outside supplies required for their inputs and those hampered in selling to outside markets.

In addition, the risks of investment inside the region will be reduced and hence the incentive to invest strengthened. If each nation pursues its own commercial and monetary policy, markets may be suddenly cut off or precipitously reduced as a result of import or foreign exchange restrictions, exchange rate changes or other measures. Regional integration provides a degree of security of selling within the region, which will stimulate investment by the MNE. At the same time, the risks of trading with and investing in other regions may be raised.

Against these forces must be set the fact that real wages will tend to be raised as a result of integration. To that extent, the incentive to invest that resulted from low wage costs is reduced. While integration will tend to lead to greater efficiency, stronger competition and economies of scale, these same forces will tend to raise labour costs and to that extent reduce the otherwise stronger incentive of the MNE to operate.

Here again, the question of the distribution of the gains from integration arises: distribution between the MNE and integrated countries as a group, and distribution between different participating countries. In oligopolistic conditions, there are no forces making automatically for lower prices of products or higher rewards to indigenous factors. If the gains are wholly absorbed by higher profits, whether open or concealed, the host countries, which created the opportunities for these gains, will not find the arrangement acceptable. But even if the countries as a group benefit, difficult problems of the distribution of these gains between the more advanced countries, which will attract the firms, and the less advanced, will have to be resolved.

In analysing the effects upon the MNE, it is important to distinguish between the incentives of a larger and securer market and those of a more rapidly growing market. The former enables investing firms to exploit economies of scale and to set up larger plants; the latter makes for the more rapid introduction of up-to-date equipment, incorporating the latest technical knowledge. Both make for unit cost reductions, but the reasons are different in the two cases.

An important difference between regional integration between advanced industrial countries and that between developing countries is the emphasis on improved *trade* patterns for the former, and on improved *investment* planning for the latter. Obviously, both trade and investment are important for both groups of countries, and equally obviously there are causal links between international trade and investment. But when developing countries seek closer regional integration, trade between them is initially relatively small and, more important, it is neither always desirable nor politically feasible to permit the mechanism of 'trade creation' to work, according to which the established high-cost industries in normally already more industrialised member countries. Resources are not as shiftable as this doctrine supposes. Moreover, countries joining a union are not concerned with maximising intra-union production, but, at the cost of some union inefficiency, in securing for themselves some of the new industries, jobs and accompanying technology, that cater for the whole market. The criterion of comparative advantage may be politically unacceptable where the location of new firms is concerned just as much as in guiding trade from existing firms.

Another important difference between regional integration among advanced countries and developing countries is that in the former case the domestic economies are already integrated. Economic opportunities are open to all, factors of production are relatively mobile, agents respond to incentives and income differentials are not too large. This is not true of most developing countries. The domestic economies of these countries are 'dualistic'. A modern sector confronts a traditional one. While it is impossible to draw a sharp line between the two and while movements and transactions between them take place, they are not as fully integrated as the market in a rich economy. If such dualistic economies pursue regional integration with reliance on the MNE, there is a danger that only the small, modern sectors of the joining countries are integrated, while the rest remains in isolated poverty. One cannot rely on the automatic effects of market forces to spread the benefits widely. It is therefore important to bear in mind the need to promote measures of greater *national* integration, side by side with a move towards *regional* integration, if the dualistic division is not to be aggravated by the operations of MNEs.

References

[1] The author is grateful to G. Helleiner, S. Lall, M. Sharpston and Frances Stewart for comments on an earlier draft.

[2] Nurkse (1953).

[3] Cameron (1967), Deane (1961), Deane & Cole (1962), and Deane (1965).

[4] cf. Baer & Hervé (1966), Burton (1965), Islam (1967), Kabaj (1969), Lewis & Solige (1965), Meier (1969), National Council of Applied Economic Research, New Delhi (1966), Power (1963, 1966), Schydlowsky (1971), Steel (1971), Thomas (1966), United States Department of Commerce (1966-8), Williamson (1969), Winston (1968, 1970, 1971a-d).

[5] Lewis (1965).

[6] Behrman (1960).

[7] See pp. 270-71.

[8] For the problem as to what consequences are to be attributed to government policy and which to the MNE, see p. 268.

[9] See pp. 268 and 275.

[10] MacDougall (1960).

[11] MacDougall (1960), p. 210. MacDougall wrote with special reference to Australia and assumed, *inter alia*, perfect competition.

[12] Balogh & Streeten (1960).

[13] MacDougall (1960), pp. 199, 203.

[14] Kindleberger (1969), Caves (1971a, b) and Diaz-Alejandro (1971).

[15] Caves (1971). See also Dunning (1973b).

[16] See p. 275.

[17] Among the contributors to this discussion are Hirsch (1967) Hufbauer (1965), Posner (1961), Linder (1961), Vernon (1966, 1971a) and Wells (1969b).

[18] Helleiner (1973).

[19] cf. Pazos (1967) writes: 'The main weakness of direct investment as a development agent is the consequence of the complete character of its contribution' (p. 196). Also Hirschman (1969). But Pazos and Hirschman emphasise the detrimental effect on the growth of indigenous factors, whereas the question treated here is the distribution of gains.

[20] The argument is developed and documented in an interesting paper by Lall (1973) and by Vaitsos (mimeo, 1970a, b; 1974).

[21] The literature on this subject is still somewhat thin. The main work has been done by Vaitsos (mimeo 1970a, b and mimeo 1972), Vernon (1971a) and UNCTAD (1972). Tugendhat discusses the problem (1971) and refers to a Ph.D. thesis by Shulman. The firms have defended their policies in Green & Duerr (1968). The US tax authorities have done a good deal of work on the subject.

[22] See below, pp. 272-5.

[23] But understatement of profits will not normally occur if the country grants generous tax concessions. Although higher tax rates than in other countries are not the only reason for underdeclaration of profits, they, together with the desire to remit profits in the face of foreign exchange restrictions, are among the most important ones.

[24] Díaz-Alejandro (1971).

[25] Stewart (1973).

[26] See Vaitsos (1974).

[27] The treatment of the government as a guardian of the interests of the whole nation is, however, misleading. See Streeten (1971). A third force in the bargain may be the government of the parent company.

28 'Return' is in quotation marks because it does not refer to the irrelevent ratio of declared profits to arbitrarily valued capital, but to the whole range of benefits over costs, some of which cannot readily or precisely be quantified.

29 As we have seen in the discussion of attribution, just as certain faults have to be attributed to government policies rather than the MNE, so certain virtues may be the result of combining capital, management and know-how, but not necessarily through the MNE. A host country has to ask itself the following questions:

(i) is the MNE wanted at all?

(ii) if so, should the particular product that it produces be available?

(iii) if so, should it be imported or produced at home?

(iv) if produced at home, how is the package most effectively assembled?

(v) if through a MNE, how can the best bargain be struck?

30 Hughes & Seng (1969) and UNCTAD Study (1969). There are several reasons for this, e.g. firms tend to regard special incentives as liable to be soon removed.

31 cf. Arrow (1962).

32 Vaitsos (1970a, b). Arrow (1970) writes: '. . . there is a fundamental paradox in the determination of demand for information: its value for the purchaser is not known until he has the information, but then he has in effect acquired it without cost'.

33 Stewart (1973).

Chapter 11

WAGE DETERMINATION AND COLLECTIVE BARGAINING[1]

Sune Carlson

INTRODUCTION

Wage determination and collective bargaining in multinational firms is a vast subject with many facets. A short paper cannot cover them all, and, from the very outset, a series of restrictions has to be made. In the first place, the problems to be discussed will be approached from the point of view of the individual multinational firm, and the theory of the firm will be the basic frame of reference. It is not the grand issues of the influences of the multinational firms on the distribution of income and welfare in a society that will be analysed, but the more pedestrian question of whether, and in what way, multinational firms behave differently from national firms, as regards wage determination and collective bargaining. Second, since such a comparison seems to be most relevant to manufacturing firms in industrialised countries, the analysis will be limited to them. The special wage or bargaining problems which may exist in the plantation, the oil or the mining industries will be ignored. Furthermore, it will be assumed that these manufacturing firms operate under conditions of full employment. Third, the discussion will centre on the factors which determine the firms' behaviour in the long run. The short-term problems of manipulating bargaining techniques and bargaining tactics will not be discussed.

On the other hand, the term 'wage determination' will be given a much wider content than the mere fixing of cash wages. It will include the determination of all the benefits which the employee gets in return for his services. A new concept—the total benefit set—will have a central place in the study.

The study starts with a discussion of the nature of the total benefit set. After a digression on the theory of managerial behaviour, there will be a review of the attitudes of managements and trade unions to the total benefit set. Thereafter follows a comparative discussion of the firms' capacity to pay (including their capacity to absorb and avoid uncertainty) and of their bargaining capacity.

WAGES, NON-CASH BENEFITS AND TERMS OF EMPLOYMENT

Wages, like rents, are contractual incomes for the rendering of certain services. Also, like rents, they are, at least in principle, agreed on by the buyers and sellers of the services before the services are performed. In most cases, the agreements cover relatively long time periods. Though the institutional characteristics of these agreements vary as between different kinds of employment, different branches of industry and different countries, they have certain common features.

But if wages have important similarities with rents, the relations between the buyers and sellers of the two types of services are entirely different. In the leasing of a house or a machine, the two parties do not need to meet in person, either when the deal is made or later during the term of the contract. Whether they like each other or not makes little difference, and if they do not trust each other, this can be taken care of by the skilful wording of the agreement. The whole thing can be an impersonal affair. This is not so in the case of labour service. On the contrary, an employment agreement always involves a relationship of continuous personal co-operation, sometimes also of subordination. Personal trust and reliance on customary procedure cannot be replaced by the clauses of an agreement and, when disagreements occur, there must be an understanding on how they are to be settled. Since the services to be rendered can seldom be specified and the conditions under which they are to be carried out cannot be fully foreseen in advance, the interpretation of how the agreement shall be applied in the day-to-day situations becomes important. But this involves problems of equity, justice and bargaining power. Thus, the economic relations between the buyers and the sellers of labour service are not only a contractual exchange of certain quantities of service against certain quantities of money.

There are two types of wage agreements, individual and collective. The individual agreement regulates the exchange of labour service against various types of cash and non-cash benefits. But it also contains some explicit or implicit rules as regards working conditions, working methods and the machinery for the settlement of disputes. Since the future cannot be fully foreseen, these rules can only be of a general character, and they can only serve as a guide for future decisions and negotiations.

The collective agreement, on the other hand, regulates the conditions under which the individual agreements will be negotiated and carried out. Often it contains certain minimum values for wages and non-wage benefits and maximum values for work loads and working hours. In particular, it specifies the roles of the individual parties and of the trade unions and employers' federations, respectively, in the wage negotiations and in the settlement of disputes. But a collective agreement contains no commitment for anyone to deliver or to receive labour service. It is a complement to the individual agreement, and the two should be considered together.

As has already been mentioned, it is not only a certain wage or salary paid in cash that the employee gets in return for the rendering of labour service. Generally he also receives certain agreed non-cash benefits, such as provision for a future pension, holidays with pay or subsidised food and housing. Generally, these non-cash benefits can be translated into cost and income terms, and for the buyer of labour service they often represent a considerable and increasing part of the total labour costs. In Belgium and France, they are, at present, calculated as being about 60 per cent of the cash wages. Thus, the term 'fringe benefits' which is sometimes used becomes less and less appropriate. But, in agreeing to render labour service, the employee also gets a promise from the buyer of the service that his employment shall be carried on according to certain terms regarding working conditions, working methods and the settlement of disputes. These terms may relate to promotion, dismissal, overtime, the fixing of work loads, etc. Even though the terms all have economic consequences both for the buyer and the seller of labour service, these consequences are not always easy to evaluate in cost and income terms.

What part and how much of the total employment benefits are determined by individual or by collective agreements varies from case to case. Often, some of them are regulated by statutory laws. In some countries there are laws on minimum wages, maximum hours, industrial welfare, paid holidays, etc., and there may also be laws regarding trade-union rights and the settlement of labour disputes. To translate these various statutes into cost and income terms is also a difficult task.

Let us, however, assume that there are no translation or evaluation difficulties, and that we can write the total benefits,

B, which the seller of labour service gets from a given employment as a set, as follows:

$$B = (c, n_1, \ldots, n_m, r_1, \ldots, n_n),$$

where c is the cash income, $n_1, \ldots, n_m$, the values of the various non-cash benefits, and $r_1, \ldots, n_n$, the values of the various terms of employment. The optimum composition of this total benefit set varies from one individual to another, according to his preferences as regards present and future income, stability of employment, etc., his attitudes to the management and the trade unions and his social and political consciousness. It also varies over time. Consequently, a trade union negotiating a collective agreement for its members must find a suitable compromise between different individual and group interests, and it must try to get this compromise accepted both within the union through a democratic process, and by the other party through bargaining. Thus, if we have to explain the wage-determination and collective-bargaining process, we cannot assume a homogeneous union which is negotiating with a homogeneous management or employers' federation, as the theorist would like to do. As Dunlop so rightly puts it:

'Collective bargaining typically involves three coincidental bargainings—the rejection of some claims and the assignment of priorities to others within the union, an analogous process of assessing priorities and trade-offs within a single management or association, and the bargaining across the table.'[2]

THE THEORY OF MANAGERIAL BEHAVIOUR AND THE MANAGEMENT PREFERENCES SET

The most striking characteristics of the multinational firms are their size and their decentralisation. This decentralisation may relate not only to the geographical location of plants but also to management policies and management techniques. The type of theory that we shall need for an analysis of the wage-determination and collective-bargaining behaviour of the multinational firms will therefore be a theory which can be applied to large and decentralised firms. But it is not the influence of size and decentralisation, as such, on this behaviour that we are interested in but whether the behaviour is influenced in any important respect by the fact that the firm has production and marketing facilities in several countries. Thus, if we want to compare the behaviour patterns of multinational and national firms, this comparison should, as far as possible, be made as between firms of similar size and degree of decentralisation.

In another paper in this volume, Horst has summarised recent developments in the theory of the firm.[3] This summary may be an appropriate starting point for some comments on management behaviour. Horst concludes this part of his presentation in the following way:

'A common practice in all the writings is to reject the notion of a firm as an agent of its shareholders and to replace it with that of an organisation with both a will and a personality all its own. Although important issues concerning the motivation of firms remain unresolved, most writers would agree that as long as the survival of the firm is not in jeopardy, the primary objective of the firm is to grow. Firms are also increasingly credited with having distinctive personalities. Although these personalities are difficult to characterise for analytical purposes, most profiles would include the distinctive resources and capabilities of the firm, the apparent preferences and inhibitions of its top management and perhaps the administrative structure through which these preferences are (or are not) implemented.'[4]

Because of their size and their decentralised structure, the multinational firms are, in most cases, characterised by a clear separation of management control and shareholder ownership. There are exceptions, such as the Johnson Group in Sweden, but they will be disregarded in this connection. One may also assume that the management behaviour in the multinational firms is influenced not directly by profit maximisation in the classical sense but by the maximisation of sales with a minimum profit constraint. But since increased sales or growth may give the firm a series of advantages in its relations with the product markets, the labour market and the capital market, it seems to me that a maximisation of sales or growth may result in pretty much the same behaviour as the maximisation of long-term profit. The difference between the recent growth theories and the classical profit-maximisation theory should not be over-emphasised. Nor should the difference between the growth theories and the behavioural theory of the Carnegie Tech school. In a long-run analysis, and that is what we are interested in here, their main postulates also lead to similar managerial behaviour as the assumption of sales or growth maximisation under a minimum profit constraint. The 'satisfying' of a given growth expectation which is increased over time is not much different from the maximisation of growth. Budget goals are generally increased.

The multinational firms may also be credited with having distinctive preferences and inhibitions among their top managements and staffs. The second postulate of the Carnegie Tech. school—that the behaviour of the firm is not determined by the objectives of an individual manager or a homogeneous management group but by a compromise between the priorities of several groups (shareholders, headquarters and local managers, employees of various kinds, etc.)—seems particularly appropriate with regard to multinational firms with their geographically decentralised structures. But there seem to be two objectives that these interest groups have in common—growth and avoidance of uncertainty—even though their various interests in these respects may lead to a preference function with more constraints than merely the profit rate.

When confronted with a concrete research problem, like the one in hand, a choice must be made between alternative theories all of which seem to lead to more or less the same results, the preference here will be determined by the availability of data. If it is necessary to study the individual units of a complex organisation, for example, sales data are easier to collect and to interpret than the profit data, and budget goals are easier to observe than profit expectations of alternative actions. To find out, *ex post*, the objectives which determined a particular managerial action is probably impossible. But by studying the kind of data which were or were not used, it may, perhaps, be possible to conclude in a negative way that certain objectives could not have been considered during the decision process.

In the present study, which is limited to the question of whether, and in what way, multinational firms behave differently from national firms, as regards wage determination and collective bargaining, the author will assume that the management objectives include the maximisation of sales with a minimum profit constraint. He will also assume that the management has a negative preference for uncertainty. But that is not all. Since, among other things, the author is concerned with the relationships between interest groups within the firm, an additional element must be introduced—control. Although this concept may be difficult to visualise for analytical purposes, it includes the procedural rules relating to the rights to take decisions. As has been mentioned, multinational firms are not only large but are also decentralised, i.e. their management consists not of a single decision-making individual or a single group of individuals but of a number of decision-making groups which are geographically and often culturally separated from one another. To understand the behaviour patterns in such an organisation without an appreciation of the control aspects is difficult. Furthermore, without an understanding of the management's attitude to control, their attitudes to the total benefit set and to collective bargaining in general cannot be understood.

The assumption here is that one of the main objectives of the management is to remain in control, and that the management will always try to safeguard its freedom of decision for the future. In a multinational firm, this means both the headquarters management and the management of a subsidiary. Whatever decisions a management group is taking, these decisions must not diminish their influence over future decisions. In so far as the diminution of future control relates to more or less known alternatives that have to be given up, the control concept can, at least theoretically, be transformed into cost and revenue terms. One thing is clear—to be in control costs money, and sometimes this money is not available. Freedom for headquarters management from shareholders' interference can be obtained only at the price of a minimum profit rate, and freedom for subsidiary management from headquarters interference only at the price of budget fulfilment. Since control is a part of the manager's job satisfaction, for the individual manager decreased control has, *ceteris paribus*, generally to be compensated for by higher salaries.[5] But, like other attitudes, the attitude to control varies both between individual managers and over time, and the control customs are different in different firms, branches of industry and societies.

In the same way as the benefits which the sellers of labour service get from a given employment by a set were described, the various objectives which influence the management's decisions will be written as a set:

$$M = (p, s, u_1, \ldots, u_m. m_1, \ldots, m_n).$$

where p is the required minimum profit, s the total sales, which are assumed to be maximised, $u_1 \ldots, u_m$ are the various uncertainty elements which have negative preference, and $m_1, \ldots, m_n$ the various procedural rules relating to the rights of decision.[6] The set M will be called the management's preference set. Since it cannot be assumed that the different members of the management group have the same preferences, the relevant management set will always be made up of compromises. This is particularly true in large and decentralised organisations.

In the same way as the components of the total benefit set may be regulated by statutory law, the procedural rules of the management preference set may also be regulated by law. Most company laws contain rules as regards the type of decisions to be taken by the stockholders' annual meeting, by the board of directors, and by the executive management, and in some countries there are legal requirements regarding employee representation on the boards of directors or on various kinds of consultative bodies.

THE MANAGEMENT, THE TRADE UNIONS AND THE TOTAL BENEFIT SET

After this digression on managerial theory, let us now compare the management's preference set:

$$M = (p, s, u_1, \ldots, u_n, m_1, \ldots m_n)$$

with the total benefit set and its three components—cash incomes, non-cash benefits and terms of employment:

$$B = (c, n_1, \ldots, n_m, r_1, \ldots, r_n).$$

By doing so, we hope to get some understanding not only of the wage-determination and bargaining processes in general, but also of possible differences, as regards the management's preference sets in national and multinational firms, and employee and union attitudes in their dealings with these two different kinds of firms.

A comparison of these two sets shows that increased cash incomes and increased costs for non-cash benefits may conflict with the objective of a minimum profit rate—at least in the short run. (If the firm can recruit better employees and get them to work harder by the offer of attractive cash and non-cash benefits, the long-run effects on profit may be different.) It is also clear that a change of the terms of employment in the direction of greater influence for the employees or the trade unions, as regards working conditions, working methods, the settlement of disputes, etc., may infringe on the management's control objective. In fact, the actual purpose of these terms is often to restrict the management's right to make decisions. On the other hand, under conditions of full employment, the maximisation of sales means that more employees have to be recruited, and that requires a total benefit set which is more attractive than those offered by competing buyers of labour service.

Since management is assumed to have a negative preference for uncertainty, in a bargaining situation it will be particularly resistant to those concessions which are difficult to evaluate, either as regards their influence on the future profit rate or future sales or as regards their interference with future management control. This means that cash payments and such non-cash benefits as are easily transformed into cash terms will be preferred to other non-cash benefits or to changes in the terms of employment. The larger the firm and the more decentralised it is geographically, the stronger this tendency will be, since the consequences of precedents will grow in importance, and the difficulties of foreseeing the total consequences of a change in a certain benefit or term of employment at the local level will increase.

But just as the optimum composition of the total benefit set varies from one employee to another, its optimum composition from the management's point of view varies from firm to firm and from one section of a firm to another. The management's preference set is always a compromise. How much the individual manager or the management group in a particular plant will have to compromise with their own preferences in a bargaining situation depends, among other things, on whether the negotiations take place at the plant, at the company or at the national level.

After these introductory observations, let us look at the particular situation of a subsidiary of a multinational firm. Although the composition of the total benefit set is determined primarily by local customs and conditions, the management of such a subsidiary must consider the set from the point of view not only of its own local operations but of the total operations of the multinational firm. The optimal composition of the total benefit set will be influenced both by local management and by headquarters-management preferences. To reach an effective compromise between these is not always easy, particularly when there are powerful minority interests in the subsidiary.

If the subsidiary is a member of a national employers association and is well integrated in the local industrial relations pattern, its situation seems little different from that of a national firm. The management has no choice but to follow the majority decisions of the association, as, for example, the American automobile companies in Germany have done.[7] When a subsidiary has been established by the acquisition of an existing local firm, such a behaviour pattern may be expected. When the subsidiary represents an entirely new operation, and when it is not a member of an employers association, the behaviour pattern may be different.

It is natural that the management's preference set should be influenced by the traditions in the parent company. In dealing with a problem, one is apt to use methods and procedures which have proved successful before. American firms are used to plant bargaining, and they will prefer plant bargaining also in countries where national bargaining has been the custom. Attitudes are built up from experience. It seems obvious, for example, that a management whose main operating experience has been gained in a high-productivity and high-wage country will look at the problems in a different way from a management with experience of a low-productivity and low-wage country. The management of an Italian subsidiary in Great Britain may react to a wage or salary demand quite differently from the management of an American firm. There will be similar attitudes to trade-union participation in wage negotiations and the settlement of disputes. Also here one must assume that a management which on the home front is used to dealing intimately with trade unions on almost every issue will have a different attitude than a management which lacks such experience. Their willingness to compensate the employees by higher cash incomes or non-cash benefits in order to safeguard their managerial prerogatives, will also be different,[8] as a comparative study of American and British or Swedish multinational firms would probably show. But it seems that multinational firms of different nationalities are also different in their capacities to adapt themselves to local traditions and customs.[9]

There is also another reason why the management's preference set may be different in multinational and in national firms. Its problems in foreseeing the total consequences of a particular non-cash benefit or a particular term of employment may be more difficult. The differences in operating conditions are generally greater between different countries than between geographically separated units in the same country. Even though the management is aware of the economic and managerial effects of an agreed concession in a particular country, the repercussions later on of similar concessions in other countries may be hard to foresee. The uncertainty component in the preference set will be different.

Thus far, I have discussed the total benefit set exclusively from the management's viewpoint. Let us once again look at the problem from the point of view of the employees and the trade unions. Is there any reason why they should want a different composition of the set when they are dealing with the local unit of a multinational firm than when they are dealing with the local unit of a large and geographically decentralised national firm? It seems that there is. But, as far as I can judge, the difference has,

K

as yet, not depended on whether or not the firm is multinational, i.e. that it has operating units in several countries, but on whether the firm has its home base in a foreign country.

Since the relationship both between the employee and the employer and between the trade union and the management is a continuous relationship, which depends, to a large extent, on personal trust and understanding of customary procedures, the very fact that the operating unit is owned by foreigners may require compensation. Even though the evidence shows that, for example, the promotion or the dismissal policies of a foreign-owned firm have been no different from those of a national firm, there is often the suspicion that one day they may be different. One of the problems that trade-union officials generally stress, as regards their dealings with multinational firms, is the difficulty of identifying the real centre of decision making,[10] and another is that the real decision maker may be unaware of or may ignore customary procedures. The same difficulties must be felt also by individual employees.

This whole discussion of the differences in the composition of the management's preference set and the total benefit set, as between multinational and national firms and between multi-national firms of different nationalities or operating in different countries, has of necessity been kept at the hypothetical level. As far as I know, there has been very little systematic empirical research on the subject. This is a field which it would be interesting to examine.

THE CAPACITY TO PAY

The total contribution which a group of employees make to the firm's revenue may be defined as the difference between the total revenue which the firm receives from the sale of the goods and services which the group produces and the costs of their pro-duction, other than the costs of the total benefit set, including the required minimum profit. This total contribution sets the upper limit to what the firm can pay for the total benefit set.

There are reasons why the total contribution may be both lower and higher in an operating unit of a multinational firm than in that of a national firm.[11] Being a 'foreigner', the multi-national firm may have to pay for its lack of local experience and local contacts and, as was mentioned above, it may have to give extra compensation to its management staff or other employees. The situation may be different in both the short and the long run, and as between subsidiaries which have been established from scratch and by the take-overs of already existing firms. On the other hand, a subsidiary of a multinational firm may be able to get capital at lower cost or its range of suppliers may be larger and more efficient. According to a survey made in the United Kingdom, multinational firms tend, for example, to purchase abroad a larger-than-average proportion of their machinery.[12] But, more important in this connection, a multinational firm with operating experience from high-productivity and high-wage countries may use labour in a different proportion to other factors than national firms and, with the same proportion of the production factors, it may also be able to get a larger output from the same amount of labour.

Since the productivity advantages may vary for different kinds of employees, the multinational firm's capacity to pay may also vary as between different employee groups. Because of more advanced managerial techniques and better training methods, American multinational firms may, for example, be able to get more out of their local managerial staff than a national firm does, and they may therefore be able to pay it better. This may lead to a different internal distribution of income from that prevailing in national firms.

But the capacity to pay will also be dependent on the reasons for which the subsidiary was established. Basically, there seem to be three types of motives for a firm to establish manufacturing subsidiaries abroad: (1) to reduce costs, (2) to avoid customs duties and other trade barriers, and (3) to get nearer to its customers. Sometimes one of these motives is enough: in others they exist in different combinations.

(1) Let us begin with the firms which start manufacturing in another country, not because they are interested in the market in question, but because the labour costs are low. This may apply to finished goods, as when Swedish firms produce ready-made clothing in Finland or Portugal for their home market, or semi-manufacturers, as when American electronic firms produce parts in Taiwan or South Korea for their assembly plants in the United States. The reason why the firms prefer to manufacture the goods themselves, with all the managerial headaches which that may bring about, instead of subscontracting, may be due to the fact that there are no local suppliers or that the quality and timing requirements are such that they can scarcely be fulfilled by an outsider. Also, in this case, subsidiaries of multinational firms may have certain cost advantages over local firms, for the reasons that have been mentioned above, but these advantages

were probably already considered when the investment decisions were made. The low labour costs are the very *raison d'être* for the establishments, and if the minimum profit requirements are to be fulfilled, the subsidiaries' capacity to pay cannot be very much higher than that of local firms, at least in the long run.

The situation must be pretty much the same also in other cases in which low labour costs are the primary motive for establishment. When, for example, a firm which has been exporting to a certain country finds it more and more difficult to compete, because of cost inflation at home, and for that reason decides to supply the market in question, wholly or partially, from a local manufacturing subsidiary, it must watch its labour costs very carefully.

(2) On the other hand, when the reason for the setting up of a local production unit is to avoid customs duties and various kinds of non-tariff barriers,[13] the conditions may be different. Here we are dealing with a protected market, and whether or not a subsidiary of a multinational firm will have a greater capacity to pay than the local firms will primarily depend on economies of scale. If the production unit is of sufficient size, the cost advantages of the multinational subsidiary may give it a lead over its local competitors.

(3) In the third case we are dealing primarily with firms producing differentiated products for markets characterised by oligopolistic or monopolistic competition.[14] Because of their high software contents, their technology-intensiveness and marketing intensity, such products require a careful co-ordination between production and marketing. In order to adapt the production to customer demand, it should preferably be located near the market, at least in its final stage. Even when a firm has excess production capacity at home, it may set up a local production unit in a particular market, if it finds that a competitor is doing so.[15] Because of their skills in differentiating and marketing their products, the multinational firms may be able to charge higher prices than local producers. If so, they may also have a greater capacity to pay, at least in the short run. How long this will last will depend on the lead it has over its competitors in the products in question and on its success in the development of new products.

One reason for the greater capacity to pay that is sometimes put forward is that multinational firms of this type will be less willing than national firms to expand operations under conditions of diminishing returns. Since they could move resources elsewhere, there would be no reason to expand. But such behaviour presupposes that the managements of multinational firms are profit maximisers, which is against the assumption made here. As long as a certain minimum rate of return is obtained and the sales can still be expanded, I find it hard to believe that the managements would worry about decreasing returns.

But also when the subsidiaries of the multinational firms have no immediate price and cost advantages over national firms, their capacity to pay may be greater because of their greater capacity to absorb and avoid uncertainty. The spreading out of operations to several national economies with different secular and cyclical patterns not only gives the multinational firm an advantage over a national firm but may also make it easier to forecast the future total contribution. Even though a national firm may have better knowledge of local production and marketing conditions, the multinational firm may be assumed to know more about the development of demand and supply in general. The existence of time-lags as between countries at different levels of industrial development is here of importance. The experience which a multinational firm has of the introduction of a product in a highly developed country may, for example, be used some years later in another country, when it has reached a similar development level.

The same advantage may exist also as regards the adaption of production techniques. When a multinational firm builds a plant in one country, it can often draw on its experience of building and running-in similar plants in other countries. For a national firm which wants to take up a new product line, the uncertainty must be greater or, if it wants to avoid the uncertainty, it must pay for the use of other people's experience. It is, for example, interesting to note that, now that the Swedish Consumers Co-operatives, which have so far only been distributors of petroleum products, are building their first refinery, they are doing so on a joint-venture basis with one of the large multinational companies.

BARGAINING POWER

The relationship between wage determination and the costs of labour conflicts has been recognised since the works of Zeuten (1930) and Hicks (1932) in the early Thirties. Today there exists a fairly extensive theoretical literature on the subject, mainly concerned with problems of manipulative bargaining behaviour and bargaining tactics. We find contributions both by mathematical economists, such as Nash (1959) and de Menil

(1971), and by behavioural scientists, such as Walton and McKensie (1965) and Gustafsson (1971). Much of this literature, with its rarefied theorising and often elegant mathematical solutions, seems, however, to be of rather limited use in the explanation of the behavioural differences which we are concerned with here. Instead, I shall base the analysis on the less sophisticated but more earth-bound works of Chamberlain (1951) and Levinson (1966).

Chamberlain relates the bargaining power of a party in a negotiation to the costs to the opposite party of disagreeing on the terms offered, relative to the costs of agreeing. In the present context, this means that the more it would cost a union to call a strike, compared with what it would cost to accept the management's offer, the greater is the bargaining power of the management. Or, if we look at the question the other way around, the greater the costs to the management of a shut-down, compared with what it would cost to agree to the union's demand, the greater bargaining power the union has. These concepts of costs of disagreement and costs of agreement are, of course, very vague and their use in the analysis of a concrete problem, like that in hand, is not made simpler by the fact that it is not the actual costs that are relevant but what the opposite party believes these costs to be. However, there seems to be no better alternative.

We have seen that the composition of the total benefit set offered by the management of a multinational firm during a wage negotiation may be different in several ways from that offered by a national firm. Reasons have also been mentioned why the total costs, measured in cash terms, of a benefit set agreed to by the unions under certain circumstances may be higher than the corresponding costs for a national firm. But what about the costs of disagreement or, more precisely, the estimates by the unions of the management's costs in the event of disagreement? Among union officials, the opinion seems to be that these costs will be of less importance for a multinational firm but that they are more difficult to estimate than the costs for a national firm.

To some extent the costs of disagreement are related to size. A large firm with vast financial resources may more easily absorb the costs of a shut-down than a small firm. But it is not the size factor that interests us here, but whether the costs of disagreement are influenced by the fact that a firm has manufacturing and marketing facilities in several countries.

At first it seems that the threat which a multinational firm may make to transfer production to another country and to stop local production altogether, if the union demand goes beyond a certain limit, may give it an advantage over national firms. It is true that the trade-union experts attending the OECD meeting on multinational companies in 1969 had to admit that so far there had been no evidence of such shut-downs.[16] Yet such threats have been made, the fear that one day they will be carried out may exist, and this may have an influence on the unions' bargaining strategies. As in other connections, such suspicions may be associated with the foreign ownership and with the difficulties of identifying the centre of decision making.

But even if we disregard this seemingly unrealistic situation, multinational firms may be less vulnerable to shut-downs than national firms. In the case of horizontally integrated firms, when the different production units serve different markets, one unit can close down without influencing the others, at least when the jurisdiction of the unions is limited by national frontiers. In 1967, for example, when there was a lengthy strike at the Ford plants in the United States, the company showed a profit of over $84 m, roughly half of which was attributed to their operations in other countries.[17] When production for the country in which the strike occurs can be shifted to another country, the situation may be even more favourable. A few years ago, for example, the American copper companies which have the greater share of their production in other countries were able to cope successfully with an eight-month shut-down in the United States by transferring production abroad.[18]

But the situation may be different in the case of vertical integration, when, for example, a subsidiary supplies production units in other countries with components. Here the costs of disagreement must include not only the local costs of a shut-down but also the repercussion costs in other units. For example, during the 1969 Ford strike in Great Britain, the Belgian Ford plant had to lay off 1500 workers and cut down production because it was not receiving British components.[19] While the multinational firm may gain in efficiency by concentrating the manufacture of certain products in a single plant, it will lose in bargaining power. For this reason some firms duplicate their manufacturing facilities, at least for the most necessary components.

As regards the possibility of the unions estimating what the employer may lose by a conflict, the difficulties will increase with the complexity of the operations. Different accounting and taxation practices in different countries, variations in transfer-pricing, the use of royalties and management fees, etc., make cost and revenue calculations for an individual operating unit difficult, particularly for an outsider who only has access to the published accounts. If this holds true for the costs of disagreement of an individual subsidiary, it is even more so for the repercussion costs abroad.

But if the bargaining power of a multinational firm is greater, the question becomes, what can the unions do to curtail this power. At the national level, it may be possible by political action to influence the law-makers in various ways. This may concern the enforcement of stricter rules on accounting procedures, the publishing of accounts, transfer-pricing, etc. It may also concern non-cash benefits and employment rules which hitherto have been issues of collective bargaining. When foreign owned companies are involved, the legislators may be more willing to act than in the case of just national firms. But union pressure on the legislature may also involve legal action to prevent the transfer of production or special tax rules.

The unions may also improve their position by international co-operation. At the headquarters of the international federation, special secretariats have been set up, the main purpose of which is to aid the national unions in their confrontations with local managements, and to disseminate information about industrial relations developments in various countries, including data on multinational firms.[20] The International Metal Workers' Federation has established a world automobile workers' committee for the exchange of information between the union members of eight of the largest automobile companies in and outside the United States, and similar attempts have been made by other international federations.

As long as the concerted action is aimed at aiding the unions in their evaluation of the costs of possible conflicts to the multinational firms and in their national bargaining strategies, there seems to be a fair chance of success. When the aspiration extends to multinational bargainings, the difficulties become much greater. The secretariats of the international federations are not organised decision centres, like the headquarters of the multinational firms, but consultative organs to national unions which operate under different legal systems and with traditions and interests which not always coincide.[21] Even within the European Community there are difficulties in getting joint action between the unions which may partly be explained by different affiliations (Christian, Social Democratic and Communist), but where different nationalistic points of view are also involved. One must also remember that, since unions in most cases are democratic organisations, any adjustment of their traditional policies will always take time.

When the subsidiaries of the multinational firms are members of employees' associations and take part in industry-wide bargainings, there is, of course, little need for international action. It is when the subsidiaries have to submit to headquarters decisions and the multinational companies insist on plant or local company bargaining that the need is felt. Some unions have refused to accept overtime in a particular subsidiary, when it was felt that this would weaken the bargaining position of the unions in another subsidiary, and there are examples of successful integrated bargaining involving unions in different countries, as in the Chrysler and St Gobain cases,[22] but these are rare. In multinational management circles, according to Günter, the view is wide-spread 'that international bargaining for whole companies is not among the issues requiring particular attention in the years to come.'[23]

In theory, the first action to be taken by the unions in order to strengthen their bargaining power must be an attempt to harmonise the rules regarding trade-union recognition and bargaining procedures. Before agreement has been reached on such things as the common commencement and termination dates of the contracts for the various unions involved, little progress can be made. Thus, if we look at the total benefit set, it is the terms-of-employment components that have priority. The non-cash benefits, such as working hours, holidays or welfare conditions come later and finally—and probably long afterwards—concerted actions regarding wages.

CONCLUSIONS

This paper has been concerned with the differences in managerial behaviour, as regards wage determination and collective bargaining, as between multinational and national firms. Such differences may actually be due to the fact that the multinational firms have operating units in a number of countries, but they may also be due to the facts that they are large and geographically decentralised and that they are owned by foreigners.

In order to understand some of the basic questions, it has been necessary to extend the concept of wage determination to what has been called the total benefit set. But this is a concept which requires further analysis, both as regards its operational meaning and as regards its composition in the concrete situations.

The attitude of the management to the total benefit set and to collective bargaining in general can only be understood, if the theory of managerial behaviour is extended to include what has here been called 'control', which includes the procedural rules relating to the rights to make decisions. This control concept also needs further study. The theoretical and operational implications of the concept are still unclear, and the concrete control situations in different firms and in different situations are too little known.

There are reasons why multinational firms may have to pay higher costs for the total benefit set than national firms. In order to survive, therefore, they must have a correspondingly greater capacity to pay. Whether this is the case will depend on, among other things, the reasons for which the subsidiaries were established. In this, as in many other respects, there are great differences as between different firms. What a subsidiary will pay, on the other hand, is influenced by its bargaining capacity. While, in principle, the analysis of the capacity to pay causes no analytical difficulties, the analysis of the bargaining capacity does. The concept, as such, is vague and its operational implications are unclear.

References

[1] While preparing this paper, the author was able to interview a number of management representatives of American and European multinational firms, both at headquarters and at subsidiary levels. The author is grateful for their co-operation. Through two young colleagues at Uppsala, Klas Levinson and Peter Sandén, the author was also able to get valuable information from the national and international trade unions. A first version of the paper was discussed in the research seminar at the Institute of Business Studies in Uppsala. It was later rewritten during a stay at the International Institute of Management in Berlin.

[2] See Dunlop (1967), p. 173.

[3] See Horst, Chapter 2.

[4] *Ibid.*, p. 40.

[5] This fact may be of particular relevance for the multinational firms. As one of the personnel directors interviewed remarked, when this question was discussed: 'If this is appreciated, it has an effect on the company's recruitment and development programmes, because the really ambitious entrepreneur will steer clear of the multinational firms, knowing that the strings are pulled in Detroit or London or wherever, and that he will never be the real boss.'

[6] In connection with a study of international financial decisions I have expressed the management objectives somewhat differently. See Carlson (1968), pp. 170–3. For a survey of management objectives, see Johnson (1968), particularly Chapters 3 and 4.

[7] See Kujawa (1971), p. 182.

[8] The Swedish subsidiary of IBM which finally became a member of the employers' association and had to accept trade-union negotiations as successfully counteracted the union's membership drive by giving all its workers the same non-cash benefits and terms of employment as the rest of the staff. See Levinson & Sandén (1972), pp. 94–5.

[9] This opinion seems to be universal among managers in multinational firms and was repeatedly expressed during my interviews. For example the personnel manager of a large multinational European firm said: 'I think it is legitimate to claim that there is quite a difference between the way the managements of American and European parent companies run their affairs. Broadly speaking, American parent companies, when operating abroad, seem to feel the need to rely on employee-relations systems and procedures which have proved successful back home to a greater extent than, for example, Dutch or British companies. American parent companies are, on the whole, less willing to allow their subsidiaries to take part in employer federations and are slower to appoint local nationals to personnel management jobs and less willing to recognise and negotiate with local trade unions.' See also Günter (1972), p. 365.

[10] See, for example, Lee (1971) and Maier (1971).

[11] Dunning has shown that American firms in the United Kingdom have a greater profitability than British firms in the same industries (see Dunning, 1969, pp. 130–9), but he has also pointed out the difficulties in the interpretation of such data (see Dunning, 1970, pp. 123–32).

[12] See *International Trade* 1967, p. 67.

[13] For a discussion of the influence of non-tariff barriers on the costs of exporting firms, see Mattsson (1971, 1972).

[14] There are the kind of firms which have been primarily considered, in recent American writing. See for example, Hymer (1960), Vernon (1966), Caves (1971) and Vernon (1971), pp. 81–98.

[15] This may hold true also in the case of more standardised products. Forsgren and Kinch found, for example, that the establishment of production subsidiaries in the EEC area by Swedish pulp and paper companies was influenced not so much by tariff considerations as by the threat from new subsidiaries set up by American firms (see Forsgren & Kinch (1970), pp. 214 ff).

[16] See Günter (1972), p. 437.

[17] See Kujawa (1971), p. 209.

[18] See Levinson & Sandén (1972), p. 98.

[19] See Perlmutter (1972), p. 44.

[20] See, for example, Barovik (1970), Blake (1972) and Levinson & Sandén (1972), Chapter 5.

[21] When, for example, under severe criticism from the British unions, Henry Ford suggested that the disruptive labour practices might cause the transfer of some of the British operations to another country and a group of Dutch business men urged that the Netherlands might be an attractive alternative for investment, no Dutch union leader protested. See Blake (1972), p. 20.

[22] See Günter (1972), pp. 433–6.

[23] *Ibid.* 432.

Chapter 12

INCOME DISTRIBUTION AND WELFARE CONSIDERATIONS[1]

Constantine V. Vaitsos

INTRODUCTION

The international sharing of direct income effects, resulting from the activities of transnational enterprises, depends on two broad causal factors. First, it depends on the decisions of firms as to the location, product mix, pricing and extent of production activities in each country, as well as on the location of R & D and marketing expenditures, administrative overheads, legal and financial services, etc., directed towards global performance. Second, income distribution depends on government policies of the home and host countries. Such policies confronted, modified and/or influenced by transnational enterprises imply accommodation of or limits to decisions undertaken by the managers of firms. The net income effect at the *national* level of the process of adjustment between these two broad causal factors, in the face of *global* strategy and financial needs by the firm, constitutes the reported value added that accrues at the country level. Furthermore, such national value added is generated in a structure where the market mechanism is often superseded by the operations of vertically and internationally integrated firms. The settlement of prices in the absence of arms'-length relationship is also a function of the two broad causal factors mentioned above.

In the presence of a wide literature on the subject of transnational enterprises, comparatively limited attention has been given to the area of the resulting income distribution effects.[2] Yet, such effects are becoming increasingly important in view of the rapid expansion of the global operations of the firms involved. From the point of view of the countries whose national firms undertake substantial foreign direct investments, the activities of the foreign located subsidiaries are taking an increasing share in the global sales of such firms.[3] For example, from

1955 to 1964 the sales of manufacturing subsidiaries owned by US transnational enterprises in the rest of the world grew by 170 per cent. The corresponding growth of sales of the same enterprises in the US market was 50 per cent.[4]

Also, from the point of view of host countries their industrial sectors are often becoming increasingly controlled by the subsidiaries of foreign corporations through competitive pressures or through outright acquisition of national firms as a mechanism of entry. The local sales of foreign subsidiaries often grow faster than those of nationally owned firms in the same or other sectors, or than the host countries' overall economic activity.[5] (Gross estimates place the foreign control of the more dynamic Latin American sectors somewhere between 50–75 per cent.) Thus, the distribution of the resulting income effects can become a critically important element of the recipient countries' growth or development strategy and achievement. Similarly for the investing firms and the countries of their origin foreign operations and income generation constitute an increasingly significant economic factor.

No doubt the foreign direct investment model involves aspects related to a non-zero sum game: benefits can accrue to one of the participants which do not necessarily imply costs for the other. For example, the host country can obtain important spillover effects through technical assistance, training and organising domestic suppliers, etc. The foreign investor can, in turn, obtain significant scale effects either in terms of risk diversification or in the spreading of production activities among various subsidiaries. Yet, a very substantial part of the effects of foreign investment involves distributable elements. Furthermore, given the thesis presented later in this paper, that foreign direct investments take place basically within a *bargaining framework*, both distributable *and* non-distributable elements enter in negotiations. This is so, since the sharing of the distributable elements can be conditioned on the non-distributable ones in a bargaining situation. Also, the sharing of returns in a non-zero sum game affects the size of the total benefits to be shared.[6]

In the first section of the present paper we will briefly discuss the income distribution and welfare arguments of standard economic theory with respect to increased factor availability. Such arguments will be extended to take into account the case where additional factors of production have a foreign origin or destination. We will also deal with the relationship that exists between inter- and intra-country income distribution effects due to the inflow (or outflow) of capital and technology. In the last part of the next section we will critically evaluate some of the basic underlying assumptions of the theory on intercountry factor flows to indicate their limited applicability or inapplicability in the foreign direct investment model undertaken by transnational enterprises. The actual market and production conditions within which foreign direct investments take place do not only violate the critical assumptions and invalidate several of the conclusions of standard factor flow theory. More than that, they raise the issue of the relevance of the type of analytical tools used.

An alternative approach will be discussed in the Foreign Factor Inflows section placing the foreign direct investment model within a bargaining model. The sharing of benefits, given alternative and mutually acceptable situations, brings into light various forms of bargaining power as well as areas where such power is exercised. Some of the specific elements related to intercountry income distribution in a bargaining context are presented in the Interdependence section. They include company needs, preferences and strategies as well as home and host country policies that affect and are, in turn, affected by company practices. The combined effects of some of the company and government policies on intercountry income distribution are presented at the end of the paper.

INCREASED FACTOR AVAILABILITY AND INTERCOUNTRY INCOME DISTRIBUTION

Given certain critical underlying assumptions, standard growth theory suggests the following about the effects of increased factor availability on trade[7] and this, in turn, on real income. Technical progress will tend to improve a country's terms of trade if such progress is introduced in the import sector and worsen them if introduced in the export industry.[8] Similarly, enhanced capital utilisation will improve a country's terms of trade if its imports are relatively capital intensive and worsen them if its exports are relatively capital intensive.[9] In both cases intercountry income distribution (expressed by real income measurements) takes place through the price effects of expansion and trade. The output effects (related to the prices ones) will depend, in addition, to the availability of other units of factors of production which, in combination with the additional capital or technology units, increase production. Thus, full employment assumptions and displacement of any existing economic activity[10] are critical in the measurement of the additional real income created.

The interdependence between increased economic activity and external trade can, under certain conditions, lead to a deterioration of the real income of the output-expanding economy with corresponding intercountry income distribution effects. This can occur if the increased supply of goods creates such a deterioration to the terms of trade of the expanding country that the gains from the increased output are more than offset by the relative price changes. Such an outcome leads to 'immiserizing growth'.[11]

There are two more examples of 'immiserising growth' that need to be mentioned which have particular relevance in the case of foreign direct investments. Both of them refer to the manner in which additional factors of production are allocated. Each one of them has varying degrees of effects on intercountry income distribution. The first case refers to the misallocation of additional factors of production in the presence of tariffs.[12] More of misallocated factors of production can result in net welfare losses rather than to additional welfare even if such factors are domestically owned.[13] If such factors of production are foreign owned, then, returns paid to them further reduce the welfare of the factor receiving country through intercountry income flows.[14] A second form of 'immiserizing growth' can occur in cases of monopoly in product or factor markets where spatial discriminatory policies could result in similar income generating and income distribution effects as the ones mentioned above with respect to tariffs.[15]

Simple, first-best arguments in the above two cases will suggest policies that should correct the corresponding market malfunctioning (e.g. reduce tariffs and introduce anti-trust or anti-monopoly policies). Yet, as it will be discussed in later pages, the existence of tariffs is not independent of the particular forms in which certain factors of production are made available (for example, foreign direct investments especially in developing countries). Similarly, particular monopoly situations arise as a direct result of the form in which additional factors of production are transferred intercountry-wise. Experience has shown that, quite often, anti-monopoly policies have either partial effects or they lead to additional policy induced distortions. Thus, they could constitute lesser best solutions.[16]

Summarising the above we can conclude that, under competitive market conditions, intercountry income distribution effects that accrue due to increased factor availability are a result of relative price changes. Additional considerations are involved in the presence of tariffs, the existence of monopoly conditions or the foreign origin of the additional factor availability. We pass now to discuss the effects of the latter case.

FOREIGN FACTOR INFLOWS AND INTERCOUNTRY INCOME DISTRIBUTION

If increased factor availability has a foreign origin then the above reached conclusions on intercountry income distribution need to be further qualified by the effects of payments to foreign factors of production. In terms of welfare considerations a distinction needs to be made between capital and already developed technology due to the public good character of the latter. In such a case payments are made for a non-exhaustible factor of production.

Under perfect market conditions and in the absence of tariffs the effects of payments to foreign factors of production can only be part or all of the income generated from the use of such foreign inputs in the host country.[17] The latter could be sharing some of the benefits in the form of higher returns to domestic factors of production and/or higher tax earnings of the host government and/or lower prices for the local consumer[18] and/or non-remitted profits by foreign investors leading to net capital formation. In the presence, though, of tariffs or under imperfect market conditions, payments to foreign factors of production will accentuate the conclusions reached above on 'immiserizing growth'. Returns to foreign factors could, in such cases, exceed host country gains leading to net negative (income) effects.

In the case of foreign capital inflows there are two terms of trade that affect intercountry income distribution. (Parallel analysis can be undertaken in the case of technology flows.) The first refers to the traditionally defined commodity terms of trade that relates to the relative prices of the traded goods as affected by capital flows. The second refers to the real value of the payments (receipts) for receiving (exporting) capital. Call it terms of borrowing. The joint effect of these two terms of trade, given prevailing market and production conditions, will determine the net effects on a country's real income resulting from capital inflows. It will also determine the relative distribution of benefits resulting from such investment activities. Furthermore, the two terms of trade are interdependent through technology, tariffs, transportation costs, etc.

As long as these two terms of trade move both in the same direction with respect to a country's gain (or loss) then the corresponding conclusions are obvious. If on the other hand the two terms of trade move in opposite directions then the net result will depend on the following two factors: (a) the degree of capital or labour intensity of the country's production function for the goods produced (foregone) due to the inflow (outflow) of foreign (national) capital and (b) the relative importance of the goods concerned in the total basket of goods and services produced and traded. Take, for example, the case of first-best policy considerations on optimum tariff level. Under incomplete specialisation, if a country is capital importing and commodity import substituting the existence and level of optimum tariff will depend on the effect that such a tariff will have on improving commodity terms of trade, on worsening terms of borrowing, the degree of capital intensity of goods produced through the foreign factor inflows under tariff protection, and their relative importance on commodity trade.[19]

The case that benefits, accruing to a country from trade, can be enhanced through unilateral restrictions (or inducements) has long been treated in the relevant literature on tariffs. Similar arguments have evolved in the case of capital flows both for borrowing and lending countries.[20] If the services of capital are considered as a traded good then interference in its flow can be incorporated in the overall analysis of the optimum tariff concept for maximising national gains. This is particularly true if the services of capital are considered as a consumption good, a usual simplification in growth theory.[21] Additional considerations, though, arise in cases where the services of capital are considered as an intermediate rather than as a consumption good. Optimal effective tax (or subsidy) rules on capital flows have been estimated in the case of different consumer valuations of traded goods in two countries.[22]

The optimum capital tax depends not only on technology (which specifies the relative factor intensity of goods produced and traded), but also on the elasticity of foreign import demand. The value of the latter depends on the price level at which it is being calculated, which in turn depends on the choice of the objective function chosen for maximisation. Thus, as in the case of optimal tariff, the optimal tax rate on capital flows is not unique.[23] The inter-dependence between the optimum tariff and optimum capital tax rates necessitate their joint estimation. It has been concluded that, although either the tariff or the tax rate can be negative, it cannot be that both of them are negative. Yet both of them can be positive.[24]

A final note needs to be raised before we leave the subject of optimal tariff and capital tax rates. It refers to the so-called 'magnification effect'.[25] According to it, returns to factors of production change by a relatively greater amount than do commodity prices. If a country exports both capital and goods or imports both of them, then the two terms of trade move in opposite directions. Thus, the net result on intercountry income distribution will depend on the extent that the magnification effect applies, the countries' commodity and capital trade, and the relative factor intensity of goods produced and traded. Also in the presence of the 'magnification effect' the absolute value of optimal tax rate will exceed that of the tariff rate.[26]

INTERDEPENDENCE BETWEEN INTRA- AND INTER-COUNTRY INCOME EFFECTS

First we will deal with the various possibilities on income effects related to the borrowing country.

(a) If all the additional income (created by the inflow of capital) or the rents (resulting from advanced technology, superior management, etc.) accrue to the foreign factor suppliers, then no direct intracountry effects occur as long as the following two conditions are met. Prices remain unchanged and full employment prevails. An exception to the direct effects can occur if final product prices facing consumers included, prior to domestic production, excise taxes which are later replaced by tariffs. Such an outcome will shift earnings from the government to the producers, while relative prices facing the consumer remain the same.

(b) If the efficiency caused by the foreign factors of production does not result in higher payments to them, but, instead, it reduces product prices, then intra-country income effects occur according to the consumption patterns of the host country nationals. Consumers whose basket of goods is more (foreign capital and/or technology intensive) will stand to gain more than others.

(c) If higher returns to foreign factors of production spill-over with resulting changes of overall relative factor prices in the host country (rather than being just foreign factor specific), then the following will occur. Given assumptions on competitive market conditions and factor substitutability, foreign capital inflows utilised in capital intensive industries could lead to relative and absolute increase in the price of capital while symmetrically causing relative *and* absolute decrease in wages.[27]

(*d*) For reasons of loyalty or if higher efficiency or monopoly rents resulting from the presence of foreign inputs are shared partly by the domestic factors of production that participate directly in economic activities with foreign capital and/or technology suppliers, the intra- as well as interfactor income effects will occur. Quite often labour working for foreign subsidiaries obtains higher salaries than the equivalent return by national firms.[28]

The above examples refer to the direct effects on host, intra-country income distribution. In the case of transnational enterprises, indirect economic effects on income distribution also exist through the influence that such firms exert on macroeconomic policies of the host governments with respect to monetary, fiscal, foreign exchange, and trade considerations. Also indirect effects on income distribution are involved through the promotion of specific local interests complementary to the activities of foreign investors (or the displacement of competitive ones) as well as through broader and direct political participation as demonstrated by the case of ITT's recent attempt to interfere with the internal political developments in Chile.

We come now to cite some of the intra-country income effects for the capital exporting economy.

(*a*) If capital outflows (and more precisely foreign direct investments) imply an expansive activity, rather than the protection of existing export markets, then capital owners could gain while wage earners could be foregoing similar returns due to the exportation of employment opportunities implied in such capital outflows. In the presence of collective bargaining in labour relations the opportunities of alternative country production through foreign direct investment could prove an important negotiating element in the hands of management and capital owners. The history of the recent UK labour strike in the plants of the Ford Motor Company demonstrated the management's intent to use the alternative-production-for-export strategy. Also the plans by foreign subsidiaries in Brazil to increase production for exports of automotive components outside of Latin America might not be independent, together with other factors, of the present labour situation in that country.

(*b*) If foreign investment is undertaken as a defensive strategy to protect already existing export markets from *third* country competition then both capital owners and labour of the capital exporting country could be obtaining gains. In the absence of such foreign investment, a foreign market could be lost. If, though, investment takes place then enhanced employment opportunities for the home country labour are made available through possible exports of processed inputs to be used by affiliated companies abroad.[29]

(c) If, on the other hand, defensive direct investment takes place so as to protect an export market against the competitive threat of an enterprise with the *same* national origin, then differences exist between firm and home country effects. For the former the analysis is equivalent to the case (b) above related to defensive investments. For the home country as a whole, though, equivalent arguments presented in the case of the expansive investments are applicable.

CRITICAL ASSUMPTIONS OF THE CAPITAL FLOWS THEORY AND THEIR INAPPLICABILITY IN THE FOREIGN DIRECT INVESTMENT MODEL

Both the analytical framework of capital flows theory as well as the conclusions on intercountry income distribution presented in the first two sections are based on several very restrictive assumptions. The latter have very limited applicability in the actual market and production conditions characterising intercountry factor and product flows in the context of foreign direct investments as well as their causal determinants. We will be briefly examining some of these assumptions.

Although the analysis presented in earlier pages referred to expanding rather than to stagnant activities or economies, many of the questions raised are of static nature. Furthermore, the answers given are at most related to comparative stationary states. As such many of the dynamic issues involved in product and factor flows are excluded.[30] For example, as discussed on p. 302 growth theory suggests that if technical progress is introduced in the export industry of a country it will tend to worsen that economy's terms of trade. Such a conclusion is correct only as far as *existing* export products are concerned. Yet, quite often technical progress is related to the export sector of a country, particularly in the manufacturing sector, through the introduction of *new* products.[31] The low price elasticity of demand that tends to characterise new products and the absence of many competitors during the initial years of their commercial exploitation,[32] could enable an innovator to obtain monopoly rents through appropriate pricing of his exports. The expectation of such rents could stimulate the allocation of further resources for technical innovation both at the firm and country level.[33] Thus, technical progress related to the export sector of new products could improve rather than worsen a country's terms of trade.

The above considerations question another critical assumption implicit in the analysis of the first two sections namely that of competitive market conditions. Theoretical and empirical analysis related to transnational enterprises have long argued that the behaviour of such firms can only be understood meaningfully if evaluated within a monopoly or oligopoly model.[34] The concentration indices in both the supply side of foreign direct investments[35] as well as in the market structure of the sectors chosen for investments in the host countries,[36] the size of firms undertaking foreign direct investments their technological and managerial capacities and requirements[38] their acquisition[39] and merger processes[40] all conduce to a structure where analytical tools related to sector-oligopoly similation models are much more representative. Although such models involve a high degree of indeterminancy, related to games between adversaries, they provide more meaningful results than maximisation models that assume at the macro level intersectorial uniformity of investment propensities and intrasectorially identity of motives by firms. Furthermore, the price and non-price monopoly effects could constitute a much more important factor on income generation and distribution than factor returns based on competitive markets as implied in most capital-flow models. The conclusions reached in such models could, thus, be significantly modified or reversed in the presence of oligopoly.

A hypothesis related to the assumptions on competitive conditions in the capital flow theory, postulates that intercountry differences in returns to capital explain investment flows even in the case of transnational firms.[41] As an extension of this hypothesis general conclusions like the following are reached, in the framework of traditional trade theory and portfolio (rather than direct) investments: 'Capital flows from relatively capital-rich to capital-poor countries tend to equalise "factor proportions" in both countries and thus to reduce the basis for commodity trade.'[42] The fact that intercountry interest rate differentials have very limited, and often, contradictory, explanatory value in the case of foreign direct investment has long been treated in the literature.[43] The presence of cross-hauling of investments among countries or even in the same sector, the appearance from the consolidated balance sheets of transnational firms, that they have larger borrowings from high interest rate countries and that they tend to invest more of their assets in low interest rate countries, as well as related findings, present contradictory evidence on the interest differential theory is the case of direct investments. More meaningful explanations have been based on monopoly or oligopoly models, with related issues of product differentiation and market concentration, defensive strategies of firms related to risk of loss of markets or of sources of supply,[44] changing technological ascendancy,[45] tariff levels,[46] organisational structures and strategies,[47] and others.

The incomes generating and distribution effects of foreign direct investment do not appear as explicit in these alternative, more valid hypotheses as they do in the interest differential one. As a result their income implications are not always sufficiently evaluated. Occasionally, despite the departure from standard capital flow theory—as far as the factors that prompt foreign direct investments are concerned—analysis, related to the alternative hypotheses, returns to rather simple maximisation models with respect to income effects both for the firm and the participating countries.

In the direct investment model capital might often be one of the least important factors involved. It is not only that foreign direct investors can obtain the largest sources of their funds from the host, 'borrowing' countries.[48] (In this case host countries are, in effect, financing to a great extent the international operations of foreign owned firms.) Of equal or greater importance is the *collective flow of a set of factors of production* whose scarcity for the firm (like management time) and effects on the host country (like the technology used) can be far more significant than capital. Furthermore, with respect to net income, it is not only that a transnational enterprise should, obviously, be maximising its global returns rather than those of each one of its corporate units. More so, the mechanisms of income generation and the channels of its remission might depend more on inter-affiliate sales of goods and services rather than on the explicitly registered returns to capital invested.[49] For example, given the particular foreign investment regulations in Colombia and the special characteristics of the pharmaceuticals industry, it was estimated that for about half of the sector which was controlled by foreign subsidiaries, declared profits amounted, in 1969, to only 3·4 per cent of the effective returns to the foreign factor suppliers.[50] Other channels of income remission appeared to be far more important in a structure where items appearing in the cost side of an affiliate's income statement show up in the revenue side of other affiliates. Such critical channels of income flows include the following:

(*a*) The pricing mechanisms on interaffiliate sales of goods.

(*b*) Royalty payments on technology sold to affiliates.

(*c*) Commissions and fees on various interaffiliate sales of services and allocation of overheads.

(*d*) Interest payments on interaffiliate loans.

The relative importance of each one of these channels will depend on a host of complex factors, including both home and host country policies as well as company needs and strategies, some of which will be examined in chapter three below. Thus, product, service and various forms of capital flows are involved in foreign direct investments which operate, basically, within oligopoly markets. As a result a proper understanding of the behaviour of transnational firms requires analysis that 'belongs more to theory of industrial organisation than that of international capital movements'.[51] It has also been noted that '. . . it is not true that these great sums flow abroad as a result of a free and enlightened calculation of self-interest. They flow as the result of a particular social organisation which . . . gives a bias in this direction.'[52] The particular 'social organisation' of foreign direct investments by transnational enterprises places the subject not only outside of *the* theory of capital movements but also, to a great extent, out of *a* theory on capital flows. As such the corresponding analysis requires an understanding of collective factor utilisation across national boundaries under an oligopolistic market structure. In this context capital itself plays only one part with, probably decreasing importance as compared to technology, managerial competence, marketing techniques and the more general and not sufficiently analysed considerations of the economies of knowledge and power.

BENEFIT-COST ANALYSIS AND INCOME GENERATION—BARGAINING AND INCOME DISTRIBUTION

The foreign investor offers capital, know-how (technological and managerial), some opportunities of commercialisation and, among other possibilities, that of a certain structure of industrial development. The host country offers access to the home market (particularly in the manufacturing sector), access to natural resources (as in the extractive industries) and access to special comparative advantages (like cheap labour). Such inputs to an investment project by both parties can lead to an agreement that is mutually beneficial. Other alternative production and ownership structures (like co-production agreements, licensing arrangements, minority equity participation, profit sharing) can result in different configurations of benefits *that could fall within the satisficing range of returns acceptable to both participants.*[53]

Economic literature on the effects of foreign direct investments uses basically tools of benefit-cost analysis applied principally to the host countries.[54] The quantifiable effects relate to income and balance of payments measurements with qualitative statements on externalities. It is of interest to observe that work using tools of welfare economics quite often concludes that, as far as non-quantifiable effects are concerned, the positive ones generally exceed the negative.[55] Political scientists or political economists often conclude exactly the opposite.[56] (Professional differences, represented by the content, ever more than the methods of their analysis, often lead to diverging conclusions on the same subject.)

The types of benefit-cost estimates applied constitute forms of project or investment analysis. In the more sophisticated cases their conceptual origins can be traced in the literature of 'optimal' interest[57] and foreign exchange rates.[58] The approaches differ in areas such as the utilisation of domestic cost estimates[59] or of 'world price' equivalents to measure costs and outputs.[60] Yet, quite generally, they follow a similar approach in applying cost-benefit analysis to each one of the participants *separately.*

On the basis of such analysis, if the net benefits for the host country exceed some minimum warranted returns, the conclusion is often reached (or implied) that foreign direct investment should be accepted rather than that it should be acceptable. The former implies that the 'alternative situation' is the absence of foreign direct investment, disregarding a multiplicity of negotiable situations where foreign direct investment could still be present. Furthermore it disregards the possibility of achieving other production and/or ownership combinations whose net benefits could be more acceptable for the host country *and* possible to achieve. Thus, the unilateral application of benefit-cost analysis, which divorces itself from the actual and/or acceptable benefits accruing to the foreign factors supplier, reduces policy considerations in a passive state even if decisions among the participants are interdependent and opportunities potentially diverse. In another area where bargaining applies, that of trade unions, the equivalent application of benefit-cost analysis (as it is presently used in extreme cases in the foreign investment model) would have implied that any wage rate above subsistence level should be accepted.

If, on the other hand, a bargaining framework is introduced

(where benefit-cost analysis is one of the various tools used rather than the only objective of evaluation) then a series of alternative approaches and needs for comparison are available. Furthermore, the horizon of policy alternatives is significantly enhanced. For example, if a foreign investor enters a country in order to protect an existing export market as a defensive strategy against other potential competitors who might plan the same or alternative production schemes in the host country (a frequent case implied in the product cycle theory), then the following occurs. From the point of view of the host country the total additional income effects from that particular investor do not constitute the relevant incremental benefits obtained. The latter amount to the difference, if any (positive or negative), between such an investment and alternative opportunities. Thus, the opportunity cost for not receiving a particular investment is smaller than the total net income generated and equally smaller than the opportunity cost, under equivalent circumstances, of an expansive, new investment. Also from the point of view of the defensive investor, decisions are undertaken not on the basis of the difference between the incremental cost of supplying a market from, let say, the home country and the average cost of producing abroad. Rather, decisions are based on the difference between total additional revenues and total additional costs in doing business abroad. Thus, in the case of a defensive investment a host country has less to gain from an additional investor than in the case of an expansive one, under comparable production situations. Also, given certain conditions of transportation costs and tariff rates, the defensive investor has more to lose if he does not undertake the investment than in the case of an expansive activity. The difference in relative magnitudes could be quite significant to imply possibilities of additional gains for the host country through intelligent use of bargaining. Even small countries can find, in relative terms, their bargaining power significally increased in confronting large transnational enterprises in situations like the one described above. A benefit-cost analysis applied unilaterally to the host country and omitting other production opportunities obscures such important policy alternatives.

In the manufacturing sector the negotiable elements involved with respect to foreign direct investments are multiple and of diverse kinds. They include the level of tariff and non-tariff protection offered to such investments, the type of know-how acquired and the existence (or displacement) of local skills that could complement or substitute foreign technological or managerial inputs, the extent of exports of goods produced by foreign subsidiaries, the degree of obligatory content of local inputs, the choice of appropriate processes given differences of social and private benefits, tax treatments (including depreciation and reserve allowances), pay/out ratios royalty and other remissions, requirements for local participants in ownership and control, internal market control and price fixing, local labour training, extent of capitalisation of intangibles, revaluation of assets due to currency devaluations, tariff rates on inputs imported by the foreign owned enterprises, subsidies such as one energy, accounting inventory valuations due to inflation, other income reporting techniques, etc. All of these can be and often are translated into net cash flow effects by the foreign investors depending on managerial sophistication. Host countries, though, often apply piecemeal policies to each one of them (since they are handled by different legislative and administrative statures or agencies) although they represent a negotiable package. The dynamics of bargaining, given the tools available, represent almost a *continuous process of distributional performance* between the host nation and the foreign investor. For example, progressive application of obligatory content of local inputs implies continous distributional effects among participants. Furthermore, host government policies with effects on such income distribution can be indirect and all encompassing, as through the effective protection offered to production activities where foreign subsidiaries participate. Or, they can be direct and specific, such as through the requirements on domestic participation in the ownership of firms[61] through direct price controls on imported intermediate products for further processing by foreign owned corporations,[62] etc.

Working within a bargaining framework in the foreign investment model implies evaluation of characteristics which are not sufficiently covered by the content as well as the tools of practised quantitative traditional economic analysis. For example, acceptable competitive market conditions assume a priori sufficient and equitably available information. Yet, in a bargaining framework information is an instrument upon which the whole system of relative power is based. The latter (i.e. bargaining power), is, among others, a function of the knowledge of what the counterpart is gaining from different configurations of policies and situations. Furthermore, acquisition of information implies certain costs which need to be evaluated in relation to the benefits to be received. The awareness of the size of distributable and non-distributable returns cannot be assumed as given but needs to be introduced as one of the policy variables in a country's confrontation with foreign investors. The economics of information in this context require more adequate cost accounting data, search for alternative sources of inputs and, among other policy or negotiable objectives, the setting of rules for more complete disclosure practices by foreign firms.

The extent of distribution of returns will also depend on an evaluation of the different comparative strengths and possibilities for applying negotiating power over different periods of time, when there exist different degrees of dependence between foreign investors and host countries. In this respect one has to distinguish between various types of bargaining. For example, the bargaining power to attract foreign investors is probably, to a large extent a function of a country's size and growth rate of the market, as well as of its access to third markets (e.g. US investments in Belgium served as an entry to the EEC. Recently a North American firm invested in Chile as a means of establishing, through Chile, a foothold and of using its trade-mark in the socialist countries of Eastern Europe). On the other hand, bargaining power to control the practices of foreign investors and to obtain more appropriate distribution of the generated benefits[63] probably depends on the degree of sophistication of government machinery as well as on the host government's political and economic decision to intervene in the operations of foreign firms.

COMPANY NEEDS AND STRATEGIES, GOVERNMENT POLICIES RELATED TO FOREIGN DIRECT INVESTMENTS AND INTERCOUNTRY INCOME DISTRIBUTION

In the present chapter we will deal with the causal factors and mechanisms that affect intercountry income distribution in the presence of vertically integrated companies operating across national boundaries. Such factors and mechanisms will include company needs (like preferences on where a firm undertakes expenditures and investments) as well as company strategies (like those on technical ascendancy and pricing, interaffiliate debt-relations, etc.). Furthermore, we will relate some of the above company propensities (particularly those on location of major expenditures) to specific home and host government policies (like taxes and their differentials, tariffs of good imported by foreign subsidiaries, etc.). The combined effect of company propensities and government policies will determine the resulting intercountry income distribution given the prevailing market imperfections.

As indicated on p. 311 the mechanisms of intercountry income flows in the foreign direct investment model include, in addition to profit remissions, the pricing of goods, technology, services and credit among affiliates. We will use the terms transfer pricing to indicate the corresponding prices for all such sales among affiliates without limiting it, as often done, to the case of commodities.

Transfer pricing of goods and services, exchanged among affiliates of transnational enterprises and the impact they have on intercountry income distribution, have been treated in the literature basically as a function of government policies.[64] If one excludes policy induced distortions on company behaviour that could result from limits on profit remissions or differences in income reporting techniques among countries, the issues of transfer pricing has been presented as amounting to a comparison between effective tax differentials on declared profits (including dividend remission taxes) and indirect charges, such as tariffs on the traded products among affiliates.[65] Since effective profit tax rates in different countries generally concentrate around the 50 per cent mark[66] and capital exporting countries, like the USA, give credit for taxes paid abroad, the conclusion is drawn that firms will minimise transfer prices so as to reduce the tariff payments of the importing affiliates. Such conclusions are reached on the basis of maximisation models which take into account only tax differentials and tariffs. Thus, they do not include a series of rather complex and interrelated factors that refer not only to government policies but also to company propensities or preferences within its objective function. Even if government policies are neutral (the meaning of which is defined on the next page) company propensities imply that management is not indifferent as to the size of transfer pricing. For example, in the absence of restrictions on profit remissions or in cases where tax rates in the host country are smaller than in that of the parent, research undertaken in four Latin American countries indicated that transfer pricing constitutes a most significant mechanism of income remission. In the particular cases examined transfer prices were being 'maximised' rather than minimised.[67]

We proceed to analyse various company needs or strategies that affect intercountry income distribution through their impact on transfer pricing. We will be assuming, at the beginning, neutral government policies with respect to transfer pricing. Later we will be introducing non-neutral policies in order to evaluate the extent by which they can modify or, in some cases, reverse corporate behaviour. By neutral government policies we mean that:

1. Effective profit tax rates are equal in all countries concerned, as are income reporting techniques.
2. Mechanisms exist for the complete avoidance of double taxation (e.g. credit is given for taxes paid abroad).
3. Governments do not scrutinise the transfer pricing of companies.
4. Indirect fiscal charges or costs are zero in the transfer pricing of imported goods (e.g. tariffs) or services.
5. No limits exist on profit remission.

We will also assume at the beginning that:

6. Local participants do not share equity in foreign affiliates (i.e. only wholly owned subsidiaries are involved).

THE RELATIVE-EXPENDITURE-REQUIREMENT

Income earned from interaffiliate sales of goods and services by a firm is not necessarily declared as profit in its income statement. Rather it is included as part of the overall receipts of the corporation as are sales in its home market or sales to non-affiliates abroad. Whether or not such earnings will result in the declaration of profits during a given year will depend on cost considerations of the firm and on the way it chooses to undertake and report expenditures or outlays as costs during that particular year, within the minimum reporting requirements set by fiscal agencies.

Given the ability of a firm to 'expense' certain outlays that are directed towards future returns (such as R & D) and given the capacity of a parent, through control, to affect or determine the degree of forward and backward linkage activities and hence, part of the costs of its subsidiaries, the parent (or some of its affiliates) declare in a fiscal year certain costs that are directed towards global operations over various periods of time. These cost include, for example, outlays for the production of components and intermediates to be further processed abroad. Or they include managerial expenses for global operations, R & D outlays, marketing costs, financial management, legal expense, etc., etc. If these expense, together with the direct costs for the operations of a given firm (assume that it is the parent), *exceed its revenues from sales in its home market and to non affiliates abroad* (R), then it will be to the overall advantage of the transnational enterprise to transfer untaxed income from its foreign affiliates through transfer pricing to cover these costs (C). In this way it reduces its global tax payments by reducing taxable income elsewhere through appropriate adjustments. It is important to note that under smaller transfer pricing the parent need not have to show losses since the difference between its revenues and costs could be more than covered by remitted profits after they have been taxed abroad. Thus, a firm's interests include not only the non-declaration of losses in any of its affiliates. More than that they include the reduction of global tax payments through the coverage of the costs of each affiliate from its revenues (which include transfer pricing) *before profits are remitted from abroad.* Even if the parent firm declares losses (in case remitted profits from affiliates abroad are not sufficient to cover the difference between R and C) then, despite the opportunity to carry forward such losses for future tax savings, it will be to the advantage of the firm not to declare (or to reduce) losses in the home country by reducing taxable profits abroad through higher transfer prices on goods and services sold to the affiliates. This is so since the corresponding future tax savings in the home country, through the carry forward, will constitute only a percentage (namely the tax rate) of the taxes paid abroad for the declared profits of the subsidiaries during the previous years. Thus, only a part of the taxes paid in the host countries will be recovered through future tax savings in the home country if the parent declares losses.[68]

Thus, If $R - C < 0$, whether or not remitted profits from affiliates are sufficiently large so as to have profits being declared in the income statement of the parent, it will be to the advantage of the latter to increase the transfer prices of the goods of services sold to its affiliates (or reduce the prices of such inputs bought from them) so as to reduce their taxable income.

The above can be seen from the following:

Let R and C stand as defined above. Also let

$Y =$ additional income of a transnational enterprise to be allocated either as repatriable taxable *profit* at the level of the foreign subsidiaries (Case A), or as *income* accruing to the parent through interaffiliate charges (Case B).

$t =$ profit tax rate in home and host countries.

Also assume that the revenues of the parent from sales in its home market and to non-affiliates abroad are smaller than its incurred costs. Hence $R - C < 0$.

Then, the net *after* tax profits of the parent from Case A (P_A) after foreign earned profits are remitted, will be:

$$P_A = R + (1 - t)Y - C.$$

No additional taxes will be paid in the home country since all declared profits, after dividend remission from abroad, have already been taxed in the host countries of the subsidiaries.

If $P_A > 0$ then, the choice between Case A and Case B will depend on the comparison between P_A and P_B, where P_B stands for the after tax profits of the parent from Case B.

$$P_B = (1 - t)(R + Y - C) \text{ if } P_B > 0.$$

Hence, optimum company policy with respect to transfer pricing will depend on whether

$$P_A = R + (1 - t)Y - C \gtreqless P_B = (1 - t)(R + Y - C)$$

or, by simplifying, it will depend on whether

$$R - C \gtreqless (1 - t)(R - C)$$

Since

$$R - C < 0 \therefore P_A < P_B$$

Thus, positive transfer pricing will be pursued up to the point where

$$R + (1 - x)Y = C,$$

where $(1 - x)$ stands for the percentage of Y that is remitted through interaffiliate charges and for which no taxes are paid anywhere, while x stands for the percentage of Y for which taxes are paid in the host or home countries. After the parent has covered its own expenses from income earned abroad, the enterprise will be indifferent as to whether it remits income through dividends or through transfer pricing, given our assumptions on neutrality of government policies. (For the proof of the same conclusion even under carried-forward losses for future tax savings in case $P_A < 0$ see Appendix A, p. 332.)

Interaffiliate charges could, thus, become an important element for optimum corporate policies. Such charges could not only cover the incremental cost of goods and services exchanged among affiliates but also pay part of the fixed expenses of an enterprise directed towards its global operations. These expenses can be called fixed in the strict sense that they do not (or need not) vary with the number of units produced during a given year. Yet, they are variable in the much broader sense according to which the use of resources by firms is conditioned by the availability of funds (or income in general) from global operations.

From the point of view of the host countries, the above considerations raise the question as to how far a particular economy should participate in covering the expenses undertaken by a transnational enterprise for the production of inputs (such as technology, managerial capacities, etc.) from which it, as well as the rest of the world, will profit. From the cosmopolitan point of view the same question can be put as follows: how should the world share in financing its overhead? If the world overhead generated by transnational enterprises is highly concentrated in particular nations, other countries, although benefiting from it, may come to question it and bargain in their payments for it. For example, in the case of US corporations it has been estimated that they spend abroad on R & D, only about 2·6 per cent of the total allocations in industrial research reported for that country, while 97·4 per cent is spent in the US. Furthermore, the R & D expenditures undertaken in the rest of the world by US transnational enterprises are highly concentrated in terms of sectors (60 per cent was spent by the automobile and other transportation equipment sectors) as well as by countries (mostly in Western Europe and Canada).[69] Similar high concentrations, even ethnocentric preferences exist for the case of top management posts related to the global direction of multinational enterprises.[70] Equally, despite some organisational, geographic or other decentralisation characterising certain dynamic transnational firms, various basic overhead allocations are realised at the home office. Such activities involve central company planning, financial management, research on industry trends, legal strategy and protection, lobbying, etc.[71] To cover these basic expenditures which are absolutely necessary for the successful survival of the world-wide activities of an enterprise over time, a firm will have a propensity to reduce its profit declaration at the level of a foreign subsidiary and to increase the revenues earned by the parent. Such increased income can in turn be used to finance the above cited expenditures in the home country.[72]

Returning to our analysis of the firm and optimum transfer pricing policy, we can estimate the additional funds (and hence resources) that accrue to the transnational enterprise by increasing interaffiliate charges on the corporate units that have comparatively lesser expenditure requirements. Let Y, t, x stand as defined earlier and $P_A > 0$: then:

(i) Additional funds available to the enterprise from its foreign operations in Case A which implies zero transfer pricing: $Y(1 - t)$.

(ii) Additional funds available to the enterprise from its foreign operations in Case B which includes transfer pricing: $Y(1 - tx)$.[73]

Hence for all cases where $x < 100$ per cent it follows that funds generated in Case B $>$ those from Case A. The difference between $Y(1 - tx)$ and $Y(1 - t)$ represents the difference of after tax profits for the parent in the two cases. This also equals the difference of global tax payments for the enterprise in the two cases. It is only when $x = 100$ per cent, that is when all foreign earned income is declared as profit by the parent, or its affiliates, that the two cases will be equivalent. This is the case when the revenues of the parent generated from sales in its home market and to non-affiliates abroad cover all the costs it incurs for domestic and foreign activities, directed towards present and future returns. For the corresponding analysis if $P_A < 0$ and if carry-forward tax credits exist see Appendix A (p. 332).

Thus, the more a firm depends on foreign earned income through subsidiaries (the more, that is, it becomes a transnational firm) *and*, the more it tends to concentrate certain fixed expenses in one country, the more likely it is that *untaxed* income will be transferred by foreign affiliates to that country. The size of the domestic market where a firm operates and its exports to non-affiliates relative to the costs it assumes for its global performance become, hence, a critical element of how such a firm distributes returns among its affiliates operating in various countries. These countries, in turn, obtain not only different returns to factors of production according to corporate strategy, but also have different tax claims depending on such strategy by transnational firms. A firm like Philips Int., given its declared fixed costs, the tax rates around the world and exports to non-affiliates, will have a higher propensity than, let us say, General Electric Co., to transfer income from its subsidiaries to the parent firm since the Dutch market is smaller than that of the US.

An obvious question still remains to be answered regarding how often transnational enterprises confront a situation where their foreign earned income is needed to cover part of the cost incurred by the parent firm. Companies guard, cerbereanly, information related to the above question. No published data exist that could give us an adequate answer to this question. Yet, a clue can be obtained in an indirect way that suggests that the above condition ($R < C$) is not an uncommon one for US

L

parent firms. For other enterprises, whose parent firm's home market is generally much smaller than that of the US, the occurrence of the above stated condition will be even more common.[74] A study published in 1966[75] indicated that for 51 out of 93 recorded enterprises, which figured among the list of the largest US owned transnational firms, the sales of their subsidiaries varied between 20 and 49 per cent of the consolidated global sales. The higher growth rates of sales experienced by many subsidiaries in their host markets, as compared to the US, since 1966, would certainly increase the above percentages of foreign content is the consolidated sales figure.

Taking, then, as a hypothetical example, an enterprise for which its foreign located subsidiaries account for one third of its global sales, the following case can be depicted. Let the parent firm charge its subsidiaries the equivalent of 20 per cent of their sales for the following purposes: royalties on technology, fees for managerial advice, charges on other headquarter services such as legal and administrative services, royalties on trademarks and other marketing intangibles, differences between prices and incremental costs of producing intermediates and capital goods sold to subsidiaries, interest charges on interaffiliate debt, commissions for exports of and/or imports by the subsidiaries that are handled by the parent, etc. Such charges imply that an equivalent of 6·6 per cent of the *consolidated* sales represent earnings registered by the parent from interaffiliate payments charged to the subsidiaries. In terms of the parent's accounts, the ratio of earnings before taxes contributed by the subsidiaries to the sales *registered by the parent* (not the consolidated sales) will be equivalent to 10 per cent (6·6 per cent compared to 66 per cent). However, the average ratio of earnings after taxes to total sales registered by the whole US manufacturing sector in the late 1960s was below 4 per cent and close to about 3·8 per cent.[76] In before tax terms this will bring the ratio to 7·3 per cent.

Thus, in our example, the net before tax contributions to the parent's earnings through charges to its subsidiaries exceed the average ratio of earnings before taxes registered in the late 1960s by the whole US manufacturing sector, all figures counted in percentage terms of the parent's sales (about 10 per cent versus 7·3 per cent). In other words, under plausible assumptions on interaffiliate charges, we found that sales to the domestic market (or to non-affiliates abroad), for our hypothetical firm, were not enough to cover the costs incurred by the parent for its *global* needs using as a base the actual figures reported on the matter for the US manufacturing sector. Hence, in our example, net earnings contributed by foreign subsidiaries covered not only *all* of the profits reported by the parent but also part of the costs undertaken by the parent. The plausibility of the assumptions used in our hypothetical example, combined with the actual profitability figures for the US manufacturing sector, lead us to conclude that the case described is not an unlikely one. It could describe the possible situation confronting various transnational firms. The non-publication, by firms, of more precise data makes this indirect way of reaching our conclusion the only possible means of analysis.

The above considerations indicate that even in the absence of profit tax differentials among countries, firms are not indifferent as to where they declare their returns. Global after tax profits can be maximised through profit minimisation (at positive levels) in certain countries with corresponding intercountry income distribution effects.

The previous pages examined the effects of transfer pricing on income distribution as a function of firms' relative-expenditures-requirements in different countries where their affiliates operate. The main causes for such behaviour are fiscal. Other factors will also tend to influence firms' preferences on transfer pricing. One of them relates to the investment opportunities available to company generated funds given different opportunities around the world. The cause under such behaviour lies on the fact that many countries allow profits to be remitted at the end of the fiscal year after payment of taxes and dividends declaration. On the contrary, transfer pricing enables a firm to shift funds between countries with greater flexibility during the course of a year to take advantage of investment opportunities. Such flexibility can become particularly important in cases of change in the relative value of the currencies where affiliates operate. Devaluation prone countries will tend to induce foreign owned affiliates to transfer funds through overpricing their imports from (or underpricing their exports to) their foreign located affiliates so as to remit their expected profitability at exchange rates that generate more foreign currency units. Such pricing policies affect the size of the transferred funds and come to complement policies with respect to the timing of payments for goods and services (advance payments or extending accounts receivable) for trade among affiliates.

OVERALL BUSINESS STRATEGY AND TRANSFER PRICING

Transfer Pricing and Revenues of Affiliates
We will discuss three specific cases of the effect that interaffiliate

charges could have on the revenues (rather than simply on profits) of the firms concerned and the impact that this has for global after tax profits of the transnational enterprise.

First, interaffiliate charges can affect the revenues of the *paying* firm, through the impact that such charges can have on tariff protection offered by the host governments on goods produced domestically. This can increase the global after tax profits of the transnational enterprise even if it may reduce the profits of the particular affiliate. In developing countries the high tariff and non-tariff protections usually applied are often based on the difficulty of sorting out, through relevant cost accounting analysis, three different elements: (*a*) the diseconomies of small scale production; (*b*) the infant industry effects whose applicability is rather limited if the local industry is dominated by subsidiaries of foreign transnational firms using few local inputs; and (*c*) the channels of effective income remission (such as transfer pricing on goods, payments for know-how, trade marks, etc.) which appear as costs in the income statements of the protected foreign wholly owned subsidiaries. (Studies undertaken by OECD in the automotive industry of various developing countries found that the import content supplied by affiliate firms, was sometimes greater than the 'international price' of the finished goods. Protection in this industry in the third world has generally been explained on the basis of scale considerations.)

Second, interaffiliate charges can affect the subsidiaries' revenues and this, in turn, can affect the parent firm's tax liabilities as in the case of depletion allowance in the petroleum industry. In such a case, transfer pricing of exports *from* the subsidiary will be increased and this, *ceteris paribus*, will increase both the before and after tax profits of the subsidiary and the after tax profits of its parent. Such a policy will be pursued as long as additional host country claims, or potential claims induced in the future due to present profitability performance, do not exceed the tax savings of the parent resulting from the increased revenues of the subsidiary.

Third, interaffiliate charges, by affecting the liquidity of subsidiaries through changes in cash revenues, can affect a particular firm's access to non-company funds, such as bank loans. This will depend on the prior liquidity requirements of each subsidiary and the effects of additional liquidity on new external funds. Furthermore, it will depend on the standards of lenders in judging each subsidiary as an independent firm or as financially covered by the transnational enterprise itself.

Technological Ascendancy, other Forms of Monopoly Power and Reporting of Returns

The technological ascendancy that a vertically integrated firm enjoys in particular processes or products can affect where it chooses to declare its profits. Such enterprises probably prefer to declare their returns, not only at the place where additional expenditures or investments are needed, but also at the level where they have a technological advantage over their competitors. They can, thus, underprice the latter in markets of easily acquired technology if market prices are influenced by the transfer pricing of the technology leaders.

Similarly, other forms of monopoly, such as patent holdings, can be used to affect profit declaration at different levels by transnational enterprises with direct effects on income distribution among countries. For example, ownership of oil pipes and monopoly of transport has proven in the past to be a key element in the carterisation of the petroleum industry.

Interaffiliate Debt-Equity Strategy[77]

Intercountry income distribution in the presence of transitional enterprises will be affected by, among other factors, the relationship that exists between interaffiliate debt and equity of their wholly owned subsidiaries. Payments for foreign debt usually imply a different tax treatment than that of remitted profits in the host countries with corresponding income effects for the latter. There are various reasons why transnational enterprises will prefer more interaffiliate debt rather than additional equity holdings as a mechanism of company originated sources of funds for the activities of their wholly owned affiliates.[78]

First, in case of company nationalisation, host countries have tended to 'honour' more the payment of the debt rather than the equity of expropriated foreign firms. This might be due to the host countries' association of debt repayment with their overall capacity for foreign indebtedness. Thus, in countries where foreign investors fear potential nationalisation, they will tend to prefer debt rather than more equity holdings in existing subsidiaries. Second, the transformation of interaffiliate debt into equity is usually possible or even welcomed by host countries. The reverse, though, is not true due to fears of decapitalisation. In this sense, companies have higher degrees of freedom by maintaining more interaffiliate debt rather than more equity investment in a wholly owned subsidiary. Third, in case corporate taxes in the host countries are smaller than at home a firm might choose the payment of the principal of the debt as a mechanism of profit remission for which no additional taxes are paid at the home country. Such tax avoidance by firms introduces the repayment of the principal, in addition to the interest payments for debt, in income calculations.

Thus, company preferences on interaffiliate debt-equity structures could have important effects on intercountry income distribution resulting from foreign direct investments cum loans from the same origin. For example, it was estimated that for every dollar invested in equity in wholly owned subsidiaries in Colombia in the late 1960s, more than $2 were lent by the parents to their Colombian affiliates.[79]

Profitability and Political Considerations

Developed countries (like Canada, more recently Australia, and, in the early 1960s, France) and almost all developing countries have translated the varying degrees of domination of their industries by foreign transnational firms into very explicit political considerations. Practically no major Latin American political movement or party exists which does not consider as one of the pillars of its platform the issue of foreign direct investement. Nationalist positions (whether by 'right' or 'left' leaning political parties), if translated into concrete economic policies can endanger, to some degree, the interests of transnational corporations in certain markets.[80]

Clearly from the economic and political point of view, the major cause of preoccupation stemming from a country's industry domination by foreign subsidiaries is the complex issue of control. Yet, the most easily identifiable element, at least for political pronouncements, is that of profitability of foreign subsidiaries. This, in turn, can be translated into statements of balance of payments and income costs or within the broader aspects of 'exploitation models'. Notions related to the determination of market shares, foreign participation, and repercussions from loss of control, are often too subtle to express or interpret. Percentages of rate of return (particularly that which is declared) consititute, on the other hand, a much more palatable political medium of expression. Thus, transnational enterprises might follow a policy of underdeclaring the returns of their subsidiaries in certain markets (particularly those of developing countries), even if this might occasionally run contrary to their tax, tariff and other interests, as a protective move for their long-run interests and acceptance in certain markets.[81]

DIFFERENCES IN GOVERNMENT POLICIES AND THEIR EFFECTS ON
TRANSFER PRICING

In the previous sections of the present chapter we assumed
neutral governments policies with respect to tariff rates on
products imported by foreign affiliates and profit tax rates.
Furthermore, we assumed that foreign affiliates did not share
equity with local investors and that no limits existed on profit
remissions. We now relax these assumptions so as to evaluate the
modifying effects they imply for our conclusions with respect to
the relative-expenditures-requirements.[82]

*External Indirect Fiscal Charges (e.g. Tariffs) and their Effects on
Transfer Pricing*
Intercountry income flows resulting from the internal pricing
practices of transnational enterprises can imply additional
indirect fiscal payments for a company. For example, charging
higher transfer prices on intermediate products or capital goods
sold by a parent firm to its foreign subsidiary can imply reduction
in the overall returns of the enterprise due to higher tariff payments paid to the host country. Or, higher royalties for technical
assistance paid by a subsidiary to its parent can result in higher
negotiation costs or remissions taxes paid to the host country.
Such indirect fiscal effects constitute an important factor that, in
some cases, could reverse the outcome of intercompany pricing
that would have resulted from the fulfilment of the relative-
expenditures-requirement analysed above.

Let Y, t and x stand as defined on p. 318. Also, let τ stand
for the average *ad valorem* tariff rate confronting the goods
imported by a given firm in a host country from its foreign
affiliates. Then, the enterprise will be indifferent as to where it
declares its foreign earned income if $\tau = [t(1 - x)]/[1 - t]$. The
enterprises will pursue maximum transfer prices possible if
$\tau < [t(1 - x)]/[1 - t]$, and minimum ones if the opposite holds
true.[83]

Hence, if the relative-expenditures-requirement applies to the
operations of a firm, transfer pricing in the presence of tariffs
does not depend only on profit tax *differentials* among countries,
as indicated in Reference 65 but also on the *absolute* level of
tax rates. Only if $x = 100$ per cent, that is, only if all foreign
earned income is declared as profit by the parent, will positive
tariff rates result in the minimisation of transfer prices in the
absence of tax differentials. If profit tax rates converge to the
50 per cent mark, then the *ad valorem* tariff rates, which will

leave the enterprise indifferent as to where it declares its profits, will be equal to the percentage of additional, foreign earned income which is *not* declared as profit by the firm.[84]

In conclusion, tariffs and other indirect fiscal charges can significantly influence the intra-company pricing policies of vertically integrated transnational enterprises. In situations of high tariffs on intermediate products imported by foreign subsidiaries and/or high percentages of profit declaration from foreign earned income and/or uniformly low corporate taxes, the indirect fiscal effects could reverse the policies that would have occurred under the strict application of the relative-expenditures-requirement. It is not surprising, then, that transnational enterprises often consider tariffs on goods imported by their subsidiaries as one of the most important negotiable elements upon which they condition their direct investments. It has been a frequent experience in Latin America that bargaining emphasis on such tariffs is more important than, for example, limits on profit remissions.

Tax differentials among Countries and Interaffiliate Charges
Let t_1 indicate the tax rate in the home country of a transnational corporation and t_2 the equivalent rate in the host country of a wholly owned subsidiary. If $t_2 > t_1$ then, in addition to the relative-expenditures-requirements, tax differential considerations will prompt income remission through transfer pricing rather than profit repatriation taxed at higher rates. If $t_1 > t_2$ and credits for taxes paid abroad apply, it is usually assumed that the enterprise will be indifferent between higher transfer pricing and profit remissions. (We still hold the assumption of zero tariff rates on goods imported.) Yet, if the relative expenditures-requirement applies to the parent's outlays (that is if $x < 100$ per cent), then maximisation of the global after tax funds available to the firm will require the transfer of income from the subsidiary to the parent through interaffiliate charges as long as $t_1 < (1 - x) + t_2$ and $t_2 > 0$. *It should be emphasised that such income transfers from the subsidiary to the parent will occur even if $t_1 > t_2$ as long as the above conditions are met.*

To indicate the secondary importance of tax *differentials* among nations as compared to the overwhelming importance of the relative-expenditures-requirement on intercountry income distribution the following numerical example is presented. Assume $t_1 = 50$ per cent, $t_2 = 45$ per cent, and a transnational enterprise that declares 70 per cent of the income repatriated from its subsidiaries as profit in the home country while the remaining 30 per cent is used to cover expenses undertaken by the parent. Then, on the basis of optimum after tax cash flow strategy the firm will be induced to transfer untaxed income from the host country to that of the parent firm since $t_1 = 50$ per cent $< (1 - 70$ per cent$) + 45$ per cent $= 75$ per cent. The government of the host country, in order to stimulate income (and/or profit) declaration by foreign subsidiaries within its tax jurisdiction decides to reduce drastically its corporate tax rate from 45 per cent to 25 per cent. Such a reduction, though, will still leave the transnational enterprise, given the above cited conditions, in a state where it will be induced to transfer untaxed income (and/or profits) outside the subsidiary's country. Despite the lower tax rate, the global financing needs of the firm will still require, in our example, the transfer of income to the parent's home country since $t_1 = 50$ per cent $< (1 - 70$ per cent$) + 25 = 55$ per cent. Thus, major tax concessions by host countries could still make very little, or no difference at all, to corporate plans as to where income is declared as long as (part) of the generated income in the host country is needed to cover expenses elsewhere.

If non-zero tariffs and other indirect fiscal charges are introduced in a situation of tax differentials among countries where $t_1 > t_2$ then the enterprise will be indifferent as to where it declares its income if

$$\tau = \frac{t_2[1 - (t_1 - t_2) - x]}{1 - t_1 + t_2(t_1 - t_2)}.$$

The Effects of Local Participants

Let p stand for the percentage participation of a transnational enterprise in the ownership of a joint venture. Then, if additional income earned by the joint venture is declared first as profit in the host country and then part of it is remitted to the foreign equity owners, the net after tax funds available to the transnational enterprise will be $Y(1 - t)p$.

If instead, income is transferred abroad through interaffiliate charges the equivalent funds available to the corporation will be $Y(1 - tx)$. Since $x \leqslant 100$ per cent, Case B will always be preferred to Case A in the absence of tariff payments. If indirect fiscal charges, though, are introduced, then the tariff rate for which the transnational corporation will be indifferent as to where it declares its income is:

$$\tau = \frac{t(p - x) + (1 - p)}{p(1 - t)}.$$

It can be shown algebraically that this tariff rate is greater than the one applying to the case of wholly owned subsidiaries, which as estimated on p. 327 is $[t(1 - x)]/[1 - t]$.

Thus, in joint ventures and in the absence of indirect fiscal charges a foreign transnational enterprise will *always* prefer remission of income through transfer pricing to profit declaration in the host country. In the presence of tariffs the latter need to be higher in the case of joint ventures than in foreign wholly owned subsidiaries, in order to reverse the decision of a transnational firm as to where it prefers to declare its income. The reason, obviously, rests on the fact that, in addition to tax payments, profit declaration by a joint-venture implies the sharing of such profits with local participants. The higher propensity of a firm to transfer untaxed profit out of a joint venture through inter-affiliate charges could be checked, though, by the potential control on decision making exercised by the local participants. If, however, local participants are not able to influence the decisions on transfer pricing, *governments pursuing explicit or implicit policies which encourage joint ventures might bring about, in the absence of other complementary policies, a higher transfer abroad of income generated in their countries by joint ventures than in the case of wholly owned subsidiaries.*

Limits of Profit Repatriation

Such limits are usually expressed as a percentage of invested capital rather than as a percentage of accrued profits. The restrictions imposed on remissions amount to an equivalent of 100 per cent taxation for profits above the repatriation ceiling if unremitted profits from affiliates are considered of no use to the transnational enterprise. Such a strategy pursued by host countries could generate most serious policy induced distortions in corporate behaviour. Firms will attempt to remit profits through any other channel that has an equivalent net result of less than 100 per cent leakage from corporate funds. Thus, countries instituting limits on remission of profits by foreign corporations have to introduce other complementary policies to achieve their balance of payments or income objectives. *Otherwise it might happen that countries with limits on profit repatriation will end up with higher income and balance of payments outflows than without such remission limits.*

QUALIFICATIONS AND CONCLUDING REMARKS

In the previous pages we presented a tax avoidance model

according to which transnational enterprises do not simply maximise yearly after tax global profits but rather after tax funds available to the firm. Such funds include not only declared returns but also income used to cover planned outlays. The latter, although constituting investments for global operations, appear as costs due to fiscal considerations. These reported costs assure the firms' long-run competitive survival and other objectives as much as business savings leading to reported investments. Furthermore, it is quite probable that during certain years firms 'create' expenditures. In the complexity of their objectives firms might not pursue a policy of reported profit maximisation. Rather they might seek stable or steadily increasing profitability, given industry standards. Reported profit maximisation could imply fluctuations of returns which during good years could attract the attention of labour unions, anti-trust authorities or competitors. During lean years, after good ones, creditors (like banks), could consider such firms credit risky due to the variance in their performance. Thus, certain expenditures could serve as a buffer for unwanted income fluctuations as much as they serve as investment outlays for future returns.

The availability of funds to finance certain key expenditures that, managed by transnational enterprises, appear to be highly country concentrated imply important direct intercountry income distribution effects. More so, though, their composition imply a particular bias in the international division of skilled labour and of knowledge with, in turn, important dynamic intercountry sharing of future global returns and intercountry dependence for growth.

Furthermore, other elements in the corporate strategy (such as technological ascendancy and barriers of entry through the effects of transfer pricing, interaffiliate debt-equity structures, etc.) imply additional considerations on intercountry income distribution. Such considerations are not easily incorporated in simple maximisation functions but are more adequately understood within simulation models. All of the previous conclusions need to be qualified by the possible effect of diseconomies of scale on company behaviour due to rigidities in administrative rules, conflicting interests between departments or affiliates of the same parent, etc. Finally, placing the above within an oligopoly model with a high interdependence of actions among participants further accentuates the complexity of corporate behaviour. Such behaviour is not only conditioned by home and host government policies but it affects such policies given the weight that such firms have in the world economy.

A better understanding of the effects of transnational enterprises will require not only an improvement on tools of economic analysis. It will also require a higher disclosure of elements of company operations such as their international cost allocations, their effects on government policies, their usage of diverse bargaining powers to affect country and factor distribution of returns, etc. Such disclosure will almost certainly affect the economic tools of analysis used.

APPENDIX A

Let: R: Revenue of parent from sales to home market and to non-affiliates abroad.

   C: Costs of parent.

   y: Net income of subsidiary which can be declared as profit and, after it has been taxed, it will be remitted to the parent (Case A) or it can be remitted directly through transfer pricing (Case B).

   t: Corporate tax rate in country of parent and subsidiary.

   P: Profits after taxes of parent firm. (P^A and P^B are after tax profits from Cases A and B, respectively.)

   1, 2: Subscripts to denote periods one and two.

Assumption: Let $R_1 < C_1$ $\hfill (1)$

PERIOD ONE

   Case A: $P_1{}^A = R_1 + (1 - t)Y_1 - C_1.$ $\hfill (2)$

No taxes will be paid in home country of parent since taxes were paid for Y in host country for which a tax credit exists and $R_1 < C_1$.

   Case B: $P_1{}^B = (1 - t)(R_1 + Y_1 - C_1).$ $\hfill (3)$

if $\qquad P_1{}^A = R_1 + (1 - t)Y_1 - C_1 > 0$ then, as shown in the text,
$$P^A < P^B \text{ or } R_1 + (1 - t)Y_1 - C_1 < (1 - t)$$
$$(R_1 + Y_1 - C_1), \text{ or}$$
$$R_1 - C_1 < (1 - t)(R_1 - C_1) \text{ since } R_1 - C_1 < 0.$$

Hence Case B will be preferred and the difference in after tax profits for the firm between Case B and Case A will be:

$$P^B - P^A = (3) - (1), \text{ or}$$
$$P^B - P^A = (1 - t)(R_1 + Y_1 - C_1) - R_1 - (1 - t)Y_1 + C_1$$
$$= -t(R_1 - C_1)$$
$$= (1 - x)Yt,$$

where $(1 - x)$ is the percentage of Y for which no taxes are paid in Case B and x is the percentage where taxes are paid in the same Case.

Note:
$$(1 - x)Y_1 = C_1 - R_1 \text{ since } R + (1 - x)Y = C$$

Furthermore (4) will represent the global tax savings of the enterprise. if $R_1 = (1 = t)Y_1 - C_1 < 0$ then there will be a carry forward in Case A. For simplicity let us assume that $P_1{}^B > 0$ so that there in no carry forward from Case B but only from A.

PERIOD TWO

Case A: Net income of parent before taxes:
$$R_2 + (1 - t)Y_2 - C_2 \tag{5}$$

Taxable income in home country will

(a) Exclude the profit remissions from subsidiary since they have already been taxed.

(b) Include a deduction equivalent to the declared losses carried forward from period one.

Hence taxable income:
$$R_2 - C_2 + [R_1 + (1 - t)Y_1 - C_1] \tag{6}$$

Taxes paid at home if (6) > 0:
$$t[R_2 - C_2 + R_1 + (1 - t)Y_1 - C_1], \tag{7}$$

$P_2{}^A$ (5) — (7)
$$= R_2 + (1 - t)Y_2 - C_2 - t[R_2 - C_2 + R_1 + (1 - t)Y_1 - C_1] \tag{8}$$
$$= (1 - t)(R_2 + Y_2 - C_2) - t[R_1 + (1 - t)Y_1 - C_1].$$

Case B: $P_2{}^B = (1 - t)R_2 + Y_2 - C_2).$ (9)

Hence $P_2{}^A > P_2{}^B$ by the tax credit from the declared losses in period one which were carried forward.

PERIODS ONE AND TWO TAKEN TOGETHER

$P_1{}^A + P_2{}^A = (2) + (8)$
$$= R_1 + (1 - t)Y_1 - C_1 + (1 - t)(R_2 + Y_2 - C_2) - t$$
$$[R_1 + (1 - t)Y_1 - C_1]$$
$$= (1 - t)[R_1 + (1 - t)Y_1 - C_1] + (1 - t)(R_2 + Y_2 - C_2) \tag{10}$$

$P_1{}^B + P_2{}^B = (3) + (9)$
$$= (1 - t)(R_1 + Y_1 - C_1) + (1 - t)(R_2 + Y_2 - C_2). \tag{11}$$

A comparison between Case A and Case B will depend on $(10 \gtrless (11)$ or after simplifying
$$(1 - t)[R_1 + (1 - t)Y_1 - C_1] \gtrless (1 - t)(R_1 + Y_1 - C_1),$$
or $(1 - t)Y_1 \gtrless Y_1$. Since $Y_1 > 0$ and $1 > (1 - t) > 0$
$$\therefore P_1{}^A + P_2{}^A < P_1{}^B + P_2{}^B.$$

Hence again Case B will be preferred. (Our conclusion would have been further strengthened had we taken into account the opportunity cost of money for the tax savings realised in period two.) The difference in after tax profits for the firm between Case B and Case A will be:

$$P_1^B + P_2^B - P_1^A - P_2^A = (11) - (10)$$
$$= (1 - t)(R_1 + Y_1 - C_1) + (1 - t)$$
$$(R_2 + Y_2 - C_2) - (1 - t)[R_1 + (1 - t)Y_1$$
$$-C_1] - (1 - t)(R_2 + Y_2 - C_2)$$
$$= (1 - t) \, Yt \text{ for } Y_1 = Y_2 = Y. \qquad (12)$$

(12) represents also the global savings in taxes for the two periods after accounting for the carry forward tax effect of Case A.

Proof:

(To simply matters and for consistency with the above let $Y_1 = Y_2 = Y$. This assumption does not alter the meaning of our conclusion.)

Taxes paid in Case A

Period One: tY paid by the subsidiary.
Period Two: tY paid by the subsidiary.

$t[R_2 - C_2 + C_1 + (1 - t)Y - C_1]$ paid by the parent as shown in (7) after taking into account the effect of carry forward from losses declared in period one.

Total taxes paid in Case A $= T^A$ where

$$T^A = t(3Y + R_2 - C_2 + R_1 - tY - C_1). \qquad (13)$$

Taxes paid in Case B

Period One: $t(R_1 + Y - C_1)$ paid by the parent.
Period Two: $t(R_2 + Y - C_2)$ paid by the parent.
Total taxes paid in Case B $= T^B$ where

$$T^B = t(2Y + R_2 - C_2 + R_1 - C_1). \qquad (14)$$

Differences in taxes paid between two cases:

$$T^A - T^B = (13) - (14).$$

After simplifying

$$T^A - T^B = t(Y - tY) = (1 - t)Yt \qquad (15)$$

As it can be seen (12 is equal to (15).

Note: The effect of carry forward (or its absence) on the difference on after tax profits between Cases A and B, other things being equal, will depend on the comparison between $(1 - x)$ and $(1 - t)$ as it can be seen, by contrasting equation $(4a) = (1 - x) \, Yt$ with equation $(12) = (1 - t)Yt$.

APPENDIX B

Let R, C, Y, x, t, t_1, t_2, p and τ stand as defined in the text and $R - C < 0$ while $R + (1 - t)Y - C > 0$. Also let P^A and P^B stand, respectively, for profits after taxes of parent firm Case A (where Y is declared as profit and is being taxed in the host country) and Case B (where Y is transferred to the parent through transfer pricing).

Tariff levels

$$t_1 = t_2 = t,$$
$$P^A = R + (1 - t)Y - C. \tag{1}$$

No taxes are paid in the home country since $R - C < 0$ and Y was taxed in the host countries for which a tax credit is applied. In Case B only a part (M) of Y will be remitted through transfer pricing while the other will cover the tariff payments in the host country resulting from the transfer pricing.

Hence

$$M + \tau M = Y \text{ or } M = \frac{Y}{1 + \tau}, \tag{2}$$

$$P^B = (1 - t)(R + M - C) = (1 - t)\left(R + \frac{Y}{1 + \tau} - C\right). \tag{3}$$

The two cases will be equivalent if $P^A = P^B$ or $(1) = (3)$ or after simplifying

$$(1 - t)Y = \frac{(1 - t)Y}{1 + \tau} - t(R - C). \tag{4}$$

According to our definition $(1 - x)$ is the percentage of foreign earned income remitted through transfer pricing to the parent for which no corporate profit taxes are paid since it goes to cover the difference between R and C. Hence $R - C + (1 - x)M = 0$ or using (2) $R - C + [(1 - x)Y]/[1 + \tau] = 0$.

Hence

$$R - C = -\frac{(1 - x)Y}{1 + \tau} \tag{5}$$

Thus (4) becomes $(1 - t)Y = [1(- t)Y]/[1 + \tau] + t[(1 - x)Y]/1 + \tau]$. Rearranging and solving for τ we find that the two Cases will be equivalent if

$$\tau = \frac{t(1 - x)}{1 - t}. \tag{6}$$

Tax differentials

Let $t_1 > t_2$ and $\tau = 0$.

Remitted profits to the parent in Case A: $Y(1 - t_2)$. The relevant tax rate in the home country will be $(t_1 - t_2)$ so as to account for the credit on taxes paid abroad.

Hence, since $R < C$,

$$P^A = [1 - (t_1 - t_2)][R - C + (1 - t_2)Y]. \tag{7}$$

Also

$$P^B = (1 - t_1)(R - C + Y). \tag{8}$$

The two Cases will be equivalent if (7) = (8). After rearranging, simplifying, using (5) and solving for t_1 we find that the two cases will be equivalent if

$$t_1 = (1 - x) + t_2. \tag{9}$$

Tax differentials and tariff rates

Let $t_1 > t_2$ and $\tau > 0$.

$$P^A = (7).$$

As deduced from (3)

$$P^B = (1 - t_1) \left(R + \frac{Y}{1 + \tau} - C \right). \tag{10}$$

The two cases will be equivalent if (7) = (10). By rearranging, simplifying, using (5) and solving for τ we find that the firm, will be indifferent on transfer pricing if

$$\tau = \frac{t_2[1 - (t_1 - t_2) - x]}{1 - t_1 + t_2(t_1 - t_2)}. \tag{11}$$

Local participants with zero tariffs

$$P^A = R + (1 - t)Yp - C = (1 - t)Yp + (R - C). \tag{12}$$

$$P^B = (1 - t)(R + Y - C) = (1 - t)Y + (1 - t)(R - C). \tag{13}$$

Since $\quad 0 < p < 1$ and $R - C < 0 \therefore P^B > P^A$.

Local participants and positive tariffs

$$P^A = (12).$$
$$P^B = (3).$$

The two cases will be equivalent if (12) = (3) or

$$R + (1 - t)Yp - C = (1 - t)(R + (Y/1 + \tau) - C)$$

or after simplifying and solving for τ we find that the firm will be indifferent on transfer pricing if

$$\tau = \frac{t(p - x) + (1 - p)}{(1 - t)p}. \tag{14}$$

References

1 Throughout this chapter the word 'transnational' (which is the author's preference) should be taken as meaning the same as 'multinational' used in the rest of the book. (Editor)

2 For some exceptions see Singer (1950). Also Penrose (1959b).

3 According to a partial survey of 200 among the principal North American transnational enterprises 40 per cent of them had more than 25 per cent of their operations abroad. The corresponding figure for 200 firms with parent companies in the UK, West Germany, Japan, Holland, Switzerland, Sweden, Canada, France and Italy was that 80 per cent of them had more than 25 per cent of their activities abroad. Figures taken from the US Government, *Congressional Record*, 'Extension of Remarks', 15 November 1971, E 12199 cited by Adam (1972).

4 Data from various years published by the Survey of Current Business as analysed by Furtado (1971). Smaller growth rates have been projected for US owned firms in the future while higher ones for European and Japanese firms. See Hymer & Rowthorn (1970).

5 See CORFO (1970).

6 See Schelling (1963), pp. 83 *et seq.*

7 See Hicks (1953), Corden (1956).

8 For example, see Johnson (1955). Also see Findlay & Grubert (1959).

9 See Johnson (1970a), p. 43.

10 This point is related to the acquisition of local firms by foreign enterprises as a vehicle of entry in the foreign direct investment model.

11 See Bhagwati (1958), pp. 201–5.

12 See Johnson (1967a).

13 See Diaz-Alejandro (1970).

14 For a numerical example see Streeten (1971).

15 If the direct investor can take over a competitor, perhaps the only competitor in a national market, he can establish a monopoly which may prove costly for the economy.' See Kindleberger (1969), p. 9.

16 For empirical examples where the combination of protection from foreign competition and domestic monopoly situations lead to income losses in the Colombian pharmaceutical industry where foreign investors control most of the local market, see Vaitsos (1970a), p. 64.

17 Penrose (1956).

18 See Johnson (1970a), p. 45.

19 For a description of the symmetrical results due to differing capital intensity of traded goods among capital exporting and importing countries in the presence of tariff policies see Jones (1967).

20 See Kemp (1962a, b, 1966). Also see MacDougall (1960) and Balogh & Streeten (1960) and (1936) pp. 160–70. Also Keynes (1924) and (1930). Also Cairncross (1935).

21 For example, in the case of three consumption goods, two commodities and the services of capital, it could pay to subsidise trade in one of them. See Graaf (1957), pp. 136–7.

22 Such differences in valuations are expressed by differences in market prices, maintained through tariffs on imports or subsidies on exports. See Jones (1967), pp. 12–14.

23 See Kemp (1966), p. 806.

24 See Jones (1967), pp. 14 *et seq.*

25 See Rybszynski (1955).

[26] See Jones (1967), p. 16.

[27] For a geometrical presentation see Johnson (1970a), pp. 46–7. Johnson related the above to the conclusions reached by Dunning on economic grounds that English capital owners welcome American capital while British labour is adverse to it. See Dunning (1969).

[28] For example, important economic and political results took place due to the fact that Chilean copper miners, who worked for foreign owned firms, used to obtain a multiple of the average wage rate of the country or the earnings of the independent miners.

[29] Research has been undertaken under the direction of R. Stobaugh at Harvard Business School on the employment generating effects for US labour due to Northamerican 'defensive' direct investment abroad.

[30] For the need of several very restrictive assumptions to handle dynamic problems given existing analytical tools, see Negishi (1965).

[31] See Gruber, et al (1967). Also see OECD (1968).

[32] See Vernon (1966).

[33] See for example fiscal treatment on royalty remissions for technology sold abroad as practised by the Japanese government.

[34] See Hymer (1960, 1966, 1967).

[35] For example, in 1957, 15 out of 1542 US firms controlled 35 per cent of the total American manufacturing investments abroad while 1463 firms, at the other end, shared 31 per cent of the total. See US Department of Commerce, US Business Investments in Foreign Countries, Washington, DC, 1960. For the UK, 46 firms controlled 71 per cent of the assets of all UK investments abroad in the manufacturing sector and three firms had practically all foreign assets in the petroleum industry abroad. See Reddaway (1967).

[36] In a sample taken on foreign owned manufacturing subsidiaries in Chile, 50 per cent had a monopoly or duopoly position in the host market; another $36 \cdot 4$ per cent were operating in an oligopoly market where they had a leader's position; finally, only $13 \cdot 6$ per cent of the foreign subsidiaries in the sample, controlled less than 25 per cent of the local market. See CORFO (1970), p. 16.

[37] See Vernon (1971a), particularly Chapter 1.

[38] See Layton (1966), Kindleberger (1966) and Servan-Schreiber (1967).

[39] For the high rate of acquisition of Latin American firms by US transnational enterprises see data from Vaupel & Curhan (1969), *The Making of the International Enterprise*, as analysed by Wionczek.

[40] See Hymer & Rowthorn (1970), p. 85. For a specific example of how scale advantages in advertising and the generated processes of acquisitions and mergers due to the entrance of a foreign direct investor in the UK tobacco industry, reduced a market of more than 13 producers to a duopoly situation, see Dunning (1958), pp. 30–1.

[41] An alternative hypothesis has been presented that direct investments will tend to equalise returns to capital among countries intrasectorially while differences will persist intersectorially. See Caves (1971).

[42] Musgrave (1969), p. 22.

[43] For one of the first and pioneering analyses on the above see Hymer (1960).

[44] See Aharoni (1966).

[45] See for example the growing literature on the product cycle theory.

[46] Horst (1969).

47 See for example Kindleberger (1969a).

48 See Furtado (1971).

49 Important conceptual and definitional issues arise on the meaning of the term 'return on investment'. Both the numerator and the denominator of R.O.I. are subject to question where, among others, accounting practices (on capitalisation of intangibles, international allocation of overheads, declaration of investments as costs and vice versa depending on pertinent fiscal treatments etc.) have a critical importance.

50 See Vaitsos (1973).

51 See Kindleberger (1969b), p. p. 9.

52 Keynes (1924), p. 585.

53 See Vaitsos (1973).

54 For example of home rather than host country effects see Hufbauer & Adler (1967).

55 See for example Schydlowsky (1970).

56 See Behrman (1971).

57 For a summary of approaches see Henderson (1968).

58 For the corresponding literature survey see Bacha & Taylor (1971).

59 See Bruno (1967).

60 See for example Little & Mirrless (1969).

61 See articles 27–37 of Decision No. 24 of the Andean Pact.

62 See policies of the Instituto de Comercio Exterior of Colombia or the equivalent policies of the US Internal Revenue Service Code No. 492.

63 Even the form or appearance by which bargaining power is excercised can in some cases be quite important. For example, a host country can decide not to permit payment of royalties for technology by subsidiaries to their foreign parents. This could be considered as quite restrictive to foreign investors. Unless there also exist limits on profit remissions, the same rate as profits to be remitted. The latter policy, having the same net effect, could be subject to different negotiable pressures by foreign firms.

64 For an analysis of the effects of optimum financial management due to differences in government policies and the advantages of centralised management in this area by transnational corporations see Robbins and Stobaugh (1973).

65 For a presentation of the above see Horst (1971). If τ_2 is the tariff rate confronting imports by a firm from its foreign affiliates and t_2 and t_1 are, respectively, the effective profit tax rates in the host country of the firm and in the countries of its affiliates abroad, Horst derives the following conclusions: If

$$\tau_2 > \frac{t_2 - t_1}{1 - t_2}$$

the corporation will be induced to minimise transfer prices in the pursuit of maximising global after tax profits. If

$$\tau_2 < \frac{t_2 - t_1}{1 - t_2}$$

the corporation will maximise global after tax profits by increasing within possible limits, transfer prices. *Ibid*, at 1061.

66 See Krause & Dam (1964). Some exceptions exist such as in the case of holding companies in developing countries and Western Hemisphere Trading Companies for which the effective tax of remitted profits in the US is 36 per cent. Also some fiscal exceptions exist in developed countries like the Japanese

treatment on 70 per cent tax exemption for royalty receipts and Netherlands' treatment on foreign earned income.

67 See Vaitsos (1973).

68 I am grateful to Paul Streeten for bringing to my attention the need to enhance my analysis by introducing the carry-forward repercussions. Yet, the latter do not alter the basis of the conclusions concerning transfer pricing if $R - C < 0$ as discussed above.

69 See McGraw-Hill (1967). For further discussion see Pavitt (1970), pp. 74–9.

70 See Simmonds (1966). Also for further discussion see Franko (1973).

71 The above consideration raise important questions about the economic meaning of the accounting definition of 'business savings' which involve reinvested profits. Other investments by the firm are reported as expenses (like R & D) due to prevailing fiscal policies. Such investments might far outweigh reinvested profits. For example the average reported retained earnings (excluding reserves) for the manufacturing sector of the US in the late 1960s were below 2 per cent of sales. Some sectors, like the pharmaceuticals, spent just on R & D about 6 per cent of sales.

72 Similar problems have been noted with respect to state income taxes paid by corporations in the US. Distribution of income for the different States in the US is settled on the basis of some crude formulas on sales and employment.

73 $Y(1 - x)$ will be available to cover the difference between R and C for which no taxes is paid and $Yx(1 - t)$, will be the after tax profits of the parent. The total funds available will be $Y(1 - tx)$.

74 For some data on the percentage share of foreign operations in the consolidated sales of multinational enterprises whose parent firms are in Europe, USA and Japan see Adam (1972).

75 Data presented by Bruck & Lees (1966), pp. 1–6, as cited by Vernon (1971), p. 122. For some definitional differences among firms see Chapter 4.

76 See for example Business Week (1971), pp. 71–90. Various transnational enterprises have not only higher growth rates on sales but also higher profit ratios than the sector averages. Thus, the $3 \cdot 8$ per cent will be an under-estimate of their returns. Yet, the figures presented above did not include the remitted declared profits of the subsidiaries. These remissions could (partly) explain the difference between profit ratios of transational enterprises and sector averages.

77 I thank Professor Louis Wells, Jr, for his suggestions on the subject.

78 Certain limits will exist due to the leverage effect of interaffiliate debt on the cost of external financing.

79 See Vaitsos (1973).

80 The reactions and pressures of the representatives of transnational enterprises against the recent Andean Pact Code on foreign investments is a well documented case. See Wionczek (1971a). Also the decision of the Argentinean ex-Minister of Economy, Aldo Ferrer, to direct government purchases to goods and services produced by Argentinean owned firms has created strong reaction by foreign firms. (Governments of developed countries have long practised similar nationalist policies.)

81 Referring to a comment in a radio broadcast from Panama on the magnitude of profits of US investments, a study published by the RAND Corporation concluded the following: 'If we seek to promote US investments in Latin America in the future as a means of furthering US national interests, it is not enough that we believe the investment works for the material benefit

of the host countries. Quite regardless of how much objective truth in our side, the position of the United States will suffer if the antagonists kindle anti-American sentiments by successfully exploiting these kind of arguments [of high profits] by US firms', Johnson (1964), p. 54.

82 The analysis that follows assumes that although $R - C < 0$ the parent firm declares profits as a result of remitted tax income from its foreign affiliates, namely $R + (1 - t)Y - C > 0$. If though the latter is negative during certain years then the analysis should include the carry forward effects on future tax savings in the home country, which will amount to a percentage of the taxes paid in the host countries for the income not remitted through transfer pricing.

83 For calculations see Appendix B (p. 335).

84 For example if $x = 70$ per cent and $t = 50$ per cent than $\tau = [t(1 - x)]/[1 - t]$ when $\tau = 30$ per cent $= (1 - x)$.

Chapter 13

SIZE OF FIRM AND SIZE OF NATION

Charles P. Kindleberger

INTRODUCTION: THE NOTION OF OPTIMUM SIZE

This paper deals with the optimum size of firm in a world of nations of various size and the optimum size of the nation in a world of firms of various size. It is assumed that it is neither possible nor desirable, at this juncture in history, to have the world one nation, with a single set of laws governing business activity, or for all firms to be of world size, selling in all regional markets. It is evident, however, that firms are getting bigger and that countries are subject to two pressures: one for integration with other countries—at least in economic matters—and one for separation of parts with different values, largely cultural, religious, language and the like. It is not obvious, however, that there is any one optimum economic size for the nation or the firm, not that the various functions discharged by the firm and the nation should all be conducted on the same scale.

There are other optima which could be discussed than size of firm, or the area within which it operates. One could deal, for example, with the optimum range of products for the firm. It is taken as axiomatic in this paper, however, that firms specialise by commodities, and achieve scale economics in production, marketing, distribution, research and the like rather than apply highly-developed management techniques to a wide range of commodities, in so-called conglomerate firms. On the basis of casual empiricism, this specialisation in a single line, or in closely-related lines, such as oil and petrochemicals, produces greater efficiency than the attempt to apply standard techniques of management to widely different production and distribution problems.

The notion of optimum size has come into economics most recently from the literature on currency areas. Mundell introduced it in the *American Economic Review* a decade ago, making the point that a currency should cover an area within which factors of production are mobile, but beyond which they do not normally move in quantity. Immobility removes a mechanism of economic adjustment; currency revaluation or depreciation provides a replacement.[1] The optimum currency area, at least for large countries like Canada may be a region, smaller than the nation. In the ensuing discussion, McKinnon argued that an optimum currency area should be a closed unit which trades mainly within its collective borders, rather than with the outside world, so that changes in the value of its currency feeding back on the prices of foreign-trade goods would not be so noticeable as to be disturbing to consuming groups.[2] On this showing, the optimum currency area would tend to be larger than a region of immobile factors, and frequently larger than a country. Countries which traded heavily with one another should join together in an optimum currency area. Finally, in private conversation, Claudio Segré has noted that the optimum currency area would be one which has control of an arsenal of macro-economic weapons, such as monetary and fiscal policy. Such an area would typically be identical with the nation state, although it might, if integration went beyond trade and factor movements to encompass monetary and fiscal policy, include wider units of integrated states.

So much is well known to economists. But the notion of an optimum area evidently has wider connotations, for example, for other social sciences. The optimum political area differs for each political function, and with changes in circumstances, such as level of income, technology, tastes, and the like. The optimum education area in France has been thought to be the nation; that in the United States has been the village, town, or city, with some functions regulated or provided by the state or nation. In some fields, there is need for successive overlapping regional coverage, e.g. local police who know the residents of an area; state police who mainly regulate highway traffic between cities; and national police who match the mobility of criminals in nation-wide operations. A fourth level of 'Interpol' develops as crime moves up to the international level.

In cultural matters, social cohesion and vitality seem to be advanced by smaller units. The late unification of Germany and Italy delayed economic development in both countries, but promoted vigorous provincial life in art, music, letters. There are economies of scale to agglomeration in a New York, Paris, or London, but these are likely to have a deadening effect on the rest of the country. Berlin failed to dominate Frankfurt, Munich, Cologne and Hamburg in the way that London did Liverpool, Manchester and York, or Paris did Marseilles, Lyon and Toulouse. Milan, Turin, Venice, Bologna and Florence testify to the fact that the optimum cultural area tends to be smaller than the optimum area of economic growth.

THE OPTIMUM PRODUCTION AND FINANCIAL AREA OF THE FIRM

The optimum production area of a firm, i.e. the size of the market which it will try to serve from a given production source, depends upon a host of considerations which will differ depending upon the nature of the outputs, inputs and their production functions, the costs of transport for outputs and inputs, and on the size of markets as determined by numbers, incomes, and tastes on the one hand, and state interference on the other. Moreover, the organisation of the firm will play a role. Economies of scale in production, marketing, finance and the like may be offset in varying degrees by diseconomies of scale in centralised administration. Our interest in the precepts derived from location theory on the one hand, or from business administration on the other, is limited. It is rather in how the optimum production area, and the optimum area of other processes within the firm, are affected by differences in the sizes of cultural and political units.

It is self-evident, even without location theory, that commodities based on natural resources which are unevenly distributed over the earth's surface, will be produced at the earliest stage where they are located in greatest abundance consonant with accessability. If processes are strongly weight-losing, or bound to specific inputs such as large amounts of power, further processing will be drawn to the particular input supply. Where on the other hand, assembly adds bulk, processes will be drawn to the market to save transport. Between the two cases whether there is little loss in weight or gain in bulk, processes may be footloose, and costs of production at separate stages—or special considerations like taste—will dominate. A remarkable feature of the postwar period is that declining transport costs and increased efficiency in production have made footloose commodities out of such previously strongly supply-oriented products as steel and veal. In steel, Japan and Italy import both iron ore and coal and produce so much more cheaply than the older regions that Japan, for one, can practically sell steel to Pittsburgh. In veal, Italy imports young calves by aeroplane from the United States, and fattens them on imported feedgrains and oilcake to the taste specifications of the Italian market.

Supply and market pulls may be affected by the intervention of the political authorities. Export taxes on primary materials may attract processing to supplies, and import duties on finished products will pull the final stages of production to the market. It is an interesting exercise to contemplate how much of international direct investment is based on the principles of location theory, plus the oligopolistic competition on which the theory of direct investment rests, and how much is owing to state intervention. The Eastman Kodak company, for example, is said to maintain that the economies of scale in production and processing of photographic film are so great, and the costs of transport so small in relation to value added by manufacture, that if there were no tariffs, it would manufacture its film for world use, and process all colour film, in the single location of Rochester, New York. In a market-oriented industry like automobiles, Volkswagen has manufacturing plants in a number of high tariff areas, such as Australia and Brazil, but none in the United States, its largest market, which is supplied from Germany because of only moderate tariffs and high labour costs in the United States and inexpensive modes of ocean transport. A number of manufacturers, like Volvo, cover the world from a single point. In a world of zero tariffs direct investment would continue in supply-oriented industries, where vertical integration is needed to reap the' economies of co-ordination in production, transport, processing and distribution of bulky commodities, difficult and expensive to store, and in the distribution facilities of differentiated products or those that required specialised servicing.[3] Doubtless in many manufactured commodities, the economies from market orientation in major markets would outweigh differences in manufacturing cost, reduce the optimum production area, and pull investment away from the innovating manufacturing area.[4]

The optimum production area is a function not only of the existence of a tariff, but of its potentiality. It has been widely noted that the formation of the European Economic Community provided foreign investors an opportunity to rationalise production within the six countries, and has offered another such opportunity since the six became nine. Apart from the International Business Machines company, however, there is little evidence that the opportunity was widely seized. French irritation with Sperry Rand and General Motors (Frigidaire) which closed down plants which became non-competitive was duly observed,[5] and the rule of thumb found expression: 'To sell in France, produce in France'. Tariffs are thus not the only facet of national policy which affect the optimal production area. Another, of course, is vulnerability to nationalisation. In petroleum, the host country wants refining facilities located within its borders, but the international oil company wants to separate production and refining to allow no sovereign jurisdiction to have a free hand in obtaining a complete unit. The consequence is that all countries which produce oil or have pipelines passing through them are host to oil refineries, most of them too small to be efficient.

Assume for reasons of location theory, of tariff barriers, or of other actual or potential exercise of political sovereignty, a manufacturer of a consumer's good has production facilities of some sort spread all over the world. What is the optimum area for a wide range of other functions that the firm performs beyond production, i.e. in personnel, capital budgeting, new product planning, research and development, marketing, finance and the like? In business administration, the question is put as to which of these functions are properly centralised in the head office, and which left to the production, marketing or service units abroad, with a middle range of regional areas—operated by a regional headquarters, for example—which co-ordinates or even makes decisions concerning the given function in several countries. For example, European marketing in some companies is divided between a German division, typically headquartered in German-speaking Switzerland, covering Germany, Austria, Scandinavia, the Netherlands, perhaps the Flemish portion of Belgium; a Latin division in Paris or Rome for France, Italy, French-Switzerland, Spain and Portugal; and a British Commonwealth group, extending overseas from Europe, operating out of London. The basis for separation is partly language, partly culture. Cultural differences or state interference may change the optimum scale. In research and development, for example, a firm may be required to undertake research and development in a given market, or may think it wise to do so even in the absence of a formal requirement. Or it may even be economical to take advantage of factor prices in the science world, giving up economies of scale for cheaper inputs. A Unilever executive at a lecture at the Harvard Business School asserted that his company performed its highly theoretical and abstract research in India, as a consequence of the abundance and modest salaries of Indian theoretical physicists.

The widest optimum area is typically in finance. For many companies finance is run from the home headquarters, with the optimum financial area the world. Where there are many subsidiaries, there may be diseconomies of scale to dictate the intervention of a layer of regional staffs, perhaps one for London, and one in Tokyo or Hong Kong, for Europe and the Far East, respectively.[6] In a world of fixed exchange rates without foreign-exchange controls, finance is one of the easiest functions on which to economise, using surplus cash in one area to make up for deficiencies in others, and reducing the need for capital through the insurance principle. Where exchange rates fluctuate or there are foreign-exchange controls, or both, finance becomes too important to be left to the separate subsidiaries, except where these possess a high degree of sophistication.

There is a tendency in Europe to think of firms as too small and operating within too small an area. Governmental pressure has been applied to encourage firms to merge, to plough-back profits, acquire other firms through takeovers, and the like, to beef up firm size. That firms may be above optimum size and produce over too wide an area—leaving aside the optimum size of the separate areas in which they produce—is evident in the failures in multinational enterprise in recent years. Gallaher in Australia, Scovill in France, Maytag in Germany, Raytheon in Italy, General Tyre in the Netherlands, Roberts-Arundel in the United Kingdom, and St Gobain in the United States, to name but a sample. Apart from empirical evidence, however, there is an *a priori* case that in a world of defensive investment, firms will spread themselves too widely. Defensive investment, it will be remembered, is undertaken not for positive profits, but to avoid losses, prospective or hypothetical. A firm feels the need to be represented in all markets lest its competitors gain an advantage over it by making large profits in one. In such cases the firm will be too large, making less than normal profits or even losses in markets where it is acting defensively. In the longer run it must serve much markets from other sources, if at all, and shrink the size of its productive span.

INTERNATIONAL BANKING AND OPTIMUM AREAS

Just as the financial function is likely to operate in the widest economic sphere within the firm, so banks may cast a wider spatial net than the normal industrial firm. Much will depend upon whether a bank is interested only in positive profits, or feels obliged as a form of defensive investment, to be represented in all important markets where its domestic customers may have occasion to look for banking assistance. This is defensive investment where the bank earns less than a normal profit in a particular market, but ascribes to the operation part of the return to operations in other lucrative markets which it might lose to a competitor if it were not on hand. Specialised banks like Barclays DSO in Africa and the Bank of London and South America

(Bolsa) serve particular clienteles. World-wide banks, moreover, operate with considerable profits in some markets, even while they react defensively in others. The subject has not been sufficently studied to enable one to say much of a positive nature. On the whole, foreign banks lack the access to demand deposits which provide the cheap raw material for loans, having in fact to buy the funds they lend out by paying interest, and missing out on the seignorage enjoyed by local banks.[7] This handicap can be over-come in some markets by aggressive competition in the provision of services ignored by local banks: instalment finance, factoring, and lately, through the one-bank holding company, computer services, management advice, and the like. Where local banking is monopolistic in character, as is alleged for example in Germany, foreign banks, if permitted entry, can earn positive profits higher than at home, though perhaps less than those enjoyed by local banks with demand deposits. The monopoly feature of the market makes the case depart from the standard theory in which the firm to operate abroad must have an advantage which enables it to earn more abroad than at home and more abroad than the local enterprise.

Major accounting firms similarly maintain offices world-wide where they may be able to render service to domestic clients, whom they would be unhappy having served by a rival firm of accountants or auditors. This is defensive investment to the extent that such firms maximise in the long run rather than the short. An accounting firm hates to lose a client, which it considers equivalent to the loss of an annuity, and will take virtually infinite pains to avoid that unhappy event.

Both location theory and economics of scale in developed money and capital markets add to the tendencies for international firms to centralise their financial operations and for international banks to be represented in major financial centres. The costs of transfer of money in space are lower than for commodities or services, thus making concentration at a few points practical. Economies of scale in financial centres derive from the fact that the broader the market, and the greater the volume, the smaller the margin between bid and asked prices for loans or existing securities, and therefore the cheaper the service to lender and borrower, buyer or seller. With greater liquidity, the lender or buyer of a security acquires a different type of asset on which he is prepared to accept a lower return. In long-term capital markets it is possible to sell new securities simultaneously in a number of locations, by means of widely-spread syndicates connected by telephone, telex, telegraph, etc. Such markets need not be concentrated. But the secondary market, the quality of which is critical for the liquidity of an issue, requires concentration in space, as the purchase, and especially the sale, of one or a few bonds will not bear the expense of searching out separated markets for the best bargain among separated sellers or buyers.

One money market also tends to dominate, currently the Eurodollar market in London unless the devaluation of the dollar and Britain's joining the European Economic Community produce a change. Note that the financial centre of a company need not be identical with its regional headquarters for decisions on production and marketing. The point is clear when one recalls that General Motors has its production/marketing headquarters in Detroit and its financial headquarters in the United States in New York. The international firm finds its European general headquarters increasingly attracted to Brussels, the seat of the Commission of the EEC. Where the financial centre of the Common Market will ultimately be located is unclear at this writing.[8] If no clearly dominant financial centre emerges quickly, the head regional offices of the large international banks, largely American, may be drawn to the head regional offices of the companies they have gone abroad to serve, rather than to an existing financial centre.

That American banks are more European than the banks of separate countries of Europe—apart perhaps from such specialised institutions as the European Investment Bank—rests on the fact that they have roots in no country in Europe to which they owe special allegiance or within which their horizon has been traditionally confined. The indigenous banks in Europe operate primarily within a single country, with limited numbers of foreign branches—except for the British overseas banks—and lacking the habit of work which would make then continuously scan opportunities outside their own borders. When the Commerzbank of Germany, the Crédit Lyonnais of France and the Banca di Roma of Italy form a consortium for European loans, it is mainly window-dressing, with no bank able to commit the group without consultation and many loans or investments, intended to be general, in which one or two of the group holds back. Whether this will change, and truly European banking will develop as the Common Market moves to monetary unification is an open question on which it is difficult to formulate an opinion with confidence. While the major banks in each country started out in a single city, and expanded to national coverage by establishing branches throughout the country, frequently moving their head office from a provincial centre to the national financial centre, it does not seem likely that the same process will be followed as integration proceeds to successively higher stages. The United States banks may remain the only truly European banks for some considerable period.

THE OPTIMUM AREA IN TECHNOLOGY

The optimum area poses a particularly critical question in the field of technology. Once the limit of efficiency in a product has been reached, it is optimal because of economics of scale in production, consumption and maintenance to adopt the same technical standard all over the world. Prior to that stage, however, there is much to be said for preserving independent, competitive technologies, so as to permit exploration of a variety of possibilities and to avoid settling prematurely on a design which will ultimately prove inefficient. The difficulties are either that one standard will be adopted widely early, and command the field through economies of scale; or that differing standards will be adopted in separate economic regions, and become so dug in that the investment necessary to shift to a common standard, if there should be a means of choosing it, becomes so large as to be prohibitive.

Examples of both tendencies are easily provided. The British standard railroad gauge of 4 ft 7·50 in. was widely adopted in Europe early, although the 5 ft, wide-gauge provided a more stable roadbed for trains at the speeds later achieved. Some countries—Russia with a wide gauge, and Australia with different standards in each state—lacked the benefits of standardisation at the international or even the national level, respectively. American-German colour television got established before the Franco–Russian standard of allegedly finer grain could be perfected and marketed. The 78 r.p.m. gramophone successfully held the field for years before the 33 and the 45 r.p.m. versions were simultaneously launched to drive it from the market. British trains drove on the left, so the British automobiles did. In Europe, France, Italy and Switzerland patterned their trains after Britain but their road traffic after the United States which first mass produced the automobile. Austria, Czechoslovakia and Sweden, which once drove on the left all changed convulsively, the first two after foreign conquest, the last after lengthy deliberation and weighing of the costs and benefits. The most pervasive example of all, however, is the British shift of its duodecimal coinage and system of weights and measures to the decimal and metric systems, the first under the influence of computer tech-

nology, the latter as a step toward efficiency in interchange-
ability and of integration in the Common Market.

The multinational enterprise plays a role in this process in
imposing the standards of the developed, frequently rich country
in which the standards are developed, to the rest of the world.
This may occur at a premature stage, and cut off a line of independent experimentation and practice which might ultimately
lead to improved designs and standards. In electricity, AEG with
the help of the Edison Company in the United States, came along
just in time with its strong current to defeat the Siemens weak
current transmission system. With smaller companies involved,
the outcome would have been probably not change to the better
standard, or a block to progress at the weaker, but failure to
standardise, as in London and New York, with various types of
current (AC and DC) and various voltages, especially 110 and
220, not to mention in London a bewildering variety of fittings.
Standards are sometimes set by government, as part of the contribution to infrastructure, and sometimes by a dominant firm.
International agreement, as on the pitch of the screwthread agreed
in World War II between the United States and Britain, is limited
primarily to the military field. But the presence of giant companies
in international trade and investment may make it difficult for
new and improved standards to be adopted, except in so far as
they originate with and are promoted by the giant firms themselves. In discussion, for example, Professor Stephen Hymer
has suggested that if Canada had had an independent Canadian
company in the field of electrical appliances, as opposed to
subsidiaries of the leading American firms, such a company might
have undertaken an independent research effort and achieved
independent results in new processes or new products, the latter
possibly more suitable to Canadian needs than the products
developed in the United States. Such a view probably exaggerates
the barriers to new entry for individuals with new ideas, who
often start small companies which grow, and do so in the backyard
of the giant companies, i.e. in the United States. It may understate
as well the international integration of the intellectual market
for science and technology which prevents research from being
completely independent anywhere in the world. Existing standards
are continuously being challenged by the introduction of new
processes and products, although the difficulties of overcoming
the head start of established standardised products must be
recognised.

The dilemma exists independently of the size of firm. Some
unpublished research of G. Cole at Oxford shows that the Bristol

bus company preferred to have it buses of the same make and model to simplify the problems of maintaining inventories of spare parts, training mechanics in maintenance, and the like. With technical improvements occurring discontinuously, but depreciation and the need for replacement taking place in a steady flow, the achievement of the (internal) economy from standardisation of equipment was virtually impossible. Similarly during war, military services are continuously faced with the choice of whether to fix on a given design and get larger and cheaper production, or keep back from long production runs while they work on improving design still further. Important to the choice is the fact that the earlier design is frozen and a standard adopted, the more difficult it will be later to replace it with better equipment, when and if developed.

On the other hand, multinational firms tend to introduce modern machinery in most cases in less developed countries, finding that the gain from standardisation of equipment within the company outweighs the loss from a technology unsuited to local factor proportions and factor prices. Size, of course, affects the gains from standardisation, but the dilemma begins at a very limited scale.

If we abstract from localisation factors and concentrate on assembly-line processes, the optimum size of firm from the viewpoint of the world economy may turn on whether at a given point in time technical change is rapid at the beginning of the introduction of a product or a process, or slowing down near the end of the product or process cycle. At early stages, the larger firm, and by definition the international firm is larger than the national one, is likely to speed up standarisation, which achieves efficiency in production, but may slow down technical change. If big firms innovate more than small firms, however, as Schumpeter believed, there is another consideration to be added to the choice.

THE MULTINATIONAL FIRM AND THE SOVEREIGNTY OF THE NATION STATE

SIZE OF ENTERPRISE AND SIZE OF STATE

Before considering the impact of the large multinational firm on the optimal size of country, it is necessary to say a few words by way of digression about the comparison, almost universally made, between the respective size of companies and states.[9] General Motors sales, for example, are said to be larger than the national income of the Netherlands, or the Standard Oil Company of New Jersey's profit for a given year larger than the national income of, say, Costa Rica.

Most of these comparisons are illegitimate. Sales of course are a gross figure, including value added and purchased inputs, whereas national income is a net figure, representing value added only. One could properly compare value added by a company and the national income of a country—though the comparison would be less striking—or gross up the national income of the country in question to include inputs bought both abroad and within the country by one firm from another—if the figures for the later were available as they would not be outside of manufactures.

One could make other comparisons, such as the value added by General Motors, its dealers and suppliers, and their suppliers, and the national income of a country, or the number of employees of General Motors, its dealers, suppliers and their suppliers, and the labour force of a country—not the population, unless one added into the first figure the employees' dependants. Possibly the comparison between the employees of General Motors alone and the labour force of say the Netherlands is relevant. Or the annual profit of a large firm and the tax receipts of a government. But why are these comparisons wanted?

There is no doubt that GM and Esso (now Exxon) are big companies compared with other companies, and that the Netherlands is relatively small in economic terms as countries go. The comparison between them in the usual case produces a statement comparable to 'this apple is bigger than this watch', of dubious interest and importance. Most people make the comparison to furnish some idea of the relative power of General Motors and the Netherlands, and this may well be incomparable.

Both GM and the Netherlands have the power of the purse. That of GM is measured less well by sales, because it has to pay its suppliers, or even value added, since it has to pay its workers, dealers and executives, than by profit—although the annually expected dividend may be regarded as an expense—and by its power to borrow in money and capital markets. The Netherlands' power of the purse could be represented by tax receipts, though normal taxation for normal running expenditure is akin to the monies GM must use for purchased inputs. Perhaps the best measure would be the Dutch governmental power to raise taxes for new expenditure, plus its capacity to borrow. One test which might be said to be fair would be the relative amounts the two bodies could borrow and the rates of interest they would have to pay, perhaps adjusted for tax discrimination and investor discrimination based upon the eligibility of government securities

M

for certain trustee purposes for which GM debt is ineligible. The argument becomes complex and uninteresting.

But the Netherlands has several powers which General Motors lacks: the power to tax, the power to issue money which may be regarded as the power to tax via inflation, and in more general terms police power. Galbraith to the contrary notwithstanding, the corporation does not have the power to compel the individual to act, against his will, in ways it chooses. The state does. The state is sovereign, General Motors is not.

THE MULTINATIONAL AND SMALLER STATES

The sovereignty of the state, surely the small state, but the large state as well, has been eroded by the international corporation, among other influences in a world of easy mobility and communication.[10] This is true in the areas of taxation, monetary policy, labour policy, regulation of shipping, and the like.

In taxation, while corporations complain of double taxation, the fiscal authorities tend to believe that the international corporation uses differences in rates of taxation, and definitions of income, to distort its operations, or transfers income, possibly through the adjustment of prices used in intra-corporation dealings—so as to avoid or evade taxation. The result is pressure to harmonise levels of taxation, definitions of income, including investment credits and the like, to reduce incentives for companies to move in ways which are uneconomic.

The pressure on the small-to-medium states to harmonise taxes, definitions of income, and perhaps one day governmental benefits, is not felt by the very small countries—Panama, the Bahamas, the Seychelles, Liechtenstein, Luxemburg and a number of Swiss cantons, which, having little to offer in the way of real economic advantages, compete to attract a portion, often minimal, of a firm's operations by offering it very low tax rates. The appeal of tax havens has been very much reduced by the Revenue Act of 1962 in the United States, which subjects to United States taxation, without the credit for foreign income taxes paid, income earned in countries with limited production facilities; and in the Swiss–German double-taxation agreement of 1971 which prevents tax avoidance by German companies through Swiss dummies. It seems likely that the pressure of the larger jurisdictions will bring the practice to a halt in a few years, and that, like Delaware, the smaller jurisdictions will lose their power to entice legal and accounting operations.

Harmonisation reduces the sovereignty of states by making

them conform to a general standard. The smaller the country, the less its capacity to produce change in the standard. Such capacity is likely to be divided asymmetrically. In the field of monetary policy, for example, the United States used to set the level of world interest rates, except for countries cut off from world money and capital markets by fluctuating exchange rates or effective exchange control, and other countries are bound to follow except for small differences. It seem likely that a similar asymmetry of power to affect the set of harmonised corporate regulations exists, pending the development of effective international institutions. The system is, of course, looser than for short-term interest rates. A change in taxes, definitions of income, investment credit, and *a fortiori* public expenditure favourable or unfavourable to corporations in one country is likely to be followed elsewhere only very slowly. Nevertheless as corporate mobility increases, the limited conformity is achieved more rapidly.

High mobility has enabled shipping companies to operate virtually independently of national regulation, except where they are paid to do so by mail contracts, construction subsidies, and the like. British shippers can ignore Plimsoll loading regulations, American tankers the labour regulations laid down by the Maritime Commission, by the device of flags of convenience. Norman notes that the shipping companies in Norway are virtually independent of government influence.[11] Other production processes are, of course, less mobile than shipping in the short run, and government can exercise it sovereignty and police power over international corporations to the extent that they have fixed assets within its borders, are organised under the laws of the state, with a preponderance of domestic officers and shareholders. It is unclear whether the location of the assets or the nationality of the corporate parent and its shareholders has the larger effect on the behaviour of a corporation in a given set of circumstances. If a company like Aramco owned in the United States but with its most important producing asset in Saudi Arabia were being pressed in opposite directions by the two governments involved, the outcome would probably depend upon the particular circumstances. But the force of circumstances, especially in the developed world but to some extent among developing countries as well, tends to produce uniformity of treatment.

It is fair to remind ourselves, however, that the multinational enterprise does not take much sovereignty away from the small state, since it is unlikely to have much in the first place. Dupriez notes that small states like Belgium not only cannot have an independent monetary policy: they cannot permit their prices and costs to get out of line with those of their neighbours, so quickly is the balance of payment likely to respond.[12] Drèze has noted that Belgium produces and exports only standardized products because its market is so small that it can achieve efficient scale of production only in products already adopted by others.[13] (This generalisation must be qualified, however, for products of high style in which a particular country develops a quality which gains acceptance abroad: Danish furniture, Swedish china and glass, Swiss watches, Italian knitted goods and shoes, French wines, Czech jewellery and glass between the wars, etc. In these products the efficient unit of production can be small if marketing is undertaken co-operatively, as in the case of Swiss watches, or the products may be bought by large international corporations, in this case the department stores and department-store chains in major cities in the larger countries, which are always on the lookout for style leadership.) The Belgian attempt to maintain a foreign-exchange control which differentiated between the trade currency and the finance currency was a failure from the start; arbitrage between the two markets was virtually perfect and prevented the rates from diverging. The international corporation may subtract something from the economic independence of the small state, but there is little enough to begin with.

The optimal size of state will vary depending on the variable concerned. In economic terms the state should be large to achieve economies of scale, in so far as these are possible in given economic circumstances—production functions, location theory and the like. If cultural identity and cohesion are sought, if should perhaps be smaller than Belgium with its antagonism between Walloons and Flamands. Within the political field, there is first the variable to be, say, maximised—whether stability, order, independence, power in world affairs, efficiency in internal administration and the like, all of which doubtless give different answers; and second, the serious question of hysteresis, which makes political institutions adapt only very slowly to changes in parameters. It has been observed before, but it may be useful to repeat, that farmers are universally overrepresented in political legislatures because of Engel's law and the lag of political behind economic change. Economic power shifts from landholding to commerce to industry and perhaps currently to the service class, or techno-structure, but political power accompanies it only with great reluctance and after a long lag (a fact not noted by Marx). The county in the United States, a political institution adapted from England and which fulfilled certain functions in eighteenth century America survives, when its *raison d'être* has disappeared. The difficulty of redrawing urban jurisdictions as people escape to the periphery is well known. Tradition, the accretion of interest in old institutions, and reluctance to induce political change for fear it may get out of hand in chain reaction,[14] tend to perpetuate political arrangements which are far from optimal.

Where the political variable is power, larger may be better. Where it is independence, the status quo, or self-determination which makes smaller units out of larger may win out. The two motives are often in conflict, as in the French attitude toward the Common Market. Independence as a political goal is also opposed to the loss of sovereignty represented by the interpenetration of efficient-sized corporations. The optimum economic organisation of America north of the Rio Grande, for example, would run north and south, instead of east and west, with separate nations for the East Coast and the Maritimes (with perhaps Quebec thrown in); a separate West Coast, covering Alaska, the Yukon, British Columbia, Washington, Oregon and California; and perhaps a single country for the rest in between. A political organisation which emphasised power would include Canada as part of the United States. With independence large in the objective function, Canada insists on independence from the United States, and French Canada is increasingly interested in separation from English Canada, which the latter resists on the basis of power. The Gray Report cannot be faulted for its insistence on a Canadian identity, if that is what Canadians choose, but only for its belief that this goal is identical with, or at least consistent with, a policy of optimal intervention in direct investment which maximises Canadian real income at the same time.[15] Most economists are prepared to recognise that optimal tariffs are based on a sometimes heroic assumption of no retaliation. A simple shift of United States policy from discrimination in favour of Canada to non-discrimination in such matters as the interest-equalisation tax, Federal Reserve lending regulations, and the automotive agreement would be costly to Canada in terms of income and growth.

THE MULTINATIONAL FIRM AND THE LARGER STATE

If the multinational enterprise does not take much power from the very small state, which has little, does it do so from those larger? Is it appropriate for the larger state to do something about it, and if so, how? Is it self-evident that as the optimum size of the corporation and corporate functions increase, the effective state must grow in size or in centralised power?

The answer to these questions cannot be given with any confidence in the present state of our knowledge of international relations. The multinational corporation is by no means the only force on the economic side making for a larger optimum size of the state; the same pressure arises from the increases in mobility of capital and labour and the reduction in transport and communication costs relative to the prices of goods and other services. On a Marxian model of economic determinism, increased mobility requires increased state size or a yielding up of the sovereign powers of the small or medium state to larger units. But economic determinism is not universally agreed. Even if it were, it is not clear whether it would be adequate to cope with the increased mobility by voluntary associations of states, as in diplomatic arrangements whether bilateral or multilateral, though formal intergovernmental agreements, like the General Agreement on Tariffs and Trade, through economic unions of the sort represented by the European Economic Community or the Andes Pact, or through political union. Harmonization to a greater or lesser degree seems inevitable. The economist would prefer to leave the analysis of the nature of such harmonisation to the political scientist, though he is unlikely to find the latter ready to make much of a positive contribution.

The cultural arguments for a smaller optimum size of state will be addressed in the next and final section. The conclusion there is that they are unlikely to prevail. Political considerations point in no particular direction. Whether they overwhelm the economic pressures for a larger state, or are in turn dominant, will vary from case to case. It is significant that Denmark joined the Common Market but that Norway did not. In these circumstances, prediction is impossible. The economic pressure is there. The state isolates itself from the pressure at its economic peril, unless it is enormously adroit as Japan has been. The choice is between losing sovereignty to the economic pressures or yielding it to larger aggregates. Which will strike political units as the preferred short-run option is impossible to forecast. In the long run, however, political agglomeration to harmonise policies and to contain economic mobility seems inevitable.

CONCLUSIONS

It seems likely then that the optimum economic area is larger than the nation state, the optimum cultural area smaller, and the optimum political area, based on the objective of independence, and subject to the hysteresis mentioned, identical with it. To the extent that corporations function beyond the confines of the state, they may serve the state's power purposes, as claimed by Gaullists, or the state may serve corporate interests, as Marxists think, but there is at least a presumption that their scope assists in the achievement of optimum economic size, and wars against cultural and political goals. The rise of the neo-mercantilist attack on the international corporation, by Gaullists, Marxists and especially political scientists reflects the view that the nation state is threatened by the growing optimum economic size of nations and of corporations. The preservation of the power of the state, a good in itself, may require restriction in the international corporations originating in other countries, if not the increase in the number of such corporations whose officers and seat are domestic and which can therefore serve as instruments of power.[16]

The most interesting contraposition of these points of view has been suggested by Hymer and Rowthorn (1970), who argue that it would be better to have companies integrated across industrial lines within a given state, than international corporations organised within industries across national lines.[17] The view implies judgement as between economic welfare and political independence for the state, though not necessarily for its citizens, and rests on a subjective basis. It may well be that for a given level of economic welfare and freedom for its citizens, more political independence is better than the same or less, and that for a given amount of political independence and freedom, more economic welfare is better than the same or less. If economic welfare is to be traded off against political independence, however, one needs an implicit series of prices to reach an equilibrium solution. It is improbable that all observers would agree on what an ideal series of trade-offs would be, much less on how in the real world one substitutes for the other in given circumstances. The problem of how much economic welfare to give up for how much nationalism is very much on the Canadian agenda today, without however, a contemplation of integration of industries in the national setting.

Perhaps the example of Eastern Europe, the Soviet Union and Comecon is too complicated by other considerations, but I find that the failures in national planning within states, and the absence of international pricing which would make possible efficient specialisation between Socialist countries make the economic cost of the Hymer solution very high, even without counting what appears to be a very high implicit price in loss of political, social and economic freedom for the individual. It is not without interest that individual voices are beginning to be raised in Eastern Europe for the establishment of convertible currencies and international corporations.[18]

In any event, cultural independence and cohesion are probably doomed. The most serious charge one can level against the international corporation is that is produces a homogenised world culture, of wall-to-wall carpeting, tasteless meals, Americanised English, traffic jams, and gasoline fumes.[19] The clash between social and economic values recalls the strictures against the industrial revolution of Karl Polanyi in *The Great Transformation* (1947), and his outrage that economic values should have dominated over social. Like Friedrich Engels, and current observers like Edward Thompson and Eric Hobsbawm, Polanyi exaggerated the delights of rural life in a Malthusian world.[20] More significant, however, where politics have made a choice in favour of preserving old values—the French peasant, the small retail shop, the guild system of artisan production, it has generally been economically unsuccessful and politically disastrous. There can be no doubt of the tragedy which befalls people displaced from performing accustomed tasks in accustomed ways. It is exceeded, however, by the tragedy implicit in the political efforts to prevent economic change, or to return, as Fascists, Nazis and Poujadists have sought, to an idyllic life that never existed.

There are Utopian solutions. At the extreme, affluence a la Galbraith eliminates scarcity and the need for economies of scale, or efficiency or international interdependence; and the brotherhood and sisterhood of man and woman eliminates the need for order, government and the state. Affluence eliminates the need for economics; true partipation with instantaneous decision-making eliminates the need for political science, and perhaps sociology. Some observers predict both by the end of the century.[21]

A personal view, again for what it may be worth, is that scarcity and the need for order are with us for the foreseeable future. This implies that the resolution of the conflict between the optimum economic area and the optimum political area should be sought not by reducing the economic dimension to the narrow political one of the nation state, but rather by building international political institutions capable of regulating the international corporation in the interest of Pareto-optimality. In the short run this means more international organisation; over the longer term, it may mean world government. But I see no virtue in the implicit position of most political scientists that the nation state as it exists today is sacrosanct and eternal and that other world forces should be bent to its preservation. If the scale of political efficiency changes, why should not the nation state follow the county not into oblivion but into the museum of antiquarian interest with the city-state.

The need to exceed the optimum cultural area saddens me. The moves to separate Bangla Desh from Pakistan, Croatia from Yugoslavia, Scotland and Wales from Britain, French Canada from Canada are understandable, possibly successful in the short run, but futile. A pity for our descendants who will find the world much more alike. Some of the now less developed countries, it should be noted, will be much better off.

References

[1] See Mundell (1961).

[2] See McKinnon (1963).

[3] Despite the fact that Volkswagen has no production facilities in the United States, it has of course a considerable investment in distribution facilities, including stocks of spare parts.

[4] In his thesis in 1960 Stephen Hymer recorded the view that when any market reached a volume of 50 000 tyres a year, it was worth while for a tyre company to invest there in productive facilities. This no longer appears to be the case, and the efficient-sized plant is said to produce 25 000 tyres a day. A new plant in Turkey, for example, starts with a capacity of 750 000 tyres a year. In some industries, on the other hand, the size of efficient plant is reduced by innovation, rather than increased. In 1964 it was said in Luxembourg that the efficient steel plant had been reduced in size from 7 or 8 m tons a year to 2 or 3 m.

[5] See Johnstone (1965).

[6] Anyone who doubts the reality of diseconomies of scale should contemplate the wartime practice of armies since the time of Napoleon of adding a new headquarters whenever the number of subordinate units exceeds three. When a fourth division is added to a corps, for example, a second corps headquarters is produced to make two corps of two divisions each. The same applies to army groups, armies, corps within armies, regiments in divisions, etc. Only the corporal who commands twelve soldiers in the American army is thought capable of managing more than three units.

[7] See Koszul (1970).

[8] The first open question is whether the financial integration of the Common Market will replace that of the North Atlantic 'community', now based in the Euro-dollar market with its primary location in London. If a European currency and a European money and capital market do develop separately from the dollar, the evident candidate for leadership in the system is London. The author has reservations, however. London dominated the Euro-dollar market because of the presence there of large American bank branches. To furnish the centre for a European money and capital market, London would have to resume international lending. The author believes that it is not sufficient to offer brokerage services: the market is made where there are financial institutions prepared to buy when demand is insufficient, and to sell when it is excessive. British savings, channelled through pension funds

and insurance companies, are normally invested in domestic government and local authority issues, and are not normally invested abroad. There is, of course, investment in British companies which themselves undertake direct investment abroad, but this is outside the capital market proper. On this showing, Amsterdam and Frankfurt are more likely candidates. It is even possible if a new currency were established, rather than an existing currency adopted by the market as a whole, that the political pull of Brussels would bring financial institutions there.

If a European currency is unable to develop in competition with the dollar, it seems unlikely that the financial centre would move back from London to New York, even if United States restrictions were removed. The convenience of a world money and capital market located in the European time zone, and largely free of government regulation, is too compelling, even though, for really large sums of money—over $125 m—New York is a much more efficient market.

[9] Seers (1963), however, carefully avoids the vulgar conparisons.

[10] See the title of Raymond Vernon's book (1971a), on the multinational enterprise.

[11] See Norman (1971), p. 36.

[12] See Dupriez (1966), pp. 281 ff.

[13] See Drèze (1960).

[14] There is a substantial literature which traces the final unwillingness of the German bourgeoisie to agree to constitutional reform after the Revolution of 1848 to the view that, terrified by the Lumpenproletariat, the bourgeoisie was unwilling to restrict the monarchy, separate justice and administration, provide for a wider franchise to dilute the aristocratic dominance of parliamentary institutions—all in its own interest—for fear it would open the flood gates of change. Historians also claim that Italian business steered away from reform of the governmental bureaucracy in Italy after World War II for fear that they could not limit reform.

[15] See Government of Canada (1972).

[16] Note that the operations of the Deutsche Bank in Italy were undertaken for political motives—to help Italy engaged in a tariff war with France—and were regarded subsequently as having had major political benefits: see Helfferich (1965), p. 543.

[17] See Hymer and Rowthorn (1970).

[18] See Vajda (1969), pp. 128 ff.

[19] Note, however, the declaration of Margaret Mead in favour of a world culture, as she received the Kalinga prize from UNESCO, *Journal de Genève*, 24 February 1972.

[20] See e.g. Braun (1965), Chapter IV.

[21] See Galtung (1970).

Chapter 14

CONCLUSIONS

John H. Dunning

What may we conclude from the contributions in this book? In our introductory chapter, we suggested that the value of economic analysis as a contribution to our understanding of the way in which resources are allocated (positive economics) or should be allocated (normative economics) rested, first, in rightly interpreting the goals which economic agents sought to achieve: second, on the choice of assumptions underlying any explanation of their behaviour: third, on correctly identifying the explanatory variables and the value attached to them: and, fourth, on the logical consistency of the argument contained in the analysis.

We also observed that the fact that multinational enterprises *do* behave differently from other enterprises, or have different consequences, does not, in itself, necessarily imply that economic *analysis* is deficient; it could simply reflect that the parameters on which analysis is based are different.

Finally, we argued that the subject for explanation was not the total behaviour of multinational enterprises but only that part which could be attributed specifically to their multinationality.

All the contributions in this book give partial answers to these questions, but it may be helpful to briefly summarise their conclusions under three headings.

(1) The extent to which received economic analysis can adequately explain the behaviour of multinational enterprises or their affiliates as economic agents.

(2) The extent to which received economic analysis can adequately explain the consequences of multinational enterprises on other economic agents or groups of economic agents, or on the institutional and market system within which they operate.

(3) The extent to which received economic analysis can adequately explain the effects of changes in exogenous variables, notably Government policy and market mechanisms on the behaviour of multinational enterprises.

THE BEHAVIOUR OF MULTINATIONAL ENTERPRISES AND THEIR AFFILIATES

The theory of the multinational enterprise is, at very least, an extension of the theory of the firm or, to be more precise, of the multi-plant firm. This is Horst's and Stevens' theme, but, in so far as the behaviour of firms is closely linked with other areas of economic theory, the chapters of Vernon, Mansfield and Vaitsos are also relevant.

Both Horst and Stevens deal with the motivation of the behaviour of firms and conclude, both on *a priori* grounds and from the empirical data available, there are no reasons for supposing multinationality, as a form of diversification of economic activity, need cause firms to modify their objectives. While accepting this from the viewpoint of the overall goals of large companies, one cannot but feel that, when comparing the goals of individual affiliates of multinational enterprises with a group of independent indigenous companies, that differences do emerge. This is because the behaviour of affiliates of multinational enterprises is geared not to meeting their own objectives (which may be very similar to those of indigenous companies), but to the enterprise of which they are part (which may be very different). This difference will affect both the operational and logistic behaviour of the firms, and distribution of their output among the participating agents of production in different countries. Moreover, the locus of decision taking is likely to be different in affiliates, and particularly interdependent affiliates, than in indigenous companies.

On the question of the assumptions underlying the analysis of the behaviour of firms, it is generally agreed that these may require modification (Government policy and market structures are two examples) and that additional ones (e.g. with respect to movements in exchange rates) need to be introduced. Several authors also make the point that, due *inter alia* to their oligopolistic interdependence and involvement in nation states of widely differing political persuasions, multinational enterprises operate a much more uncertain environment than do most domestic companies.

The introduction of new explanatory variables offers perhaps the most important variation to the received theory of the firm. Considerations which do not affect the financial and operating behaviour of domestic firms may be crucial to an understanding of multinationals or of their affiliates. The essays of Horst,

Stevens and Vaitsos illustrate this: it is relevant both in efficiency and equity type decisions. The authors conclude that, while most new variables can be easily incorporated into established theory, additional complications arise whenever the prices of goods traded between different parts of the multinational enterprise are arbitrarily fixed. This is one of a number of areas in which most authors in this book call for more research; in this case because variations in the intra-group prices, where they are in response to changes in exogenous or endogenous variables, make it difficult to predict the behaviour of affiliates.

To my mind, one of the most important conclusions which follow the papers in this volume is the need to distinguish between the behaviour of the individual operating units of multinational enterprises and the behaviour of multinational enterprises *in toto*. Most authors agree that existing theories of the managerial enterprise, appropriately modified, are adequate to deal with the latter question. But to explain the behaviour of the individual operating units of multinational enterprises, e.g. compared with that of independent indigenous companies, the state of received theory seems less satisfactory. For, here one needs to turn to an explanation of the branch plant activities of firms, extended to include the specific characteristics of multinationalisation. But it is precisely in this area where existing theory has so little to offer and the need for new thinking is so pressing.

THE IMPACT OF MULTINATIONAL ENTERPRISES ON THE LEVEL AND PATTERN OF RESOURCE ALLOCATION

The actions of any institution (or groups of institutions) may have *micro-* or *macro-*economic consequences. Here, we are concerned with the extent to which the distinctive characteristics and behaviour of multinational enterprises require modification to the accepted analysis of the level and pattern of resource allocation. Chapter 1 suggested that, because of their significance in the world economy and their unique economic characteristics, an *a priori* case could be made out for this. The chapters on the behaviour of multinational enterprises confirmed this. Most of the rest of the book has sought both to identifying this impact, and evaluating its implications for various branches of economic theory. Can we summarise their conclusions? Perhaps, three main points stand out.

(i) Though it is generally accepted that, in some areas, the predictive value of received analysis may be weakened by the emergence of multinational enterprises, it is strongly felt that, in most cases, this is primarily due to the changes in the character and value of the endogenous or exogenous variables occasioned by the phenomenon, rather than any fundamental defect of the theories themselves. Clearly, the operational value of any theory is as good as the assumptions underlying it. If these are false or inappropriate, then so will be the relationship established between economic variables. New production management or marketing techniques are constantly causing firms to modify their supply functions; which, in turn, may influence other economic agents and resource allocation in general. Most of the contributors to this book accept that, in this sense, the multinational enterprise does have a distinctive impact on resource allocation. New variables do need to be introduced to satisfactorily explain the pattern of international production and the trade flows of multinational enterprises; their impact on market structure and collective bargaining, on the determinants of investment and on the distribution of income between nations.

(ii) On the other hand, it is quite clear that many of the assertions about the behaviour and impact of multinational enterprises have little to do with their multinationality *per se* but to other of their structural characteristics, e.g. size, geographical origin, industry, organisational strategy. Mansfield's and Caves' essays bring this point out very clearly; the main consequences of multinational enterprises on the production and diffusion of technology and on market structure and economic power arises *both* because they are large and diversified firms *and* that they engage in activities across national boundaries. To this extent, the impact of multinational enterprises may be little different from that of multi-regional national firms, or international trading firms. The spatial diversification of production across national boundaries has many common characteristics with other forms of diversification and much of the behaviour of multinational enterprises reflects these. The effects of these companies which can be specifically attributed to their multinationality are probably much smaller than is popularly thought, and the differences are more ones of degree than kind. This is not to say they are insignificant, but their impact is probably more of macro- than micro-economic consequence. Once one accepts this, it is not surprising that many economists should conclude that the multinational enterprise *qua* multinational enterprise should necessitate no major changes to much of economic analysis. What is, perhaps, surprising is that, in the past, so little attention has been paid to these features associated with the multinational enterprise. In his essay, Caves suggests that the multinational enterprise may give the theory of industrial organisation a new lease of life, as it is so relevant to our understanding of the behaviour of firms. The same, one suspects, may be true of the theories of location and international trade, while many of one's ideas about economic power and diversification are affected by the ownership and control by firms of income generating assets across national boundaries.

(iii) In some areas, the introduction of the multinational enterprise underlines the validity of economic principles which have long stood the test of time. The principle of division of labour and comparative advantage is one of these. In others, it has focused attention, thrown new light on, or helped to reappraise the value of known theories. The theories of oligopoly, of decision taking under conditions of uncertainty, of corporate strategy and of bargaining are examples of these. In still others, it has emphasised the weaknesses of existing explanations, e.g. of the product composition of international trade and the geographical structure of capital flows; or indicated the need for new thinking, e.g. about the economics of the production and dissemination of proprietary knowledge, and the determinants of the international distribution of economic welfare.

But what about more fundamental modifications to economic doctrine? The consensus of opinion of the authors in this book seems to be that the emergence of the multinational enterprises should cause economists to rethink the validity or relevance of two basic micro-economic assumptions and one basic macro-economic assumption.

MICRO-ECONOMIC ASSUMPTIONS

In explaining the way in which resources are allocated in a free society, economists have tended to assume that (a) prices of both inputs and outputs are determined by the market viz, by independent buyers and sellers and that (b) resources are immobile across national boundaries.

(a) This assumption is valid as long as transactions of goods and services between different parts of the same economic agent are small in relation to all transactions, or that, when these do occur, prices are fixed at the same level as those which would be charged to independent purchasers, i.e. open market or arm's-length prices. The fact that arm's-length prices may, themselves be affected by the presence and behaviour of multinational enterprises is not at issue. Moreover, one recognises that intra-group corporate pricing *within* a country is widely practised by multiplant or multiproduct firms and is probably growing. Normally, however, the way in which a firm chooses to invoice the goods it internally trades will not affect its profits,[1] nor, indeed, the volume of goods traded. Whether transactions are invoiced at market or some other prices is mainly a matter of accounting convenience and, for this reason, economists have not been greatly concerned.

In an international context, the situation is different. States are sovereign bodies and operate their own fiscal and monetary policies. No longer is a firm indifferent to where its income is earned. If it is to minimise its tax burden, and by manipulating its intra-group prices a profit maximising firm can reduce its tax burden, it will attempt to do so. In such situations prices will not reflect market forces, but the desires of firms to record net profit in one country rather than another.

Quite apart from this, as Vaitsos points out, there may be other reasons why firms may wish to trade with each other at other than arm's-length prices. How far this is, in practice, achieved will depend on the willingness of authorities in host or investing countries to allow it or their ability to control it. But, as Corden shows, whenever prices are arbitrarily fixed, the terms of trade, and hence the total value of trade between countries, may be affected. Vertical integration may have other implications on the conditions of trade, through creating barriers to entry.

(*b*) Taken literally, the second micro-economic assumption, viz. the immobility of factor inputs, negates the existence of the multinational enterprise. It suggests that the only way in which firms may exploit foreign markets is through trade. A pattern of international trade based on this assumption is obviously likely to be different from one where there is some mobility of resources. International production sometimes substitutes for trade; sometimes it is complementary to it; sometimes it creates it. Some economists have argued that because the multinational enterprise trades in inputs of tools of location rather than international trade are better suited to explain the distribution of its resources. Corden does not accept this: he argues that (most) national boundaries create a barrier to the movement of, at least, *some* factor inputs—and, therefore, there is a case for having a body of theory which deals with this situation. At the same time, he acknowledges that the growth of international production calls for a much closer alliance between location and trade theory.

Taken with Vernon's and Caves' contributions, this might suggest that the orientation of trade theory may move from considering reasons *countries* trade with each other to why *firms* trade across national boundaries.

MACRO-ECONOMIC ASSUMPTIONS

The basic macro-economic assumption questioned by the presence of the multinational enterprise is that the use of resources of a society are controlled by the institutions and mechanisms set up by, and answerable to that society. This is implicit in both the theories of monetary and development policies, dealt with, respectively, by Maynard and Caves. It is true that any form of 'openness' both influences the use of a country's resources, and makes the task of macro-economic management more difficult. But, in the absence of international production, and assuming a competitive environment, then, on efficiency grounds, decisions taken by national firms will usually benefit the national economy. If the distribution of the proceeds of the output is not in accord with Governments' social objectives or if the sections of firms lead to social costs, then Governments can take remedial action.

In the case of international production by foreign or domestically-owned multinational companies, the situation is different. Decisions by multinational enterprises on the use of resources by their foreign affiliates may be taken, which are neither in the latter's interests nor of those of the countries in which they operate. Moreover, because multinational enterprises are likely to be influenced by changes in international economic conditions more than are indigenous firms and are generally more flexible in their response to these changes, their behaviour may be different from national firms and not always in the interests of the country in question.

Partly because of this, and partly because the behaviour of affiliates is geared to that of the enterprise of which it is part, traditional macro-economic policies, appropriate to deal with national firms, can be circumvented or thwarted by multinational enterprises and their affiliates. Maynard illustrates some of the dilemmas facing governments, in the pursuance of monetary and exchange rate policies. Streeten points out that patterns of economic development induced by affiliates of multinational enterprises in less developed countries will be different from, and not always as desirable as, those caused by indigenous companies. Again, many of these differences arise because the behaviour of affiliates is geared to the goals of their parent companies.

The macro-economic consequences of multinational enterprises will, of course, depend on the particular types of strategies they pursue and the extent to which host or investing governments seek to control or influence their behaviour. It is not surprising that economies which are insulated and centrally planned will be more concerned about the effects of this form of openness than those which are internationally and market oriented. The size, political power and wealth of an economy, and its bargaining strength with large firms are also likely to affect their policies.

In other areas, both micro- and macro-economic policies may need to be modified because of the activities of multinational enterprises or their affiliates. Corden and Borts cite tariff policy; Mansfield, policy towards industrial property rights and research and development; Maynard, interest rate and exchange rate policies; Caves, competition policy; Vaitsos, fiscal policy; and Kindleberger, policy towards the formation of regional currency and/or trading blocs. Because of the particular form of the openness which the multinational enterprise introduces, existing policies covering these questions may no longer be adequate to achieve the goals set by nations.

One area where this is being felt concerns the relation between nation states. Kindleberger concludes that, in a variety of directions, the optimum size of nation states (or more correctly the functions performed by nation states) may be enlarged by the operations of the multinational enterprise. Behrman (1972) has suggested that policies towards industrial integration of nations need to be rethought if the contribution of such enterprises to efficiency and equity goals is to be fully realised.

One issue of policy which uniquely arises from the operations of multinational enterprises is that of inter-country income distribution. This is because, however much the spatial distribution of income within an economy is affected by multi-regional firms, national governments have the final responsibility for the welfare of the regions, while the terms of trade between economic agents exchanging goods across national boundaries are mainly fixed by the market place, which governments (except by manipulation of tariffs or exchange rate) can do little about.

However, the multinationals do have power to affect intra-country income distribution, and the conclusion from Vaitsos' paper is that this power can be very important in countries whose economies are dominated by foreign affiliates, which have the ability to earn rent over and above the opportunity cost of the resources invested. In such cases, Governments are more than usually concerned with increasing their bargaining strength and minimising the opportunities for foreign affiliates to exploit their economic power. As yet, as Vaitsos points out, we have no adequate theory of bargaining to predict the likely outcome of any negotiations between country and firms. Streeten, in his essay, suggests the framework of one particular approach.

THE IMPACT OF OTHER ECONOMIC AGENTS ON THE MULTINATIONAL ENTERPRISE

The final question of interest to economic analysis—which is an extension of the first—concerns the extent to which any response of multinational enterprises to exogenous forces might be different from that of national firms.

Most of the discussion in the book on this question has centred on the impact of macro-economic policy of host Governments. Maynard, for example, believes that certain aspects of domestic monetary and exchange rate policy have different effects on resource allocation when the affiliates of multinational enterprises are present than when they are absent. Elsewhere (Dunning, 1973c), we have suggested that the reasons for this lie in the ability of multinational enterprises to adjust their resource allocative patterns across national boundaries and, by doing so, affect the ability of Governments in *individual* countries to achieve their objectives.

Such policies might induce various responses on the parts of governments. Some of these are set out by Streeten, Vaitsos and Kindleberger. Basically, however, the problem arises because the economic bargaining strength of smaller nations is becoming less in relation to large international companies, due *inter alia* to the latter's faster rate of growth. Such unilateral policies which Governments do take, tend to do as much harm as good; the alternatives of (i) controlling inward investment or the behaviour of foreign affiliates, (ii) encouraging more competition from domestic firms, and (iii) the formation of regional economic blocs and/or the framing of bilateral policies, have been successful up to a point, but each has its costs (Behrman, 1970). Again, it is in these areas where the theory of bargaining needs restructuring.

Among other contributions, Caves and Mansfield also consider the effects on the behaviour of multinational enterprises and their affiliates of changes in the values of exogenous variables. Both agree that responses may differ, mainly because of the power and flexibility which stem from branch plant and multinational effects of their operations: but neither believe that any *basic* modification to economic analysis is required; indeed they argue that branches of analysis neglected in the past, can make a more positive contribution to our understanding of economic behaviour.

FURTHER RESEARCH ON THE MULTINATIONAL ENTERPRISE

Most authors in this book have called for more research into the character and behaviour of multinational enterprises, and into their economic consequences; a few, notably Vaitsos and Maynard, have argued international production has posed new issues for economic analysis; but none has asserted the need for a wholesale reappraisal of economic doctrine.

We believe this is the way in which most research on the multinational enterprise may proceed in the future. For the main claim to uniqueness of this phenomenon is that it has introduced a new dimension into the world economic order. On the one hand, it has acted as a powerful integrating force for factor, product and financial markets; on the other, it has posed a challenge to national economic sovereignty. It is not, by accident, that the greatest concern about foreign direct investment is felt by recipient countries which are strongly nationalistic in ideology or have different cultural backgrounds than those of investing countries.

It is for this basic reason that the multinational enterprise provokes such a love-hate relationship wherever it operates. Welcomed for the package of technology, capital and management expertise it provides, it is resented for the control it exercises over these and local resources; and is disliked for its apparent ability to influence or circumvent economic policies and national aspirations. In spite of the impressive evidence of the economic benefits of foreign direct investment to both developed and developing countries, these attitudes remain, and are exacerbated whenever cases are reported of large multinationals using their power in ways contrary to the interests of Governments.

One difficulty of any calculation of the effects of foreign direct investment is that its costs and benefits are often interdependent; and that policies of individual Governments to maximise the net benefits are sometimes frustrated by the competition between them to attract new investment. It is in this light that attention is currently being focused by such international and regional organisations as the United Nations, OECD, EEC and the Andean Group, on evaluating the extent to which multinational enterprises, *because of their multinationality*, affect national and international goals; and to devise appropriate multilateral machinery to ensure that their actions, and those of the Governments involved, are better harnessed to meet these goals. Already, for example, it has been suggested that a new Commission on Multinational Corporations should be established within the United Nations, and that one of its tasks should be to consider whether or not a General Agreement on Multinational Enterprises (GAME) on the lines of the General Agreement on Tariffs and Trade (GATT) is a feasible proposition. In this kind of work, the professional economist can play a vital role. It is precisely because the subject is such a politically charged one, that his assistance to policy makers, in the careful interpretation and analysis of economic data, is vitally needed.

More serious research is also needed to better understand the effects which multinationals have on the global allocation of resources and on the ability of the existing international economic order to do this efficiently and equitably. The essays in this book have illustrated some of the ways in which they *do* affect the location of economic activity, trade flows and market structure, and also their impact on national economic policies. But so far, little attention has been given on how international bodies, e.g. the IMF or GATT, or international systems, e.g. on tax harmonisation and patent protection, are affected by the operations of multinational enterprises; or in what way these organisations and machineries need to be modified to achieve their original goals.

Like international trade, international production introduces openness into the participating economies. Unlike trade, it does not involve a change in ownership and is often concentrated in the hands of a few large companies, competing under oligopolistic conditions. What of the resulting division of labour and patterns of production and trade? Are these likely to advance or retard global economic welfare or the interests of the individual countries in which the multinationals operate? These are some basic issues which are both intellectually challenging and of vital practical importance.

Academic economists have often been accused of neglecting real-life issues, and of concentrating on abstract and esoteric model building. There is some truth in this contention. But the subject of the multinational enterprise does offer a unique opportunity for professional economists to, at least partly, dispel this accusation. These essays have sought to review some of the main lines of current thinking and to offer suggestions for new research.

References

[1] The exception is where there are differential taxes charged on different products or stages in production process or regions.

Bibliography

ADAM, G., 1971, 'New Trends in International Business: Worldwide Sourcing and Dedomicling', *Acta Oeconomica*, **7**, 3–4, pp. 349–67; 1972, 'Las Corporaciones Transnacionales en la Década de los Sententa', *Comercio Exterior (Mexico)*, p. 1038.

ADELMAN, M. A., 1972, *The World Petroleum Market*, Baltimore: Johns Hopkins Univ. Press.

ADLER, M., 1970, 'Specialisation in the European Coal and Steel Community', *Journal of Common Market Studies*, **8**, pp. 175–91.

AHARONI, Y., 1966, *The Foreign Investment Decision Process*, Boston: Harvard Univ. Press.

AIGRAIN, P., 1969, 'Some Factors Inhibiting Technological Innovation in France', Symposium sponsored by National Association of Engineering, *The Process of Technological Innovation*, Washington: National Resources Council.

ALIBER, R. Z., 1970, 'A Theory of Direct Foreign Investment', in C. P. Kingleberger (ed.), *The International Corporation*, Cambridge, Mass.: M.I.T. Press.

ALMON, S., 1965, 'The Distributed Lag Between Capital Appropriations and Expenditures', *Econometrica*, **33**, pp. 178–96.

ANDERSON, W. H. L., 1964, *Corporate Finance and Fixed Investment*, Boston: Harvard.

ANDREWS, M. E., 1972, 'A Survey of American Investment in Irish Industry', Unpublished Senior Honours thesis, Harvard College.

ANSOFF, H. I., 1965, *Corporate Strategy*, New York: McGraw-Hill.

ARCHIBALD, G. C. (ed.), 1971, *The Theory of the Firm*, Harmondsworth: Penguin.

ARROW, K., 1962a, 'The Economic Implications of Learning by Doing', *Review of Economic Studies*, **29**, 80, pp. 155–73: 1962b, 'Economic Welfare and the Allocation of Resources to Invention', *The Rate and Direction of Inventive Activity: Economic and Social Factors*, National Bureau of Economic Research, Princeton Univ. Press, pp. 609–26 (reprinted in D. M. Lamberton (ed.), *Economics of Information and Knowledge*, Penguin Modern Economics Readings).

BACHA, E. & TAYLOR, L., 1971, 'Foreign Exchange Shadow Prices: A Critical Review of Current Theories', *Quarterly Journal of Economics*, **85**, 2, pp. 197–224.

BAER, W. & HERVÉ, M., 1966, 'Employment and Industrialisation in Developing Countries', *Quarterly Journal of Economics*, 80.

BAIN, J. S., 1956, *Barriers to New Competition*, Cambridge, Mass.: Harvard Univ. Press; 1966, *International Differences in Industrial Structure*, New Haven & London: Yale Univ. Press; 1968, *Industrial Organisation*, 2nd ed., New York: John Wiley.

BALASSA, B., 1965, 'Tariff Protection in Industrial Countries: An

Evaluation', *Journal of Political Economy*, **73**, pp. 573–94; 1966, 'American Direct Investments in the Common Market', *Banca Nazionale del Lavoro Quarterly Review*, **77**, pp. 121–46.

BALASSA, B., *et. al.*, 1971, *Structure of Protection in Less-developed Countries*, Baltimore: Johns Hopkins Press.

BALDWIN, R. E., 1969, 'The Case Against Infant-Industry Tariff Protection', *Journal of Political Economy*, **77**, pp. 195–305; 1970, 'International Trade in Inputs and Outputs', *American Economic Review*, **60**, pp. 430–4.

BALOGH, T., & STREETEN, P. P., 1960, 'Domestic versus Foreign Investment', *Bulletin of the Oxford University Institute of Statistics*, **22**.

BANDERA, V. W., & WHITE, J. T., 1968, 'US Direct Investments and Domestic Markets in Europe', *Economia Internazionale*, **21**, pp. 117–33.

BANNOCK, G., 1971, *The Juggernauts*, London: Weidenfeld & Nicolson.

BARANSON, J., 1966, 'Transfer of Technical Knowledge by International Corporations to Developing Economies', *American Economic Review*, **55**, pp. 260–6; 1967a, *Technology for Underdeveloped Areas*, Oxford: Pergamon Press, pp. 9–22; 1967b, *Manufacturing Problems in India: the Cummings Diesel Experience*, Syracuse Univ. 1967, *Industrial Technologies for Developing Economies*, Praeger; 1970, 'Technology Transfer through the International Firm', *American Economic Review*, Papers and Proceedings, **60**, pp. 435–40.

BARLOW, E. R., & WENDER, I. T., 1955, *Foreign Investment and Taxation*, Englewood Cliffs: Prentice-Hall.

BAROVIK, R., 1970, 'Labour Reacts to Multinationalism', *Columbia Journal of World Business*, **5**, pp. 40–6.

BAUMOL, W. J., 1959, *Business Behavior, Value and Growth*, New York: Macmillan Co.; 1962, 'On the Theory of Expansion of the Firm', *American Economic Review*, **52**, pp. 1078–87.

BAUMOL, W. J., & MALKIEL, B., 1967, 'The Firm's Optimal Debt-Equity Combination and the Cost of Capital', *Quarterly Journal of Economics*, **81**, pp. 547–78.

BAUMOL, W. J., & STEWART, M., 1971, 'On the Behavioural Theory of the Firm', in R. Marris & A. Wood (eds), *The Corporate Economy*, Boston: Harvard.

BEHRMAN, J., 1960, 'Promoting Free World Economic Development Through Direct Investment', *American Economic Review*, **50**, pp. 271–81; 1962, 'Foreign Affiliates and Their Financing', in R. Mikesell (ed.), *US Private and Government Investment Abroad*, Eugene, Oregon: Univ. Oregon Books; 1969, *Some Patterns in the Rise of the Multinational Enterprise*, Chapel Hill: Graduate School of Business Administration, Univ. North Carolina; 1970, *National Interests and the Multinational Enterprise*, Prentice-Hall; 1971, 'Government Policy Alternatives and the Problem of International Sharing', in J. H. Dunning (ed.), *The Multinational Enterprise*, Allen & Unwin; 1972, 'Industrial Integration and the Multinational

Enterprise', *Annals of the American Academy of Political and Social Studies*, **403**, September.

BERLE, A. A., & MEANS, G. C., 1932, *The Modern Corporation and Private Property*, New York: Commerce Clearing House.

BERLIN, P. D., 1971, *Foreign Affiliate Financial Survey*, 1966–9, Washington, DC: US Department of Commerce, Office of Foreign Direct Investments.

BHAGWATI, J., 1958, 'Immiserizing Growth: A Geometrical Note', *Review of Economic Studies*, **25**, 3, pp. 201–5; 1964, 'The Pure Theory of International Trade: A Survey', *Economic Journal*, **74**, pp. 1–84; 1969, *Trade, Tariffs and Growth*, Cambridge, Mass.: M.I.T. Press.

BILLSBORROW, R. E., 1968, 'The Determinants of Fixed Investment by Manufacturing Corporations in Colombia', Unpublished Doctoral thesis, Michigan.

BISCHOFF, C., 1969 'Hypothesis Testing and the Demand for Capital Goods', *Review of Economics and Statistics*, **51**, pp. 354–68; 1971a, 'Business Investment in the 1970's: A Comparison of Models', *Brookings Papers on Economic Activity*, **1**, pp. 13–64; 1971b, 'The Effect of Alternative Lag Distribution', in G. Fromm (ed.), *Tax Incentives and Capital Spending*, Washington, D.C.: Brookings.

BLAKE, D. H., 1972, 'Corporate Structure and International Unionism', *Columbia Journal of World Business*, **7**, pp. 19–26.

BOHLEW, J., *et al.*, 1961, *Adopters of the New Farm Ideas*, North Central Regional Extension Publications, No. 13.

BORTS, G. H., & KOPECKY, K. J., 1972, 'Capital Movements and Economic Growth in Developed Countries', in F. Machlup, W. Salant & L. Tarshis (eds), *International Mobility and Movement of Capital*, New York: National Bureau for Economic Research.

BRANSON, W., & HILL, R. D., 1971, 'Capital Movements in the *OECD* Area, An Econometric Analysis', *OECD Economic Outlook*, Occasional Studies.

BRASH, D. T., 1966, *American Investment in Australian Industry*, Cambridge, Mass.: Harvard Univ. Press.

BRAUN, R., 1965, *Soziale und kulturelle Wandlung in einem ländlichen Industriegebiet im 19. und 20. Jahrhundert*, Stuttgart: Eugen Rentsch Verlag.

BROOKS, H., *et al.*, 1967, *Applied Science and Technological Change*, National Academy of Sciences.

BROWN, L., 1970, *The Interdependence of Nations*.

BRUCK, N. K., & LEES, F. A., 1966, 'Foreign Content of US Corporate Activities', *Financial Analyst's Journal*, **22**.

BRUNO, M., 1967, 'The Optimal Selection of Export-Promoting and Import-Substituting Projects', *Planning the External Sector Techniques, Problems and Policies*, ST/TAO/SERC/91, New York: United Nations.

BURTON, H. J., 1965, 'On the Role of Import Substitution in Development Planning', *Philippine Economic Journal*, First Semester.

BURNS, T., & STALKER, G. M., 1961, *The Management of Innovation*, Tavistock.

BUSINESS WEEK, 1971, 'Third Quarterly Survey of Corporate Performance', Nov.

CAIRNCROSS, A. K., 1935, 'Home and Foreign Investment 1807–1913', *Review of Economic Studies*, Oct., pp. 67–78.

CAMERON, R., 1967, 'Some Lessons of History for Developing Nations', *American Economic Review, Papers and Proceedings*, **57**, 2, p. 313.

CANNON, C. M., 1968, 'Private Capital Investment: A Case-study Approach Towards Testing Alternative Theories', *Journal of Industrial Economics*, **16**, pp. 186–95.

CARLSON, S., 1968, 'A Note on the Use of Models in the Study of Business Finance', *Acta Universitatis Upsaliensis, Skrifter rörande Uppsala Universitet 17*, Uppsala, pp. 162–73; 1969, *International Financial Decisions*, Stockholm: Scandinavian Univ. Books.

CATY, G., *et al.*, 1972, *The Research Systems*, Vol. 1, Paris: OECD.

CAVES, R. E., 1960, *Trade and Economic Structure*, Harvard Univ. Press; 1971a, 'International Corporations: the Industrial Economics of Foreign Investment', *Economica*, **38**, 149, pp. 1–27; 1971b, 'Industrial Economics of Foreign Investment: The Case of the International Corporation', *Journal of World Trade Law*, **5**, 3, pp. 303–14.

CHAMBERLAIN, N. W., 1951, *Collective Bargaining*, New York: McGraw-Hill.

CHANDLER, A. D., JR., 1962, *Strategy and Structure: Chapters in the History of the American Industrial Enterprise*, Cambridge, Mass.: M.I.T. Press.

CHENERY, H., 1952, 'Overcapacity and the Acceleration Principle', *Econometrica*, **20**, pp. 1–28.

CHIPMAN, J., 1971, 'International Trade with Capital Mobility: A Substitution Theorem', in J. N. Bhagawati, *et al.*, (eds), *Trade, Balance of Payments and Growth: Papers in Honor of Charles P. Kindleberger*, North-Holland.

CLAGUE, C., 1970, 'The Determinants of Efficiency in Manufacturing Industries in an Underdeveloped Country', *Economic Development and Cultural Change*, **18**, 2, pp. 188–205.

CLEE, G. H., & WILBUR, M. S., 1964, 'Organizing a Worldwide Business', *Harvard Business Review*, **44**, 6.

COEN, R. M., 1971, 'The Effect of Cash Flow on the Speed of Adjustment', in G. Fromm (ed.), *Tax Incentives and Capital Spending*, Washington, D.C.: Brookings.

COHEN, K. J., & CYERT, R., 1965, *Theory of the Firm: Resource Allocation in a Market Economy*, Englewood Cliffs: Prentice-Hall.

COMANOR, W. S., 1967, 'Vertical Mergers, Market Power and the Antitrust Laws', *American Economic Review*, **57**, pp. 254–65.

COMANOR, W. S., & WILSON, T. A., 1967, 'Advertising Market Structure and Performance', *Review of Economics and Statistics*, **49**, pp. 423–40; 1972, *Advertising and Market Power*. Cambridge, Mass.: Harvard Univ. Press.

CONFERENCE BOARD, 1970, *R & D in the Multinational Company*, New York.

COOPER, C., 1968, 'Science and Underdeveloped Countries', *Problems in Science Policy*, Paris: OECD.

COOPER, R. N., 1971, 'Technology and US Trade: A Historical Review', *Technology and International Trade*, National Academy of Engineering; 1972, 'Towards an International Capital ¡Market', in C. P. Kindleberger & A. Shonfield (eds), *North American and Western European Economic Policies*, Macmillan.

CORDELL, A. J., 1971, *The Multinational Firm, Foreign Investment and Canadian Science Policy*, Background Study No. 22, Ottawa: Science Council of Canada.

CORDEN, W. M., 1956, 'Economic Expansion and International Trade: A Geometric Approach', *Oxford Economic Papers*, N. S., **8**, 2, pp. 223–8; 1965, *Recent Developments in the Theory of International Trade*, Special Papers in International Economics, No. 7, Princeton Univ. Press; 1967, 'Protection and Foreign Investment', *Economic Records*, 43, pp. 209–32; 1971, *The Theory of Protection*, Oxford Univ. Press; 1972, 'Monetary Inegration', *Essays in International Finance*, No. 93, Princeton Univ. Press.

CORFO, 1970, *Comportamiento de las Principales Empresas Industriales Extranjeras Acogidas al D.F.L. 258*, Publication No. 9–1/70, Santiago, Chile.

CRAINE, R., 1971, 'Optimal Distributed Lag Responses and Expectations', *American Economic Review*, **61**, pp. 916–24.

CYERT, R., & MARCH, J. G., 1963, *A Behavioral Theory of the Firm*, Englewood Cliffs: Prentice-Hall.

DANIELS, J. D., 1971, *Recent Foreign Direct Manufacturing Investment in the United States*, New York: Praeger.

DEANE, P., 1961, 'Capital Formation in Britain Before the Railway Age', *Economic Development and Cultural Change*, No. 3; 1965, *The First Industrial Revolution*, Cambridge.

DEANE, P., & COLE, W. A., 1962, *British Economic Growth, 1688–1959; Trends and Structure*, Cambridge.

DENISON, E., assisted by POLLIER, J., 1967, *Why Growth Rates Differ*, Washington D.C.: Brookings Institution.

DIAZ-ALEJANDRO, C. F., 1970, 'Direct Foreign Investment in Latin America', in C. P. Kindleberger (ed.), *The International Corporation*, Cambridge, Mass.: M.I.T. Press, 1971, 'The Future of Direct Foreign Investment in Latin America', *Yale Economic Growth Center Discussion Paper*, No. 131.

DRÈZE, J., 1960, 'Quelques réflexions sereines sur l'adaptation de l'industrie belge au Marché Commun', *Comptes rendus de Travaux de la Société d'Economie Politique de Belgique*, No. 275.

DUNLOP, J. T., 1967, 'The Social Utility of Collective Bargaining', in L. Ullman (ed.), *Challenge to Collective Bargaining*, Englewood Cliffs: Prentice-Hall.

DUNNING, J. H., 1958, *American Investment in British Manufacturing*

Industry, Allen & Unwin; 1966, 'US Subsidiaries and their UK Competitors', *Business Ratios*, Autumn; 1969, *The Role of American Investment in the British Economy*, London: P.E.P.; 1970a, *Studies in International Investments*, Allen & Unwin; 1970b, 'Technology, United States Investment, and European Economic Growth', in C. Kindleberger (ed.), *The International Corporation*, Cambridge, Mass.: M.I.T. Press; 1971, *The Multinational Enterprise*, Allen & Unwin; 1973a, *The Location of International Firms in an Enlarged EEC*, Manchester Statistical Society; 1973b, 'The Determinants of International Production', *Oxford Economic Papers*, 25, 289–336; 1973c, Multinational Enterprises and Domestic Capital Formation, Manchester School of Economic and Social Studies, 38, 283–310.

DUNNING, J. H., and PEARCE, R. D., 1974, *The World's Largest Companies*. An EAG Business Research Study. Financial Times, London.

DUNNING, J. H., & STEUER, M., 1969, 'The Effect of United States Direct Investment in Britain and on British Technology', *Moorgate and Wall Street*, Autumn, pp. 5–33.

DUPRIEZ, L. H., 1966, Principles et problèmes d'interpretation', *Diffusion du progrès et convergence des prix, études internationles*, Louvain; Editions Nauwelaerts.

EASTMAN, H. C., & STYKOLT, S., 1967, *The Tariff and Competition in Canada*, Toronto: Macmillan.

EDGREN, G., FAXEN, K. O., & ODHNER, C. E., 1970, 'Lonebildning och samhälls-ekonomi', S.A.F., LO and TCO, Stockholm: Raben & Sjögren. English translation (somewhat revised) *Wage Formation and the Economy*, Allen & Unwin.

EISNER, R., 1956, *Determinants of Capital Expenditures*, Urbana: Univ. Illinois.

EISNER, R., & NADIR, M. I., 1968, 'Investment Behavior and the Neoclassical Theory', *Review of Economics and Statistics*, 50, pp. 369–82.

EISNER, R., & STROTZ, R. H., 1963, 'Determinants of Business Investment', in Commission on Money and Credit, *Impact of Monetary Policy*, Englewood Cliffs: Prentice-Hall.

ENGLISH, H. E., 1964, *Industrial Structure in Canada's International Competitive Position*, Montreal: Canadian Trade Committee.

FAITH, N., 1971, *The Infiltrators*, London: Hamish Hamilton.

FINDLAY, R., & GRUBERT, H., 1959, 'Factor Intensities, Technological Progress, and the Terms of Trade', *Oxford Economic Papers*, N.S., 11, 1, pp. 111–2.

FOREIGN POLICY RESEARCH INSTITUTE, 1971, *The Multinational Enterprise and the Nation State*; an annotated bibliography.

FORSGREN, M., & KINCH, N., 1970, *Företagets anpasning till förädringar i omgivande system. En studie av massaoch pappersindustrin*, Uppsala:

FRANKO, L., 1969, 'Strategy Choice and Multinational Corporate Tolerance for Joint Ventures with Foreign Partners', Unpublished

DBA dissertation, Harvard Business School; 1971, *European Business Strategies in the United States*, Geneva: Business Int.; 1973, *Who Manages the Multinational Enterprise?*', Geneva: Centre d'Etudes Industrielles (mimeo).

FREEMAN, C., 1963, 'The Plastics Industry: A Comparative Study of Research and Innovation', *National Institute Economic Review*, **26**, pp. 22–62; 1965, 'Research and Development in Electronic Capital Goods', *National Institute Economic Review*, No. 34, pp. 40–91; 1971, 'A Study of Success and Failure in Industrial Innovation', *Conference of International Economic Association*, San Anton, Australia:

FREEMAN, C., *et al.*, 1971, 'The Goals of R & D in the 1970s', *Science Studies*.

FROMM, G. (ed.), 1971, *Tax Incentives and Capital Spending*, Washington, D.C.: Brookings.

FURTADO, C., 1971, *Los Estados Unidos y el Subdesarrollo de América Latina*, Lima: Instituto de Estudios Peruanos.

GALBRAITH, J. K., 1967, *The New Industrial State*, Boston: Houghton Mifflin.

GALTUNG, J., 1970, 'The Future of Human Society', *Futures*, **2**, 2, pp. 132–42.

GEHRELS, F., 1971, 'Optimal Restrictions on Foreign Trade and Investment', *American Economic Review*, **59**, pp. 147–59.

GENNARD, J., 1972, *Multinational Corporations and British Labour: A Review of Attitudes and Responses*, British North American Committee.

GOLDBERG, M. A., 1972, 'The Determinants of US Direct Investment in the EEC: Comment', *American Economic Review*, **62**, pp. 692–9.

GOLDFELD, S., 1969, 'An Extension of the Monetary Sector', in J. Duesenberry, G. Fromm, L. Klein, & E. Kuh (eds), *The Brookings Model: Some Further Results*, Chicago: Rand McNally.

GORDON, R. A., 1945, *Business Leadership in the Large Corporation*, Washington, D.C.: Brookings.

GOULD, J. P., & WAUD, R., 1970, *The Neoclassical Model of Investment Behavior: Another View*, Report 7054, Center for Mathematical Studies in Business and Economics, Univ. Chicago.

GOVERNMENT OF CANADA, 1972, *Foreign Investment in Canada* (The Gray Report), Ottawa: Queen's Printer.

GRABOWSKI, H., & MUELLER, D. C., 1972, 'Managerial and Stockholder Welfare Models of Firm Expenditures', *Review of Economics and Statistics*, **54**, pp. 9–24.

GRAAF, J. DE V., 1957, *Theoretical Welfare Economics*, C.U.P.

GRAYSON, C. J., 1960, *Decisions Under Uncertainty: Drilling Decisions by Oil and Gas Operators*, Boston: Harvard Business School Div. of Research.

GREENE, J., & DUERR, M. G., 1968, *Intercompany Transfers in Multinational Firms*, New York: The Conference Board.

GRILICHES, Z., 1957, 'Hybrid Corn: An Exploration in the Economics of Technological Change', *Econometrica*, **25**, 4, pp. 501–22.

GROO, E., 1967, *Technology and World Trade*, National Bureau of Standards.

GRUBEL, H. G., 1967, 'Intra-Industry Specialization and the Pattern of Trade', *Canadian Journal of Economics and Political Science*, **33**, pp. 374–88; 1968, 'Internationally Diversified Portfolios: Welfare Gains and Capital Flows', *American Economic Review*, **58**, pp. 1219–1314.

GRUBER, W. D., MEHTA, D., & VERNON, R., 1967, 'R & D Factor in International Trade and International Investment of US Industries', *Journal of Political Economy*, **75**, 1, pp. 20–37.

GUSTAFSSON, L., 1971, *Förhandlinger*, Stockholm.

GUNTER, H. (ed.), 1972, 'The Future of Transnational Industrial Relations', *Transnational Industrial Relations*, London: Macmillan.

HALL, G., & JOHNSON, R., 1970, 'Transfer of US Aerospace Technology to Japan', in R. Vernon (ed.), *The Technology Factor in International Trade*, National Bureau of Economic Research.

HANSON, W., & RUMKER, R. VAN, 1971, 'Multinational R & D in Practice: Two Case Studies', *Research Management*, January.

HELFFERICH, K., 1965, *Georg von Siemens*, Krefeld: Richard Serpe.

HELLEINER, G. K., 1973, 'Manufactured Exports from Less Developed Countries and Multinational Firms', *Economic Journal*, March.

HELLER, H. R., 1973, *International Trade: Theory and Empirical Evidence*, 2nd ed., Englewood Cliffs: Prentice-Hall.

HELLMAN, R., 1970, *The Challenge to US Dominance of International Corporation*, New York: Dunnellen.

HENDERSON, P. D., 1968, 'Investment Criteria for Public Enterprises', in R. Turvey (ed.), *Public Enterprise*, Penguin.

HEXNER, E., 1945, *International Cartels*, Chapel Hill: Univ. North Carolina Press.

HICKS, J. R., 1932, *The Theory of Wages*, London: Macmillan: 1953, 'An Inaugural Lecture', *Oxford Economic Papers*, N.S., **5**, 2, pp. 117–34; 1962, 'Liquidity', *Economic Journal*, **72**, pp. 787–802.

HIRSCH, S., 1967, *Location of Industry and International Competitiveness*, Oxford Univ. Press.

HIRSCHMAN, A. O., 1969, 'How to Divest in Latin America and Why', *Princeton Essays in International Finance*, No. 76, November.

HOLLAND, S. (ed.), 1972, *The State as Entrepreneur*, London: Weidenfeld & Nicolson.

HOLLANDER, S., 1965, *The Sources of Increased Efficiency*, Cambridge, Mass.: M.I.T. Press.

HOOVER, E. M., 1948, *The Location of Economic Activity*, New York: McGraw-Hill.

HORST, T. O., 1969, 'A Theoretical and Empirical Analysis of American Exports and Direct Investment', Unpublished Ph.D. dissertation, Univ. Rochester; 1971, 'The Theory of the Multinational Firm: Optimal Behaviour under Different Tariff and Tax Rates', *Journal of Political Economy*, **79**, 5, pp. 1059–72; 1972a, 'The Industrial Composition of US Exports and Subsidiary Sales to the Canadian Market', *American Economic Review*, **62**, pp. 37–45; 1972b, 'Firm and Industry Determinants of the Decision to Invest Abroad: an Empirical Study', *Review of Economics and Statistics*.

HSIA, R., 1971, 'Technological Change in the Industrial Growth of Hong Kong', *Conference of the International Economic Association*, San Anton, Australia:

HUFBAUER, G. C., 1965, *Synthetic Materials and the Theory of International Trade*, London: Duckworth; 1970, 'The Impact of National Characteristics', in R. Vernon (ed.), *The Technology Factor in International Trade*, New York: Columbia Univ. Press.

HUFBAUER, G. C., & ADLER, M. H., 1967, *Overseas Manufacturing Investment and the Balance of Payments*, US Treasury Department.

HUGHES, H., & SENG, Y. P., 1969, *Foreign Investment and Industrialisation in Singapore*, University of Wisconsin Press.

HUI, C., & HAWKINS, R., 1972, 'Foreign Direct Investment and the US Balance of Payments', *Proceedings of the Business and Economics Section*, American Statistical Association, pp. 21–8.

HYMER, S., 1960, 'The International Operations of National Firms: A Study of Direct Investment', doctoral dissertation, Mass. Institute of Technology; 1966, 'Direct Foreign Investment and National Interest' in P. H. Russell (ed.), *Nationalism in Canada*, Toronto: McGraw Hill; 1966, 'Anti-trust and American Direct Investment Abroad', *International Aspects of Antitrust* (Hearings before the Sub-committee on Anti-trust and Monopoly of the Committee of the Judiciary, US Senate, 89th Congress, Second Session), Washington, D.C.: US Government Printing Office; 1970, 'The Efficiency (Contradictions) of Multinational Corporations', *American Economic Review*, **60**, May, pp. 441–8.

HYMER, S., & ROWTHORN, R., 1969, *Multinational Corporations and International Oligopoly: the Non-American Challenge*, Economic Growth Center Discussion No. 75, New Haven: Yale Univ.; 1970, 'Multinational Corporations and International Oligopoly: The Non-American Challenge', in C. Kindleberger (ed.), *The International Corporation*, Cambridge, Mass.: M.I.T. Press.

INTERNATIONAL MONETARY FUND, 1967, *International Financial Statistics*, Suppl. 1966/7 issues, Washington, D.C.

INTERNATIONAL TRADE, 1967 (published 1968), 'Development of World Trade and Export Specialization in Engineering Products since 1853–1954', Geneva.

ISLAM, N., 1967, 'Comparative Costs, Factor Proportions and Industrial Efficiency in Pakistan', *Pakistan Development Review*, Summer.

IVERSEN, C., 1935, *Aspects of International Capital Movements*, London & Copenhagen: Levin & Munksgaard.

JOHNS, B. L., 1967, 'Private Overseas Investment in Australia: Profitability and Motivation', *Economic Record*, **43**, pp. 233–61.

JOHNSON, E., 1968, *Studies in Multiobjective Decision Models*, Lund.

JOHNSON, H. G., 1955, 'Economic Expansion and International Trade', *Manchester School of Economic and Social Studies*, **23**, 2, pp. 95–112; 1967, 'The Possibility of Income Losses from Increased Efficiency or Factor Accumulation in the Presence of Tariffs', *Economic Journal*, **77**, 305, pp. 151–4; 1967b, 'International Trade Theory and Monopolistic Competition Theory', in R. E. Kuenne (ed.), *Monopolistic Competition Theory: Studies in Impact*, New York: Wiley; 1968, *Comparative Cost and Commercial Policy Theory for a Developing World Economy*, Stockholm: Almqvist & Wiksell; 1970a, 'The Efficiency and Welfare Implications of the International Corporation', in C. Kindleberger (ed.), *The International Corporation*, Cambridge, Mass.: M.I.T. Press; 1970b, 'The State of Theory in Relation to the Empirical Analysis', in R. Vernon (ed.), *The Technology Factor in International Trade*, Columbia Univ. Press; 1972, 'Survey of the Issues', in P. Drysdale (ed.), *Direct Foreign Investment in Asia and the Pacific*, Australian National Univ. Press.

JOHNSON, L. L., 1964, *US Private Investments in Latin America: Some Questions of National Policy*, RAND Corporation.

JOHNSTONE, A. W., 1965, *US Direct Investment in France*, Cambridge, Mass.: M.I.T. Press.

JONES, R. W., 1967, 'International Capital Movements and the Theory of Tariffs and Trade', *Quarterly Journal of Economics*, **81**, 1, pp. 10–11; 1970, 'The Role of Technology in the Theory of International Trade', in R. Vernon (ed.), *The Technology Factor in International Trade*, Columbia Univ. Press.

JORGENSON, D., 1963, 'Capital Theory and Investment Behavior', *American Economic Review*, **53**, pp. 247–59; 1966, 'Rational Distributed Lag Functions', *Econometrica*, **34**, pp. 135–49; 1971, 'Economic Studies of Investment Behavior: A Survey', *Journal of Economic Literature*, **9**, pp. 1111–47.

JORGENSON, D., HUNTER, J., & NADIRI, M. L., 1970a, 'A Comparison of Alternative Econometric Models of Corporate Investment Behavior', *Econometrica*, **38**, pp. 187–212; 1970b, 'The Predictive Performance of Econometric Models of Quarterly Investment Behavior', *Econometrica*, **38**, pp. 213–24.

JORGENSON, D., & SIEBERT, C., 1968, 'A Comparison of Alternative Theories of Corporate Investment Behavior', *American Economic Review*, **58**, pp. 681–712.

JORGENSON, D., & STEPHENSON, J., 1967, 'Investment Behavior in US Manufacturing, 1947–60', *Econometrica*, **35**, pp. 16–27; 1969, 'Issues in the Development of the Neoclassical Theory of Investment Behavior', *Review of Economics and Statistics*, **51**, pp. 346–53.

KABAJ, M., 1969, *Problems of Shift Work as a Means of Improving Capacity Utilisation*, Vienna: United Nations Industrial Organization.

KATZ, E., 1961, 'The Social Itinerary of Technical Change', *Human Organization*, Summer.

KAYSEN, C., 1958, 'Basing Point Pricing and Public Policy', in R. B. Heflebower & G. W. Stocking (eds), *Readings in Industrial Organization and Public Policy*, Homewood, Ill.: R. D. Irwin.

KEESING, D. B., 1969, 'The Impact of Research and Development on United States Trade', *Journal of Political Economy*, 75, 1, pp. 38–48.

KEMP, M. C., 1962a, 'Foreign Investment and the National Advantage', *Economic Record*, 38, March, pp. 56–62; 1962b, 'The Benefits and Costs of Private Investment from Abroad: Comment', *Economic Record*, 38, March; 1966, 'The Gains from International Trade and Investment: A Neo-Heckscher–Ohlin Approach', *American Economic Review*, 56, pp. 788–809; 1969, *The Pure Theory of International Trade and Investment*, Prentice-Hall.

KEYNES, J. M., 1924, 'Foreign Investment and National Advantage', *The Nation and Atheneum*, pp. 584–7; 1930, *Treatise on Money*, Vol. 1, London: pp. 343–6.

KIDRON, M., 1965, *Foreign Investment in India*, Oxford Univ. Press.

KINDLEBERGER, C. P., 1966, 'European Integration and International Corporation', *Columbia Journal of World Business*, 1, 1, pp. 65–76; 1969a, *American Business Abroad*, New Haven, Conn.: Yale Univ. Press; 1969b, 'Restrictions on Direct Investments in Host Countries', Unpublished discussion paper for the Univ. Chicago Workshop on International Business; 1970, *The International Corporation*, Cambridge, Mass.: M.I.T. Press.

KLEIN, L. R., & TAUBMAN, P., 1971, 'Estimating Effects Within a Complete Econometric Model', in G. Fromm (ed.), *Tax Incentives and Capital Spending*, Washington, D.C.: Brookings.

KLEIN, R. W., 1973, 'A Dynamic Theory of Comparative Advantage', *American Economic Review*, 63, 1, pp. 173–84.

KNICKERBOCKER, F. T., 1973, *Oligopolistic Reaction and the Multinational Enterprise*, Graduate School of Business Admin., Harvard Univ. Press.

KOPITS, G., 1972, 'Dividend Remittance Behavior Within the International Firm: A Cross-country Analysis', *Review of Economics and Statistics*, 54, pp. 339–42.

KOSZUL, J.-P., 1970, 'American Banks in Europe', in C. P. Kindleberger (ed.), *The International Corporation*, Cambridge, Mass.: M.I.T. Press, pp. 273–89.

KRAINER, R., 1972, 'The Valuation and Financing of the Multinational Firm', *KYKLOS*, Fasc. 3, 25, pp. 553–73.

KRAUSSE, L. B., & DAM, K. W., 1964, *'Federal Tax Treatment of Foreign Income'*, Brookings.

KUJAWA, D., 1971, *International Labour Relations Management in the Automotive Industry: A Comparative Study of Chrysler, Ford and General Motors*, New York: Praeger.

KWACK, S., 1971, 'A Model of US Direct Investment Abroad: A Neoclassical Approach', *Western Economic Journal*.

LADENSON, M., 1972, 'A Dynamic Balance Sheet Approach to American

N

Direct Foreign Investment', *International Economic Review*, **13**, pp. 531–43.

LALL, S., 1973, 'Transfer Pricing by Multinational Manufacturing Firms', Oxford Bulletin of Economics and Statistics, **35**, pp. 173–195.

LAURSEN, S., & METZLER, L. A., 1950, 'Flexible Exchange Rates and the Theory of Employment', *Review of Economics and Statistics*, **32**, pp. 281–99.

LAYTON, C., 1966, *Trans-Atlantic Investments*, The Atlantic Institute Boulognesur-Seine; 1969, *European Advanced Technology*, Allen & Unwin.

LEAMER, E. E., & STERN, R. M., 1970, *Quantitative International Economics*, Int. Series in Economics, Allyn & Baran.

LEA, D., 1971, 'Multinational Companies and Trade Union Interests', in J. H. Dunning (ed.), *The Multinational Enterprise*, Allen & Unwin, pp. 147–63.

LEVINSON, C., 1970, 'The Answer to the Giant Company', *Voice of the Unions* (Published at 73 Ridgeway Place, London, SW19).

LEVINSON, H. M., 1966, *Determining Forces in Collective Bargaining*, New York: Wiley.

LEVINSON, K., & SANDÊN, P., 1972, *Kapitalets international*, Stockholm.

LEWIS, S., & SOLIGE, R., 1965, 'Growth and Structural Change in Pakistan Manufacturing Industry', *Pakistan Development Review*, Spring.

LEWIS, W. A., 1965, 'A Review of Economic Development', The Richard T. Ely Lecture, *American Economic Review*, **60**, 2, pp. 1–4.

LINDER, S. B., 1961, *An Essay on Trade and Transformation*, New York & Stockholm: Wiley and Almqvist & Wiksell.

LINTNER, J., 1965, 'The Valuation of Risk Assets and Selection of Risky Investments in Stock Portfolios and Capital Budgets', *Review of Economics and Statistics*, **47**, pp. 13–37.

LITTLE, I. M. D., & MIRLESS, J. A., 1969, *Manual of Industrial Project Analysis in Developing Countries*, Vol. II, Social Cost Benefit Analysis, Paris: OECD.

LUNDGREN, N., 1973, 'Multinational Enterprises and Economic Stability', Unpublished paper presented to SUERF Conference at Nottingham.

LYNN, F., 1966, 'An Investigation of the Rate of Development and Diffusion of Technology in our Modern Industrial Society', *Report of the National Commission on Technology, Automation and Economic Progress*, Washington, D.C.

MACDOUGALL, G. D. A., 1960a, 'The Benefits and Costs of Private Investment from Abroad', *Economic Records*, **36**, pp. 13–35; 1960b, 'The Benefits and Costs of Private Investment from Abroad: A Theoretical Approach', *Bulletin of the Oxford Univ. Institute of Statistics*, **22**, 3, pp. 189–211 (Reprinted in R. E. Caves and H. G.

Johnson (eds), *Readings in International Economics*, Allen & Unwin, Chapter 10, pp. 172–94).

McGraw-Hill, 1967, *Survey of Business Plans for Research and Development Expenditures*, 1967–70.

Machlup, F., 1946, 'Marginal Analysis and Empirical Research', *American Economic Review*, **36**, pp. 519–77; 1948, *The Basing Point System*, Philadelphia: Blakiston; 1967, 'Theories of the Firm: Marginalist, Behavioral, Managerial', *American Economic Review*, **57**, 1, pp. 1–33.

McKinnon, R. I., 1963, 'Optimum Currency Areas', *American Economic Review*, **53**, 4, pp. 717–25.

McKinnon, R. I., & Oates, W. E., 1966, *The Implications of International Economic Integration for Monetary, Fiscal and Exchange Rate Policy*, Princeton Studies in Int. Finance, No. 16.

McManus, J. C. 1972, 'The Theory of the Multinational Firm', in G. Paquet (ed.), *The Multinational and the Nation State*, Don Mills, Canada: Collier-Macmillan.

Maddison, A., 1965, *Foreign Skills and Technical Assistance in Economic Development*, Development Centre of OECD.

Maier, H., 1971, 'The International Free Trade Union Movement and Multinational Corporations', *Personnel Management Review*, March, pp. 14–19.

Maison Rouge, J., 1971, 'Computers and International Trade', *Technology and International Trade*, National Academy of Engineering.

Mann, H. M., 1966, 'Seller Concentration, Barriers to Entry, and Rates of Return in Thirty Industries, 1959–60', *Review of Economics and Statistics*, **48**, pp. 296–307.

Manser, W., 1973, *The Financial Role of Multinational Enterprises*, Int. Chamber of Commerce.

Mansfield, E., 1961, 'Technical Change and the Rate of Imitation; *Econometrica*, **29**, 4, pp. 741–66; 1968a, *The Economics of Technical Change*, W. W. Norton; 1968b, *Industrial Research and Technological Innovation*, The Cowles Foundation for Research in Economics at Yale Univ., W. W. Norton; 1971, 'Determinants of the Speed of Application of New Technology', *Conference of the International Economic Association*, San Anton, Australia. 1972, 'Contribution of Research and Development to Economic Growth in the United States', *Science, N.Y.*, **175**, 4021, pp. 477–86.

Mansfield, E., Rapoport, J., Schnee, J., Wagner, S., & Hamburger, M., 1971, *Research and Innovation in the Modern Corporation*, W. W. Norton.

Markowitz, H., 1959, *Portfolio Analysis*, New York: Wiley.

Marquis, D. Q., & Allen, T. J., 1966, 'Communication Patterns in Applied Technology', *American Psychologist*, **21**, pp. 1052–60.

Marris, R., 1964, *The Economic Theory of 'Managerial' Capitalism*, New York: Macmillan; 1971, 'An Introduction to Theories of

Corporate Growth', in R. Marris & A. Wood (eds), *The Corporate Economy*, Cambridge Mass.: Harvard Univ. Press.

MARRIS, R., & WOOD, A., 1971, *The Corporate Economy: Growth, Competition and Innovation Potential*, Cambridge, Mass.: Harvard Univ. Press.

MARSCHAK, T., GLENNAW, T., & SUMMERS, R., 1967, *Strategy for R & D*, Springer Verlag.

MASON, R. H., 1971, *The Transfer of Technology and the Factor Proportions Problem: The Philippines and Mexico*, Research Report No. 10, New York: UNITAR.

MATTSSON, A., 1971, *Handelshinder som exportproblem*, Stockholm: 1972, *Dumping och antidumpingatgärder*, Uppsala.

MEADE, J. E., 1952, *A Geometry of International Trade*, Allen & Unwin; 1955, *The Theory of International Trade*, Allen & Unwin; 1955, *The Theory of International Economic Policy*, Vol. 2, Trade and Welfare, Oxford Univ. Press.

MEIER, G., 1969, 'Development Without Employment', *Banca Nazionale del Lavoro Quarterly Review*, **22**, pp. 309–319.

MELVIN, J., 1968, 'Production and Trade with Two Factors and Three Goods', *American Economic Review*, **58**, pp. 1249–68.

MENIL, G. DE, 1971, *Bargaining: Monopoly Power versus Union Power*, Cambridge, Mass.: M.I.T. Press.

MEYER, J., & KUH, E., 1957, *The Investment Decision: An Empirical Study*, Cambridge, Mass.: Harvard Univ. Press.

MIKDASHI, Z., 1966, *A Financial Analysis of Middle East Oil Concessions: 1901–65*, New York: Praeger; 1971, *A Comparative Analysis of selected Mineral Exporting Industries*, Vienna: OPEC (mimeo); 1972, *The Community of Oil Exporting Countries: A Study in Governmental Co-operation*, Ithaca: Cornel Univ. Press.

MILLER, M., & MODIGLIANI, F., 1966, 'Some Estimates of the Cost of Capital to the Electric Utility Industry', *American Economic Review*, **56**, pp. 333–91.

MILLER, R., & WEIGEL, D. R., 1971, 'Factors Affecting Resource Transfer Through Direct Investment', College of Business Administration, *Univ. Iowa Working Paper* series.

MODIGLIANI, F., & MILLER, M., 1958, 'The Cost of Capital, Corporation Finance and the Theory of Investment', *American Economic Review*, **48**, pp. 261–97.

MOOSE, J., 1968, 'US Direct Investment Abroad in Manufacturing and Petroleum—A Recursive Model', Unpublished Doctoral thesis, Harvard.

MORLEY, S., 1966, 'American Corporate Investment Abroad Since 1919', Unpublished Doctoral thesis, Univ. California at Berkeley.

MUELLER, D., 1972, 'A Life Cycle Theory of the Firm', *Journal of Industrial Economics*, **20**, pp. 199–219.

MUNDELL, R. A., 1957, 'International Trade and Factor Mobility', *American Economic Review*, **47**, pp. 321–35; 1961, 'A Theory of

Optimum Currency Areas', *American Economic Review*, **51**, 4, pp. 657–65.

MUSGRAVE, P. B., 1969, *United States Taxation of Foreign Investment Income: Issues and Arguments*, Harvard Law School.

MYERS, S., & MARQUIS, D. G., 1969, *Successful Industrial Innovations*, National Science Foundation.

NADIRI, M., & ROSEN, S., 1969, 'Interrelated Factor Demand Functions', *American Economic Review*, **49**, pp. 457–71.

NASBETH, L., 1971, 'The Diffusion of Innovations in Swedish Industry', *Conference of the International Economic Association*, San Anton, Australia.

NASH, J. F., 1959, 'The Bargaining Problem', *Economica*, **27**, pp. 155–62.

NATIONAL BUREAU COMMITTEE FOR ECONOMIC RESEARCH, 1962, *The Rate and Direction of Inventive Activity*, Princeton.

NATIONAL COUNCIL OF APPLIED ECONOMIC RESEARCH, 1966, *Underutilisation of Industrial Capacity*, 1955–64, New Delhi.

NATIONAL SCIENCE FOUNDATIONS, 1967, *Proceedings of a Conference on Technology Transfer and Innovations*.

NEBON, R., 1971, 'World Leadership, the Technology Gap and National Policy', *Minerva*, July.

NEGISHI, T., 1965, 'Foreign Investment and the Long-run National Advantage', *Economic Record*, Dec., pp. 628–31.

NELSON, R., PECK, M. J., & KALACHEK, E., 1967, *Technology and Economic Growth and Public Policy*, Brookings.

NERLOVE, M., 1972, 'Lags in Economic Behavior', *Econometrica*, **40**, pp. 221–52.

NORMAN, V. D., 1971, *Norwegian Shipping in the National Economy*, Bergen: Institute for Shipping Research.

NURKSE, R., 1953, *Problems of Capital Formation in Underdeveloped Countries*, Blackwell.

OECD, 1968a, *Gaps in Technology: General Report*, Paris; 1968b, *Gaps in Technology: Electronic Components*, Paris; 1969a, *Gaps in Technology: Pharmaceuticals*, Paris; 1969b, *Gaps in Technology: Plastics*, Paris; 1970, *Gaps in Technology: Analytical Report*, Paris; 1971, *Science, Growth and Society*, Paris.

OHLIN, B., 1933, *Interregional and International Trade*, Harvard Univ. Press; 1967, *Interregional and International Trade* (revised edition), Harvard Univ. Press.

PALMER, J., 1971, *The Extent of the Separation of Ownership from Control in Large US Industrial Corporations'*, Research Report No. 7129, Univ. Western Ontario.

PAPO, M., 1971, 'How to Establish and Operate Multinational Laboratories', *Research Management*, January.

PARKER, J., 1973, 'Diffusion and the Multinational Enterprise', Unpublished Ph.D. thesis, Univ. Exeter.

PAVITT, K., 1970, 'Multinational Enterprise and the Transfer of Technology', in J. H. Dunning (ed.), *The Multinational Enterprise*,

Allen & Unwin; 1971, *The Conditions for Success in Technological Innovation*, OECD.

PAZOS, F., 1967, 'The Role of International Movements of Private Capital in Promoting Development' in J. H. Adler (ed.), *Capital Movements and Economic Development*, Macmillan.

PECCEI, A., 1967, *Technology and World Trade*, National Bureau of Standards.

PECK, M. J., 1968, 'Science and Technology', in R. Caves *et al.* (eds), *Britain's Economic Prospects*, Brookings.

PENROSE, E., 1956, 'Foreign Investment and the Growth of the Firm', *Economic Journal*, 66, 262, pp. 220–35; 1959a, *The Theory of the Growth of the Firm*, New York: Wiley; 1959b, 'Profit Sharing Between Producing Countries and Oil Companies in the Middle East', *Economic Journal*, 69, pp. 238–54; 1968, *The Large International Firm in Developing Countries: The International Petroleum Industry*, Allen & Unwin.

PERLMUTTER, H. V., 1972, 'Toward Research and Development of Nations, Unions and Firms as Worldwide Institutions', in H. Günter (ed.), *Transnational Industrial Relations*, London: Macmillan.

PIGOU, A. C., 1935, *Protective and Preferential Import Duties*, London School of Economics (first published 1906).

POLANYI, K., 1947, *The Great Transformation*, Philadelphia: Blakiston.

POLK, J., 1971, *World Companies and the new World Economy*, New York: Council for Foreign Relations.

POLK, J., MEISTER, I. W., & VEIT, L. A., 1966, *US Production Abroad and the Balance of Payments*, New York: National Industrial Conference Board.

POPKIN, J., 1965, 'Determinants of Foreign Investment Behavior of US Manufacturing Firms', Unpublished Doctoral thesis, Univ. Pennsylvania.

POSNER, M. V., 1961, 'International Trade and Technical Change', *Oxford Economic Papers*, 13, pp. 323–341.

POTTER, B., 1971, 'Effective Information and Technology Transfer in Multinational R & D', *Research Management*, January.

POWER, J. H., 1963, 'Industrialisation in Pakistan: A Case of Frustrated Take-off', *Pakistan Development Review*, Summer; 1966, 'Import Substitution as an Industrialisation Strategy', *Philippine Economic Journal*, 2nd Semester.

PRACHOWNY, M. J., 1969, *A Structural Model of the US Balance of Payments*, Amsterdam: North Holland; 1972, 'Direct Investment and the Balance of Payments of the United States: A Portfolio Approach', in F. Machlup, W. Salant & L. Tarshis (eds), *The International Mobility and Movement of Capital*, New York: National Bureau of Economic Research.

PRICE, W., & BASS, L., 1969, 'Scientific Research and the Innovative Process', *Science, N.Y.*, 164, 3881, pp. 802–6.

PRYOR, F. L., 1972, 'An International Comparison of Concentration Ratios', *Review of Economics and Statistics*, 54, pp. 130–40.

QUINN, J. B., 1969, 'Technology Transfer by Multinational Companies' *Harvard Business Review*, **47**, pp. 147–61.

RAY, G., 1969, 'The Diffusion of New Technology', *National Institute Economic Review*, No. 48, pp. 40–83.

REDDAWAY, W. B., in collaboration with POTTER, S. J., & TAYLOR, C. T., 1968, *Effects of UK Direct Investment Overseas: Final Report*, Cambridge Univ. Press.

REISS, H., 1969, 'Human Factors at the Science-Technology Interface', in D. G. Marquis & W. H. Gruber (eds), *Factors in the Transfer of Technology*, Cambridge, Mass.: M.I.T. Press.

REUBER, G., 1973, *Private Foreign Investment in Development*, Oxford: Clarendon Press.

RHOMBERG, R., 1968, 'Transmission of Business Fluctuations from Developed to Developing Countries', *IMF Staff Papers*, **15**, pp. 1–29.

RICHARDSON, H. W., 1969, *Regional Economics*, London: Weidenfeld & Nicolson.

RICHARDSON, J. D., 1971, 'Theoretical Considerations in the Analysis of Foreign Direct Investment', *Western Economic Journal*, **9**, pp. 87–98.

RIESSER, J., 1911, *The Great German Banks and their Concentration*, Washington, D.C.: US Government Printing Office, National Monetary Commission.

ROBBINS, S., & STOBAUGH, R., 1973, *Money in the International Enterprise: A Study of Financial Policy*, Basic Books (Particularly Chapter 4 on 'A Systems View of the Multinational Enterprise').

ROBERTSON, D., 1971, 'The Multinational Enterprise: Trade Flows and Trade Policy', in J. H. Dunning (ed.), *The Multinational Enterprise*, Allen & Unwin.

ROGERS, E., 1962, *Diffusion of Innovations*, New York: Free Press.

ROLFE, S., 1969, *The International Corporation*, Paris: International Chamber of Commerce.

ROSENBLUTH, G., 1970, 'The Relation between Foreign Control and Concentration in Canadian Industry', *Canadian Journal of Economics*, **3**, pp. 14–30.

RUCKDESCHEL, F., 1971, 'The Determinants of a Direct Investment Outflow with Emphasis on the Supply of Funds', Unpublished Doctoral thesis, Univ. Pennsylvania.

RYBCZYNSKI, T. M., 1955, 'Factor Endowment and Relative Commodity Prices', *Economica*, **22**, pp. 336–41.

SAFARIAN, A. E., 1966, *Foreign Ownership of Canadian Industry*, Toronto: McGraw-Hill.

SAMUELSON, P. A., 1965, 'Equalization by Trade of the Interest Rate Along with the Real Wage', *Trade, Growth and the Balance of Payments; Essays in honour of G. Haberler*, Chicago.

SANDMO, A., 1971, 'On the Theory of the Competitive Firm Under Price Uncertainty', *American Economic Review*, **61**, pp. 65–73.

SAVING, T. R., 1961, 'Estimation of Optimum Size of Plant by the Survivor Technique', *Quarterly Journal of Economics*, **75**, pp. 596–607.

SCAPERLANDA, A. E., & MAUER, L. J., 1969, 'The Determinants of US Direct Investment in the EEC', *American Economic Review*, **59**, pp. 558–68; 1972, 'Reply', *American Economic Review*, **62**, pp. 700–4.

SCHELLING, T. C., 1960, *The Strategy of Conflict*, Cambridge, Mass.: Harvard Univ. Press; 1963, *The Strategy of Conflict*, Oxford Univ. Press.

SCHERER, F. M., 1969, 'Market Structure and the Stability of Investment', *American Economic Review*, **59**, pp. 72–9; 1970, *Industrial Market Structure and Economic Performance*, Chicago: Rand McNally.

SCHMOOKLER, J., 1966, *Inventions and Economic Growth*, Cambridge, Mass.: Harvard Univ. Press.

SCHON, D., 1967, *Technology and Change*, Delacorte.

SCHREIBER, J. C., 1970, *US Corporate Investment in Taiwan*, New York: Dunellen.

SCHYDLOWSKY, D., 1970, 'Benefit-Cost Analysis of Foreign Investment Proposals', Paper presented at the Dubrovnik Conference of Harvard Development Advisory; 1971, 'Fiscal Policy for Full Capacity Industrial Growth in Latin America', *Economic Development Report*, No. 201, Development Advisory Service, Centre for International Relations, Harvard Univ.

SEERS, D., 1963, 'Big Companies and Little Countries', *KYKLOS*, **26**, 4, pp. 599–607.

SERVAN-SCHREIBER, J. J., 1967, *Le Defi American*, Paris: Editions de Noel.

SEVERN, A., 1972, 'Investment and Financial Behavior of American Direct Investors in Manufacturing', in F. Machlup, W. Salant, & L. Tarshis (eds), *The International Mobility and Movement of Capital*, New York: National Bureau of Economic Research.

SHARPE, W., 1964, 'Capital Asset Prices: A Theory of Market Equilibrium Under Conditions of Risk' *Journal of Finance*, **19**, pp. 425–42.

SHEARER, R. A., 1964, 'Nationality, Size of Firm and Exploration for Petroleum in Western Canada, 1946–54', *Canadian Journal of Economics and Political Science*, **30**, pp. 211–27.

SHERMAN, R., & TOLLISON, R., 1972, 'Technology, Profit Risk, and Assessments of Market Performance', *Quarterly Journal of Economics*, **86**, pp. 448–62.

SIMMONDS, K., 1966, 'Multinational? Well Not Quite', *Columbia Journal of World Business*, Fall, pp. 115–22.

SIMON, H., 1957a, *Administrative Behavior*, New York: Macmillan; 1957b, *Models of Man*, New York: Wiley; 1962, 'New Developments in the Theory of the Firm', *American Economic Review*, **52**, 2, pp. 1–15.

SINGER, H. W., 1950, 'The Distribution of Gains between Investing and Borrowing Countries', *American Economic Review*, **40**, pp. 473–85.

SLATER, W. E. G., 1960, *Productivity and Technical Change*, Cambridge Univ. Press.

SMITH, A., 1937, *The Wealth of Nations*, New York: Modern Library.

SOLOW, R. M., 1971, 'Some Implications of Alternative Criteria for the Firm', in R. Marris & A. Wood (eds), *The Corporate Economy*, Cambridge, Mass.: Harvard Univ. Press.

SPITÄLLER, E., 1971, 'A Survey of Recent Quantitative Studies of Long-term Capital Movements', *IMF Staff Papers*, **18**, pp. 189–220.

STAUFFER, T. R., 1971, 'The Measurement of Corporate Rates of Return: A Generalised Formulation', *Bell Journal of Economics and Management Science*, **2**, pp. 434–69.

STEEL, W., 1971, 'Import Substitution and Excess Capacity in Ghana', *Economic Development Report*, No. 198, Development Advisory Service Centre for International Relations, Harvard Univ. Press.

STEUER, M., & GENNARD, J., 1971, 'Industrial Relations, Labour Disputes and Labour Utilization in Foreign Owned Firms in the UK', in J. H. Dunning (ed.), *The Multinational Enterprise*, Allen & Unwin.

STEUER, M., *et al.*, 1973, 'The Impact of Foreign Direct Investment on the United Kingdom: H.M.S.O.

STEVENS, G. V., 1967, 'Fixed Investment Expenditures of Foreign Manufacturing Affiliates of US Firms: Theoretical Models and Empirical Evidence', Unpublished Doctoral thesis, Yale Univ.; 1969a, 'Fixed Investment Expenditures of Foreign Manufacturing Affiliates of US Firms: Theoretical Models and Empirical Evidence', *Yale Economic Essays*, **9**, 1, pp. 137–200; 1969b, *US Direct Manufacturing Investment to Latin America: Some Economic and Political Determinants*, A.I.D. Research Paper (multilithoed); 1971, 'Two Problems in Portfolio Analysis: Conditional and Multiplicative Random Variables', *Journal of Financial and Quantitative Analysis*, **6**, pp. 1235–50; 1972, 'Capital Mobility and the International Firm', in F. Machlup, W. Salant & L. Tarshis (eds.), *The International Mobility and Movement of Capital*, New York: National Bureau of Economic Research; 1973, 'On the Value of the Firm, Discounting, and Optimal Investment under Uncertainty', *Special Studies Paper*, No. 26, Washington, D.C.: Federal Reserve Board.

STEWART, F., 1973, 'Trade and Technology', in P. Streeten (ed.), *Trade Strategies for Development*, Macmillan.

STOBAUGH, R. B., 1968, 'The Product Life Cycle, US Exports and International Investment', Unpublished DBA thesis, Harvard Business school; 1969, 'Where in the World should We Put that Plant', *Harvard Business Review*, **46**, pp. 129–36; 1970a, 'Utilizing Technical Know-how in a Foreign Investment and Licensing Program', *Proceedings of the Chemical Marketing Research Association*, February; 1970b, 'Financing Foreign Subsidiaries of US-Controlled Multinational Enterprises', *Journal of International Business Studies*, Summer, pp. 43–64; 1972, 'US Multinational

O

Enterprises and the US Economy', Washington: US Department of Commerce.

STONEHILL, A., 1965, *Foreign Ownership in Norwegian Enterprises*, Oslo: Central Bureau of Statistics.

STOPFORD, J. M., 1968, 'Growth and Organizational Change in the Multinational Firm', Unpublished DBA dissertation, Harvard Business School.

STOPLER, W. F., & SAMUELSON, P. A., 1941, 'Protection and Real Wages', *Review Economic Studies*, 9, pp. 58–73.

STRASSMANN, W. P., 1968, *Technological Change and Economic Development*, Ithaca, New York: Cornell Univ. Press.

STREETEN, P., 1971, 'Costs and Benefits of Multinational Enterprises in Less-developed Countries', in J. H. Dunning (ed.), *The Multinational Enterprise*, Allen & Unwin.

STUBENITSKY, F., 1970, *American Direct Investment in the Netherlands Industry*, Rotterdam: Rotterdam Univ. Press.

SUNDELSON, J. W., 1970, 'US Automotive Investments Abroad', in C. P. Kindleberger (ed.), *The International Corporation*, Cambridge, Mass.: M.I.T. Press.

SVENNILSON, I., 1964, 'The Transfer of Industrial Know-how to Non-industrialized Countries', in K. Berrill (ed.), *Economic development with Special Reference to East Asia*, Macmillan.

TANNENBAUM, M., *et al.*, 1966, *Report of the Ad Hoc Committee on Research engineering Interaction, Materials Advisory Board.*

TELER, L. G., 1966, 'Cut-throat Competition and the Long Purse', *Journal of Law and Economics*, 9, pp. 257–77.

TEUBAL, M., 1972, 'Heavy and Light Industry in Economic Development', Unpublished manuscript, Hebrew Univ., Jerusalem.

THOMAS, P., 1966, 'Import Licensing and Import Liberalization in Pakistan', *Pakistan Development Review*, 6.

TILTON, J. E., 1966, 'The Choice of Trading Partners: An Analysis of International Trade in Aluminium, Bauxite, Copper, Lead, Tin and Zinc', *Yale Economic Essays*, 6, Fall; 1971, *International Diffusion of Technology: The Case of Semiconductors*, Brookings.

TINSLEY, P., 1970a, 'Capital Structure, Precautionary Balances, and the Valuation of the Firm: The Problem of Financial Risk', *Journal of Financial and Quantitative Analysis*, 5, pp. 33–62; 1970b, 'On Ramps, Turnpikes and Distributed Lag Approximations of Optimal Intertemporal Adjustment', *Western Economic Journal*, 8, pp. 397–411.

TOBIN, J., 1958, 'Liquidity Preference as Behavior Towards Risk', *Review of Economic Studies*, 26, pp. 65–86.

TRAVIS, W., 1972, 'Production, Trade and Protection, When there are Many Commodities and Two Factors', *American Economic Review*, 62, pp. 87–106.

TSURUMI, Y., 1972, 'Profiles of Japan-based Multinational Firms', *Journal of World Trade Law*. 6.

TUGENDHAT, C., 1971, *The Multinationals*, Eyre & Spottiswoode.

UNITED NATIONS, 1973, *Multinational Corporations in World Development*, New York, ST/ECA/190.

UNCTAD, 1969, *Queen Elizabeth House Study on Private Foreign Investment;* 1972, *Policies Relating to Technology in the Countries of the Andean Pact: Their Foundations*, Santiago, TD/107.

UNITED NATIONS INSTITUTE FOR TRAINING AND RESEARCH, 1971, *The International Transfer of Technology in the Establishment of the Petrochemical Industry in Developing Countries.*

UNITED STATES DEPARTMENT OF COMMERCE, 1960, *US Business Investments in Foreign Countries*, Washington; US Government Printing Office; 1966, *Overseas Business Reports* (May 1966–April 1968); 1967, *Technological Innovation: Its Environment and Management.*

UNITED STATES FEDERAL TRADE COMMISSION, 1952, *The International Petroleum Cartel Report*, Washington, D.C.: US Government Printing Office.

UNITED STATES SENATE COMMITTEE ON FINANCE, 1973, *The Multinational Corporation in the World Economy*, US Government Printing Office.

UNITED STATES TARIFF COMMISSION, 1973, *Implications of Multinational Firms for World Trade and Investment and for US Trade and Labor*, Washington, D.C.: US Government Printing Office.

VAITSOS, C. V., 1970a, 'Transfer of Resources and Preservation of Monopoly Rents', *Economic Development Report*, No. 168, Centre of International Affairs, Harvard Univ. (mimeo); 1970b, 'Bargaining and the Distribution of Returns in the Purchase of Technology by Developing Countries', *Bulletin of the Institute of Development Studies*, **3,** 1; 1973, *Income Generation and Income Distribution in the Foreign Investment Model*, Oxford Univ. Press and Fondo de Cultura Economica.

VAJDA, I., 1969, 'The Problems of East-West Trade', in P. A. Samuelson (ed.), *International Economic Relations*, London: Macmillan.

VAN DEN BULDKE, 1973, *The Foreign Companies in Belgian Industry*, Belgium Productivity Centre.

VAUPEL, J. W., 1972, 'The Multinational Expansion of US Manufacturers', Unpublished Ph.D. thesis, Kennedy School of Government, Harvard Univ.

VAUPEL, J. W., & CURHAN, J. P., 1969, *The Making of the International Enterprise*, Boston, Mass.: Harvard Business School.

VERNON, R., 1966, 'International Investment and International Trade in the Product Cycle', *Quarterly Journal of Economics*, **80,** pp. 190–207; 1970, 'Future of the Multinational Enterprise', in C. Kindleberger (ed.), *The International Corporation*, Cambridge, Mass.: M.I.T. Press; 1971, *Sovereignty at Bay*, Basic Books; 1971b, 'Organization as a Scale Factor in the Growth of Firms', in J. P. Markham & G. F. Papenek (eds), *Industrial Organization and Economic Development*, Boston: Houghton Mifflin.

VINER, J., 1966, *Dumping: A Problem in International Trade*, New York: Kelley (originally published 1923, Univ. Chicago).

WALTON, R. E., & McKENSIE, R. B., 1965, *A Behavioral Theory of Labor Negotiations*, New York: McGraw-Hill.

WARNER, M., & TURNER, L., 1971, *Trade Unions and the Multinational Firm*, Research Publication, London: Graduate Business School.

WATKINS, M., 1970, *Foreign Ownership and the Structure of American Industry*, Ottawa: Queens Printers.

WEIGEL, D., 1966, 'The Relation Between Government Economic Policy and Direct Investment in Developing Countries', Unpublished Doctoral thesis, Stanford Univ. Graduate School of Business Administration.

WELLS, L. T., 1966, 'Product Innovation and Direction of International Trade', Unpublished DBA thesis, Harvard Business School; 1969a, 'Vehicles for the International Transfer of Technology', *Technology and Economic Development*, Istanbul: The Economic Research Foundation; 1969b, 'Tests of a Product Cycle Model of International Trade: US Exports of Consumer Durables', *Quarterly Journal of Economics*, **83**, pp. 152–63; 1972, (ed.), *The Product Life Cycle and International Trade*, Boston: Division of Research, Harvard Business School.

WILKINS, M., 1970, *The Emergence of Multinational Enterprise*, Cambridge, Mass.: Harvard Univ. Press.

WILLIAMSON, J., 1966, 'Profit, Growth and Sales Maximization', *Economica*, **33**, pp. 1–16; 1969, *Capital Accumulation, Labour-Saving and Labour-Absorption: A New Look at Some Contemporary Asian Experience*, SSRI Workshop Series EDIE 6932, Univ. Wisconsin.

WILLIAMSON, O., 1964, *The Economics of Discretionary Behavior: Managerial Objectives in a Theory of the Firm*, Englewood Cliffs: Prentice-Hall; 1971, 'Managerial Discretion, Organizational Form and the Multidivisional Hypothesis', in R. Marris & A. Wood (eds), *The Corporate Economy*, Boston: Harvard Business School.

WINSTON, G. C., 1968, *Excess Capacity in Underdeveloped Countries: The Pakistan Case*, Centre for Development Economics, Williams College; 1970, 'Overinvoicing, Underutilisation and Distorted Industrial Growth', *Pakistan Development Review*, Winter; 1971a, *The Four Reasons for Idle Capital*, Oxford (mimeo); 1971b, 'Capital Utilisation in Economic Development', *Economic Journal*, March; 1971c, *Capital Utilisation and Development: Physiological Costs and Preference for Shift Work*, Williams College, February (mimeo); 1971d, *A Comparison of Capital Utilisation in Pakistan and the United States*, Karachi, February (mimeo).

WIONCZEK, M. S., 1971a, 'Hacia el Establecimiento de un Trato Comun para la Inversion Extranjera en el Mercado Comun Andino', *El Trimestre Economico*, **38**, April/June; 1971b, 'La Reaccion Norteamericana ante el Trato Comun a los Capitales Extranjeros enel Grupo Andino', *Comercio Exterior*, May.

WOLF, B., 1971, 'Internationalization of US Manufacturing Forms:

A Type of Diversification', Unpublished Doctoral thesis, Yale Univ.

WORCESTER, D. H., 1967, *Monopoly, Big Business and Welfare in the United States*, Seattle: Univ. of Washington Press.

WORTZEL, L., 1971, *Technological Transfer in the Pharmaceutical Industry*, UN Institute for Training and Research.

YEOMAN, W. A., 1968, 'Selection of Production Processes for the Manufacturing Subsidiaries of US-based Multinational Corporations', Unpublished DBA thesis, Harvard Business School.

ZEUTHEN, F., 1930, *Problems of Monopoly and Economic Welfare*, London: Routledge.

Author Index

Adam, G. 114*n*, 337*n*, 340*n*
Adelman, M. A. 113*n*
Adler, M. H. 144*n*, 339*n*
Aharoni, Y. 30*n*, 39, 56, 60, 62, 63, 64, 85, 86*n*, 87*n*, 174, 182*n*, 388*n*
Aigrain, P. 113*n*
Aliber, R. Z. 56, 85*n*, 146*n*
Allen, T. J. 113*n*
Almon, S. 52
Anderson, W. H. L. 76
Andrews, M. E. 146*n*
Ansoff, H. I. 38
Archibald, G. C. 31

Bacha, E. 339*n*
Baer, W. 278*n*
Bain, J. S. 117, 143*n*, 146*n*
Balassa, B. 56, 113*n*, 144*n*, 233*n*
Baldwin, R. E. 23, 181*n*, 228
Balogh, T. 260, 278*n*, 337*n*
Bandera, V. W. 56, 69, 85*n*
Bannock, G. 113*n*
Baranson, J. 114*n*, 161, 174, 181*n*, 182*n*
Barlow, E. R. 57, 66, 67, 85*n*, 86*n*, 87*n*
Barovik, R. 299*n*
Bass, L. 180*n*
Baumol, W. J. 33, 34, 46*n*, 50, 84*n*, 87*n*
Behrman, J. 57, 60, 61, 66, 67, 68, 85*n*, 86*n*, 144*n*, 180*n*, 181*n*, 278*n*, 339*n*, 370, 371
Berle, A. A. 32, 49
Berlin, P. D. 57, 77, 85*n*, 87*n*
Bhagwati, J. 114*n*, 209*n*, 337*n*
Billsborrow, R. E. 57, 69, 85*n*, 87*n*
Bischoff, C. 49, 52, 84*n*, 85*n*, 87*n*
Blake, D. H. 299*n*
Bohlew, J. 181*n*
Borts, G. H. 19, 211–33, 214, 370
Branson, W. 215
Brash, D. T. 30*n*, 57, 85*n*, 87*n*, 143*n*, 144*n*, 182*n*
Braun, R. 362*n*
Brooks, H. 180*n*
Brown, L. 13

Bruck, N. K. 14, 240*n*
Bruno, M. 339*n*
Burns, T. 180*n*
Burton, H. J. 278*n*

Cairncross, A. K. 337*n*
Cameron, R. 278*n*
Cannon, C. M. 86*n*
Carlson, S. 19, 26, 27, 57, 87*n*, 280–99
Caty, G. 112*n*
Caves, R. E. 19, 20, 24, 57, 75, 85*n*, 87*n*, 112*n*, 115–46, 190, 209*n*, 260, 278*n*, 299*n*, 338*n*, 366, 367, 369, 370, 371
Chamberlain, N. W. 105, 294
Chandler, A. D. Jr 40
Chenery, H. 52, 69
Chipman, J. 191, 192
Clague, C. 114*n*
Coen, R. M. 54
Cohen, K. J. 38, 84*n*, 85*n*
Comanor, W. S. 143*n*, 146*n*
Cole, G. 351
Cole, W. A. 278*n*
Cooper, R. N. 162, 173, 181*n*, 182*n*, 183*n*, 236
Cordell, A. J. 113*n*
Corden, W. M. 19, 22, 23, 114*n*, 184–210, 247, 337*n*, 368, 370
Craine, R. 85*n*
Curhan, J. P. 338*n*
Cyert, R. 38, 60, 62, 63, 84*n*, 85*n*

Dam, K. W. 339*n*
Daniels, J. D. 144*n*, 145*n*
Deane, P. 30*n*, 278*n*
Denison, E. 157, 181*n*
Diaz-Alejandro, C. F. 1 260, 267, 278*n*, 337*n*
Drèze, J. 356, 362*n*
Duerr, M. G. 278*n*
Dunlop, J. T. 283, 298*n*
Dunning, J. H. 13–30, 14, 21, 30*n*, 143*n*, 146*n*, 171, 175, 180*n*, 181*n*, 182*n*, 210*n*, 185, 251*n*, 278*n*, 299*n*, 338*n*, 363–72
Dupriez, L. H. 355, 362*n*

Eastman, H. C. 146*n*
Edgren, G. 251*n*
Eisner, R. 84*n*, 85*n*, 86*n*
English, H. E. 145*n*

Faith, N. 113*n*, 114*n*
Findlay, R. 337*n*
Forsgren, M. 299*n*
Franko, L. 113*n*, 340*n*
Freeman, C. 113*n*, 178, 180*n*, 181*n*, 182*n*, 183*n*
Fromm, G. 84, 85*n*
Furtado, C. 337*n*, 339*n*

Galbraith, J. K. 50, 354
Galtung, J. 362*n*
Gehrels, F. 193, 204
Gennard, J. 244
Goldberg, M. A. 76, 212
Gordon, R. A. 32, 33
Gould, J. P. 84*n*
Grabowski, H. 51, 62
Graâf, J. de V. 337*n*
Gray, H. 16
Grayson, C. J. 114*n*
Green, J. 278
Griliches, Z. 180*n*
Groo, E. 182*n*
Grubel, H. G. 144*n*, 237
Gruber, W. D. 112*n*, 338*n*
Grubert, H. 337*n*
Gunter, H. 297, 299*n*
Gustafsson, L. 294

Hall, G. 174, 182*n*
Hamburg, M. 165
Hanson, W. 182*n*
Hawkins, R. 87*n*
Heckscher, E. 185
Helfferich, K. 362*n*
Helleiner, G. K. 278*n*
Heller, H. R. 209*n*
Hellman, R. 114*n*
Henderson, P. D. 339
Herve, M. 278*n*
Hexner, E. 112*n*
Hicks, J. R. 86*n*, 293, 337*n*
Hill, R. D. 215
Hirsch, S. 298*n*
Hirschman, A. O. 278*n*
Holland, S. 114*n*
Hollander, S. 180*n*
Hoover, E. M. 112*n*

Horst, T. O. 19, 31–46, 57, 63, 73, 74, 75, 85*n*, 87*n*, 144*n*, 145*n*, 210*n*, 211, 284, 298*n*, 338*n*, 339*n*, 364
Hsia, R. 180*n*
Hufbauer, G. C. 113*n*, 114*n*, 157, 181*n*, 185, 278*n*, 339*n*
Hughes, H. 30*n*, 278*n*
Hui, C. 87*n*
Hymer, S. 57, 60, 61, 74, 75, 85*n*, 112*n*, 144*n*, 145*n*, 181*n*, 182*n*, 299*n*, 337*n*, 338*n*, 351, 359, 361*n*, 362*n*

Islam, N. 278*n*
Iverson, C. 85*n*

Jewkes, J. 165
Johns, B. L. 57, 146*n*
Johnson, H. G. 144*n*, 174, 181*n*, 182*n*, 186, 187, 201, 208, 209*n*, 210*n*, 215, 337*n*, 338*n*
Johnson, L. 341*n*
Johnstone, A. W. 30*n*, 361*n*
Jones, R. W. 186, 191, 192, 193, 197, 204, 337*n*, 338*n*
Jorgenson, D. 49, 51, 52, 53, 54, 61, 69, 70, 84*n*

Kabaj, M. 278*n*
Kaysen, C. 113*n*
Kessing, D. B. 112*n*, 181*n*
Kemp, M. C. 188, 191, 192, 193, 204, 337*n*
Keynes, J. M. 337*n*, 339*n*
Kidron, M. 30*n*
Kinch, N. 299*n*
Kindleberger, C. P. 28, 30*n*, 57, 85*n*, 180*n*, 182*n*, 260, 278*n*, 337*n*, 338*n*, 339*n*, 342–62, 370, 371
Klein, L. R. 54, 211
Knickerbocker, F. T. 57, 75, 85*n*, 87*n*, 113*n*, 133, 145*n*
Kopecky, K. J. 214
Kopits, G. 57, 69, 70, 71, 85*n*, 86*n*
Koszul, J.-P. 361*n*
Krainer, R. 87*n*
Krausse, L. B. 339*n*
Kuh, E. 52
Kujawa, D. 298*n*, 299*n*
Kwack, S. 57, 69, 70, 77, 85*n*, 86*n*

Ladenson, M. 87*n*
Lall, S. 278*n*
Laursen, S. 232*n*

Layton, C. 181*n*, 338*n*
Leamer, E. E. 237
Lee, D. 299*n*
Lees, F. A. 14, 240*n*
Leibenstein, H. 40
Levinson, C. 245
Levinson, H. M. 294
Levinson, K. 299*n*
Lewis, W. A. 278*n*
Linder, S. B. 113*n*, 143*n*, 278*n*
Lintner, J. 65, 66
Little, I. M. D. 30*n*, 339*n*
Lösch, L. 89
Lundgren, N. 24
Lynn, F. 180*n*

MacDougall, G. D. A. 192, 259, 260, 278*n*, 337*n*
McGraw-Hill 340*n*
Machlup F. 31, 85*n*, 113*n*
McKensie, R. B. 294
McKinnon, R. I. 236, 343, 361*n*
McManus, J. C. 145*n*, 146*n*
Maddison, A. 183*n*
Maier, H. 299*n*
Maisonrouge, J. 182*n*
Malkiel, B. 87*n*
Mann, H. M. 143*n*
Manser, W. A. P. 28
Mansfield, E. 19, 20, 24, 112*n*, 113*n*, 144*n*, 147–83, 180*n*, 364, 366, 370, 371
Markowitz, H. 64, 78, 86*n*
March, J. G. 50, 62, 63, 84*n*
Marquis, D. Q. 113*n*, 151, 180*n*
Marris, R. 31, 36, 50, 62, 84*n*
Marschak, T. 180*n*
Marshall, A. 188
Mason, R. H. 114*n*
Mattsson, A. 299*n*
Mauer, L. J. 58, 69, 74, 85*n*, 87*n*, 212
Maynard, G. 19, 23, 24, 28, 234–51, 369, 370, 371
Meade, J. E. 185, 189, 190, 207
Means, G. C. 32, 49
Mehta, D. 112*n*
Meier, G. 278*n*
Meister, I. W. 58
Melvin, J. 219
Menil, G. de 293
Metzler, L. A. 232*n*
Meyer, J. 52
Mikdashi, Z. 112*n*, 113*n*

Miller, M. 54, 57, 62, 63, 73, 74, 76, 85*n*, 87*n*
Mirless, J. A. 30*n*, 339*n*
Modigliani, F. 54, 76
Moose, J. 58, 69, 85*n*, 86*n*, 87*n*
Morley, S. 58, 69, 85*n*
Mueller, D. C. 51, 62
Mundell, R. A. 112*n*, 190, 191, 196, 342, 361*n*
Musgrave, P. B. 338*n*
Myers, S. 113*n*, 151, 180*n*

Nadiri, M. 85*n*, 86*n*
Nasbeth, L. 180*n*
Nash, J. F. 293
Negishi, T. 338*n*
Nelson, R. 157, 180*n*, 181*n*
Nerlove, M. 84*n*
Norman, V. D. 355, 362*n*
Nurkse, R. 278*n*

Oates, W. E. 236
Ohlin, B. 112*n*, 185, 190, 195

Papo, M. 181*n*, 182*n*
Parker, J. 30*n*
Pavitt, K. 112*n*, 113*n*, 164, 171, 178, 179, 180*n*, 181*n*, 182*n*, 183*n*, 340*n*
Pazsos, F. 278*n*
Peccei, A. 181*n*
Peck, M. J. 182*n*
Penrose, E. 34, 35, 46*n*, 58, 66, 67, 86*n*, 113*n*, 337*n*
Perlmutter, H. V. 299*n*
Pigou, A. C. 190
Polanyi, K. 360
Polk, J. 58
Popkin, J. 58
Posner, M. V. 185, 278*n*
Potter, B. 181*n*
Power, J. H. 278*n*
Prachowny, M. J. 58, 60, 64, 65, 72, 85*n*
Price, W. 180*n*
Pryor, F. L. 146*n*

Quinn, J. B. 171, 179, 181*n*, 182*n*

Ray, G. 180*n*
Reddaway, W. B. 145*n*, 146*n*
Reiss, H. 113*n*
Reuber, G. 58, 85*n*
Rhomberg, R. 58, 85*n*

Richardson, H. W. 112n
Richardson, J. D. 58, 87n
Robbins, S. 339n
Robertson, D. 24, 209n, 210n
Rogers, E. 181n
Rolfe, S. 58, 180n
Rosen, S. 85n
Rosenbluth, G. 146n
Rowthorn, R. 57, 60, 85n, 112n, 144n, 145n, 337n, 338n, 359, 362
Ruckdeschel, F. 58, 77, 85n, 86n, 87n
Rumker, R. Van 182n
Rybczynski, T. M. 225, 337n

Safarian, A. E. 30n, 143n, 145n, 182n
Samuelson, P. A. 112n, 185, 189, 218
Sanden, P. 299n
Sandmo, A. 85n
Saving, T. R. 146n
Scaperlanda, A. E. 58, 69, 74, 85n 87n, 212
Schelling, T. C. 144n, 337n
Scherer, F. M. 87n, 112n, 143n, 144n, 181n
Schmookler, J. 113n, 180n
Schon, D. 180n
Schreiber, J. C. 146n
Schumpeter, J. 352
Schydlowsky, D. 278n, 339n
Seers, D. 362n
Segre, C. 343n
Seng, M. H. 30n, 278n
Servan-Schreiber, J. J. 338n
Severn, A. 58, 68, 69, 71, 72, 77, 85n, 86n, 87n
Sharpe, W. 65, 66
Sherman, R. 143n
Siebert, C. 52, 84
Simmonds, K. 340n
Simon, H. 31, 38, 39, 63, 84n
Singer, H. W. 337n
Smith, A. 34
Solige, R. 278n
Spitaller, E. 58, 85n
Stauffer, T. R. 144n
Stalker, G. 180n
Steel, W. 114n, 278n
Stern, R. M. 237
Steuer, M. 30n, 143n, 145n, 244
Stevens, G. 19, 22, 27, 41, 47–88, 144n, 364, 365
Stewart, F. 278n, 279n
Stewart, M. 84n

Stobaugh, R. B. 59, 67, 87n, 113n, 164, 181n, 338n, 339n
Stonehill, A. 30n, 59, 144n
Stopler, W. F. 189
Strotz, R. H. 84n
Strassmann, W. P. 114n
Streeten, P. 19, 26, 252–79, 337n, 340n, 369, 371
Stubenitsky, F. 30n, 59, 60, 61, 85n
Stykolt, S. 146n
Sundelson, J. W. 145n
Svennilson, I. 181n

Tannenbaum, M. 180n
Taubman, P. 54
Taylor, L. 339n
Telser, L. G. 144n
Teubal, M. 233n
Thomas, P. 278n
Tilton, J. E. 114n, 181n
Tinsley, P. 84n, 87n
Tobin, J. 64, 86n
Tollison, R. 143n
Travis, W. 219, 231
Tsurumi, Y. 113n
Tugendhat, C. 278n
Turner, L. 246

Vaitsos, C. V. 19, 20, 23, 24, 25, 26, 271, 278n, 279n, 300–41, 364, 365, 368, 370, 371
Vajda, I. 362n
Van der Bulke, 30n
Vaupel, J. W. 112n, 338n
Veit, L. A. 58
Vernon, R. 19, 20, 59, 61, 85n, 89–114, 139, 140, 157, 169, 180n, 181n, 182n, 185, 195, 198, 240n, 261, 278n, 299n, 338n, 362n, 364, 369
Viner, J. 113n

Walton, R. E. 294
Warner, M. 246
Watkins, M. 30n
Waud, R. 84n
Weber, M. 89
Weigel, D. 57, 62, 63, 73, 74, 85n, 87n
Wells, L. T. 113n, 181n, 278n
Wender, I. T. 57, 66, 67, 85n, 86n, 87n
Whight, J. T. 56, 69, 85n

Williamson, J. 50, 53, 278n

Williamson, J. G. 278n

Williamson, O. 34, 40, 46n, 84n

Wilson, T. A. 143n

Winston, G. C. 278n

Wionczek, M. S. 338n, 340n

Wolf, B. 59, 63, 73, 74, 85n

Worcester, D. H. 143n

Wortzel, L. 181n

Yeoman, W. A. 114n

Zeuthen, F. 293

Subject Index

Affiliates of the multinational enterprise 14, 15–16, 364–5, 369
industrial organisation 130
intra-firm trading 264–5
location 109–11
technology 154–6, 165–7, 175, 177
welfare considerations 315–30

Balance of payments, impact of the multinational enterprise 48, 240, 246–9
Bargaining power
between management and unions in the multinational enterprise 27, 293–7
between multinational enterprise and host country 24–7, 256, 263, 265–75, 312–15, 366, 371
Behavioural theory of the firm 38–40, 50
see also Determinants of Investment
Bureau of Economic Analysis 87–88n

Capital Movements 186, 211–33
capital flows theory 302, 308–11
definition and model 213–15
future research 230–2
impact of multinational enterprise 216–17
in International trade theory 189–95
Competition and restrictive practices in product and pricing policies 100–1, 122–6, 133–4
Cost-benefit analysis 25–6, 270, 312–13
Currency areas 246–9, 342–3

Development policy, theory of 252–77, 369

Economic efficiency 17, 19–24, 136–8
Entry barriers of multinational enterprises 97–99, 116–20, 124, 128, 132–4, 136–8, 140, 142
Equity considerations 17, 24–8

Euro-dollar market 237–9
European Economic Community 211–13, 231–2, 250
Exchange rate policies 23, 24, 77, 235–40, 249–50, 323, 369–71

Factor costs
implications for multinational enterprises 107–9
increased availability of 302–8
Financial structure of the multinational enterprise 76–7
Financial theory of the firm 76–7
Firm, theory of 18–22, 29, 31–46, 49–50, 364–5
Foreign Research Policy Institute 28

General Motors 217
size of enterprise 352–4
Government policy 20–1, 24, 27–8, 315–30, 363, 369, 371
Growth maximisation, economic theory of 33–8, 41–6, 49–51, 284
see also Determinants of investment

Heckscher-Ohlin-Samuelson Theory
see International trade theory
Horizontal integration 117–20, 138

Income distribution
inter-country 24–7, 291, 300–41, 370–1
intra-country 27–8, 276, 306–8, 370–1
see also Welfare
Industrial organisation 114–46
future research 141–3
International firm, definition 84n
International trade, theory of 22, 23–4, 29, 184–209, 217–30, 368–9
International trade unions 245–6
Investment, determinants of
future research 77–83
impact of multinational enterprises 55–75
theory and evidence 48–54, 308–11

Location of economic activity 21–2, 89–114, 139, 195–9, 217

Managerial behaviour, theory of 283–90
Markets, elements of conduct, performance and structure 116–28
  impact of multinational enterprise 24, 129–41, 366
  impact of tariffs 201–3
  models of market structure 128–9
  optimum size 344–7
  see also Oligopolistic market structure
Monetary policy, impact of multinational enterprise 234–50, 369
  domestic monetary policy 236–9
Multinational enterprise
  economic importance 13–15
  impact on economic analysis and policy 16–30, 361–72
  related enterprises 15
  study of objectives 56–68

National firms
  comparison with multinational enterprises 21, 25, 107–11, 366

Office of Foreign Direct Investment 88*n*
Oil, pricing conventions 98–100
Oligopolies
  location behaviour 90–109
  theory of 20, 112, 367
Oligopolistic market structure 74–5, 90, 122–3, 132–3, 187–8
Optimum areas of the firm
  banking and accounting 347–50
  finance 346–7
  production 344–6
  technology 350–2
Optimum areas of the state 28, 249–50, 352–61, 370
Optimum currency areas 342–3
Organization for Economic Co-operation and Development (OECD) 159–62, 164, 178–9, 181–3*n*

Portfolio theory and risk 58, 64–6, 78, 215–16

Product differentiation 118, 120, 123–4, 133
Production activities, location of 94–7
Profit maximisation, economic theory of 32–5, 41–6, 49, 121, 284
  see also Determinants of Investment

Regional integration and the multinational enterprise 275–7

Sovereignty 17, 28–9, 352–61
Stability of multinational enterprises 97–104
Steady state analysis 36–7
Stock market share values, theory of 36
Subsidiaries of multinational enterprises, *see* Affiliates
Synergy 38

Tariff policy 74, 211, 231–2, 275–6, 370
  effect on foreign borrowing and investment 217–30
  effect on transfer pricing 327–8
Tariff theory and the multinational enterprise 199–204
Tariffs, optimum theory of 193–5
Taxation
  tax differentials 197, 203–4, 327–32
  tax harmonisation 264–5, 354–5
  tax policy 239, 370
  theory of optimal trade and capital taxes 204–8
  optimal tax rate 193–5
Technological gap 156–8, 162, 172
Technology
  future research 174–9
  geographic location 350–2
  importance of multinational enterprise in innovation and production 95–6, 155–6, 164–70, 366
  innovation 150–2
  problems for the host country 170–4
  production of 148–50

Technology—*cont.*
transfer between countries 24, 152–5, 158–64, 180*n*, 186–7, 256, 272–5, 366
Total benefit set 280, 287–90, 297–8
Transfer pricing 126, 203–4, 264–5, 316–30

United States, Department of Commerce 82, 166

Vertical direct investment 117, 187, 368
explanatory market models 138–41

Wage determination and collective bargaining 26–7, 29, 280–99, 370–1
Wage inflation 241–6, 248
Welfare 24, 188–9, 204–8, 315–30, 367